The Virtuoso Liszt

The greatest virtuoso career in histo_
told in countless biographies. But what does that career look like
when viewed from the perspective of European cultural history? In
this study Dana Gooley examines the world of discussion,
journalism, and controversy that surrounded the virtuoso Liszt, and
reconstructs the multiple symbolic identities that he fulfilled for his
enthusiastic audiences. Gooley's work is based on extensive research
into contemporary periodicals – well-known and obscure journals
and newspapers – as well as letters, memoirs, receipts, and other
documents that shed light on Liszt's concertizing activities.
Emphasizing the virtuoso's contradictions, the author shows Liszt
being constructed as a model aristocrat and a model bourgeois, as a
German nationalist and a Hungarian patriot, as a sensitive romantic
artist and a military dictator, as a greedy entrepreneur and as a
leading force for humanitarian charity. His popularity, Gooley argues,
was not an inevitable result of his musical genius, but depended on
specific ways in which his playing intersected with the concerns of
his contemporary world.

DANA GOOLEY is Assistant Professor of Music at the Case Western
Reserve University, Ohio. He is a music historian specializing in
music of the nineteenth century. He has presented numerous papers
on virtuosity and on issues of gender and music, and has published
in the journal *19th Century Music* and the *Journal of the American Liszt
Society*. Dana Gooley is also an accomplished pianist who plays in
jazz clubs and concert halls around the world.

New perspectives in music history and criticism

GENERAL EDITORS
JEFFREY KALLBERG, ANTHONY NEWCOMB, AND RUTH SOLIE

This series explores the conceptual frameworks that shape or have shaped the ways in which we understand music and its history, and aims to elaborate structures of explanation, interpretation, commentary, and criticism which make music intelligible and which provide a basis for argument about judgments of value. The intellectual scope of the series is broad. Some investigations will treat, for example, historiographical topics, others will apply cross-disciplinary methods to the criticism of music, and there will also be studies which consider music in its relation to society, culture, and politics. Overall, the series hopes to create a greater presence for music in the ongoing discourse among the human sciences.

PUBLISHED TITLES

Leslie C. Dunn and Nancy A. Jones (eds.), *Embodied voices: representing female vocality in Western culture*

Downing A. Thomas, *Music and the origins of language: theories from the French Enlightenment*

Thomas S. Grey, *Wagner's musical prose*

Daniel K. L. Chua, *Absolute music and the construction of meaning*

Adam Krims, *Rap music and the poetics of identity*

Annette Richards, *The free fantasia and the musical picturesque*

Richard Will, *The characteristic symphony in the age of Haydn and Beethoven*

Christopher Morris, *Reading opera between the lines: orchestral interludes and cultural meaning from Wagner to Berg*

Emma Dillon, *Medieval music-making and the 'Roman de Fauvel'*

David Yearsley, *Bach and the meanings of counterpoint*

David Metzer, *Quoting music within music: quotation and cultural meaning in the twentieth century*

Alexander Rehding, *Hugo Riemann and the birth of modern musical thought*

Dana Gooley, *The Virtuoso Liszt*

The Virtuoso Liszt

DANA GOOLEY

John Michael Cooper
Denton, Texas
3 June 2011

CAMBRIDGE
UNIVERSITY PRESS

CAMBRIDGE UNIVERSITY PRESS
Cambridge, New York, Melbourne, Madrid, Cape Town, Singapore, São Paulo, Delhi

Cambridge University Press
The Edinburgh Building, Cambridge CB2 8RU, UK

Published in the United States of America by Cambridge University Press, New York

www.cambridge.org
Information on this title: www.cambridge.org/9780521108720

First published 2004
Reprinted 2006
This digitally printed version 2009

A catalogue record for this publication is available from the British Library

Library of Congress Cataloguing in Publication data
Gooley, Dana A. (Dana Andrew), 1969–
The virtuoso Liszt / Dana Gooley.
    p.   cm. – (New perspectives in music history and criticism)
Includes bibliographical references and index.
ISBN 0 521 83443 0
1. Liszt, Franz, 1811–1886 – Appreciation.   2. Liszt, Franz, 1811–1886 – Public opinion.
3. Liszt, Franz, 1811–1886 – Performances.   4. Virtuosity in music.   5. Music –
19th century – Social aspects.   I. Title   II. Series.
ML410.L7G68   2004
786.2´092 – dc22   2003065426

ISBN 978-0-521-83443-8 hardback
ISBN 978-0-521-10872-0 paperback

In memory of my mother, Judith Ann Gooley

CONTENTS

ILLUSTRATIONS

All reasonable effort was made to contact the original holders of these images.

MUSIC EXAMPLES

TABLES

ACKNOWLEDGMENTS

I would like to thank first Carolyn Abbate, who advised the dissertation on which this book is based. It would have gone nowhere without her sustained encouragement, and she remains an inspiration. William Weber selflessly offered his mentorship, and his insights about European concert life provided an excellent frame for thinking about Liszt's career. I have incurred a huge debt to Gabriela Cruz, who read and reread these chapters more times than I care to remember. David Kasunic and Rob Wegman gave me valuable feedback on individual chapters. Fellow Lisztians Geraldine Keeling, Michael Saffle, and Rena Mueller kindly responded to specific inquiries about sources. Nada Bezić and Mirjana Šimundža helped me with the documents concerning Liszt's visit to Zagreb. I have received crucial support for this project from numerous colleagues and friends, including Tom Walker, Karen Painter, James Deaville, David Schneider, Klara Moricz, and Robin Draganic.

I wish to thank Penny Souster, Jeffrey Kallberg, Ruth Solie, and Anthony Newcomb for the interest they have all shown in this book. Conversations with Jeff helped steer this book as I was conceiving it. With his uncanny eye for detail, he picked up on numerous errors in the text, and then he did it all over again for the next draft.

I have received generous financial support from several institutions. A fellowship from the German Academic Exchange Service (DAAD) allowed me to spend a year in Berlin and to make research visits to other parts of Germany. The American Musicological Society helped me finish the dissertation with an AMS 50 award. I am grateful to the following libraries and research institutions for the use of their resources: in Paris the Bibliothèque nationale, the Bibliothèque de l'Opéra, and the Bibliothèque de la Ville de Paris; the Municipal Library of Versailles, the Berlin Staatsbibliothek, the Vienna Österreichische Nationalbibliothek, the Frankfurt Stadt- und Universitätsbibliothek, the Hamburg Staats- und Universitätsbibliothek, the Goethe- und Schiller-Archiv of Weimar, and the Herzogin Anna Amalia Bibliothek of Weimar.

Acknowledgments

Chapter 2, "Warhorses," appeared in *19th Century Music* 24/1 (Summer 2000), and I would like to thank them for permission to reprint it here.

Liszt knew to save something special for the end. Mai Kawabata has contributed to the writing of this book in innumerable ways. She read it and critiqued it more closely than anyone. She has been a dedicated editor, my toughest critic, and my closest friend.

NOTE ON PERIODICAL CITATIONS

Hundreds of reviews of Liszt's concerts bear generic titles such as "Liszt" or "Concert de Liszt." Many others have no title at all, or lie embedded in reviews of several miscellaneous concerts (for example, "Concerts de la semaine"). As a rule, I leave such titles out of my citations. Most concert reviews also leave the author undesignated. When the author is known, I put the name in parentheses at the end of the citation. Some periodicals do not contain specific dates, or were later reprinted in volumes with the dates removed. Citations without page numbers are from journals and newspapers that were not through-numbered and contain just three or four pages per issue. They will be easily found by date. Most translations from German or French are my own. I have given the original French or German only in cases where the translation proved difficult.

Introduction: a virtuoso in context

Virtuosity is about shifting borders. The musician, the athlete, and the magician are potentially virtuosos as soon as they cross a limit – the limit of what seems possible, or what the spectator can imagine. Once this act of transgression is complete, the border shifts, and the boundaries of the possible are redrawn. If the performer does not cross a new, more challenging one, he will no longer be perceived as a virtuoso. He can move the border along either a qualitative or quantitative axis. A magician, for example, may astound his audience by pulling a dove out of a black hat resting on the table, then go on to pull *two* doves out of the hat. And then, to top it all off, he might pull three doves out of a hat that is not resting on the table, perhaps even with his coat off. But this movement of the border to the next quantitative level of difficulty, however integral to virtuoso performance, cannot go on for long. Soon the spectator will demand a new trick, indeed a whole repertory of new tricks: the border must be moved qualitatively. So the virtuoso magician then makes things float, disappear, reappear, or explode. He reads hidden cards. He detaches limbs from the body. It is all amazing, and yet these tricks, still, are only the clichés of the professional magician – mere craft. To be a truly surpassing virtuoso, he must have his own tricks, inventing new impossibilities to be transcended, for these are the only impossibilities that will any longer seem truly impossible.

Franz Liszt remains the quintessential virtuoso because he was constantly and insistently mobilizing, destabilizing, and reconstituting borders. In terms of sheer skill of pianistic execution – the quantitative border – he was evidently surpassed within his lifetime. None of his protegés and imitators, however, came even close to him in extending the virtuoso's relevance qualitatively – beyond the sphere of music and into the social environments he entered. It is well known that the range of musical materials Liszt absorbed and reconstituted through his virtuosity was unusually wide, encompassing nearly every genre and style in the contemporary world. Yet he also absorbed a great deal from his non-musical environment – social styles, literary currents, political movements, ethical fashions – and worked these elements into his

1

persona and performing style. He was constantly redefining himself, playing off and adapting to the varied local contexts he encountered.

Described this way, Liszt can sound like a figure of absolute omnipotence – a supreme master of himself and of everything in his environment, a manipulator of the symbolic resources of his day. The virtuoso Liszt has, indeed, always served as a figure for fantasies of omnipotence: over pianos, women, and concert audiences. His concert career is imagined as an effortless march from one capital to another, where audiences wait to drink in his transcendent genius and send him off with roars of applause. A cursory reading of Liszt's correspondence, however, exposes this image as a fantasy. Reading his letters, it becomes clear that he was constantly watching his audiences, measuring out his prospects for success, and actively shaping his reputation in the press. He worried about audiences, approaching every new city with a measure of trepidation. If he felt uncertain that a concert or concert series would be well attended, he would cancel it, look for a smaller hall, or turn it into a private concert. On several occasions he suspected that opponents were conspiring to ruin his concerts with sneers or booing, and in some cases these suspicions turned out to be justified.

Liszt's relationship to audiences was thus far from omnipotent. He had to win them over. He explored the resources for gaining the public's approval, and because the audiences were so varied from place to place, he developed multiple strategies. Aristocrats and intellectuals, men and women, wealthy bourgeois and poor beggars, learned connoisseurs and humble amateurs, Frenchmen and Germans all looked to him for something different, and he rarely failed to deliver. Liszt became one of the most widely admired figures of his time not because his enormous musical talent made such popularity inevitable, but because his audiences made symbolic demands upon him that he was willing and able to fulfill. He successfully carved out identities specific to the different worlds he entered. His relationship to the social world was one not of mastery, but of dynamic, responsive contact. We know that Liszt possessed a remarkable capacity to pick up musical materials and recast them according to his own individual stamp. But in the virtuoso years, he was working almost exclusively with materials not of his own invention, materials that form a veritable compendium of contemporary musical life. Viewed this way, Liszt appears to be a *carte blanche* on which the world of the 1830s and 1840s wrote itself. Liszt can seem to stand above and beyond his environment, but to an important extent he was a product of it, and occasionally it swallowed him entirely.

This book is a reconstruction of the virtuoso Liszt through the eyes and ears of contemporary audiences, critics, and readers. The result is several Liszts, each developed according to the priorities and emphases of particular audiences and writers. Many of these constructions could not peacefully coexist and came into conflict with one other. I intentionally throw the spotlight on controversies he provoked to show how the larger social, political, and cultural debates of the time played themselves out in his reception. Furthermore, I counterpoint the reception of Liszt with his own, considerably self-conscious attempt to construct and control his public identity, an endeavor in which he did not always succeed. Liszt's virtuoso identity was in perpetual flux as he and his audiences tried to make him mean different things. Each chapter tells a story of how he, journalists, and audiences together negotiated his significance or identity. Not all of the multiple layers of his identity were rooted directly in his virtuoso performances. They also emerged from his social affiliations, personal behavior, literary publications, concertizing strategies, and press publicity. But in chapters 1, 2, and 5, I make efforts to show how Liszt's performing style – both its visual and aural dimensions – became infused with social meaning and addressed the symbolic needs of his audiences.

The biographical tradition

Until recently, nearly all studies of the virtuoso Liszt emerged from the biographical tradition established by Lina Ramann and recently updated by Alan Walker.[1] The vision that informs these biographies is the "greatness" of Liszt's concert career, just as "greatness" serves as master theme of all traditional biography. To convey the greatness of his virtuoso travels, it sufficed to describe the episodes with the highest public profile, such as the Liszt–Thalberg contest of 1837, the return to Pest in 1839, and the "Lisztomania" of Berlin in 1842. Ramann and Walker, the most important biographers, left many gaps in the chronicle of Liszt's concert tours, and numerous recent studies have filled in these gaps. They form the foundation on which this book builds. Geraldine Keeling has uncovered many previously unknown Parisian concerts, Michael Saffle has filled in huge gaps in the German chronicle, and the *Liszt Society Journal* has traced his English tours thoroughly.[2] The more we find out about his concert career, however, the less glamorous it appears. We encounter shabby, out-of-tune pianos, half-empty halls, tiny provincial towns where Liszt played only to pick up extra cash, petty local musicians who plot against him out of professional jealousy, audiences who can't make heads or tails of Weber's *Konzertstück*, and

[1] Lina Ramann, *Franz Liszt als Künstler und Mensch* (Leipzig, 1880–94), 3 vols. Alan Walker, *Franz Liszt* (Ithaca, 1987–97), 3 vols.
[2] Geraldine Keeling, "Liszt's Appearances in Parisian Concerts, 1824–1844," *Liszt Society Journal* 11 (1986), 22–34, and *Liszt Society Journal* 12 (1987), 8–22. Michael Saffle, *Liszt in Germany, 1840–1845* (Stuyvesant, NY, 1994). The documents on Liszt in England are found under various titles in volumes 6–13 of the *Liszt Society Journal*.

devastating financial losses. The thoroughness of the biographical tradition has, paradoxically, nearly undone the premise of Liszt's "great" concert career.

But if Liszt's concert career was not uniformly great and spectacular, what made the great moments truly great? Biographers implicitly answer this question with reference to his merits as an artist. His genius and his virtuosity are the generators, the engines of his great moments. Audiences appear in biographies only to pay witness to, and affirm, the artist's supreme talent, while we, the readers, are implicitly asked to clap along. Yet we only know of Liszt's great moments at all because we have traces of the public enthusiasm they generated. Biographers deduce Liszt's greatness, that is, from the demonstrations of his audiences. They are thus caught in a circular logic: on the one hand, Liszt's audiences applaud enthusiastically because he is a great artist; on the other, Liszt is a great artist because the audiences applaud enthusiastically.

The only way to break out of this circle is to show that the applause of his audiences does not simply reflect the artist's genius, but also reflects the interests and values of the applauders. I begin from the assumption that Liszt's great moments can only be explained by taking into account the tastes, dispositions, and symbolic needs of contemporary audiences. His appeal was rooted in aspects of the social and public life of the 1830s and 1840s that have nearly disappeared from view. Contemporary audiences cared deeply about charity for the poor and unfortunate, marveled at Napoleon's prowess and brilliance, attended theatres where aristocrats and bourgeois were battling for social terrain, or witnessed their countries developing into nation-states – and each of these things powerfully mediated their reactions to Liszt. Much of this book is devoted to reconstructing these historical trends, in an attempted archaeology of Liszt's phenomenal popularity. It thus lays emphasis on his public faces and personas, which look quite different from the dreamy romantic artist we encounter in various young portraits.

Traditional biographies place Franz Liszt, conceived as a person or self, at the center of attention. Here I consider Liszt, in contrast, as a figure of public discourse – a cluster of ideas, meanings, and projections that led critics and audiences to react to him in particular ways. This anti-subjective move has been made in several recent studies. Lawrence Kramer, adopting a broadly new historicist approach, interweaves Liszt's virtuosity with various strains of contemporary cultural practice, including theatrical life, the carnivalesque, balls, and monarchical ritual. Richard Leppert and Stephen Zank assess the virtuoso Liszt as a figure of the emergent modernity of the early nineteenth century, focusing on industrialization, masculine domination, militarism, and the formation of bourgeois subjectivity. Susan Bernstein discusses

Liszt's virtuosity in relation to romantic philosophy, with its remarkable privileging of music over language. Drawing from the theoretical perspective of Paul de Man, Bernstein argues that his performances and published writings radically destabilized the music-writing hierarchy that served as a precondition for elevating music to the status of pure, self-originating meaning.[3]

The hermeneutic, cultural, and historical emphasis of these studies has shed entirely new light on Liszt and the cult of the virtuoso, and the dialectical methods they employ are particularly well suited to their subject. While my interests are similar, my approach and results are more expository in character. I am concerned to present the universe of discourse that surrounded Liszt in its documentary richness, bordering sometimes on anthropological "thick description" of single concerts or episodes, as well as the diachronic trajectory of his career. This book is thus less explicitly theoretical, and more historically detailed, than these other recent studies. And although I share the anti-subjective premises of recent studies, Liszt-as-subject remains an important, active contributor to the discursive matrix that surrounded him. I emphasize that Liszt was directly engaged in public discourse about himself. In the cultural field he was just one among many players wrestling for the authority over his significance, but he was an unusually important one.

Sources

The historical emphasis of this study has led me to draw on an eclectic range of documents from Liszt's time – scores, periodicals, illustrations, correspondence, memoirs, and monographs – to recover major themes and debates in the press, previously unexplored dimensions of Liszt's performing language, individual episodes of his career, and audience dispositions. The body of evidence I am working with is unusually fragmented. Its main unit is the concert review or concert report, usually just a few paragraphs or a column in length. My reconstruction of larger patterns therefore entails a citation-heavy accumulation of details

---

[3] Lawrence Kramer, "Franz Liszt and the Virtuoso Public Sphere: Sight and Sound in the Rise of Mass Entertainment," in *Musical Meaning: Toward a Critical History* (Berkeley, 2002), 68–99. Richard Leppert and Stephen Zank, "The Concert and the Virtuoso," in *Piano Roles: Three Hundred Years of Life with the Piano*, ed. James Parakilas (New Haven, 1999), 237–81. Susan Bernstein, *Virtuosity of the Nineteenth Century: Performing Music and Language in Heine, Liszt, and Baudelaire* (Stanford, 1998). Jacqueline Bellas' study of Liszt's trip toward the Iberian peninsula ("Un virtuose en tournée: Franz Liszt dans le Sud-Ouest en 1844" [*Littératures* 9 (1960), 5–50]) is unique among Liszt studies in that it includes analysis, in the style of traditional literary criticism, of the motifs and ideas that appear in the press reports.

from diverse sources. This has the disadvantage of leaving less room for the analysis of verbal rhetoric and of the motivations of individual authors. Such fragmentation has the advantage, however, of offering a greater diversity of viewpoints. Furthermore, concert reviews are usually loosely framed, lacking a strong agenda. They respond to the concert event with little intellectual mediation. Unconstrained by specific demands or themes, reviewers often isolate the details that strike them, and these details can be the most valuable ones. The more synthetic books and pamphlets on Liszt that appeared during his career – those of d'Ortigue, Christern, Duverger, Schober, and Rellstab, for example – were mostly written by his close friends and probably in consultation with him. They are in many ways less reliable, as an index of more general perceptions, than individual concert reviews.

The greatest difficulty of using periodicals extensively is gauging the degree to which they reflect opinions and attitudes of the larger public. Determining the relevance or authority of periodical articles demands consideration of the author's priorities, the journal's profile, and the prospective readership. Musicological studies have too often offered journal citations to describe how past musical cultures "thought" about an artist or a work, or about music in general. Katherine Ellis, in her study of the *Revue et gazette musicale de Paris*, has challenged this tendency by showing the wide range of institutional and economic pressures to which the editor and publisher, Maurice Schlesinger, had to respond. While it is important to approach journals skeptically when writing music history, however, their contents cannot be reduced to the idiosyncratic impressions of individual writers. In general I consider motifs and patterns that appear repeatedly in contemporary writings to reveal a more general cultural interpretation of Liszt, and in discussing such motifs I give less attention to individual writers. At other times I focus on highly idiosyncratic writings about Liszt, in which he is blatantly appropriated for particular ideological ends.

Although my historical approach is not narrative, much of the material to be presented is anecdotal. At times I accumulate anecdotes in order to show the recurrence of certain responses to Liszt, and in such places the reader may note a certain disconnectedness. This disconnectedness is inherent in the subject matter, for Liszt was constantly playing to new audiences, each of which was forming fresh impressions of his playing. In pursuing Liszt's relationship to audiences, my main unit of analysis is not the individual concert, but his visit to an individual locale – which I refer to as an "episode." Liszt's visits tended to become civic events, accompanied by a wealth of press reports and public activity, and this is the framework within which it is most useful to evaluate his public identity. My presentation of detailed "local" studies contrasts sharply with the traditional biographical approach, which emphasizes the "universal" Liszt and romanticizes his wandering virtuoso existence.

Who were Liszt's audiences?

To study the symbolic investments of contemporary audiences in Liszt, it is necessary to get a sense of who attended his concerts. In the absence of detailed records showing who bought tickets, we can only determine who they were by conjecture. Studies of concert life in the early nineteenth century have consistently emphasized the prominence of the prosperous bourgeoisie in concert audiences, and it is often assumed that Liszt's audiences were accordingly bourgeois. In terms of sheer numbers, it seems incontrovertible that the middle bourgeoisie was the core of his audience. He filled his halls with hundreds of people, and the middle bourgeoisie was by far the most numerous social level among those that had the financial means to attend.

There are, however, major problems with assimilating Liszt's audience to that of the growing sphere of public concerts, for his concerts bore a distinctive, and rather exclusive, social tone. Tickets to his concerts were typically slightly more than *double* the going prices for public concerts, and he usually restricted the prices to two levels. Such prices filtered out those families from the lower bourgeoisie that did attend public concerts, and were even a strain for the middle bourgeoisie. The lower social classes, however, did occasionally have the opportunity to hear Liszt in performance. When he played in very large halls, such as Vienna's *grösser Redoutensaal* or the theatre in St. Petersburg, there were a number of quite inexpensive tickets available, probably to fill in areas that would otherwise remain empty (due to bad lines of vision or an association with the lower classes). Such occasions are not nearly as common as concerts with two price tiers. Liszt tended to place them at the end of an extended stay in a single city, to help give his departure a grand public profile.

While the high ticket prices of his normal concerts siphoned off the lower bourgeoisie, they in no way scared away the more prosperous middle level of the bourgeoisie. On the contrary, the prices made his concerts *most* attractive to this class by conferring high prestige upon the event. The elite classes, too, sought social distinction at Liszt's concerts, but they were able to generate it in private contexts as well, and did not particularly need a virtuoso for this purpose. The middle bourgeoisie, on the other hand, was excluded from the private halls of high prestige, and Liszt's concerts compensated for this exclusion, making it available to them for the purchase of a ticket. Liszt incarnated the concert hall as a temple of prestige through several means. He often surrounded himself on stage with a semicircle of distinguished women, or alternatively, reserved the first few rows of the orchestra section for them. During the pauses he would circulate and converse with them. On several recorded occasions he mingled with the women in the orchestra section before playing, and made his entrance onto the stage from there. In the cities with a francophone aristocracy (most of the large capitals) or with a court, these women were the same people with whom he had been circulating in private society.[4] This importation of the aristocratic salon into the concert hall is unique to Liszt, and constitutes one of the unrecognized valences of his famous invention: the solo recital.

While the middle bourgeoisie predominated numerically among Liszt's listeners, then, they did not predominate symbolically. The tone of the concert was built around an idea of exclusive, elite distinction, to which the middle bourgeoisie could aspire only in fantasy.[5] There was thus a difference between who Liszt's audiences actually were and who they appeared to be. In reality they were a shade more prosperous than the general concert-going public, but otherwise they were not substantially different. What is crucially different with Liszt's audiences is how they were *represented*, for this representation inflected their experiences and symbolic investments.

Liszt's audiences include not only those who heard him in the concert hall or the private salon, but also those who read about him in newspapers and journals, and those who heard about him in public conversation, for Liszt was a figure of public discourse independently of his concerts. His fame always preceded his arrival, and audiences waited for his performances with immense anticipation. This made it possible for people who could not afford his concerts – namely students and the lower classes – to participate in his reception. They lined the streets when he left a city, or gathered around his hotel balcony and cheered or sang songs for him. They gave his reception a public scope that ticket prices precluded.

Concert reviews of Liszt include many comments about the behavior of his audiences. While these comments are sometimes believable as plain facts, they more often bear an implicit polemical or rhetorical

---

[4] There were of course also men – intellectuals and aristocrats – with whom Liszt mingled in private society, but they were not part of the stage scenery in his concert hall.

[5] For quite some time Liszt himself measured his success according to his popularity among the aristocratic women. From Vienna he wrote to Marie d'Agoult: "Tout le public féminin et aristocratique est pour moi partout, et chaudement et violemment. Avec cela on va loin" (*Correspondance de Liszt et de Madame d'Agoult*, ed. D. Ollivier [Paris, 1933–35], 2 vols., I: 382; letter of 12 February 1840). Shortly thereafter he wrote from Prague: "L'aristocratie de Bohême, la plus fière de la Monarchie a été charmantissime pour moi. Ici, comme ailleurs, les femmes sont pour moi" (*Correspondance de Liszt et de Mme. d'Agoult*, I: 405).

purpose, and must be treated as representations. For Liszt's concerts raised the question of the *legitimacy* of audience behavior to an unprecedented degree. His audiences displayed levels of enthusiasm that appeared aberrant or excessive even by the more relaxed standards of concert etiquette that then prevailed. Most critics evaluated public entertainments – musical or otherwise – along a continuum between aesthetic pleasure and sheer sensual pleasure, the former legitimate and the latter illegitimate. All virtuoso concerts evidently fell somewhere in the middle: they were neither too severe nor too light, neither high art nor low entertainment. Liszt's concerts, however, starkly posed the endpoints of this continuum against one another. His performances seemed at once drenched in fantasy and overcharged with nerve-shaking stimulation, making it difficult to separate the aesthetic and the corporeal, the legitimate and the illegitimate.

Faced with this destabilized hierarchy of legitimacy, critics made redoubled efforts to maintain it. They urged audiences to remain civil, or mocked those who let their enthusiasms stretch too far. Gradually they were installing in contemporary audiences what I would call a "concert-superego" – an internal voice that would say "no" to the sensual transports of exciting virtuosity. This resonates strongly with the larger cultural project of promoting the model bourgeois subject: an individual who masters his pleasures and maintains a modest demeanor in public. Yet critics declared the behavior of Liszt's audiences illegitimate for other reasons, and in the chapters that follow we will see the category of "bad enthusiasm" being put to various ends. The Parisians will use it to affirm their superiority over the "provincial" Hungarians; the south Germans will reaffirm their liberal political orientation by criticizing the Berlin public; and within Berlin, many critics will rescue the legitimacy of their own pleasures by assigning the excesses of enthusiasm to women. The management of pleasure is, in short, one of the main themes of the story of Liszt's reception. Because of this, we have to treat portrayals of his audiences as figures of discourse. In doing so, we will find out as much about the newly developed authority of the music critic as about Liszt's virtuoso powers.

Liszt and the listener

The figure of the listener, a newcomer to musicology, inhabits several pages of this study. Studies of how people in the past listened is motivated principally by a rejection or suspicion of idealist aesthetics, according to which the listener and the music come into contact in the disinterested realm of pure mind or *Geist*. This model of listening is institutionalized in the customs of today's concert life, and it is only through historical investigation of the concert event that we can understand how people in the past experienced music differently. James H. Johnson, focusing on Paris in the years 1750–1850, shows listening as a mode of social behavior aimed at the production and reproduction of social status.[6] Leon Botstein has proposed that silent reading was such a pervasive activity among concert audiences in the nineteenth century that literature mediated their understanding of instrumental music.[7] However incomplete these studies may be, they have begun to identify the assumptions, priorities, and investments with which audiences came into the concert hall, and the perceptual filters through which they processed musical information.

In this book I will propose no general theory of how Liszt's audiences listened, but I will often discuss larger cultural dispositions that directly affected their perceptions of him in performance. Chapter 1, for example, delves into the vocally centered listening preferences of some factions in Paris, which played an important role in Liszt's rivalry with Sigismond Thalberg. In chapter 2 I explain how the cult of Napoleon and the celebration of military valor bolstered Liszt's popularity. And in chapter 4 I emphasize the pervasiveness of charity in the everyday lives of Liszt's audiences, which made them respond enthusiastically to his aura of benevolence and Christian virtue. All of these audience dispositions have faded since Liszt's time. In examining them we see elements of his virtuoso identity that are today obscure, and we see his popularity not as an inevitable consequence of a transcendental genius, but as contingent upon circumstances specific to his historical period.

Although Liszt's audiences brought symbolic and aesthetic dispositions with them to the concert hall, he had a remarkable ability to make listeners focus their attention on him and him alone. He absorbed his listener so completely in the sound and spectacle of his virtuosity that the listener lost all awareness of the concert environment. With the institution of solo recitals he reconstituted the performance space to encourage the highest degree of visual, aural, and psychological concentration. Even when he played with an orchestra, I argue in chapter 1, he could hold in check the orchestra's diffuseness by projecting himself as the leader, hierarchically subordinating the other performers to his performing self. In this study, then, I also consider the effect of Liszt's playing on the "absorbed" spectator, bracketing off levels of mediation implicit in the concert as a social event.

This does not constitute a return to the assumptions of idealist aesthetics. First, I account for differences in habits of spectatorship:

[6] James H. Johnson, *Listening in Paris: A Cultural History* (Berkeley and Los Angeles, 1995).
[7] Leon Botstein, "Listening through Reading: Musical Literacy and the Concert Audience," *19th Century Music* 16 (1992), 129–45.

connoisseurs, men of letters, the Parisian dilettantes, and amateurs all entered into the experience of Liszt with different eyes and different ears. Liszt's performances presented a plethora of visual and sonic data, and listeners took in this information through differently configured filters. Second, I discuss the role of unaestheticized sound (the sheer volume and density of sonority) and unaestheticized sight (his violent approach to the keyboard) in shaping the listener's experience. My method for reconstructing the listener's experience might loosely be described as phenomenological, as it attempts to represent how an individual listener processed all the stimuli coming from Liszt's virtuoso performance. Carolyn Abbate has shown how the interpenetration of opera's separate discursive levels – sight, sound, voice, orchestra, plot, narrative – renders opera's meanings radically overdetermined and often internally contradictory. The range of discursive variables in Liszt's performance is narrower than in operatic performance: my analyses will work mainly with the elements of sound, sight, and musical codes. I will argue, nevertheless, that Liszt's virtuosity was, like operatic performance, an indeterminate, untidy discourse with a surplus of meanings, posing the very difficulty of reading rather than presenting to listeners an object for reading.

The experience of Liszt in performance was as much about watching as about listening, and this study returns repeatedly to the visual dimension of his virtuosity. Lisztians have been shy about discussing this side of his playing because, from the perspective of idealist aesthetics, the visual is inherently a compromise of sound. Furthermore, attention to the visual threatens to compromise his legitimacy, since his bodily movements were often caricatured and criticized as charlatanism. The suppression of the visual, however, poses a major block to a full understanding of what he meant for his audiences, and the recent studies by Kramer and by Leppert and Zank have helped redress the balance. There is very little evidence that Liszt's audiences felt a conflict of interest between the visual and the aural. On the contrary, several writers claimed that Liszt's appearance in performance was essential to comprehending his music, and no one listened to him with closed eyes.[8] There were critics who invoked idealist aesthetics to delegitimate his facial expressions and active body, but their victory over public opinion had to wait well into the era of recorded music.

---

[8] Schumann's words on this point are often quoted: "But he must be heard – and also seen; for if Liszt played behind the screen, a great deal of poetry would be lost" (*Robert Schumann on Music and Musicians*, ed. Konrad Wolff, trans. Paul Rosenfeld [New York, 1946], 156).

Liszt as strategist

In spite of my emphasis on synchronic history, Liszt's reception in Paris requires an occasional turn to the narrative historical mode. His relationship to the French capital extends from 1824, when he arrived as a prodigy, to at least 1845, when he tried to make an impact with his Beethoven Cantata (the failure thereof nearly extinguished his hopes of rescuing his reputation there). His struggle to maintain a reputation in Paris over this long period is a tormented narrative, filled with upswings and downswings, ill-willed plotters, heated confrontations, and an outcome with a nearly tragic protagonist. This narrative is especially valuable for challenging the myth of Liszt's easy victory over contemporary audiences and critics. The Parisian story reveals, furthermore, just how self-consciously he was managing his public identity. He tailored his repertory and ticketing practices to particular audiences, asked journalists and publishers to write certain things about him, and took other steps to shape himself as a particular type of public figure.

The Liszt that emerges from the Parisian narrative is a *strategist*, working within the constraints of a skeptical, critical public to maximize his impact as a virtuoso. Although Paris offers the clearest case study, Liszt was strategizing throughout his concert travels. He was constantly on the lookout for ways to broaden and deepen his appeal. At times he can even appear to be a chameleon, assuming whatever identity seems most suited to his audience's wishes. In chapter 3, for example, I describe a rapid metamorphosis from a thoroughly cosmopolitan identity (marked to some degree as French) to a personality rich in characteristics coded German. Toward what end was all of this strategic activity aimed? There is a line of Liszt biography (Newman and Perenyi, for example) according to which the virtuoso travels were largely an exercise in self-aggrandizement, and this has left a strong imprint on the popular image of Liszt. It has unfortunately put Liszt's admirers on the defensive, provoking the overstated counterclaim that he placed little value on his popularity as a virtuoso, and that his true desire was to compose.

It is true that Liszt had a long-range plan of settling down to devote himself more fully to composition. As he traveled he was considering in what location, and in what capacity, he could best realize this goal. There is evidence that Pest, Vienna, Weimar, and Paris were all prospective sites for the continuation of his musical career.[9] He manifestly took

---

[9] In the early 1840s Liszt thought that he would probably settle down in Vienna or Pest within a few years. Sharon Winklhofer has shown that as late as 1846 Liszt was angling to replace Donizetti at the Vienna Royal Opera, thus revising the idea that he had been set on Weimar for some years (*Liszt's Sonata in B minor: A Study of Autograph Sources and Documents* [Ann Arbor, 1980], 15ff.). As Liszt's concert career came to an end there were also rumors that he might settle in Paris and start a school for piano instruction.

steps to foster his connections with these locations in ways that might offer opportunities for the future. Yet described this way, Liszt's virtuoso career sounds like a mere stepping stone toward the achievement of his compositional goals. It does not leave room to consider how Liszt might have gained satisfaction, or felt he was making an artistic statement, through his activities as a virtuoso. We still lack an interpretation of Liszt's strategizing that does not reduce it to mere vanity, on the one hand, and does not suppress it defensively in favor of Liszt's goals as a composer, on the other. And yet these are the alternatives offered by the biographical tradition, with its emphasis on Liszt as a moral being.

My view is that Liszt's goals as a virtuoso were fundamentally *negative*. He transformed himself, diversified his affiliations, and intervened in the formation of his reputation in reaction to a major crisis in the musical life of his time. This crisis merits a brief exposition. Liszt came of age during the most intense period of anti-virtuosity backlash in the history of instrumental music. Both of the major music journals that established themselves around 1830 – the Leipzig *Neue Zeitschrift für Musik*, and the Parisian *Revue et gazette musicale* – made opposition to instrumental virtuosity a cornerstone of their aesthetic and professional platforms. This war against virtuosity, which was coterminous with the elevation of Beethoven's works as the standard of musical value, merits a study of its own. It began in the reviews of newly published compositions, with Schumann (at the *Neue Zeitschrift*) and F.-J. Fétis (at the *Revue musicale*) taking full-fisted swipes at the compositions of Henri Herz. Around 1840, critics started waging the war more directly against performers and the entire profession of the touring virtuoso, culminating in Carl Gollmick's condemning article "Virtuosity Today" ("Das heutige Virtuosenwesen"), which appeared in the *Neue Zeitschrift* on 2 December 1842.

The wave of anti-virtuoso polemics that swept into the music world in the 1830s could only have shaken Liszt to the core. His executive skill was such a remarkable element of his talent that it threatened to overwhelm him – to become his mark of distinction. Such an achievement, toward which he had devoted most of his youth, was being declared illegitimate from all sides. Liszt absorbed the values that debased "sheer virtuosity," and he announced it publicly in his essays. In his obituary of Paganini, for example, he made the extraordinary gesture of accusing the violinist of vanity. It is one of the baldest imaginable examples of the need to kill the father – not Paganini the person, but the bad demon of unproductive, self-directed virtuosity that the violinist seemed to emblematize. Thalberg's compositions provided Liszt with yet another occasion to knock down the edifice of superficial virtuosity. Clearly, sheer executive skill was something Liszt felt he had to define himself against.

13

The first step Liszt took to carve out a space for himself beyond that of *exécutant* was his essay "De la situation des artistes" (1835), in which he fused the role of the virtuoso with that of the priest, prophet, and humanitarian. However effective this essay might have been, it could not realistically define his public identity during his concert travels. Its rhetoric speaks to and from the heady utopian ferment of artistic Paris in the early 1830s, and would have been nearly incomprehensible to readers outside Paris. The surest way for a virtuoso to avoid sinking in the quicksand of "mere virtuosity" was to distinguish himself as a composer. Thalberg, for example, rose to preeminence in Paris by convincing a leading critic that his compositions were of outstanding quality. Liszt tried bolstering his reputation with compositions, but as I show in chapter 1, this strategy simply did not work. He was therefore constantly on the lookout for ways to expand his significance beyond his keyboard prowess. A variety of possible roles offered themselves: interpreter of "classical" works, German patriot, Hungarian patriot, man of letters, the composer-pianist, the artist as aristocrat, as prophet, as humanitarian, or as revolutionary. He took on all of these guises self-consciously in the course of his concert career. This is not to say that he bore the cynical attitude that he would simply give the people what they wanted. He wanted, rather, to make the virtuoso pianist mean something more than the ongoing debasement of super-virtuosos seemed to allow.

It is worth emphasizing here that Liszt's motivations were largely negative. He had a strong vision of the virtuoso he did *not* want to be, but he was not so clear what form the new virtuoso might take. He therefore experimented, in an ad hoc fashion, with the virtuoso's identity, trying out different possibilities for making him newly significant in the world. It is for this reason that his roles and identities have a miscellaneous quality to them, and on some occasions even contradict one another. His identity was not informed by a singular, sharply focused vision that he set out to realize. As he traveled around the world his audiences asked him to mean different things, offering him a variety of resources for shaping his identity. The fluid, chameleonic nature of Liszt's identity does not so much evince his supreme self-mastery as its opposite. His environments and audiences pressed themselves upon him, serving materials from which he could construct an identity, and also defining the borders he would have to work within, or transcend.

Orientations

The time period of this study, 1835–47, marks approximately the boundaries of Liszt's career as mature virtuoso performer. The latter date, 1847, is unproblematic because he ceased giving public concerts for his own benefit in the fall of that year. The earlier date is more arbitrary. Before

1835, the most concentrated performing period was 1824 to 1828, when he appeared often as a child prodigy in London, Paris, and the French provinces. From 1829 to 1834 he kept a relatively low profile on the public concert scene of Paris, making cameo appearances at the benefit concerts of other musicians, but not mounting his own public concerts. In the season of 1835, however, he made a decisive "comeback," after which a lengthy biography of him appeared in the *Revue et gazette musicale*. This biography recognized and established Liszt as an artist of international stature. It gave him a degree of public exposure – especially in Paris but also abroad – that he had not previously enjoyed, and it effectively capped off his youthful achievements. For these reasons 1835 serves as a useful starting point for the consideration of Liszt's mature reputation.

Liszt's years of itinerant concertizing did not begin until late 1839, but in the intervening years he gave two groups of highly publicized concerts (Paris in 1837, Vienna in 1838), and he performed not infrequently in Switzerland (1836–37) and Italy (1838–39). He was thus less dormant during these years than the usual "years of pilgrimage" image suggests. The "years of pilgrimage" were less a retreat from his life as a virtuoso than a period of experimentation, in which he attempted to complement his keyboard virtuosity with comparable achievements in the spheres of composition and letters. They were therefore extremely important in the development of his public reputation, although this reputation was still disseminated largely in Paris. Most of my discussion concerns the years 1837 to 1843, the period in which his international reputation was in formation and therefore most unstable. By 1844 writers were saying little about Liszt that had not already been said.

A few critics are cited especially often in the chapters that follow, and they merit brief introductions here. Heinrich Adami, who wrote for the *Allgemeine Theaterzeitung* of Vienna, left the single largest body of concert reviews.[10] He tried to cover every concert Liszt played in Vienna during his three extended concert series (1838, 1839–40, 1846). Adami knew very little about music, and after the first four or five reviews he ran out of things to say. His reviews are valuable because he makes a point of commenting on each individual piece Liszt played, leaving behind some fascinating details, and because he is attentive to the social tone of the concerts. Another Viennese writer who wrote often about Liszt was Moritz Saphir, editor of *Der Humorist*. Saphir was obviously very fond of Liszt and his playing, and his florid essays are probably the best example we have of how Liszt could animate a writer's fantasy.

---

[10] Many of Adami's reviews are printed in *Franz Liszt: unbekannte Presse und Briefe aus Wien, 1822–1866*, ed. Dezsö Legány (Vienna/Graz, 1984).

The largest number of concert reviews in Paris were written by Henri Blanchard, who covered many concerts for the *Revue et gazette musicale*. His reviews are markedly literary, sprinkled with references to classical literature and rich in piquant metaphors. His writing is impressionistic, attempting to evoke the mood or feeling of a musical event. Musical learning is almost entirely absent from his comments. He did not show a decided preference for Liszt over other virtuosos. Parisian readers also read several reviews by Berlioz and Jules Janin, all of them uniformly positive. Janin, in particular, went to extra lengths to defend Liszt in print when the Parisian press turned against him. Heinrich Heine's three essays from Paris are, in my opinion, the richest and most insightful writings about the virtuoso Liszt.[11] He clearly felt the imaginative power of Liszt's playing, but he also found it unpleasantly overbearing, and his ambivalence toward the pianist never disappeared. Heine was one of the only writers who, in metacritical style, followed and commented upon the development of Liszt's international image.

In the German states the reviews of Robert Schumann, Carl Gollmick, and Ludwig Rellstab were probably the most widely read. Rellstab wrote many reviews and essays during Liszt's visits to Berlin and published them in book form shortly thereafter. He harbored a strong bias against traveling virtuosos, but Liszt's playing won him over. He only kept his reservations with regard to Liszt's performances of Beethoven. Rellstab's book is an unusually thorough presentation of Liszt and his virtuosity, and it contains several insights found nowhere else in the review literature. A final critic worth introducing is Henry Chorley, who wrote about Liszt for English audiences. Chorley was principally an opera critic, but he wrote lucidly about Liszt's personality, his creative goals, and his place in the international artistic scene. He is far more useful with regard to Liszt than the influential London critic John Davison, whose hard line on classical musical values led him to reject Liszt almost out of hand.

With the exception of John Davison, all of the critics just described were personal friends of Liszt. There is hardly a negative comment to be found in all of their writings combined. When they hint at dissatisfaction, as Chorley and Rellstab occasionally do, they usually employ euphemistic or evasive phrases. Berlioz helped Liszt with exaggeratedly glowing reviews, partly in friendly exchange for efforts to propagate his compositions. Liszt also provided his journalist-friends with free tickets to his concerts, a favor that to some extent obliged them to write positive reviews. Mutual support of this kind was standard for its time, and it would be anachronistic to view such practices as a travesty of

---

[11] These essays are collected in *Heinrich Heine und die Musik*, ed. Gerhard Müller (Leipzig, 1987).

the critic's independence or authority. Nevertheless, Liszt's friendship with these critics had a muffling effect on the negative voices that might have left us with a more complete picture of contemporary responses to his playing. There are a few cases, such as his dealings with Ernest Legouvé and Maurice Schlesinger, where Liszt was demonstrably trying to silence negative opinions from the press, and biographers have naturally tended to follow suit. Here I will emphasize negative and controversial views of Liszt not to discredit him, but because they help reveal the value systems that critics and writers brought to their work.

In chapter 1 I revisit the famous Liszt–Thalberg rivalry of 1837, showing how the performing styles of the two pianists addressed rather different listening habits within the Parisian audiences, and delving into their complex social affiliations. In chapter 2 I show how Liszt's virtuosity projected an image of heroic military domination, epitomized in his performances of Weber's *Konzertstück*, and consider its place in a larger cultural valorization of military prowess, especially the cult of Napoleon. Chapters 3 and 4 discuss Liszt's national affiliations with France, Hungary, and Germany, which led to several controversies that changed the course of his future career. Chapter 3 focuses on conflicts that surrounded the famous "sabre of honor" concert in Pest, which served as a cornerstone of Liszt's relationship to Hungary. Chapter 4 explains how Liszt's concerts in Germany bound him to the German national movement, paving the way toward the prestigious position he eventually occupied in Weimar. In chapter 5 I investigate why Berlin was home to the most intense public enthusiasms of Liszt's career, giving rise to the word "Lisztomania." Readers looking for detailed discussions of Liszt's playing will find them in chapter 1, chapter 5, and to a lesser extent chapter 2.

These chapters do not even come close to exhausting the possibilities for studying Liszt's relevance to contemporary social, political, and musical life. I deal mainly with the well-known highlights of his career – his extended visit to Berlin, the "duel" with Thalberg, the "sabre of honor" concert in Pest – and investigate them in the context of European history. I work almost exclusively with German-, French-, and English-language sources, and with Liszt's visits to places where those languages were spoken. A complete study of Liszt and his audiences would require a scholar who could cross borders and press boundaries as effectively as he did with his virtuosity. I will have accomplished my goal if I have offered at least some new ways of getting around the instrument.

1

Liszt, Thalberg, and the Parisian publics

Virtuoso contests and rivalries are sprinkled throughout the music-historical lore. Handel and Scarlatti had a youthful confrontation in Rome, J. S. Bach and Louis Marchand were said to have sparred in Dresden, Clementi and Mozart alternated rounds at the Vienna court, Beethoven dueled with Joseph Wölffl, and Paganini and Lafont traded solos before the public of Milan in 1816. The narratives through which these contests are related all thematize rival musical idioms and performing traditions of their times. Handel represented the church style against Scarlatti's court style. The Bach–Marchand contest, which probably did not take place, was a narrative about the ongoing battle between galant and contrapuntal styles. Clementi and Mozart staked out claims for the two major keyboard schools of the time, the English and the Viennese, while Lafont and Paganini juxtaposed the two dominant schools of violin playing, the French and the Italian.

The sensational meeting of Liszt and Sigismond Thalberg at a Parisian soirée in 1837 is by far the best known and most fully documented of all such contests. Yet it is hardly better understood than its historical predecessors. What stake did the organizers and audiences have in staging such an event? What aesthetic or stylistic currents were being negotiated? Without answers to these questions the contest seems to represent little more than a battle of egos, a highly charged game of one-upmanship between two popular public figures. For generations, biographers presented it just that way. It was a triumph of art over charlatanism, with Liszt brushing away his rival like an annoying flea. In their zeal to demonstrate Liszt's superiority, they completely passed over the aesthetic and social dimensions of the contest. When Alan Walker tackled the affair, he refreshingly pointed out that in 1837 Liszt did not really "win" the contest. But citing posterity's judgment, he crowned Liszt with a still greater victory:

The "battle" was a perfect illustration of that deeper historical process which governs change throughout all human activity; the Old had to defend itself against the New, and the New won. If history had not brought Liszt and

Thalberg together during that spring of 1837, and turned them into symbols of her purpose, she would doubtless have found other pianists through whom to work out her age-old dialectical ritual.[1]

If Liszt was weakened by the challenge of Thalberg, in this account he is strengthened by a quasi-Hegelian historical will.

Interpreting the Liszt–Thalberg rivalry according to the question "who was better than whom?" – whether in 1837 or in the long run – can only produce limited results. It reduces Thalberg and Liszt to their executive skill, and attributes the enthusiasms and passions of their fans to small-minded partisanship. Here I would like to reexamine the contest in the context of Parisian musical life, in hopes of restoring the musical, ethical, and social dimensions that gave the controversy such weight. I argue that the rivalry was closely related to pianistic styles, to the social physiognomy of the Parisian concert scene, and to the listening habits of Paris audiences. A discussion of the visual and sonic properties of Liszt's and Thalberg's playing forms the first part of the chapter. Each virtuoso had a unique way of relating musical sound, the performing body, and the listener. Thalberg's playing, by virtue of its sonority and melodic construction, conjured up an operatic singing voice, and his immobility at the keyboard made the vocal presence stand out with particular relief. His playing was addressed to the Parisian listeners whose musical pleasures centered on opera and voice: the *dilettanti*. Liszt's virtuosity, on the other hand, assaulted the listener with a dense, scattered sonorous field, and a performing body on the brink of physical dismemberment. It demanded that the listener seek coherence among this barrage of signals, through an imaginative engagement in the performance. His playing was in this way aimed at the sensibilities of the *literati*, the *artistes*, and the younger musicians of Paris. Thalberg's vocality tapped into a strong, already existing aesthetic predilection of the Parisian publics, while Liszt asked his audiences to listen in new ways, and thereby presented a challenge to his general acceptance. For this reason Thalberg posed a powerful challenge to Liszt's reputation in Paris. Indeed, Thalberg gained the upper hand in the rivalry of 1837, a possibility biographers have never even entertained.

The second part of this chapter offers a social interpretation of the Liszt–Thalberg contest. Its social meaning followed partly from aesthetic

---

[1] Alan Walker, *Franz Liszt* (Ithaca, 1987–97), 3 vols., I: 237. Although Walker goes out of his way to present Thalberg more fully, there remain strong traces of the condescending attitude that characterizes earlier biographies. He writes: "Liszt was asked his opinion of Thalberg's playing and retaliated, 'He is the only man I know who plays violin on the piano.' Such comments set the whole of Paris laughing" (ibid.). Walker thus interprets Liszt's comment as an insult, and assumes that it encouraged the Parisians to mock Thalberg. Liszt's comment strikes me, however, as a generous compliment.

Table 1.1 *Outline of the Liszt–Thalberg rivalry*

	Prelude
June 1835	Joseph d'Ortigue's lengthy biography of Liszt appears in the *Gazette musicale*. Two weeks later, Liszt begins an extended absence from Paris.
Winter 1836	Thalberg concertizes in Paris and the public lionizes him.
May 1836	Liszt makes an unexpected return to Paris, gives two concerts at the Érard salons for an exclusive audience. He programs his most recent fantasies, and the "Hammerklavier" Sonata of Beethoven.
December 1836	Liszt returns to Paris for the concert season and appears on a Berlioz concert.
	Rivalry
8 January 1837	Liszt publishes article in *Gazette musicale* judging Thalberg's compositions harshly, enraging Thalberg's fans and even some of Liszt's.
January–February 1837	Liszt puts on four concerts featuring Beethoven's piano trios, with Urhan and Batta.
March 1837	Thalberg and Liszt each give their big benefit concert of the season. On 31 March, the two appear together at a charity concert at the salon of Cristina Belgiojoso.
23 April 1837	Long article by Fétis, comparing Liszt and Thalberg, sparks off a hot polemical exchange between Liszt and Fétis in the pages of the *Gazette musicale*.
	Postlude
Spring 1838	Liszt and Thalberg simultaneously concertizing in Vienna.
Spring 1840	Liszt returns to Paris for the first time since 1837.

differences between the two virtuosos, and partly from their methods of social networking. Prominent among the *dilettanti* who adored Thalberg were conservative aristocrats, while Liszt's strongest advocates were in the worlds of literature and music. The rivalry thus pitted two distinct factions of the *beau monde* against each other – the "aristocracy of birth" and the "aristocracy of talent." The divisiveness that emerged between these groups, however, stemmed less from aesthetic differences than from a moral issue. Liszt's condescending article on Thalberg's compositions, published early in the 1837 concert season, offended the conservative aristocrats who had lauded Thalberg; and because their influence in the *beau monde* had recently become distressingly weak, they needed to defend themselves. Cristina Belgiojoso sought to resolve this social tension by staging the famous contest at her home. The *beau monde* needed a ritual to affirm its fundamental unity as a political, social, and intellectual elite, which the contentious debates over Liszt and Thalberg were putting under stress. By framing the contest as a charity function – an inherently collective elite effort – Belgiojoso thought she could fill this need.

Prelude: Liszt's Parisian reputation in the 1830s

The rivalry between Liszt and Thalberg was ignited by an article Liszt published in the *Gazette musicale* on 8 January 1837. If the article had never been published, it is likely that no controversy would ever have flared up. In it, Liszt methodically attacked Thalberg's music, describing it as vapid, uninspired, and mediocre. That Liszt would be accused of professional jealousy and faulted for bad journalistic ethics was predictable enough. Why, then, did he feel compelled to publish such a strongly worded article? Why was he willing to put his reputation at risk? Answering this question requires some biographical preliminaries.

In the middle 1830s Liszt had little reason to be insecure about his Parisian reputation. In the public's opinion he was unquestionably the leading virtuoso of the city. An 1834 article in the *Gazette* had declared him the peak of a pyramid of virtuosos consisting of Chopin, Hiller, and Bertini.[2] Yet he was far from being unanimously accepted or admired, and he was anything but indifferent to public opinion. His manner of speaking, dressing, and behaving were often mocked in the caricature press.[3] The powerful critic F.-J. Fétis insisted that his playing still suffered from the same faults as in earlier years, claiming that Liszt lost control of color and expression through bodily convulsions, and that he destroyed the intentions of the classical masters.[4] Even Joseph d'Ortigue's 1835 biography – which is overwhelmingly positive – spoke frankly of the young virtuoso's faults, singling out exaggerations of expression, modifications of tempo, and "a certain charlatanism in his manner and in his playing."[5]

---

[2] A. Guemer, "Exécution musicale: Liszt, Ferd. Hiller, Chopin et Bertini," *Revue et gazette musicale* 1/1 (5 January 1834), 4–7.

[3] J. Duverger, *Notice biographique sur Franz Liszt* (Paris, 1843), 27.

[4] Two of Fétis's most cutting reviews are in the following issues: *Revue musicale*, 26 January 1833 and 16 March 1833. Fétis dropped his reservations when Liszt, in the same season, minimized his bodily motions, apparently in direct response to Fétis's criticism (*Revue musicale*, 30 November 1833, 349). It is easy to imagine that this too would be dissatisfying to Liszt: he was not temperamentally suited to letting someone like Fétis dictate his performing style.

[5] *Revue et gazette musicale* 2/24 (14 June 1835), 196.

21

Although these criticisms were not a serious threat to Liszt's pre-eminent status, they unsettled him. In the early 1830s especially, he needed affirmation that his artistry had been positively transformed by the inspiration of Paganini, by his vaunted commitment to Beethoven, and by the dramatic intellectual and literary ferment he was experiencing. He held an uncompromising attitude toward the sympathy and support of his friends and critics that led him to exaggerate the bad intentions of his detractors. F.-J. Fétis, for example, had always found things to praise in his playing, and his critical remarks are clearly stated with a constructive purpose. Yet Liszt found the criticisms unacceptable: "up until this period in his artistic life [1835]," Fétis wrote, "M. Liszt considered me his enemy because I tainted his triumphs with my severe criticism."[6]

These insecurities led Liszt to downplay his identity as a "mere" virtuoso pianist. He did not give even one public benefit concert for himself between 1828 and 1835, astonishing for a virtuoso of his stature. He occasionally appeared at benefit concerts for other musicians, but was not making conspicuous public appearances and asserting himself as a professional musician. In a discussion of this phase, Fétis noted: "There is reason to think that he was himself little satisfied with the effect that he made, because his appearances in public as well as in society were rare."[7] Where Liszt *was* asserting himself in these years was in the salons of the *literati*. He preferred to be recognized by a rarified, educated elite than by a concert-hall audience; he wanted to be thought of as an *artiste*, not just a pianist. He even seems to have developed a disdain for his identity as a virtuoso. The following report from 1843 could easily have surfaced a decade earlier: "M. Liszt has declared that he considers a pianist's talent a talent of such little importance that he would much prefer to be known as a good writer capable of handling musical matters than a celebrated performer on the piano."[8]

Liszt's dissatisfaction with his Parisian reputation provoked him to transcend his identity as a "mere virtuoso" by distinguishing himself in pursuits that were accorded more prestige – namely composition and letters. He pursued this goal not with a sense of vague aspiration, but in the form of a premeditated master plan. As early as 1833, he

---

[6] *Revue et gazette musicale* 4/17 (23 April 1837), 137–42. Ernest Legouvé, in a letter to Liszt from around 1840, apologized for having placed Chopin above Liszt in a published article. Legouvé had learned from a mutual friend, a certain Schoelcher, that Liszt was upset by this.

[7] *Revue et gazette musicale* 4/17 (23 April 1837), 137–42.

[8] *La Belgique musicale*, 9 March 1843; quoted in Charles Suttoni, *An Artist's Journey: Lettres d'un bachelier ès musique* (Chicago, 1989), xii.

had decided that his touring career would begin in the year 1840.[9] The intention never left his mind, for he reiterated it in letters from 1836 and 1839, and he realized it with uncanny precision, launching his itinerant career late in 1839.[10] According to this master plan – it was nothing less than that – he would set aside the latter part of the 1830s for the purpose of establishing himself as a man of letters and as a serious composer. These transformations, as he saw it, would prepare him for a spectacular performing career far more significant than that of the usual virtuoso.

When in the spring of 1835 Liszt and his companion Marie d'Agoult planned an extended absence from Paris, he had barely begun this process of transformation. He could no longer afford to delay, because in his absence he would only be able to sustain his visibility and status in Paris by means of articles and music publications. It is thus not surprising that his first major statements as a man of letters coincide with his departure from Paris. The first three installments of "De la situation des artistes" appeared in the *Gazette musicale* the month before he left, and the remaining installments were published at regular intervals throughout the rest of the year. As if to keep the literary ball rolling, he published the first of the "Lettres d'un bachelier ès musique" just a few weeks after the last installment of "Artistes." A further publishing event that coincided with his departure was the appearance of Joseph d'Ortigue's biography of Liszt in the *Gazette musicale* (14 June). The exceptional length of the document, fifteen columns in unusually small print, was far beyond the ordinary for the *Gazette*. It served as a consecration of Liszt – still only twenty-three years old – as a major figure in the Parisian artistic world, and it was exactly what he needed to secure his musical position while he was away from the city. In these ways Liszt was using his connections and editorial influence at the *Gazette* to protect and reshape his Parisian reputation.

After all these efforts to keep himself in the Parisian public eye, to minimize his insecurities, and to preserve his position, the worst possible thing happened: in late 1835 Thalberg appeared in Paris, and within a few weeks the public had lionized him. Three aspects of Thalberg's reception were particularly troublesome for Liszt. First, praise for Thalberg was unanimous, something he could not claim for himself. There is not a single negative comment to be found in any of the 1836 reviews of Thalberg. Second, the Parisian audiences had shown that they could universally admire a virtuoso who was not in any sense a literary or

---

[9] The letter in which he states this is from October 1839; Liszt tells Cristina Belgiojoso that he made the decision "six years ago." See *Autour de Mme. d'Agoult et de Liszt*, ed. D. Ollivier (Paris, 1941), 181.

[10] Jacquéline Bellas, "La tumultueuse amitié de Franz Liszt et de Maurice Schlesinger," *Littératures* 12 (1965), 13.

philosophical *artiste*, throwing into severe doubt the value and outcome of Liszt's master plan. Third, Thalberg was praised for his compositions as well as his virtuosity, whereas Liszt had not yet received recognition as a composer.

The third of these problems, Thalberg's success as a composer, needs special emphasis, because Liszt's fateful article – the document that initiated the rivalry – was aimed directly at Thalberg's compositions. Almost instantly upon his arrival Parisians were reading that "M. Thalberg is not only the leading [*premier*] pianist in the world, he is also a very distinguished composer."[11] Liszt could not yet compete as a composer, and this was a source of intense anxiety. The original large-scale compositions he had published by 1835 – the *Apparitions*, the *Harmonies poétiques et réligieuses*, and the *Clochette* fantasy – had convinced Parisians that he could not compose.[12] Just after hearing about Thalberg's successes in Paris, Liszt sent an article he had clipped from a Geneva newspaper to the editor of the *Gazette*, Maurice Schlesinger, and asked him to publish it. It spoke of his gifts as a composer, and not only his "tours de jonglerie musicale," as he deprecatingly put it.[13] It was the perfect vehicle to counteract the force of Thalberg in Paris. Schlesinger refused to print it, and Liszt wrote back angrily: "*My position is not that of just anybody; the same goes for my talent and my ambition.* I'm asking you again for my three or four years – then we shall see."[14] Thalberg, evidently, was ruining Liszt's master plan. What brand of virtuosity did he offer up that was capable of making such a potent impact on the Parisians?

1.   Liszt and Thalberg in comparison

Thalberg's vocality

Thalberg's early reputation in Paris centered on a single composition: his fantasy on themes from Rossini's *Moïse*. People were talking about it in the salons not long after his arrival: "The fantasy . . . is, according to all the connoisseurs, ingeniously composed . . . never was the melody interrupted."[15] Although they heard it at virtually every appearance he

---

[11] *Ménestrel* 3/15 (13 March 1836).

[12] This is shown in Dieter Torkewitz, "Die Erstfassung der 'Harmonies poétiques et réligieuses' von Liszt," *Liszt-Studien* 2 (Munich, 1981), 228. The reception of these pieces in Germany was also unfavorable.

[13] Bellas, "Tumultueuse amitié," 11; undated letter. The article praising Liszt's compositions was by Émile Prym.

[14] Ibid., 13; emphasis original. This letter also shows that Schlesinger had given Liszt "advice" on his compositions, which is probably a euphemism for criticism. The reference to three or four years shows that Liszt still planned to start concertizing around 1840.

[15] *Gazette des salons* (1836), 190.

made in the 1836 and 1837 seasons, Parisian audiences could not get enough of the fantasy. Publishers raced to capitalize on its popularity by producing several "simplified" editions.[16] By 1838 it was palpably intruding upon the glory of other virtuosos. Theodor Döhler's benefit concert, attended by Thalberg, was interrupted by a note dropped onto the stage: "'Mr. Thalberg is requested by the public to play the fantasy on *Moïse*. – Bravo! bravo! yes, *Moïse, Moïse!'* – And Thalberg, responding to these flattering invitations, came with that modest air you know in him and played the piece with his two hands."[17] Döhler could not have resented the request too much: without Thalberg's presence the concert hall might have been half empty from the start.

The *Moïse* fantasy is still the basis for Thalberg's reputation. He is best known for supposedly inventing the "three-hand technique," in which a melody is sustained in the middle register using both hands, while arpeggios cloud around it from above and below (Example 1.1).[18] The association of Thalberg with the three-hand technique was codified in an article Fétis wrote in 1837, and because of Fétis's emphasis on compositional technique and historical development, this technique has drawn the most attention from musicologists. Yet the lionization of Thalberg in Paris began in 1836, and the articles from that season are much more concerned with the sound and feeling of his playing. Henri Blanchard's article of May 1836 – presumably a resume of ideas that had been circulating in the salons during the concert season – makes no reference at all to the technical "advances" of Thalberg's art. Furthermore, the novelty of Thalberg's innovation does not explain why this *particular* technique triggered a reaction much more profound than the innovations of other virtuosos in Paris. We must therefore look beyond the technique-centered emphasis of Fétis and open our ears to Thalberg's sonorous aesthetic, for it was ultimately his vocality, not the three-handed technique per se, that anchored his reception in Paris. Indeed, when he was eventually prevailed upon to produce a treatise, he entitled it *L'art du chant appliqué au piano*.

Thalberg's vocality – his manner of sustaining the *chant* (both "song" and "voice") throughout a piece – gave his playing a character quite distinct from Liszt's. It was already noted by the *Gazette*'s Vienna correspondent in 1834, when Thalberg's existence was barely known to Paris: "When he plays the theme *Là ci darem la mano* on the piano, it is impossible not to think you are hearing the same song being sung; the

---

16 Katharine Ellis, "Female Pianists and their Male Critics in Nineteenth-Century Paris," *Journal of the American Musicological Society* 50 (1997), 356n.

17 *Revue et gazette musicale* 5/16 (22 April 1838), 168 (H. Blanchard).

18 For a full discussion of the three-hand technique, which was in fact not invented by Thalberg, see Isabelle Bélance-Zank, "The Three-hand Texture: Origins and Use," *Journal of the American Liszt Society* 38 (1995), 99–121.

Example 1.1 Thalberg, *Célèbre fantaisie pour le piano sur "Moïse"*

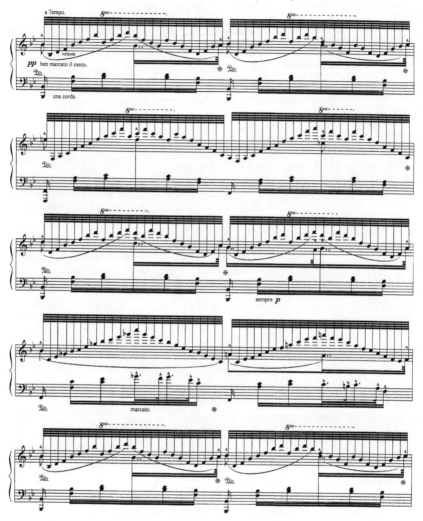

full sounds, her delayed submission, the piano expresses all of that as if it were the most dramatic voice."[19] Blanchard was impressed by the same, nearly iconic presence of the human voice: "you forget the dryness of this mechanical instrument, and you are completely surprised to hear the sound held, singing, crying like Grisi, Malibran, de-Beriot,

---

[19] *Gazette musicale de Paris* 1/43 (26 October 1834), 346–48 (A. Z.).

or Rubini . . . No one has ever sung on the piano like Thalberg."[20] The vocality of Thalberg's playing was singled out as its distinguishing mark just a couple of months after his arrival:

All of these difficulties, which seem to play themselves under his fingers, are only the accompaniments and embellishments of a firm song, sustained and penetrating, which despite the prodigious traffic of notes seduces the ear and charms the heart like the sounds of Rubini's or Mlle. Falcon's voice.[21]

This vocal aesthetic had such appeal for the Parisian audiences that he was almost immediately named "le premier pianiste du monde," the phrase that, after finding its way around the salons, prompted Liszt to come back to Paris and find out who this mysterious rival was.[22]

The vocality of Thalberg's playing did not consist in a "singing tone" of the kind Cramer, Field, and Chopin were famous for, and which had a firm hold in piano pedagogy. The traditional "singing tone" was produced by a legato touch, phrasing, fingering, and nuanced dynamics. Thalberg, however, played the internal melody of his compositions *bien marcato*; it had to be hammered out firmly in order to emerge above the acoustic wash of the arpeggios and figuration. The sense of connection in the melody was created not by the fingers alone, but by the sonorous tissue, mainly arpeggios, between the melodic tones. As Fétis later let on, "the vocal character that he managed to give to the singing part [was achieved] by the resources of the pedals."[23] By opening up a wide range of sympathetic vibrations and by placing the melody in a lower register than usual, Thalberg evoked the voice as a sonorous plenitude rather than as an elegantly shaped line. Thalberg's voice was also differently gendered. While the "singing tone" voice was almost invariably a soprano, Thalberg evoked on the piano the sound of a male voice, filling in the registers of tenor and contralto (as Fétis pointed out). The "singing tone" voice was analogous to the voice heard in private salons – in genres such as the Lied, the romance and the nocturne. Thalberg's voice, in contrast, was full and rich, able to project into large spaces; it was the voice of an opera singer.[24] And to the extent that Thalberg's reputation was made and sustained on the basis of a fantasy on themes from Rossini's *Moïse*, it was a voice from *Italian* opera.

Contemporary writers rarely commented on Liszt's tone, suggesting that tone per se was less central to his aesthetic. And the few comments

---

[20] *Revue et gazette musicale* 3/19 (8 May 1836), 153–54 (H. Blanchard). De Beriot's place in this list can be explained by the fact that he was a noted representative of the French violin school, which took pride in its melodic, vocal approach to the instrument.

[21] *Abeille musicale* (March 1836), 3.   [22] *Ménestrel* 3/15 (13 March 1836).

[23] *Revue et gazette musicale* 8/32 (9 May 1841), 261–64 (Fétis).

[24] Adjectives such "powerful," "penetrating," "full," and "sonorous" appear repeatedly in descriptions of Thalberg's delivery of melodies.

we do have tend to be negative. Henry Chorley, who was fond of Liszt and his pianism, put it most diplomatically: "In uniform richness and sweetness of tone he may have been surpassed."[25] Another commentator noted this weakness, but drew attention to the compensating advantages: "Liszt has no touch, but he makes the tones awaken, live, grow, and soar through a subtle handling of the keys."[26] This evocation of a living being, of an animated character, is the main feature separating Liszt's approach to melody from that of Thalberg and that of the "singing tone" school. Compare the above description of Thalberg playing the melody of *Là ci darem la mano* with descriptions of Liszt playing the same melody (in his *Don Giovanni* fantasy). Thalberg's performance evoked a material icon of the singing voice, and only secondarily the character's feelings. Liszt's performances, however, evoked the dramatic character singing the song, rendering it even more sharply than the original operatic scene: "No, you have never heard the motif of the duo *La ci darem la mano* sung with such soul and tenderness, never heard the song *Fin ch'an d'al vino!* with such gaiety and wildness. And the applause and acclamations often interrupted the artist."[27] A Vienna critic was similarly swept away by the vividness of character in Liszt's performance, signaled here by a plethora of adjectives:

How tasteful and charming sounded the "La ci darem la mano" under his hands, how it sang ever more beautiful, more intimate, more sweet; how serious and forceful arose the stone guest's warning voice in pressed chords of the strings, then in between the cheerful loose joke of the happy couple, and at the close the energetic champagne song, performed with all fire, stirring in the highest degree through boldness and bravura.[28]

---

[25] Henry Chorley, *Music and Manners in France and Germany* (London, 1844), 3 vols., III: 45n. Chorley was kind enough to put this comment in a footnote. The disregard of tone in the Parisian press may result from the fact that almost all the virtuosos in Paris, like Liszt, had emerged from the Viennese "brilliant" school, which laid much less emphasis on melodic continuity and beauty than the rival English school. This is also suggested by the unusual focus on his tone and touch in the English reception, of which Chorley's comment is a trace. A Norwich critic claimed that "his tone is inferior to Thalberg's, whose means are all adapted to the one end of making the most of his instrument, and towards which tone is the first requisite" (*Norwich Mercury*, 26 September 1840; quoted in *Liszt Society Journal* 7 [1982], 13).

[26] *Pester Tageblatt*, 31 December 1839. "Liszt hat keinen Anschlag; sondern durch graduelles Betesten der Klappern macht er die Töne entstehen, leben, wachsen, und entschweben."

[27] *Revue et gazette musicale* 11/26 (30 June 1844), 223 (P. Smith).

[28] *Allgemeine Theaterzeitung*, 3 March 1846. Yet another example of the same idea appears in the Leipzig *Zeitung für die elegante Welt*, 17 December 1841: "As he played the arias from *Don Juan*, they stepped palpably forward into the scene, the tones became action, as though the figures, Zerlina and the others, wanted to emerge out of them." The remarkable consistency of this response to Liszt's *Don Giovanni* fantasy is also attributable to the familiarity of the opera.

The clarity with which Liszt realized the dramatic character of a melody was enhanced by his facial and bodily expressions, which often mimicked the feeling or emotion in the music:

Là ci darem la mano he rendered in a way that I shall never forget . . . Everything he did on the keys was mirrored in his features, flashed in his eyes and electrified by all his movements; especially in the duet between the Don and Zerlina, in which at one moment he looked timid and the next leapt from his seat into the air for joy.[29]

The dramatic, character-centered orientation of Liszt's playing, evident in these descriptions of the *Don Giovanni* fantasy, extends beyond his approach to melody. Drama was basic to his aesthetic even when there was no specific dramatic subject. In his rendition of the Scherzo of Beethoven's sixth symphony, a piece he played often in public, he slowed down to about half the previous tempo when he arrived at the D major melody at measure 9 (Example 1.2).[30] He thereby treated the two eight-bar phrases as two radically opposed images or characters, rather than as a pair of complementary syntactical units that must temporally balance each other. Although Thalberg performed the *Moïse* fantasy at almost every concert he gave in Paris, not one critic ever mentioned the stage characters whose melody was being sung, or the emotional quality of the melody, either in its operatic or pianistic context. The difference between Liszt and Thalberg's delivery of melodies, then, was not only that Thalberg's was more stamped with a vocal element. More important still, Liszt made his melodies paint a character, or signify, whereas with Thalberg the melody was presented for the sake of gorgeous vocal sonority alone – the grain of the voice.

Thalberg and the dilettantes

According to this interpretation of Thalberg's aesthetic, his ideal listener was the fan of vocal music, especially Italian opera. In Paris such listeners were abundant. Instrumental music had on the whole made much less headway there than in other musical capitals, and Beethoven was only beginning to be heard on a regular basis.[31] Because listening habits of the Parisian concert-going audiences were still quite thoroughly opera-centered, Thalberg appealed to them at the core of their tastes and preferences: "enveloping like a region the theme, which M. Thalberg usually

---

[29] Curd von Schloezer, *Römische Briefe, 1864–1869* (Stuttgart and Berlin, 1926); quoted in "Liszt in Rome (iii)," *Liszt Society Journal* 10 (1985), 30. Schloezer wrote this in a letter from Göttingen dated 29 November 1841.

[30] *The Autobiography of Charles Hallé*, ed. Michael Kennedy (London, 1972), 58. The date of Hallé's recollection is apparently 1836.

[31] On the limited presence of instrumental music in France, see chapter 6 in Jean Mongrédien, *La musique en France des lumières au romantisme, 1789–1830* (Paris, 1986).

Example 1.2 Beethoven, Symphony no. 6, III, opening

has the good sense to choose from Rossini or Meyerbeer, [he makes] an infallible call to the applause of the Parisian public, always happy to discover in concert music its memories of the Théâtre-Italiens and the Opéra."[32] Thalberg's choice of thematic material for his fantasies, indeed, stands out for its nearly exclusive focus on opera, avoiding the popular songs or folk songs other virtuosos were drawing upon.

Yet Liszt, too, was playing many fantasies on opera melodies, so opera alone was insufficient to anchor Thalberg's reception. To understand Thalberg's special appeal we need to look at a particular kind of opera listener addressed by his playing: the dilettante. Beginning in the late eighteenth century the word "dilettante" was being used to designate passionate fans of Italian opera.[33] The enormous success of Rossini during the Restoration increased both the number of dilettantes in Paris and the degree of enthusiasm they displayed. Although the dilettantes were often mocked, they had considerable power as trendsetters, and were able to spread the taste for Rossini to a larger social spectrum. Not

---

[32] *Le monde* 4/7 (6 April 1838).

[33] This discussion of the *dilettanti* is based mostly on James H. Johnson, *Listening in Paris: A Cultural History* (Berkeley and Los Angeles, 1995), 190–92.

all fans of Italian opera were as demonstrative as the dilettantes, but the dilettante revealed most explicitly the aesthetic priorities of the Italian opera listener.

The dilettante listener was fixated on melody and the voice, less on the words, dramatic emotions, or stage machinery. As James H. Johnson has put it, Rossini's music at the Italiens "aroused great emotion without conveying it. It created an effect without wrapping it in an image."[34] The dilettante disdained a "learned" way of listening; for him the musical response should be based exclusively on sentiment. He strove to acquire, and to display in the theatre, a direct, unmediated response to the melody. He demonstrated his uninhibited response by sending out resounding *bravos* at every high note or virtuosic passage. In between these climactic moments he was quiet and concentrated, visually absorbed in the music.

Although not all dilettantes were aristocrats, dilettante listening was socially coded as "aristocratic." They held court at the Théâtre des Italiens, the public theatre in Paris most identified with the nobility, and the "house composer" Rossini was symbolically linked with the Restoration political order. The dilettante's demonstrations of enthusiasm were thus a social gesture, signaling that he possessed an elevated taste, which in turn defined or confirmed his elite social status. Other listeners at the Italiens who listened intensely and claimed an elevated taste – namely the men of letters who frequented the orchestra region of the theatre – also laid claim to dilettante status. It is precisely because dilettante listening was socially coded, available for appropriation by non-aristocrats, that it preserved distinct, consistent boundaries, allowing us to identify it as a "type" of listening.

There was thus in Paris a distinct segment of listening public, housed at the Théâtre des Italiens, that was predisposed to the aesthetic Thalberg presented. This helps explain his very unusual decision to give his first public concert in Paris at the Italiens. While it was not uncommon for the house singers to give their benefit concerts in the hall, it was unheard of for a piano virtuoso to give his benefit there, especially since so many new spaces for piano concerts had recently opened.[35] Thalberg's choice was both a recognition that his aesthetic would appeal to the dilettantes and a strong gesture of affiliation with the aristocracy that lorded over the theatre. He continued to play at the Italiens as often as he could when he revisited Paris. Indeed, he established the hall as the venue for

---

[34] Johnson, *Listening in Paris*, 220.

[35] Concert spaces commonly used by virtuosos included the Salle Pleyel, the Conservatoire, and the Gymnase musicale. As a young boy Liszt had in fact played at the Italiens, but these concerts were presented between acts of an opera performance.

the very top virtuosos of the future, starting with Döhler in 1838 and continuing with Liszt in 1844.

Liszt was aware of Thalberg's appeal for the Parisian dilettantes, and had no desire to try to win them over to his own aesthetic. In an outline for an article he asked Marie d'Agoult to complete, he wanted it mentioned that the audience at his four chamber music soirées of 1837, which featured Beethoven's music, were evidence of a substantial public for serious music, and that his concert programs "were not of the sort to seduce the dilettantes or the dandies in the balcony of the Italiens."[36] This was written at the height of his rivalry with Thalberg. Liszt was defining himself against his rival by associating himself with a distinctly different, more serious-minded listening public. Thalberg's dilettante public was further mentioned in a review of his 1837 benefit at the Conservatoire: his fantasy on *God Save the Queen* "did not make much of an impression, a deduction gathered from the obligatory enthusiasm of the dilettantes, who so insisted on behaving like dilettantes."[37] And when Thalberg came back to Paris in 1838, a German journal admiringly reported, his public concerts at the Italiens were attended by "all the dilettantes of the high aristocracy."[38]

Two great dilettantes, both legitimists and both high on the social scale, betrayed a musical preference for Thalberg over Liszt: Henry Chorley and Count Armand de Pontmartin. Chorley was descended from the Lancashire gentry, and his social circles were significantly higher than those of most music critics of his time.[39] Chorley genuinely enjoyed Liszt's playing, but he could not give himself over to Liszt entirely because he associated him with the French romantics, for whom he had a distaste typical of his social class. He was able to enjoy Thalberg, however, without restraint:

There are things the right appreciation for which no comparison is needed – such as the "Sono innocente!" of Pasta in "Otello" . . . [Chorley gives examples of passages sung by Duprez, Malibran, and Lablanche] . . . or Thalberg's hand upon the piano. They go to the heart at once as supreme, and not to be surpassed of their kind; and if our enthusiasm for them becomes a prejudice, it is one which, in the first instance, has been startled into life by some display which so entirely satisfies as well as startles, that a slight tenacity in yielding it up on any new temptation is surely excusable.[40]

---

[36] *Correspondance de Liszt et de Madame d'Agoult*, ed. Daniel Ollivier (Paris, 1933–35), 2 vols., I: 193.

[37] *Courrier des théâtres*, 13 March 1837. The review is generally negative. This critic, clearly despising the virtuoso phenomenon as a whole, has no kinder words for Liszt.

[38] *Europa* (1838/2), 140.

[39] Jennifer Lee Hall, "The Refashioning of Fashionable Society: Opera-going and Sociability in Britain, 1821–1861" (Ph.D. dissertation, Yale University, 1996), 284, 288.

[40] Chorley, *Music and Manners*, III: 17.

This passage is a distillation of the priorities of the dilettante. He has a list of favorite moments from Italian opera performers, his taste is elevated ("right appreciation"), he focuses on sentiment ("go to the heart," "so entirely satisfies"), and his response is passionate (his enthusiasm becomes a prejudice that he refuses to give up). That Chorley should drop Thalberg's name alongside those of the most famous singers of Italian opera is an unmistakable sign that the virtuoso is being valued for his vocality. The three-hand technique could not be further from his mind.

The other dilettante who clearly preferred Thalberg to Liszt was Count Armand de Pontmartin, an aristocrat. In his book *Souvenirs d'un vieux mélomane* (1879) – whose title itself gives away his dilettante bias – Pontmartin talks almost exclusively about singers of Italian opera, waxing particularly rhapsodic over Malibran. Like Chorley, Pontmartin bore an aversion to the romantics, and this led him to prefer Thalberg to Liszt: "In 1840 romanticism still dominated, and an illustrious example persuaded us that a pianist who was not frenzied [i.e., Thalberg] could only be considered mediocre."[41] Pontmartin gives a poetic account of Thalberg enrapturing a small audience at his Avignon home with the fantasy on *Moïse*. He describes the three-hand effect, but as though to remind the reader of his unprofessional, dilettante orientation, he attaches a footnote attributing the "technical details" to another author. In another anecdote, Pontmartin recalls a concert by Liszt at the home of Émile Zimmerman. On this occasion, Pontmartin offered a merely tepid opinion of Liszt's playing. Zimmerman was baffled, and Pontmartin was forced to explain himself by alluding to Thalberg's concert at his home: "since my last trip to Paris I have heard another virtuoso quite as extraordinary, and in circumstances much more suited to exalting the imagination."[42] Pontmartin highlights his preference for the private context, the aristocrat's privilege that allows him to listen in a nobler, more exalted manner.

Chorley and Pontmartin represent the dilettante orientation in its purer form, but they are only the tip of the iceberg. Paris was filled with vocally centered listeners who did not share the dilettante's social status or habits, but who leaned heavily toward Thalberg, and their tastes found voice in several of the widely circulating journals. Henri Blanchard of the *Revue et gazette musicale* was Thalberg's most enthusiastic fan, and although his main task was to review concerts, the human voice was at the center of his listening pleasures. In a sonnet he wrote for

---

[41] Count Armand de Pontmartin, *Souvenirs d'un vieux critique* (Paris, 1881), 10 vols., I: 271–72. In the passages that follow this quotation, the identities of the musicians being discussed are revealed to be Liszt and Thalberg.

[42] Ibid., 296.

Cristina Belgiojoso, he lauded the pianist alongside the leading opera singers: "To listen to Rubini, Thalberg, or Damoreau / Is to know the most beautiful things in the art."[43] His articles on Thalberg are stamped with a dilettante orientation: he elaborates on the aura of Thalberg's personality and on his vocality, or on the sentiment he conveys to his audiences, and they are for the most part void of musical learning.[44] Blanchard's reviews of Liszt's concerts, while generally positive, are uninspired in comparison.

Thalberg was also the favorite of *La France musicale*. From its earliest issues (1838) this journal made itself the headquarters of Thalberg advocacy, and in the 1840s it acquired an institutional weight matched only by the *Gazette musicale*. As the organ of the publishing firm of the Escudier brothers, it focused on Italian opera and vocal music, and its criticism reflected the Italian emphasis.[45] Its main readership, we can therefore presume, was the dilettante-derived Italian opera public. The Escudiers took advantage of Thalberg's appeal to the Italian opera fans by publishing his compositions and promoting his talent in the journal with large articles and regular reports.[46]

The vocality of Thalberg's playing also gave him a more powerful stronghold among amateurs of vocal music than Liszt. This is evident in the outstanding support that he received in 1836 from the journals *Ménestrel* and *Abeille musicale*. Both were romance journals, whose primary purpose was to offer regular installments of a song or vocal romance. Their subscribers were amateurs of vocal music. Articles and news items in the *Ménestrel* were customarily very short and often light or humorous, but an exception was made for Thalberg. He was blessed

---

[43] *Revue et gazette musicale* 9/17 (24 April 1842), 181 (H. Blanchard). "Écouter Rubini, Thalberg ou Damoreau, / C'est connaître de l'art ce qu'il y a de plus beau."

[44] Blanchard's writing style is that of the dilettante critic: his criticisms are consistently sensitive to social implications, interlaced with classical references, literary in tone, and prone to brief summarizing phrases.

[45] Ellis, *Music Criticism*, 46.

[46] It should be noted, however, that *La France musicale* championed Thalberg with little reference to his vocality. It derived much of its rhetoric about Thalberg from Fétis's articles from 1837, thematizing the novelty of his pianism and its connection with a classical "school." It is surprising that a journal with vocally oriented readers would not have taken advantage of Thalberg's vocality to promote his compositions. A possible explanation is that the Escudiers had a purely commercial interest, and did not particularly care on what grounds they promoted him. Another possible explanation is that Léon Escudier, the author of the Thalberg articles, felt the authority of Fétis's musical expertise – rooted in uncompromising professionalism – to be stronger than his more impressionistic, dilettantish writing style. The *France musicale* and the *Gazette* were in the midst of heavy competition, and Escudier could not risk falling behind. In spite of their lack of emphasis on Thalberg's vocality, the articles in the *France musicale* had the effect of spreading and buttressing his reputation among the broader Italian opera public.

with an article that was by far the most extended and intellectual article to appear in the journal, and its peroration was the first appearance in print of the *bon mot* that would set off Liszt's reaction: "M. Thalberg is not only the best pianist in the world, he is also a very distinguished composer."[47] The *Ménestrel* became a permanent supporter of Thalberg and a critic of Liszt. A satire of Liszt appeared in November 1836, some months after Thalberg's first wave of success in Paris. At the height of the virtuoso rivalry in 1837, it reprinted a segment of one of Fétis's damaging articles on Liszt.[48] The *Ménestrel*, furthermore, hailed Thalberg's return to Paris in 1842, after an absence of four years, as a major event. He was praised for his "suavity, sensitivity, expression and warmth without impetuosity," the latter comment clearly implying a comparison with Liszt.[49] At about the same time, the journal began reporting on Liszt with restless mockery, and continued to do so for several years. The *Ménestrel*'s conspicuous advocacy of Thalberg against Liszt may have been tied to commercial interests, since the editor Heugel might have been publishing Thalberg's compositions. Nevertheless, it helped forge a bond with its vocally oriented readership by promoting a pianist whose aesthetic was more voice-centered than that of his contemporaries.

Thalberg's vocality was the secret of his immense success in Paris. He had come to Paris at a time when the Parisian publics had not yet had depth of experience with instrumental music. They remained voice-centered, opera-centered, and nothing could have disposed them better to Thalberg's aesthetic of singing on the piano. The journals circulating among the vocally inclined segments of the Parisian public – be they old-fashioned aristocratic dilettantes or modern sheet-music consumers – disseminated his reputation and strengthened his support base. Fétis's claims about Thalberg's historical importance and compositional innovations strengthened his status, especially among the more serious-minded musicians and listeners in Paris, but they did not provide its foundation.

Liszt's orchestrality

Liszt's playing was altogether more diverse, and poses more problems for characterization. Yet just as the leading metaphor for Thalberg's playing was the voice, so Liszt's playing drew in the metaphor of the orchestra. Shortly before leaving Paris in 1835, he thrilled audiences at the Conservatoire with his arrangement of the "Bal" and "Marche" from

---

[47] *Ménestrel* 3/15 (13 March 1836). This article is likely to have been commissioned from outside or lifted from another source, as the *Ménestrel* occasionally did in later years.
[48] *Ménestrel* 4/22 (30 April 1837).   [49] *Ménestrel* 9/19 (17 April 1842).

Berlioz's *Symphonie fantastique*, thus inviting audiences to compare the original with his transcription. Joseph d'Ortigue, perhaps prompted by this recent event, observed that an orchestral conception pervaded his piano music: "in everything Liszt has had the goal of applying orchestration to the piano, that is, to render the piano *instrumental* and diversified [*concertant*] with itself."[50] The main orchestral transcriptions in Liszt's repertory in these early years were the excerpts from Berlioz's *Symphonie fantastique* and the last three movements of Beethoven's sixth symphony, the latter appearing much more frequently than the former. Every time he was in Paris audiences heard either the Beethoven or the Berlioz. Critics were consistently amazed at how perfectly Beethoven's orchestra was transferred to the piano:

Just listen to Liszt, orchestra on the piano! See in each of his fingers the capacity of a whole association of people! . . . He successively conjures up in their magnificence all the faces, the grandiose monologues of the winds, the demonic pizzicatos of the basses; from the trembling pianissimo to the fortissimo tempest! and you will admit that Liszt has transformed the piano, that he has metamorphosed it into an orchestra.[51]

Liszt was equally successful at capturing the varied effects of Berlioz's more colorful, more variegated orchestra: "It is really prodigious to hear the piano reproduce so powerfully and with such charm all the effects of [the *Symphonie fantastique*], all the little details of the instrumentation."[52]

Yet the impression of a reproduction of orchestral sound, however prominent in these descriptions, was not the most important aspect of Liszt's orchestrality. In these quotations, as in most other reviews, the orchestra is evoked in its heterogeneity and multiplicity – as a potpourri of sounds, characters, and dynamic levels – rather than as an organic unit. It was thus Liszt's tendency – both in his compositions and his playing – to multiply timbres, stratify registers, differentiate dynamics, and recompose textures that made the orchestra an appropriate metaphor for his playing as a whole. Théophile Gautier drew attention away from the literalness of the orchestral comparison, highlighting in Liszt's playing the richness of details, the sheer quantity of impressions, each of them forcefully evoked:

Not that he enticed from the body of his piano a volume of sonority equal to the noise of all the instruments, but he articulated all its melodies, evoked the most

---

[50] *Gazette musicale de Paris* 2/24 (14 June 1835), 202 (J. d'Ortigue); emphasis original. Vienna critic Heinrich Adami drew the same conclusion: "many passages from his compositions suggest that one of his primary goals is to orchestrate the piano as much as possible" (*Allgemeine Theaterzeitung*, 5 May 1838).

[51] *Revue et gazette musicale* 6/67 (12 December 1839), 531.

[52] *Monde musical* 5/19 (9 May 1844), 76.

delicate nuances, the most fleeting intentions with an incredible charm, relief, and penetration.[53]

It is because of this richness of color, character, and detail that Liszt was best heard solo, rather than accompanied by orchestra:

The intervention or rather cooperation of the orchestra often prevents the appreciation of a thousand finesses, a thousand lovely caprices, like fleeting thoughts, varied and fleeting like the nuances with which the sun colors the mist which rises around rushing cascades, and these infinite delicacies so rarely accompanied by *strength,* and which Liszt, the *strongest* of all pianists, nevertheless possesses to the highest degree.[54]

As these passages show, Liszt's orchestrality consisted in sonorous and expressive multiplicity, in the dispersion and restless shift of sensations and impressions. The metaphors that come up repeatedly are images of violent fragmentation: cascades, sparks, flames, meteors, and storms. This splintering effect is registered in visual representations of his music (Figures 1.1 and 1.2).

Liszt's *Grande fantaisie di bravura sur la clochette de Paganini,* which he performed often in the 1830s, is a composed-out example of his orchestral approach to the piano (Example 1.3). There is hardly a moment in the fantasy where the texture does not have three or four independent layers. A single hand can be responsible for managing two contrasting types of attack or articulation (mm. 88–89, 95–98, 118–20). Both hands are constantly shifting registers, crossing each other, and switching roles (mm. 91–93, 99–104, 118–25). Liszt's notation practices are revealing: there is an almost ridiculous density of notated information on dynamics, accentuation, articulation, tempo, and character. Measure 127 alone contains four types of articulation marks, a separate dynamic marking for the lower voice (just one shade down from the other voices), specific pedaling indications, and four verbal instructions. The score reads more like a transcription of a performance than a prescription for performance. This is a virtuoso style that pursues complexity of texture, richness of detail, and bodily choreography to the maximum. Continuity is undesirable: no pianistic idea is pursued for more than four measures, and abrupt shifts are the rule (mm. 109–12, 125–27, and 131–36).

Writers also brought in the orchestra to describe Thalberg's playing, but it was an orchestra of a different kind. When Fétis wrote of Thalberg: "the instrument acquired under his fingers the power and fullness [*ampleur*] of a large orchestra,"[55] he was thinking of the orchestra as a

---

[53] *La presse,* 13 May 1844 (T. Gautier).

[54] *Revue et gazette musicale* 4/13 (26 March 1837), 103; emphasis original. The piece under review is Liszt's *Divertissement sur la cavatine "I tuoi frequenti palpiti."*

[55] *Revue et gazette musicale* 4/17 (23 April 1837), 137–42. This was also the basis for the occasional comparison of Thalberg's sonority to that of the organ.

Figure 1.1 Caricature of Liszt, 1842

Figure 1.2 "'General Bass' is taken unawares in his fixed lines, and overpowered by Liszt," 1842

Example 1.3 Liszt, *Grand fantaisie di bravura sur la clochette de Paganini*

full-bodied, integrated sonority that activated several registers simultaneously. Another *Gazette* writer made the same comparison:

We don't know how to express with what charm the deeply melancholic and impassioned melodies of the andante [from Beethoven's fifth symphony] were exhaled from Thalberg's piano. It is to be wondered whether the orchestra of the Conservatory, whether the human voice has more intimate eloquence, more true, penetrating accent.[56]

---

[56] *Revue et gazette musicale* 5/12 (25 March 1838), 131–32 (E. M.).

Example 1.3 (*cont.*)

Thalberg's playing could only evoke comparison with the orchestra as a unified whole. The orchestra cited here, that of the Conservatoire, was legendary throughout Europe for its precision ensemble and homogeneous power. It performed as if with a single "voice," facilitating the comparison to a human voice in this quotation. The Conservatoire orchestra appeared as a mass of performers whose coordination produced a unified enunciation, and this unity was often symbolized by reference to the orchestra's leader, François Habeneck.[57]

[57] It is important to differentiate this sense of enunciation from that conveyed by modern conductors, who have come to embody near complete authorial power in orchestral

Example 1.3 (*cont.*)

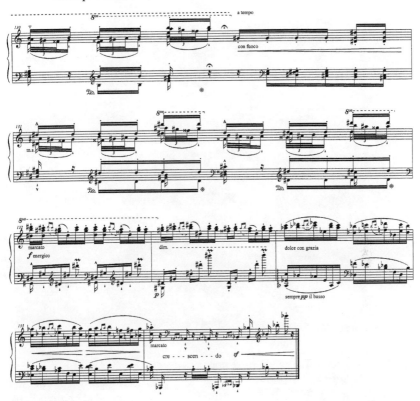

Liszt's playing, however, conveyed an image of the orchestra quite different from that of the Conservatoire orchestra, which was the prevalent ideal in the minds of contemporary Parisians. From a single performer emerged the sounds of a multitude of enunciators usually distributed among the orchestra: "Liszt, orchestra on the piano! See in every finger the capacity of a whole association of people." In this passage Liszt's fingers are singled out as the bodily analogy for that division of self, or dispersal of enunciation, that his pianistic style enacted.[58] Through the involvement of his body in his performing style,

performances. Habeneck was not a modern conductor, and did little more than keep time. He was the *symbol* of the Conservatoire orchestra's unified utterance, not its *source*.

[58] The term "enunciation" here refers to the effect of a subject or speaker, a speaking "I," being present in the material signs of language. Linguist Emile Benveniste theorized enunciation in relation to the grammatical "I," and Susan Bernstein has used his ideas to explore Liszt's problematization of the "I" in his writings. See especially the introduction, and the chapter "Liszt's Bad Style," in *Virtuosity of the Nineteenth Century: Performing Music and Language in Heine, Liszt, and Baudelaire* (Stanford, 1998).

41

Figure 1.3 Parisian caricature of Liszt, 1855

Liszt maximized the sense of dispersal already inherent in his sound. When he played "La ci darem la mano," we have seen, he "became" Zerlina temporarily, then "became" Don Giovanni. Liszt realized the dialogue as if he was himself two characters, a dispersal of enunciation effected partly by mimetic facial gestures.

Bodily dispersal is a common theme in contemporary caricatures of Liszt. Such images almost always focus on the hands, for obvious reasons a concentrated site of visual attention in virtuosic performance. Not only do Liszt's fingers multiply, but they also divide within themselves; their joints become detached and take on a radically independent movement (Figures 1.3, 1.4, 1.5). With this division the fingers challenge the sovereignty of the hand, and by extension Liszt's sovereignty over his body: "his fingers seem to lengthen and stretch out by means of a spring, and often to separate from the hands."[59] Liszt contributed to this effect by experimenting with "incomprehensible interweavings of the fingers" such as crossing the fourth finger over the fifth.[60] These experiments were radical at a time when "correct fingering" was still a

---

[59] *Europa* (1836/1), 381. The article quotes this passage from a French source that I have not identified.
[60] *Musical World* 10/138 (1 November 1838), 134–35.

Figure 1.4 "Galop chromatique," 1843

rather dogmatic aspect of piano pedagogy. A close associate of Liszt in Vienna observed that he achieved his effects "through a quite personal method of fingering, in which the thumb assumes a wide variety of functions."[61]

The independence that characterized Liszt's hands and fingers extended to his body as a whole. In performance he stamped his feet, lifted his arms far above the keyboard, and on the whole denied his body a stable center of gravity. In the caricatures his limbs and hair are in restless motion: one foot is in the air, the other on the ground, the toes pointing different ways, his hair blowing in one direction, his head looking upward while his limbs spread out, octopus-like, in all directions (Figures 1.4 and 1.5). This is a body on the verge of

---

[61] *Humorist*, 28 May 1838 (M. Saphir).

Figure 1.5 "Le magicien Liszt au piano"

Figure 1.6 J.-P. Dantan, "Liszt"

complete dismemberment, a body abandoned by a sovereign will. Dantan's well-known sculpture epitomizes this sense of sovereign breakdown by burying Liszt's head – the site of rational control – altogether in his hair (Figure 1.6). Liszt's bodily division, moreover, was never easily separated from the sonorous complexity of his music:

45

No system of words can accurately describe the power which Liszt possesses of *dividing* himself, as it were, into two, or sometimes, even, three performers . . . obviously unreachable extensions; playing figures of opposite character, widely-contrasted power, and running through and intersecting each other with the utmost freedom of motion, an arpeggio bass of large dimensions meanwhile continuing uninterrupted.[62]

Liszt's bodily motions – surely one of his most remarkable contributions to the history of performance in general – provoked mixed responses. There were critics who said the motions were the result of a willful *bizarrerie* that he had adopted through his association with the romantics, and they occasionally urged Liszt in print to get rid of the excessive motions (F.-J. Fétis and A. Specht are examples). These critics assumed that Liszt had control over his bodily motions, that he *could* stop them, that they were indeed subordinate to his sovereign will. As listeners they were doomed to dislike Liszt's playing, since they perceived the fragmented, disjointed language of his virtuosity as an artistic intention. The people who enjoyed Liszt's playing most were those who felt that, in performance, his body was in fact abandoned by a sovereign will and occupied by a new force, usually described as inspiration or enthusiasm: "the artist's fever seemed to take him as if by an electric commotion from the instant his hand touched the keyboard."[63] It is important to emphasize that Liszt's inspiration was always, in descriptions of his playing, inferred back from his bodily motion, not from the sounds of his playing. Once the inspiration had been inferred, it was then reinscribed as the origin of the musical sounds. What listeners called "Liszt's inspiration" thus stood in for the unified enunciating source that the sounds of his playing lacked; it was his inspiration that brought unity, in their minds, upon the dispersive sonorous mass he delivered.

Descriptions of Liszt's inspiration locate it both within him and outside of him. This double source could also give rise to confusions: "what he plays comes so completely *out of his soul*; it is the expression of the highest passion, fiery inspiration. It is quite natural that such unrestrained playing, *originating outside of himself* . . . would make a deep impression."[64] In a strange circulation of power, Liszt was both source and recipient of his music, both creator and audience: "Whatever he plays, he truly does not play to show his virtuosity, but – this is clear from his whole manner of execution – because the composition stirs him up, and *among his listeners he is perhaps the most inspired*."[65] The enunciating

[62] *Musical World* 13/220 (11 June 1840), 361–64.
[63] *Revue musicale* 6/52 (26 January 1833), 413.
[64] *Allgemeine Theaterzeitung*, 1 May 1838, 383 (H. Adami). Quoted in D. Legány, *Franz Liszt: Unbekannte Presse und Briefe aus Wien, 1822–1866* (Vienna, 1984), 31–32.
[65] *Allgemeine Theaterzeitung*, 5 May 1838, 399–400 (H. Adami); emphasis original. Quoted in Legány, *Franz Liszt*, 399–400.

source of his virtuosic discourse, then, was double: it was Liszt fused with, and vastly expanded by, an exogenous, transcendental force.

The unusually powerful subjective force of Liszt's playing, I am arguing, was an effect created by the involvement of his body in his performing style. For those listeners who did not read his body language in the way above described, his playing lacked subjective force and was simply strange or incoherent. For those who did follow his discursive logic, the visual aspect of his playing was crucial. Many writers, even someone with good ears such as Schumann, asserted that he could not be fully understood until he was *seen*; the sounds themselves did not communicate what it was that Liszt had to communicate: "he must be heard – and also seen; for if Liszt played behind the scenes, a great deal of the poetry of his playing would be lost."[66] A Vienna critic pointed out in quite explicit terms how Liszt's subjectivity compensated for the fragmentation and incoherence of the sounds of his music:

As a composer Liszt is distinguished by deeply-grasped contents and an energetic wealth of ideas. Yet the exemplariness of the form leaves something to be wished . . . He has perhaps not found the time to make his works more vocal and more comprehensible to the general public through a greater degree of polish. *Perhaps it is simply because of his all-powerful subjectivity that they are in their perfection only comprehensible and playable by him.*[67]

The subjective power of Liszt's playing would not have been greater if the sonorous aspect of his music had projected a more unified mode of enunciation (such as Thalberg's). On the contrary, the subjective force of his performance was directly proportional to the degree to which his musical discourse resisted rendering a coherent "voice." The sheer quantity of information he put forth was far beyond what audiences were accustomed to hearing and seeing at a virtuoso concert, and exceeded what their minds could reasonably process. Listening to him was the aural equivalent of the experience of the sublime, often overwhelming or terrifying the listener: "When his keys tremble . . . his audience is suddenly dominated by the unheard-of power of the artist."[68] In reaction to this unsettling experience, the listener would reflexively participate in a search for coherence, a search for the enunciating voice: "after the first blank astonishment with which he is listened to . . . the mind as well

[66] *Robert Schumann on Music and Musicians,* ed. Konrad Wolff, trans. Paul Rosenfeld (New York, 1946), 156. An English journalist, arguably working from Schumann's article, observed that Liszt's playing "is of that extraordinary character that cannot be described; it must be heard and witnessed to be truly appreciated" (*Cheltenham Looker-On,* 5 September 1840).

[67] Carl Tausenau, "Liszt und Thalberg," *Allgemeine musikalische Anzeiger,* 7 February 1838; emphasis added. Quoted in Legány, *Franz Liszt,* 53–56.

[68] *Revue et gazette musicale* 7/35 (10 May 1840), 301 (A. A.).

as the ear are perpetually on the alert, to enter into the story he means to tell."[69] This psychological mechanism, drawing the listener into the drama of his playing, had no parallel in Thalberg. As one German critic put it, "[Thalberg] turns the heart increasingly away even while he is astonishing the mind [*Verstand*], whereas his rival Liszt, when he conjures a forceful sea-storm in notes, at least brings forth an animation of the mind."[70]

Carl Dahlhaus has made a similar interpretation of how piano virtuosos brought coherence into their improvisations: "the fantasy . . . was dominated by expressive rhetorical gestures, played with a subjective verve that swept over the cracks and fissures inherent in rhapsodic form . . . lines of fracture were hidden by the expressive powers of the improviser."[71] But do "subjective verve" and "expressive powers" lie outside and apart from musical fissures and cracks, as Dahlhaus implies? In Liszt's virtuosity the interruptions of continuity were not a threat to, but rather the very condition of, the subjective impact of his playing. This aspect of his virtuosity was not a projection or emanation of Liszt's powerful mind or persona, although that is exactly how listeners experienced it. It was an effect created on and in the minds of his listeners by means of his bodily motions and his dispersive, orchestral approach to the keyboard.

Thalberg, to offer a counterexample, had his own way of communicating inspiration. Contrary to received wisdom, his calm demeanor at the keyboard did not translate into expressive frigidity. Many of his contemporaries saw glimpses of inspiration and emotion through his serenity:

Thalberg sits very close to the piano. His posture is severe . . . In the most virtuosic moments he does not allow any contortion. But his features, ordinarily calm and imprinted with a modest dignity, gradually become animated and betray the violent commotion that he feels.[72]

Thalberg's appearance was a mix of inspiration and Apollonian calm: "[it] is the symbol of profound but calm conviction, of ardent but concentrated enthusiasm, of fire without smoke, but not without heat."[73] Joseph d'Ortigue continued the list of antinomies by describing Thalberg's "calm force, this tranquil power, this exaltation at the same time measured and serene."[74] Thalberg's calmness did not cancel out his

[69] *Norwich Mercury* (1840, no date specified); quoted in *Liszt Society Journal* 6 (1981), 13.
[70] *Vossische Zeitung*, 14 February 1842.
[71] Carl Dahlhaus, *Nineteenth-Century Music*, trans. J. Bradford Robinson (Berkeley and Los Angeles, 1989), 137.
[72] *France musicale* 1/12 (18 March 1838), 1.
[73] *Revue et gazette musicale* 3/22 (29 May 1836), 180–81 (E. M.).
[74] *Revue et gazette musicale* 4/12 (19 March 1837), 96–98 (J. d'Ortigue).

Figure 1.7 Caricature of Thalberg, *c.* 1840

internal emotions; rather, it exerted "pressure" upon them. By visibly holding back the emotions, he preserved himself as a sovereign subject, and gave inspiration a location *within* the body, as well as within the domain of the subject – something internal to be resisted or conquered. The difference between Liszt and Thalberg was thus not that one appeared to be inspired, and the other cold. This is a view that has been perpetuated by an overly rigid opposition between the two pianists. Inspiration was crucial to both, but the inspiration was channeled differently in their respective virtuosities. Thalberg let the traces of inspiration show on his face, but whatever disruptive power that inspiration might carry was firmly centered in, and contained by, a nearly motionless body.

We can take this point to a more general level: Thalberg's virtuosity did not completely lack the sonorous and bodily dispersiveness we observed in Liszt, as some of the caricatures show (Figure 1.7). In an important sense bravura is inherently dispersive. The speed and density of his right-hand activity placed him technically far beyond the pianism of the previous generation, leading writers to call him a "romantic" musician in spite of Fétis's emphasis on the "classical" elements of his playing. His way of maintaining a texture in several registers simultaneously inspired dispersive images such as "twenty harps in a piano." It was often observed that Thalberg had a remarkable independence of the fingers, inspiring the sculptor Dantan to render him with twenty fingers. The name of his three-handed technique itself conveys the sense in which he was dividing or redistributing the body.

Yet in Thalberg's playing, unlike Liszt's, each of these elements was subject to recuperation. His runs and arpeggios were hierarchically subordinated to the melody: "in all his compositions the mechanism is always the servant of the melody . . . the idea is the melody; the form is the melody; the inspiration is the melody; the music altogether is the melody."[75] Writers never independently analyzed the non-melodic components of his music, which were simply "everything else," and this "everything else" pointed insistently back to the melody:

M. Thalberg preserves, in the middle of the most rapid execution, the purest taste and style; all the difficulties which play under his fingers are *only* the accompaniments and embellishments of a firm, sustained, and penetrating melody, which *despite* the prodigious traffic of notes seduces the ear and charms the heart.[76]

At the level of the body, we find a recuperation in Dantan's famous bust. The pianist's twenty fingers are towered over by his large, concentrated, controlling head, so that the fingers preserve the unity of purpose and obedience to a sovereign will so conspicuously absent in Liszt's body and fingers (Figure 1.8). Liszt's head, tellingly, was never rendered this way.

We have seen, in this analysis of their respective performing styles, that Liszt and Thalberg had very different ways of establishing the performer–spectator relationship. Thalberg's virtuosity delivered a highly refined vocal conception that required only of its audience that it be receptive to vocality. The depth of vocally centered listening in Paris made it effortless for him to win unanimous applause. Liszt's style worked on its audiences assertively and psychologically, and its vocal elements were subsumed under the more general dramatic, gestural orientation of his playing. It demanded that the listeners activate their minds to find coherence in a radically dispersed musical field. If the listener misinterpreted Liszt's bodily motions, or did not wish to listen actively, or had his eyes closed, Liszt would lose his listener. Liszt's ideal listener was one predisposed to letting his virtuosity provoke a flight of the imagination. Berlioz and George Sand can be cited

---

[75] *France musicale* 3/40 (4 October 1840), 359–60 (L. Escudier).
[76] *Abeille musicale*, March 1836, 2–3; emphasis added.

Figure 1.8 J.-P. Dantan, "Thalberg"

as examples; they were among his most earnest devotees and left some of the most eloquent testimony to the power of his playing. Outside the *artistes*, however, there was no group in Paris whose listening dispositions made Liszt's reception unproblematic like Thalberg's. He was demanding new habits of listening and experiencing music. He had to win audiences over to his aesthetic, with the result that his reception was much more ambivalent and conflicted than that of his rival.

Press comparisons

Thalberg's vocality, I have been arguing, gave him significant advantages over Liszt by addressing a wider social base in the Parisian publics. It stacked the rivalry in Thalberg's favor, and if Liszt knew this, he was powerless to change it. More importantly, Thalberg retained his advantage throughout the 1837 season in spite of Liszt's efforts to challenge it. The duel did not end in a "draw" as is often claimed. On the contrary, Thalberg remained the favorite of the Parisian publics at least until 1840. In order to see how these circumstances affected Liszt's ambitions and the virtuoso rivalry, we need to return to the main problem: Thalberg's reputation as a composer. Liszt was not yet prepared to compete as a composer, and he strategically decided to wage his battle with the resources he had: the pen and the piano.

Liszt's use of the pen did not help at all. Early in the 1837 concert season he published his critique of Thalberg's compositions in the *Gazette*, and it was soon notorious. With this article he not only opened himself to attack on ethical grounds, but also invited critics to consider his own achievements in composition. None of the responses to Liszt's article, not even Fétis's, attempted to demonstrate the real merits of Thalberg's compositions. Rather, they focused on Liszt's own defects as a composer:

The great accusation formulated by M. Liszt against Thalberg consists in reproaching him of playing mediocre compositions with genius. Let me just ask you this: What then is M. Liszt himself, if not an able performer of very mediocre compositions? Where are the culminating and fulminating works of M. Liszt? . . . Liszt's way of writing in music is a stew of languages, and the eighth and sixteenth notes . . . resemble the accompaniment of a barbarous song, which he sings anyway with enough skill.[77]

The exact same rhetoric appeared in another major counterattack:

We call directly upon the grand judge, the public, which has already decided on the incontestable merit of Thalberg's works, but which does not yet know exactly what those of Liszt contain . . . What then has M. Liszt done to judge so severely his colleague or his imitators?[78]

[77] *Vert-vert*, 16 January 1837.
[78] Christian Baumgartner, "Thalberg et M. Liszt," *Gazette des salons*, 25 January 1837.

The continuation of this article went beyond all others in subjecting Liszt's *Serenata e Orgia* to the same type of analysis Liszt had carried out on Thalberg's compositions. The author singles out "unparalleled monotony" in the second motive, a "lack of ideas," a "new idea that has no relationship to the previous ones," and transitions that are "too brusque" or "bizarre." With Thalberg as the implicit comparison, the writer complains that Liszt "destroys the simplicity of the melody" by placing dense chords in the bass. His analysis closes with mockery of the excessive pedal and verbal expressive indications, "this immense romantic and fantastic nomenclature."

Objections such as these had a long-term impact on Liszt's reception as a composer. The compositions he published in the later 1830s did little to improve things, and the comparisons to Thalberg continued. The *France musicale* sharpened its stance against Liszt's compositions because it was promoting Thalberg's music. An 1839 performance of Liszt's *Niobe* fantasy by Messemaeckers prompted one of its writers to reflect on Liszt as virtuoso and composer. The author associated him with everything awful in the virtuoso phenomenon, and regretted that he had not transcended his virtuoso identity in his compositions. Thalberg was not only cited as a counterexample, but was also strongly implied in the peroration: "We will only say that Liszt is not a composer, that he has no school and that he will never form one, because he has no method."[79] Escudier, the journal's chief editor, could not have made his own opinion plainer: "M. Liszt was born a pianist, but only a pianist . . . Thalberg is a composer of the first rank."[80] With his article on Thalberg, Liszt had virtually ruined the compositional wing of his master plan – he unwittingly spotlighted his weaknesses as a composer.

Liszt's initial strategy for challenging Thalberg as a virtuoso pianist, rather than as a composer, was to advance himself as a proponent of Beethoven. Before 1836, the only Beethoven he had ever performed in public, as far as we know, was the "Moonlight" sonata. In Thalberg's wake, however, he gave two unplanned concerts and made the extraordinary move of programming the "Hammerklavier" sonata. It was a gesture of separation from Thalberg and his dilettante public, which was least likely (he thought) to be interested in the Beethoven. He was asserting himself as a serious *artiste* in order to make Thalberg look like a charlatan. His four chamber music *séances* of 1837, also featuring nearly unknown large-scale works by Beethoven, were part of the same strategy. *Le monde* described the audience of the first *séance* in a way that is conspicuous for its absence of aristocrats: "The famous pianist's name had attracted a brilliant crowd, among whom were many of our

[79] *France musicale* 2/6 (20 January 1839), 478.
[80] *France musicale* 3/40 (4 October 1840), 359.

literary and political figures."[81] It is possible that Liszt was using his close connection to the editors at *Le monde* to propagate the impression that he was not playing for superficial, dilettante aristocrats. He had in fact specifically instructed Marie d'Agoult to make that very point in an article she was in the process of writing for him.[82]

Liszt's attempt to separate himself from Thalberg could not, however, have kept critics from making comparisons when both virtuosos were in Paris in 1837. Thalberg's presence made Liszt's deficiencies more obvious and easier to criticize. The most severe criticism of Liszt's playing during the 1837 season came not long after the famous contest:

> We will say to M. Liszt that it is time he temper his hot enthusiasms with order and method . . . When M. Thalberg is at the piano, one feels sure of him, as he feels sure of himself; one feels that he sees from the beginning the goal that he seeks and will attain, for the route is planned in advance; it is not the same with M. Liszt; he is a bold navigator who throws himself into the sea with his boat and his sail, and who seeks his route in the stars of the sky; but if the sky gets cloudy the navigator loses his way; M. Thalberg, for his part, carries a compass.[83]

Critics had voiced disapproval of Liszt's *entraînements* before, but the experience of Thalberg made them less tolerant. This critic's emphasis on the listener's feelings is important; Thalberg had opened up a range of musical feeling and pleasure that seemed outside the scope of Liszt's playing. On the occasion of Liszt's 1840 return to Paris, Escudier compared the two virtuosos and found this basic, easy pleasure missing: "M. Liszt still lacks this perfumed poetry which charms and makes one dream . . . this natural expression of the pleasures or the sorrows of the soul, which soothe you while at the same time raising your enthusiasm."[84] Blanchard's report from the same season is intended to praise Liszt's delivery of melody, but it misses its mark and unintentionally divulges a preference for Thalberg:

> It is his transformation into a melodist that is really astonishing. This is not at all to say that he has that plastic, large, and tranquil melody which cradles you with confidence and quietude; you feel the nervous man, impatient, tight [*l'homme nerveux, impatient, sec*], wanting above all to dazzle, to win approval by assault and not to conquer by sweetness and persuasion: it is in no way the melody of the soul which emerges from him, it is that of the mind, of the imagination.[85]

[81] *Le monde*, 29 January 1837.   [82] *Correspondance de Liszt et de Madame d'Agoult*, I: 193.
[83] *La presse*, 10 April 1837 (F. Soulié).
[84] *France musicale* 3/40 (4 October 1840), p. 359. The date of the concert is not given, but it was clearly late in the season. Escudier had since 1838 been heavily promoting Thalberg, but never explicitly at Liszt's expense.
[85] *Revue et gazette musicale* 7/33 (26 April 1840), 285–86 (H. Blanchard). This praise sounds so forced as to raise the suspicion that Liszt, or one of his advocates, may have solicited a puff from Blanchard.

Whether it was sureness and control, a certain *poésie*, or melodiousness, all these critics felt in Thalberg's music something that made it difficult for them to accept fully Liszt's playing.

Liszt's playing, in turn, drew attention to Thalberg's deficiencies. Joseph d'Ortigue, in a generally positive review of Thalberg's 1837 benefit, wrote: "We cannot ask of M. Thalberg a fire, an impetuosity, a passion which are clearly not in his temperament; but one might hope that his playing gain in variety; it is to be feared that the too-continuous ringing of the same strings will only result in engendering monotony."[86] Critical recognition of Thalberg's weaknesses, however, was not enough to prevent him from coming back to Paris with complete success during the following season. Furthermore, Liszt was more injured by the comparison than Thalberg. Thalberg's playing realized a sharply delimited conception with great refinement; it did not aspire beyond that, so it was not tainted by what it lacked. Liszt's playing, however, aspired to inclusiveness at all levels, including those at which Thalberg excelled. As a result, his playing suffered from the aural comparison to a greater degree.

Liszt thus began the rivalry in 1837 with a disadvantage relative to Thalberg. He made it worse with his article on Thalberg's compositions, and competed with only moderate success as a pianist. His attempt to challenge Thalberg was simply a failure. It was Thalberg who had the majority of the public favor in 1837, and he held on to it for fully three years. In 1840 Blanchard explained this in completely unambiguous terms: "Previously Liszt was only the Pompey, the Antony, the Moreau of the piano vis-à-vis Thalberg, who was its Caesar, Octavian, or Napoleon."[87] The anxiety this produced in Liszt is evident in his letters to Lambert Massart, who was something of a publicity agent for Liszt during his absence. Massart suggested strategies for keeping his reputation alive in the Parisian press, but Liszt had lost his trust in the Parisian critics:

I wrote to d'Ortigue because I feel like he is a friend. The same cannot be said of several other people to whom you would like me to perhaps make great advances (I'm not naming them, but you know whom I'm talking about). These fine men have never been but three-quarters on my side . . . I need frank and devoted friends who, when the occasion arises, have the courage to say in front of anyone, as you did, that I am incapable of a vile act [*une bassesse*].[88]

[86] *Revue et gazette musicale* 4/12 (19 March 1837), 96–98 (J. d'Ortigue).
[87] *Revue et gazette musicale* 7/33 (26 April 1840), 285–86 (H. Blanchard).
[88] *Franz Liszt: l'artiste, le clerc*, ed. J. Vier (Paris, 1950), 54. Schlesinger is probably implied in the comment in parentheses. The "bassesse" to which he refers is most likely his article criticizing Thalberg's compositions.

The rivalry, therefore, did not cease with the legendary duel, nor with the close of the 1837 season. Liszt had to continue to deal with Thalberg's effect on his status in Paris, not in the least because the Viennese virtuoso had scored another wave of triumphs in 1838. He first concentrated on defeating Thalberg as a virtuoso. Under the pretense of responding to the tragic 1838 flood in Budapest, he left from his retreat in Italy and gave a "spontaneous" series of concerts in Vienna in 1838. His letters to Marie d'Agoult, however, show that he was watching the lines of support in Vienna's audiences very closely, and that he was competing more successfully with his rival: "A good majority of people have pronounced themselves unanimously in my favor. The Ostrogoth has been quite relegated to the second rank."[89] This observation was confirmed by London's Vienna correspondent: "The effect of his performance at Vienna has certainly been such as to unseat Thalberg from the throne of the piano."[90] Finally, after confronting Thalberg on his home ground, Liszt felt able to put him out of his mind as a serious virtuoso rival.

Immediately after playing in Vienna, Liszt returned to his objective of producing a steady wave of music publications in Paris. His letters to Massart are urgent: the *Grand galop chromatique* and *Hexaméron*, he insists in 1838, must be published as soon as possible:

Get to it then, so that the same will be done in Paris and we don't have to speak any more about this unfortunate piece, which in any case will not really be published until I play it in Paris. For some years this will be the inevitable misfortune of all the pieces I write; I call it a misfortune, but it's also an advantage. As I have told you often before, for me everything is *future*. But it's not necessary that this future be forever put off. *In two or three years, my cause will be definitively lost or won*, at least as far as the piano is concerned.[91]

This is the most explicit articulation we have of Liszt's master plan: he is planning a return to Paris around 1840, and its success or failure depends on the publication of his compositions. In his 1839 letters to Massart he has settled definitively on 1840: "I would like Bernard to publish [the *Album d'un voyageur*] next autumn so that my return to Paris is somewhat prepared."[92] Later in the same letter he adds the *Hexaméron* and the transcriptions of Beethoven's fifth and sixth symphonies: "All of this . . . must appear in the course of this year."[93]

Did Liszt's master plan succeed? He did make up for ground he had lost to Thalberg, especially by the year 1844, when he made his last Parisian appearances as a virtuoso. Yet this was not because he was

[89] *Correspondance de Liszt et de Madame d'Agoult*, I: 227–28.
[90] *Musical World* 10/138 (1 November 1838), 134–35.
[91] Vier, *Franz Liszt*, 48–49; emphasis original. This letter is undated, but is from 1838. His instructions about the *Grand galop* are from a letter dated 3 June 1838.
[92] Ibid., 50.   [93] Ibid.

newly recognized as a major compositional talent, nor because he had established himself as a man of letters. Furthermore, there is an important sense in which Thalberg's pianistic aesthetic achieved deeper penetration among the Parisian publics: Thalberg's playing, much more than Liszt's, became the ideal toward which many young virtuosos aspired, as well as the conception Parisian audiences most responded to. Almost every pianist who made an impression in Paris was seen as a disciple of Thalberg. Theodor Döhler appeared on the scene in 1838, when Thalberg was again in Paris and Liszt in Vienna. *La France musicale* frankly described Döhler as Thalberg's imitator. Döhler not only played like Thalberg, but also apparently had the personal gracefulness of character so central to his appeal. The *Gazette musicale* attempted to carve out an independent space for Döhler, and established Liszt, Thalberg, and Döhler as the "trinity" among pianists. Yet the claim of Döhler's distinctiveness was made with a conspicuous lack of explanation and detail. The summary statement subtly assimilates him to Thalberg: "[he is] above all an elegant melodist and an original harmonist."[94] The assimilation of Döhler to Thalberg was especially marked during the 1841 season, since Liszt was also part of the Parisian soundscape that season.[95]

After Döhler the examples multiply. Henri Blanchard and Léon Escudier, in particular, could hardly miss an opportunity to make comparisons with Thalberg. In 1839 Clara Wieck was described, in Thalberg's absence, as "the musical lion of the moment, the feminine Thalberg of the piano." Both Escudier and Fétis associated Émile Prudent, who made a powerful impression in the 1842 season, with the Thalberg school. The lion of the 1843 season was Alexander Dreyschock. His playing fell somewhere "between" Thalberg's and Liszt's, but reports from both London and Paris said that the balance tipped in Thalberg's direction.[96] Even Charles Kontski, who was once described as a "diabolic pianist," was credited with "placing himself, by his sure and brilliant style, in the first rank of the school of Thalberg."[97] And who was Mlle. Guénée? "It is

---

[94] *Revue et gazette musicale* 5/16 (22 April 1838), 166–67 (S.).

[95] *Artiste*, Ser. 2, No. VII/16 (1841), 268–69 (A. Specht).

[96] *Revue et gazette musicale* 10/4 (22 January 1843), 27–29 (H. Blanchard). A London correspondent reported: "He is more like Thalberg than Liszt . . . His passages in the amorous and tender style came out ravishingly beautiful" (*Revue et gazette musicale* 10/18 [30 April 1843], 152). The comment on Clara Wieck is from the *Revue et gazette musicale* 6/16 (21 April 1839), 125.

[97] *France musicale* 2/25 (28 March 1839), 197. This is surely an example of the *France musicale*'s pro-Thalberg propaganda, but it in fact seems closer to the truth than the earlier passage. Kontski made his career primarily in aristocratic salons. In a report on a concert at which both he and Liszt played, it is suggested that Liszt appealed to the male public and Kontski to the female, this coded through a contrast between bravos and bouquets.

Thalberg himself who, like a new Tiresias, has become a woman."[98] An 1847 overview added to the list of Thalberg disciples almost all the other major virtuosos of the middle 1840s: Schulhof, Rosenhain, Heller, and Ravina.[99] Only rarely was a pianist seen as a disciple of Liszt, and none of them – Louis Messemaeckers, Henri Litolff, and Leopold Meyer – had the prominence of Döhler, Prudent, or Dreyschock.[100]

It was thus Thalberg who made a deeper mark on his profession, and whose aesthetic was being propagated in Paris and the rest of Europe during the late 1830s and 1840s. This does not mean that Thalberg was necessarily more popular or better liked; Thalberg's reputation as a pianist, in fact, fell steadily in the course of the 1840s. Yet the degree to which his aesthetic was adopted by other virtuosos strengthened the sense that he had founded a "school," a theme that had been introduced by Fétis in 1837, was heavily promoted by the *France musicale*, and was becoming a commonplace opinion. This gave Thalberg what Liszt had always wanted and never quite achieved: recognition by an official or semi-official organ in the Parisian musical or artistic establishment, some kind of permanent foothold to mark his status there, such as the Legion of Honor or the exclusive support of the *Gazette musicale*.

In this examination of the effects of Thalberg's reception on that of Liszt, we have seen just how deeply and lastingly Thalberg cut into Liszt's status as a composer and pianist. Liszt had reserved the years before 1840 for transcending, through writing and composing, what he considered his "mere" virtuoso status. Thalberg affected Liszt's Parisian publics in ways that made it much more difficult for them to accept that he was in fact achieving this transcendence. Liszt felt this, and made his anxiety evident in his letters and negotiations with the press. He wanted the public to feel he had transcended his virtuoso identity *before* he went on his concert tours. As it turned out, he achieved that goal fully only by ending his concert tours and reinventing himself as a composer in Weimar.

---

[98] *Revue et gazette musicale* 7/2 (5 January 1840), 16–17 (H. Blanchard).

[99] *France musicale* 10/45 (7 November 1847), 366.

[100] Litolff had the misfortune of making a major public appearance in 1840, thus competing with Liszt. The *Gazette* saw in Litolff a Liszt imitator who simply lacked his artistic completeness. The most obvious point of resemblance was his physical comportment at the keyboard, for which he, like Liszt, was taken to task in the *Monde musical* (December 1840): "Mr. Litolff is a young, talented pianist who unfortunately has a habit of *exerting* himself too much in public. What is the point of these rollings of the eye, these turns of the head, these waves of blond hair that cover his face?"

2.   Virtuosos in the Parisian *beau monde*: the social significance of the Liszt–Thalberg contest

In the 1830s and 1840s, Parisian audiences and critics were ideally situated to survey the world of pianism. Paris was the principal city in
which virtuosos made and sustained their reputations, and even the
most established pianists were obliged to make regular visits to preserve their place. Starting in the later 1830s, virtuoso traffic in Paris
was so heavy that one could count on at least two or three of the most
outstanding European performers every concert season. By 1845 the
saturation had become so high that the socialite Mme. Girardin could
write: "This week was the week of pianists: each day was designated
for one of their names. Everyone talked only about the piano, quality of
sound, style and method: there were quarrels without end."[101]

As Girardin's words suggest, the appearance of so many virtuosos
made them the subject of fashionable or even learned conversation in
salons. A virtuoso was not just somebody to listen to, but someone to talk
about, a figure around whom people could negotiate style and status.
This was especially true when the virtuoso had not yet been heard in
the city. As Léon Escudier wrote not long after Alexander Dreyschock's
arrival:

As soon as you walk into a salon you are asked: Have you heard Dreyschock?
What is he like? Does he have long or short fingers? Is he like Thalberg, or
E. Prudent, or Liszt? Is he big or small?[102]

It was thus in the forum of salons that the reputation of a virtuoso was
created, shaped, contested, andpotentially lost. Music journalists, who
were not yet professional music critics in the way we understand them
today, picked up the ideas and opinions heard in salon conversation
and spread them among the larger public. Only a highly professional
organ such as the *Gazette musicale* could compete with salon conversation for authority over general musical opinion. Through this conversational activity, each virtuoso developed a "performing identity"
that determined his or her future reception. At one salon, a prominent
judge was heard comparing the Parisian pianists as follows: "At the
piano, Thalberg is a king, Liszt is a prophet, Chopin is a poet, Herz is a
judge, Kalkbrenner is a minstrel, Madame Pleyel is a sibyl, Döhler is a
pianiste."[103] The map of pianists was even richer in the early 1830s, when

---

[101] Delphine Girardin, *Oeuvres complètes* (Paris, 1860), 6 vols., V: 399; journal entry from
5 May 1845.

[102] *France musicale* 6/7 (12 February 1843), 40–50.

[103] Girardin, *Oeuvres complètes*, V: 400.

members of the older generation were still around: "We have Bertini, the dramatic pianist; Liszt, the fantastic pianist; de Kontsky, the diabolical pianist; Chopin the elegiac; Henri Herz, brilliant and dry; Döhler, clear, limpid, not less brilliant and more inspired; Thalberg the singing enchanter; Rosenhain's prudent manner . . ."[104]

The oral character of a pianist's reputation needs special emphasis if we are to understand the rivalry of Liszt and Thalberg. Salon conversation was stimulated by comparisons, and the simultaneous presence of the two leading virtuosos in 1837 was bound to become a major affair. More importantly, the social context of the salon gave such conversations special significance within the *beau monde*, the world of elite socializing. Both Liszt and Thalberg had a special relationship to the *monde* – Liszt as a friend of the Parisian romantics, Thalberg as a friend of the legitimist aristocrats. This created a complex layering of their performing identities with their social affiliations, and it gave the famous virtuoso contest a competitive subtext in the elite world. Something similar had occurred forty years previously, when the young Beethoven and Joseph Wölffl kicked up some dust in the salons of Vienna. As Tia DeNora has shown, this pianistic contest became a symbolic battleground for different groups within Viennese society, who linked themselves to the two pianists, and to musical styles, in ways strongly tied to their social status.[105] Liszt and Thalberg were thus not the first performers to engage the link between musical and social politics.

The *monde* after 1830

The term *"monde"* is used here to designate the Parisian elites generally. The various factions of the *monde* were unified by a range of contexts (salons, balls, opera houses, cafes, etc.) in which their members typically met, by certain coded patterns of behavior (such as dress, conversation, applause, consumption), and perhaps most of all by their possession of financial, political, legal, and intellectual power. During the 1830s the members of the *monde* were described in two rather different ways. In one description it consisted of three "aristocracies": the aristocracy of birth (nobility), the aristocracy of wealth (primarily bankers and merchants), and the aristocracy of talent (artists, men of letters, doctors). In another description the *monde* consisted of the Faubourg Saint-Germain (the old aristocracy with ultra-royalist politics), the Faubourg

---

[104] *Revue et gazette musicale* 6/28 (7 July 1839), 217–19 (G.-E. Anders).

[105] See the chapter "The Beethoven–Wölffl Piano Duel: Aesthetic Debates and Social Boundaries," in Tia DeNora, *Beethoven and the Construction of Genius* (Berkeley and Los Angeles, 1995).

Saint-Honoré (old aristocracy with more liberal politics), and the Chaussée d'Antin (wealthy bourgeoisie).[106]

The divisions of opinion, taste, and lifestyle within the *monde* were substantial, but as a unit they were distinct from the middle bourgeoisie.[107] It can even be said that the *monde* defined itself *against* the lack of cultivation and refined manners it perceived in the middle bourgeoisie. The distinction between the *monde* and the middle bourgeoisie is important to keep in mind, because the virtuoso phenomenon of the first half of the nineteenth century straddled the two social spheres. Music historians have long observed that the rise of popular piano virtuosos was connected with the development of an enlarged middle class.[108] The prosperity of the middle class led to an explosion in the industries of piano manufacture, sheet music for piano amateurs, and public virtuoso concerts. But the multiple ways in which the culture of pianos and of piano virtuosos developed out of middle-class economic conditions should not lead us to misread virtuosity as *symbolically* bourgeois or mass-oriented. As James H. Johnson has put it:

The artist-as-iconoclast is a well-worn cliché of Romanticism, but seldom are the effects of that image upon the public considered, a public composed of so many stock traders, lawyers, bureaucrats, well-to-do merchants, who wouldn't dare risk dashing clothes or displays of passion. They just might have harbored a touch of jealous admiration for those who did.[109]

Johnson's emphasis on the disjunction between the virtuoso's projected image and the self-image of bourgeois listeners is a welcome revision of traditional clichés about Liszt's popular appeal. The appeal of virtuoso concerts to the middle bourgeoisie rested significantly on the fleeting access it gave them to *bon ton* glamor. And *bon ton*, in turn, was created by the virtuoso's status in the world of high society, transmitted top-down. Virtuosos remained, in spite of the social changes that had transformed the musical world, symbolically elite. Their popularity was in this way fundamentally different from that of today's popular-music stars, who if anything derive their appeal from the oppositional relationship to "legitimate" prestige.

106 Anne Martin-Fugier, *La vie élégante, ou la formation du Tout-Paris, 1815–1848* (Paris, 1990), 107–8. This latter triad conceals the close social relationships that existed between the Saint-Germain and Saint-Honoré groups, which were basically unified in spite of their political differences.
107 William Weber, *Music and the Middle Class* (New York, 1975), 7–9.
108 The better among these studies are Arthur Loesser, *Men, Women, and Pianos: A Social History* (New York, 1990 [1958]); Marc Pincherle, *Le monde des virtuoses* (Paris, 1961), and Robert Wangermée, "Tradition et innovation dans la virtuosité romantique," *Acta Musicologica* 42 (1970), 5–32.
109 Johnson, *Listening in Paris*, 268.

I make this point because Liszt and Thalberg have too often been interpreted as polar opposites, so that if Thalberg was the "aristocracy's pianist," Liszt must have been a populist, or the "bourgeoisie's pianist." In a comparison of the two pianists, for example, Ralph Locke has claimed that Liszt resented the upper classes and willingly allied himself with large public audiences and the working classes.[110] Liszt did once vaunt his sympathy for the oppressed workers of Lyons, but he never wanted in any general sense to associate himself with the bourgeois masses or the general public. Indeed, he made efforts to distance himself from the bourgeois public. In the following discussion of Liszt's and Thalberg's social connections, it will become evident that the two pianists shared much more social space than is usually acknowledged, and that it was precisely the proximity of their social spheres that gave their rivalry such intensity.

Thalberg's social network

From even before the French revolution, aristocrats and wealthy non-aristocrats in Paris had bonded socially into a unified elite and shared territory in the *monde*. The revolution of 1830, however, was overwhelmingly favorable to the bourgeois elite and generated a violent, if temporary, feeling of hostility between the two groups. The bitter aristocrats retreated, wishing to distance themselves as much as possible from the new order, and taking refuge in their newly narrowed sphere. Not all aristocrats had this reaction; it was mainly those who belonged to the older, higher lines of nobility, and whose legitimist opinions had been left unmodified by the revolution, that most felt a need to retreat. In the ensuing discussion they will therefore be referred to as the "ultras." The socializing habits of the bourgeois elites were less altered by the revolution: they had nothing to lose from continuing to mix with aristocrats and to imitate their manners of socializing.

The ultras, cut off from the *monde* and living under a regime that did little to recognize their noble status, needed new resources for affirming their distinction. It was into this context that Sigismond Thalberg stepped in November 1835. Thalberg was the court pianist in Vienna, thus a representative from the most powerful legitimist regime in Europe. He had been furnished with a noble lineage, and his manners were elegant and unaffected. His appearance, as related by Blanchard, recalled that of a classical Greek deity: "the blond streaks of his hair, softly tossed to one side of his head ... the rose tints of his smooth and fresh cheeks."[111] These aspects of Thalberg's persona alone would have

---

[110] *The Early Romantic Era*, ed. Alexander Ringer (Englewood Cliffs, NJ, 1990), 67ff.
[111] *Revue et gazette musicale* 3/22 (29 May 1836), 180 (Ed. M.).

been enough to guarantee him an enthusiastic welcome from the ultras, but he was also in possession of a virtuosic style with a clear dilettante orientation, which made him even more attractive to their class.

Thalberg was soon circulating in the Parisian ultra circles. Rudolph Apponyi, the secretary to the Austrian embassy and the embassy's main representative in the *monde*, paved Thalberg's way into the salons of the Faubourg Saint-Germain. This is significant because the Austrian embassy had forged a new alliance with the Parisian aristocracy after the events of 1830. After the revolution Apponyi was circulating among aristocrats who wished to avoid social events in which they would have to mix with the newly empowered bourgeois elites. In 1832, for example, the embassy held a concert in self-conscious Restoration style: Rossini held the piano and accompanied the three top singers at the Théâtre-Italiens, while the leading piano virtuosos of the city were also invited. Apponyi wrote of his pleasure at the exclusiveness of the affair: "all the people of the same rank, of the same caste, no mixing, you could greet everyone, something which seems no longer possible in a non-public event since the Glorious Days."[112]

Although there is no proof that Apponyi served as Thalberg's protector, it is hard to imagine otherwise in light of the fact that virtuosos were typically introduced into Parisian society by their compatriots. In addition, Apponyi often went out of his way for Thalberg. He attended the pianist's public début in 1836 and wrote about it with enthusiasm, in spite of the fact that he was not fond of public concerts. During the intrigues of 1837, Liszt noted that Apponyi was championing a team of support in Thalberg's favor: "The Apponyis are caballing (that is the only word for it) for Thalberg and against me."[113] The fact that Apponyi turned against Liszt in the rivalry is all the more remarkable because he had been a friend of Liszt from his earliest days in Paris, and remained benevolent toward him in later years (by facilitating his bid for the Legion of Honor). It suggests that taking sides in the Liszt–Thalberg rivalry had less to do with musical aesthetics than with social partisanship.

We have seen that the Théâtre-Italiens, as the home of the dilettantes, was the perfect setting for Thalberg's vocal aesthetic. His choice of the Italiens for his public début was also ideal for consolidating his affiliation with the aristocracy. For aristocrats, public virtuoso concerts had become virtually off limits, since one was likely to encounter a mixed, lower-status public. The audience at the Italiens had always been aristocratic,

---

112 Rudolph Apponyi, *Journal. Vingt-cinq ans à Paris (1826–50)* (Paris, 1914), 3 vols., I: 305. The Austrian embassy preserved its exclusiveness partly by its refusal to recognize titles conferred during the empire.

113 *Correspondance de Liszt et de Madame d'Agoult*, I: 198.

but after 1830 the theatre's importance for the aristocracy was magnified because it was one of the few venues where audiences had not become substantially mixed.[114] This was perhaps the one public space in Paris where an aristocrat, especially an ultra, could still feel completely at home. Thalberg chose the Conservatoire for his 1837 benefit solely because he wanted his concert to be on the same date as Liszt's, and the Théâtre-Italiens was not available. The relatively small size and elite status of the Conservatoire made it the best alternative for his ultra fans.

Two of the journals that enthused over Thalberg, the *Abeille musicale* and the *Gazette des salons*, were aristocratic in tone. Both focused their reporting on private salons, turning their eyes away from the less exclusive spheres of socializing. It is unlikely that their readers included many aristocrats; the editors were probably trying to make their product attractive by offering a slice of *bon ton* to those who did not have direct access to it. Nevertheless, it is a sign of Thalberg's association with the aristocracy that he was given special attention in these journals. The *Gazette des salons* was unusual in covering Thalberg's activities in high society: his appearances at the court, his playing and behavior in private soirées, and even an anecdote about a princess who sought piano lessons from him. The journal was an early and passionate Thalberg advocate, describing him on several occasions as superior to all other pianists.[115] In response to Liszt's article on Thalberg's compositions, it published three harshly critical articles on Liszt as a person, as a composer, and as a pianist, respectively.[116]

Although information on Thalberg's private appearances is scarce, we know that they were not exclusively concentrated in the salons of ultras. In 1836 he was the featured artist on a concert at the home of a music pedagogue, certainly a low-status event.[117] Another journal from the same season praised his willingness to lend his talents on various

---

[114] The new bourgeoisie had plenty to keep itself occupied at the new Opéra. Louis Veron, who was admittedly prone to exaggeration, said that the high aristocracy "fled" to the Théâtre-Italiens (Géraldine de Courcy, *Paganini the Genoese* [Norman, OK, 1957], 2 vols., II: 10–12).

[115] *Gazette des salons*, 22 February 1836. In this article there appears for the first time the idea that would precipitate the rivalry with Liszt: "when one has heard Thalberg, one can say, without fear of being wrong, that he's the best [*premier*] of them all." It should be pointed out that both the *Gazette des salons* and the *Abeille musicale* were small-scale publications whose content was for the most part controlled by a single editor. Their advocacy of Thalberg thus amounted to the favoritism of two individuals, who may have been motivated by a desire to sell Thalberg's sheet music. This does not change the fact that the journals served as a channel for the dissemination of Thalberg advocacy among the public.

[116] *Gazette des salons*, 18 January, 25 January, and 8 February 1837.

[117] *Gazette des salons* (1836), 188–90.

64

types of occasions, especially for the sake of charity.[118] Ferdinand Hiller featured him at his music soirées, where the musical elite of Paris gathered and where Liszt had often appeared.[119] Finally and most significantly, he made several appearances at the salon of Mme. Girardin, a literary salon, at the very height of the rivalry with Liszt.[120] These activities suggest that, although Thalberg had a definite alignment with the ultras, he hardly closed his doors to other social affiliations.

Liszt's aristocratic connections

If Thalberg was claimed symbolically by the high aristocrats, what social group claimed Liszt? In an obvious way, Liszt became the token virtuoso of the world of letters – the "aristocracy of talent."[121] In the public concert spaces of Paris, the artists, *literati*, and musicians made their presence most felt at the Conservatoire, both at the famous subscription concerts and at Berlioz's "appendixes" to the series. Liszt only performed once at the Conservatoire Concerts, but he was associated with the Conservatoire and its *artiste* public by conduit of Berlioz. In the 1835 season, just before he left Paris, Liszt had effectively declared his alliance with the young composer before the Parisian public. Not only did he play in Berlioz's benefit concerts of December and May, but he also played parts of the *Symphonie fantastique* and the newly written *Lélio* fantasy at his own concerts. Berlioz became from this point forward an important institutional support for Liszt. Not only did he continually praise Liszt in the press, but he also made Liszt a regular guest of honor at his self-mounted orchestra concerts. The Conservatoire thus became a forum in which Liszt could make public appearances and preserve his alignment with *Paris artiste*. Liszt's symbolic association with the Conservatoire was by 1837 strong enough to have become material for a satirical article.[122]

Liszt's public at the Salle Érard also included many artists. The *literati* were in force at his last benefit concert of the 1837 season – a crucial moment in the public eye, since it took place soon after the duel: "it was among all the poets, all the intelligent writers, all the famous and eminent men, all the elegant and enthusiastic women contained within the capital, that Liszt made his farewell to the public."[123] His audience was described in almost identical terms at a Salle Érard appearance three years later: "a small audience composed of his friends, which made a very large group assembled in the Érard salons. In the middle of the

[118] *Abeille musicale*, March 1836, 3. [119] *Europa* (1836/2), 333.

[120] *La presse*, 10 April 1837.

[121] Liszt's relations with the literati are thoroughly explored in Léon Guichard, "Liszt et la littérature française," *Revue de musicologie* 1 (1970), 5–34, and in Thérèse Marix-Spire, *Les romantiques et la musique: le cas George Sand* (Paris, 1954).

[122] *Gazette des salons*, 18 January 1837. [123] *Le monde*, 10 April 1837.

most intelligent and most beautiful women, the celebrities of the day, perfumes and flowers, Liszt played five pieces all himself."[124]

In both of these passages Liszt's public is represented as a combination of *literati* and aristocratic women. Liszt's symbolic affiliation with aristocrats was, indeed, equally as strong as his affiliation with *Paris artiste*. It is even arguable that aristocrats, by their greater number and more stable position in social life, constituted his main affiliation. Delphine Girardin, writing in 1844, noted that Liszt's concert attracted an outstandingly elite crowd:

It is important to point out that there were many attractive women the other day at Liszt's concert. All circles [*tous les mondes*] and all nations came together there; each society was represented by its famous beauty. This soirée was wonderful. Fashion is not inconstant as some say; since his childhood, Liszt has been its favorite. It admired him then by calling him the little Liszt, now it admires him in proclaiming him the great Liszt. That cannot be called a change. All the rivals that were supposed to have challenged him have only confirmed his glory.[125]

If Liszt's aristocratic support had undergone a significant change during the thirties, Girardin would have been the first to notice it, since she was one of the most astute social observers of her time. What stood out for her was the long-term continuity of Liszt's social affiliation. That she is talking specifically about the aristocratic public here is evident not only from the mention of Liszt's Restoration public (who called him "le petit Litzi"), but also from her mention of the various nations represented, a sign that this audience was the international, cosmopolitan elite of Paris, the highest of the aristocrats. The fact that both of Liszt's benefit concerts of 1844 were held at the Théâtre-Italiens strengthened his symbolic association with the aristocracy, since that theatre was still aristocrat-identified.

Liszt kept up his appearances in aristocratic salons throughout his career. Henry Chorley marveled at "his unsparing prodigality of his talent in private society," implying not only the number of salon performances but also his lively participation in salon conversation.[126] Liszt had played regularly at the Apponyis' private concerts before the revolution, and was still appearing there after the revolution, when Apponyi

---

[124] *Artiste*, Ser. 2, No. V/18 (1840), p. 316. The aristocratic tone of the Érard salons was casually mentioned in *France musicale* 1/2 (7 January 1838), 3: "salons aristocratiques de M. Érard."

[125] Girardin, *Oeuvres complètes*, V: 269; journal entry from 20 April 1844.

[126] Chorley, *Music and Manners*, III: 43. It is possible that Chorley's impression is derived specifically from Liszt's visits to London, when he dabbled in dandyism. He spent much time in the company of the Comte d'Orsay, who virtually defined the dandy style, and Lady Blessington, who played a major leadership role in the elite social life of London.

was circulating almost exclusively with the Faubourg Saint-Germain.[127] In 1833, Liszt was playing regularly to a small company at the house of Marquise Le Vayer of the Faubourg Saint-Germain, and it is there that he met Marie d'Agoult, also of Saint-Germain caste. Whatever sympathy Liszt felt for the revolution, then, it did not keep him from visiting or performing in aristocratic salons.

In the early 1830s Liszt was developing a new channel of access to the aristocrats. Where he previously networked with them as an in-demand piano teacher, he was now emerging as a figure in intellectual and literary society. This was not an easy entry, since some aristocrats, most of them ultras, bore an aversion to artists. Rudolph Apponyi is an example. He was revolted upon encountering Liszt and other artistic company at a salon of Cristina Belgiojoso in 1836: "I was so astonished and dumbfounded by all these extravagances surrounding me that I could scarcely start a conversation . . . in the end one pities her."[128] Marie d'Agoult remembered hearing the same prejudice against artists from a member of the Le Vayer family: "Her relative, a discreet and sober-minded man, ventured a few remarks on the eccentricities of artists and the inconvenience of admitting them to one's home on an equal footing. These observations displeased me, and I was grateful to the Marquise for ignoring them."[129] Yet aristocrats had much to gain from cultivating relationships with artists. An alliance between the "aristocracy of birth" and the "aristocracy of talent" reached back into the 1820s, when the latter had emerged as an independent social group. The bond was possible in spite of their ideological differences because artists possessed the qualities of intelligence and verbal brilliance – *ésprit* – that were so central to the self-definition of the aristocracy. As the examples of Belgiojoso and Le Vayer suggest, most of the aristocrats who linked themselves with artistic circles were women. It was they who presided over the salons, and because men were more likely to center their conversation on politics, male aristocrats and artists did not easily come to terms.

There was a group of younger aristocratic women who responded to the 1830 revolution creatively by opening up their salons to non-aristocrats and artists, Marie d'Agoult among them.[130] The main difference with pre-1830 times was that the artists were received as equal

---

127 Apponyi recorded two embassy concerts at which Liszt appeared in 1832.

128 Apponyi, *Journal*, III: 265; entry from 8 June 1836.

129 Agoult, Comtesse d', *Mémoires 1833–1854*, ed. D. Ollivier (Paris, 1927); quoted in *Portrait of Liszt: by Himself and his Contemporaries*, ed. Adrian Williams (Oxford, 1990), 56. In addition, the aristocrats who lorded over the prestigious Jockey Club showed their aversion to artists by refusing admittance to even the most admired men of letters. See Martin-Fugier, *La vie élégante*, 366.

130 Jacques Boulenger, *Sous Louis-Philippe: les dandys* (Paris, 1932), 190ff.

participants among the regular aristocratic salon company. One such woman who had Liszt as a guest was the Duchess of Rauzan (again Faubourg Saint-Germain).[131] Rauzan, continuing a practice initiated by her mother (the Duchess of Duras) during the Restoration, reserved her afternoon salons for conversations with prominent men of letters.[132] She valued conversing with artists because philosophical and literary discussion helped cultivate *ésprit* and thereby reaffirm her social distinction. That Liszt possessed the quality of *ésprit* in abundance was undoubtedly the reason he was invited to Rauzan's salon; he did not necessarily make any music there. Thus, while Liszt was clearly identified as a member of the artistic elite, this identity kept him much closer to the aristocratic world than to the world of the bourgeois elite. As an artist he was especially valued by that part of the aristocracy that took advantage of artists to reinforce social prestige, rather than shying away from them as a threat.

For further evidence of Liszt's social proximity to the aristocracy we need look no further than his notorious supporter Cristina Belgiojoso. The princess was to Liszt what Apponyi was to Thalberg: a symbolic representative in the *monde*, a protector and champion. With the exception of Marie d'Agoult, she was Liszt's closest and most faithful friend in Parisian high society. Liszt made many musical appearances at her salons, and he seems to have spent time with her whenever he was in Paris. Belgiojoso's society was that of the Faubourg Saint-Honoré – aristocrats with a more liberal political orientation than their Saint-Germain counterparts. Differences between the two aristocratic quarters, however, remained minimal, and they mixed with little conflict.[133] The fact that the Belgiojosos had fought passionately against the legitimacy of Austrian rule in Milan, for example, or that the princess had many left-leaning intellectual guests in her salon, did not prevent them from circulating primarily among the highest aristocratic society. The Belgiojosos' status as members of the nobility was more important, as far as their position in the *monde* is concerned, than their political views.

Aristocratic society, in sum, had two different social tendencies. Many of them found traffic with artists uncomfortable if not disturbing, but others sought out their company, whether because of shared political convictions or for the sake of cultivating *ésprit*. It is along this social division – very far from an aristocrat–bourgeois dichotomy – that the respective social affiliations of Liszt and Thalberg should be understood. And although it was a division, it was a difference of degree that did not substantially affect the unity of the aristocracy. Liszt and Thalberg

---

[131] Serge Gut, *Franz Liszt* (Paris, 1989), 35.   [132] Martin-Fugier, *La vie élégante*, 92.
[133] Boulenger, *Sous Louis-Philippe*, 190ff.

were both, in rather different ways, "pianists of the aristocracy." They were "the two great names that share the admiration and the applause of the musical world of salons."[134]

Liszt did not, of course, only play to aristocrats and artists. He was also part of the world of public concerts, especially from the year 1833, and was therefore playing for middle bourgeois listeners as well. Yet he seems to have assiduously avoided the bourgeois-identified world of public concerts at this time. As noted earlier, he did not offer even a single concert for his own benefit between 1828 and 1835, although he fulfilled his obligations to other musicians by participating in theirs. Had he given concerts, he would undoubtedly have had the choice of the best musicians and attracted full houses, but he preferred not to. Furthermore, Liszt did not take advantage of his virtuoso popularity to exploit the sheet-music market, an extraordinary choice given the conventions of the day. Pianists such as Kalkbrenner and Herz had become favorites of the bourgeois audiences largely through the momentum of sheet-music publishing. In these ways Liszt prevented himself from being claimed by the bourgeois public. He kept his social networks and activities thoroughly elite.

Liszt shared with his romantic colleagues, notably Berlioz, a contempt for the bad taste of the bourgeoisie, and this is reflected in some of his concert practices.[135] He tried to siphon out the middle bourgeoisie with high ticket prices. In 1837 he was heavily criticized for charging a barely affordable twelve francs for his chamber-music concerts.[136] In 1840, upon his long-prepared return to Paris, he avoided the larger public altogether by giving only private concerts. In 1841 he returned to the public, but announced a ticket price of twenty francs. The price was so high that Schlesinger reproached him in the pages of the *Gazette* and suggested that he lower it, an act that cost him Liszt's friendship.[137] His 1841 appearances at the Érard salons were by invitation only, an unprecedented practice there. Finally, he capped off his Parisian career

---

[134] *France musicale* 3/40 (4 October 1840), 359–60 (Escudier). Jennifer Hall has made a similar argument with regard to London's opera houses in this time period. She shows that Covent Garden was pitted against Her Majesty's Theatre as bourgeois vs. aristocratic, even by critics who probably knew it was an exaggeration. The audiences at the two theatres are much more accurately described, she shows, as different segments of the aristocracy. See Hall, "The Re-fashioning of Fashionable Society," 384–403. Together with recent work by William Weber, Simon McVeigh, Tia DiNora, and others, there has emerged a strong sense of the continuing power of aristocrats in the musical life of the period 1780–1840, and correspondingly, a revision of the notion that the bourgeoisie assertively and abruptly appropriated that power.

[135] For Berlioz's anti-bourgeois attitude, see *The Memoirs of Hector Berlioz*, trans. David Cairns (London, 1969), 271, 286.

[136] *Gazette des salons*, 8 February 1837.

[137] The details of this affair are related in Bellas, "Tumultueuse amitié."

in 1844 at the Théâtre-Italiens, which had not at all lost its aristocratic identification.

Liszt was not entirely unwilling to play for mixed audiences, but it had to be on terms that set him apart from the "usual" virtuoso. In May 1835 he was the featured artist in a concert celebrating the opening of the Gymnase musical. The Gymnase was the first hall in Paris built for the purpose of public concerts. It was conceived as a democratic, bourgeois answer to the Conservatoire Concerts. Its series would feature works by the classical masters and therefore carry special prestige, but the ticket prices and availability of seats would not be so exclusive.[138] According to Liszt, the middlebrow social profile of the Gymnase had turned Thalberg off: "he does not yet know where he will give his concert. It seems that the *Gymnase musical* is not aristocratic enough for him."[139] Liszt was willing to play for the larger audiences as long as he could do so as artist and educator, and not in "the role of public amuser," as he once put it.[140] In keeping with this principle, he consecrated the Gymnase with the one major "classical" work in his repertory, Weber's *Konzertstück*.

This discussion of Liszt's social connections and concertizing practices shows that his reputation as a "popular" virtuoso, turning away the upper classes and allying himself with the large public, is misleading, at least in relation to Paris.[141] His social profile was consistently and deliberately elite, and he took measures to ensure that it remained that way. In private society he circulated among *literati* and aristocrats, and it was these two groups, themselves forming something of an alliance, that "claimed" him for their own interests. For this reason the Liszt–Thalberg contest could not have been socially coded along a bourgeois/aristocrat axis, as has often been implied. The contest did have an important social meaning, but it was precisely because Thalberg and Liszt occupied a common territory within the *monde*. Having established this, we are now in a position to examine the social thematics of history's most famous musical contest.

---

[138] Weber, *Music and the Middle Class*, 99–100.

[139] *Correspondance de Liszt et de Madame d'Agoult*, I: 191.

[140] Ibid., I: 194.

[141] It is of course true that Liszt resented the low status some aristocrats accorded to musicians, but this did not give over into a general resentment toward the aristocracy. Caroline Boissier wrote, to the contrary, that "he sees the *savants*, the celebrated men of letters, the artists, the fashionable women, and talks about it all in the most piquant manner, claiming that society offers him a thousand different ways of enriching and developing his art" (*La Comtesse Agénor de Gasparin et sa famille: Correspondance et souvenirs 1813–1894* [Paris, 1902], 2 vols., II: 199; quoted in *Portrait of Liszt*, 50).

Charity and social reconciliation

The Parisian *beau monde* had its internal divisions, but these factions were not supposed to come into conflict over musical issues. Music, as a non-verbal and non-representational art, was valued as a force of reconciliation among the divergent political opinions within the elite world. Recalling the politically and socially mixed salons of the 1830s, Virginie Ançelot thus wrote: "We saw the adversaries gathered together under the charm of the harmonious improvisations of Chopin and the irresistible voice of M. Duprez."[142] It is because music played such an important role in healing social divisions that Liszt's article on Thalberg's compositions caused so much trouble. Liszt had insulted not only his rival but the entire Parisian *monde*, which had lionized Thalberg the previous season. In the years after 1830, social cohesion was fragile enough without such provocations.

It is therefore not surprising that no one but Liszt himself defended the article. Several journals that normally kept relatively quiet on musical matters raised their voices against him, and nearly all of these reproaches ignored the musical substance of Liszt's critique. Their argument with Liszt was moral and social, not aesthetic. In the weeks immediately following the appearance of the article, a dark cloud of social disharmony descended upon the *beau monde*. At the salon of Émile Zimmerman, Thalberg played with Liszt in the audience. One listener was disturbed by the tense air that resulted from the simultaneous presence of the two virtuosos: they seemed to avoid each other "instead of mutually appreciating each other and offering a fraternal hand, as these two young artists should."[143] The same person explicitly pointed his finger at Liszt's article as the cause of the problem.

The article also had the effect of making people take sides who normally would have supported both virtuosos. Rudolph Apponyi had been on good terms with Liszt but suddenly made himself an exclusive Thalberg supporter, and was using his power in the *monde* to turn others against Liszt. Fétis, never an enemy of Liszt, was motivated to exaggerate Thalberg's superiority. The most interesting case of partisanship is that of Delphine and Émile Girardin. The Wednesday-evening salons at the Girardin residence had immense prestige in the *monde*, and they were exactly the kind of event at which Liszt might have been welcome. Featuring music and dramatic readings, they were frequented by aristocrats and the most famous men of letters. Liszt was in fact a favorite

[142] Virginie Ançelot, *Les salons de Paris* (Paris, 1858), 245.
[143] *Ménestrel* 4/12 (19 February 1837).

guest of the Girardins in later years.[144] Yet it was Thalberg whom they featured in 1837, inviting him for several salon appearances at the peak of the rivalry with Liszt. The fact that the Girardins were one-sidedly in favor of Thalberg is evident from the appearance in their newspaper, *La presse*, of the strongest anti-Liszt and pro-Thalberg polemic of the season. This article makes it clear that Liszt's article, now months old, was still considered the origin of the debates: "M. Liszt was wrong to publish in the *Gazette musicale* an excessively critical article against his rival M. Thalberg, a man of superior talent."[145] These words were penned by Fréderic Soulié, a man of letters: Liszt had even estranged members of his own social network.[146]

The pro-Thalberg faction, then, was anchored in the elite world. The pro-Liszt faction, from what we can tell, consisted primarily of professional musicians, and was thus situated outside the *beau monde* proper. While Thalberg was appearing at the Girardin salons, Liszt was appearing at benefit concerts of Labarre, Massart, Batta, and Géraldy – local virtuosos all – and apparently not in the salons. His one exclusive supporter in the press, Berlioz, represented the younger musicians' establishment and had a relatively weak influence in the *monde*.[147] Liszt had courted the Parisian musicians in February by featuring Beethoven's chamber music in a series of four concerts, and Schlesinger helped promote the concerts among the musically educated readership of the *Gazette* by publishing regular, positive reports.[148] Liszt attempted to elicit additional support within the left-wing faction of the *monde* by means of the liberal press – *Le temps*, the *Journal des débats*, and *Le monde* – but among them only *Le monde* took a decidedly partisan approach in his favor.[149] Liszt was on good terms with the editors of *Le monde* because of his friendship with its editor-in-chief, Alphonse de Lamartine. It is thus not surprising that the most significant pro-Liszt and anti-Thalberg article of the season, signed by Louis de Ronchaud, appeared there.[150]

[144] This is evident in an 1844 caricature of the Girardin salon (Robert Bory, *La vie de Franz Liszt par l'image* [Geneva, 1936], 122). Delphine Girardin was also publishing positive reports on Liszt in *La presse* during the 1844 season.

[145] *La presse*, 10 April 1837.

[146] Liszt had only one exclusive supporter in the press: Berlioz. Liszt's delicate management of the rivalry in the press is evident in his correspondence with d'Agoult (*Correspondance de Liszt et de Madame d'Agoult*, I: 183ff.).

[147] The key article Berlioz contributed to the rivalry appeared in the *Chronique de Paris* on 19 March, the day of his concert at the Opéra.

[148] Liszt wrote to d'Agoult that "Schlesinger is also going a little bit out of the way for me" (*Correspondance de Liszt et de Mme. d'Agoult*, I: 183).

[149] Liszt's dealings with the press are described in his correspondence with Marie d'Agoult (*Correspondance de Liszt et de Madame d'Agoult*, I: 182ff.).

[150] Bernard Gavoty, *Liszt: le virtuose* (Paris, 1980), 183.

In the long run, Liszt's reputation was apparently more harmed by his article than Thalberg. Tickets to his four Beethoven-centered soirées of chamber music did not sell well, perhaps also because of the high prices.[151] Thalberg was confident enough of his greater public support to schedule his benefit concert for the same day as Liszt's, even though it meant he would not be able to play at his favorite hall, the Italiens. Evidently recognizing the severity of the competition, Liszt responded by postponing his benefit one week. His choice to play his benefit at the Opéra has always been interpreted as a bold gesture, "outdoing" Thalberg by venturing a much larger concert space. But upon closer inspection, it turns out to have been a safe choice, and a brilliant piece of damage control. It was quite unlike Liszt to schedule a concert at the intermission of a ballet performance, as he did on 19 March. Yet by choosing the Opéra he was assured of a large audience, for the extremely popular celebrity dancer Maria Taglioni would be performing that evening.

In order to understand the social thematics of the Liszt–Thalberg concert it is essential to acknowledge its charity function. The concert closed off a three-day event initiated by Cristina Belgiojoso for the benefit of the Italian refugees in Paris. Walker dismisses the charitable significance of the event: "Shrewdly observing the mounting tension between the Liszt and Thalberg factions, she invited both pianists to play in her home, together with other artists, in aid of the Italian refugees. Everybody in Paris saw through this piece of diplomatic bluff."[152] According to Walker the real motivation for the concert was a public hungry for a virtuoso confrontation: "So fierce was the demand to see Liszt and Thalberg 'take turns' that the princess was able to charge 40 francs a ticket."[153] If the concert was as charged with competitive significance as Walker suggests, why were many newspapers and journals uninterested in the contest itself? The *Constitutionnel* mentioned that Liszt and Thalberg played but said nothing in relation to their rivalry; the *Journal de Paris* did not even mention the musical portion of the charity events; and Girardin reported with a yawn in *La presse*: "a fashionable soirée but rather cold . . . too expensive."[154] These and other reports *do* mention, however, the fund-raising sale and the huge sum of money brought in for the sake of the Italian refugees. The charity function of the concert was neither unnoticed nor irrelevant to the rivalry of Liszt and Thalberg.

---

151 Ellis, *Music Criticism*, 151. The bad ticket sales might also have motivated Berlioz's puffs in the *Gazette*.

152 Walker, *Franz Liszt*, I: 238.   153 Ibid., I: 239.

154 *Constitutionnel*, 2 April 1837; *Journal de Paris*, 2 April 1837; *La presse*, 6 April 1837.

Charity events were numerous and highly important to the self-justification of the Parisian *monde*. Almost any disaster that came to their attention could become an occasion for a charity ball, concert, or dramatic reading among the elites, usually initiated by aristocratic women.[155] Philanthropy was an aristocratic tradition practiced partly to show that financial privilege did not ruin their moral sensibility. It gave them a sense of moral distinction and portrayed the elites – always in danger of being considered useless – as a socially productive force. Charity was thus heavily loaded with social significance: "To practice philanthropy was to legitimate oneself as a member of the directing class."[156] The attraction of the concert, then, did not consist in the rivalry of Liszt and Thalberg alone. Belgiojoso was able to charge forty francs per ticket partly because charity was legitimating to the members of the *monde*. If we recall that Schlesinger, a few years later, reproached Liszt for charging twenty francs for a public concert, we get a sense of just how exclusive the audience must have been. The contest was an event of unusually high status and relatively low public profile.[157] In the *beau monde*, musical events functioned like charity events, bridging political divisions and reaffirming the fundamental unity of the elites as a cultural and political leadership. The charitable significance of Belgiojoso's concert was thus the perfect setting in which to resolve the social disharmony that had emerged from the rivalry of the two virtuosos.

This is probably how Belgiojoso envisioned the concert, and Jules Janin helped her out with his press report: "In this brilliant crowd were mixed, *in the same admiration and same sympathy*, M. and Mme. Apponyi, Mme. the Duchess of Sutherland . . . M. Thiers, M. Berryer, Mme. de Mouchy, all the opinions that divide the *monde*, and who reunited on this neutral territory of philanthropy and benevolence."[158] A close look at this list of attendees shows that Janin is deliberately pointing up oppositions. The Apponyis represented the Austrian embassy; the Duchess of Sutherland the English embassy.[159] Since the events of 1830 these two embassies, the most important in Paris, had been politically opposed: "The two great embassies had separated political colors: at the Austrian the legitimists, at the English sympathizers of the new regime."[160]

---

[155] Martin-Fugier, *La vie élégante*, 162.   [156] Ibid., 155.
[157] The concert received far less coverage in newspapers than, for example, Liszt's four chamber-music soirées. The concert and the bazaar were covered more fully in periodicals targeted at exclusive readerships.
[158] *Journal des débats*, 2 April 1837; emphasis added.
[159] The Duchess of Sutherland was the niece of Lady Granville, wife of the English ambassador and the keeper of the Granvilles' position in the Parisian world.
[160] Martin-Fugier, *La vie élégante*, 153.

The next pair of names, Thiers and Berryer, forms a similar opposition. Adolphe Thiers, minister of foreign affairs and chief of the government between 1836 and 1840, symbolized the liberal direction of the *Juste Milieu* government. Pierre-Antoine Berryer, on the other hand, was a legitimist lawyer and an orator whose extraordinary eloquence made him the chief spokesman for legitimist politics, both in and outside the chambers.

Janin thus strove to paint the contest as a peaceful and affirmative meeting of the two diverging political factions in Paris. But his picture smacks of idealization. Girardin's comment that the concert was "rather cold" suggests that there was not much social warmth in the audience. The word "cold" was standard vocabulary for describing the tone of social settings in which strong political rivals met.[161] Janin may also have been idealizing when he reported that the audience applauded the virtuosos in the "same admiration and same sympathy." For according to another report, the applause was indeed equal, but only because half the audience applauded for Liszt and the other half for Thalberg, meaning the audience remained divided.[162] Janin presents a rosy picture of the event not as a reporter, but to fulfill the uplifting requirements of the *feuilleton* genre.

The setting of the concert in Belgiojoso's salon gave Liszt a significant home field advantage. This important fact was noted in a useful article from the journal *Vert-vert*:

The applause was frenetic for both of them . . . It is hard to say which way the balance tipped. One part of the public preferred Mr. Liszt, the rest of the audience pronounced itself in favor of Thalberg, so that there was an equal division of bravos . . . We would note here, however, that if the advantage was to one side, it was that of Thalberg, who might not have expected such a great favor from an audience composed almost entirely of exclusive admirers of Liszt.[163]

The princess's regular salon company was composed of literary and intellectual figures, including Liszt, and as a close friend she may have been able to arrange that the audience be favorable to Liszt. Belgiojoso was in fact credited with the famous *bon mot* that spread the rumor of Liszt's triumph over his rival: "Thalberg est le prémier pianiste du monde, Liszt est le seul." But she admitted to Liszt a few years later, as if to retract the phrase, that she had been unfairly biased against Thalberg: "I often tell myself that I was unjust with regard to Thalberg, and that my admiration for you muddled my judgment."[164] Furthermore, the

---

[161] Apponyi once described the salons of the Comtesse de Ségur, famous for their mixed attendees, as "horribly cold" (quoted in ibid., 185; journal entry dated 9 March 1836).

[162] *Vert-vert*, 1 April 1837. [163] Ibid.

[164] *Autour de Madame d'Agoult et de Liszt*, 184; letter dated 9 November 1841.

Vert-vert passage confirms that Belgiojoso may not have been speaking for the opinion of the audience as a whole when she uttered her *bon mot*. If the concert did not entirely succeed in its purpose of achieving social reconciliation, then, it may be because the setting was heavily weighted in Liszt's favor.

Belgiojoso's concert, in sum, invoked charity in order to heal a social wound that Liszt had inflicted in the *beau monde* with his article on Thalberg. The mixed and unusually exclusive composition of the audience gave the event great potential as a symbolic affirmation of the unity of the elites. Yet the concert did not close the social infighting, and neither did it mark the end of the virtuoso rivalry. Most press debates over the two pianists, including the heated exchanges between Liszt and Fétis, were waged after the famous duel took place. Liszt and Thalberg incarnated virtuoso identities of such a pronounced individuality that even the pressing needs of elite social power could not find between them a common ground.

Musicians and writers have often had a difficult time taking the virtuoso Liszt seriously. If he famously rode the line between the sublime and the ridiculous, we tend to opt for the ridiculous. We seem to be more convinced by the rollicking caricatures than by the proud, ennobling portraits, and we balk at the extreme virtuosity or inflated rhetoric of those interminable opera fantasies. Audiences who heard Liszt during his concert career were evidently of a different frame of mind. They not only accepted but vociferously affirmed his seriousness and idealism. There exists, then, a basic historical disconnection between how Liszt appears to us today and how he appeared to his contemporaries. Something in the fabric of social life made figures like Liszt or Thalberg richer and more meaningful to their contemporaries than we can easily imagine.

In this chapter I have attempted to restore some of this social dimension to Liszt and his pianistic style. The Liszt–Thalberg contest needs such treatment because it has always been imagined in the preferred humorous vein. It circulates popularly as a sensational, appealingly trashy episode in which Liszt briefly steps away from his utopian pulpit and enters the earthy terrain of professional competition and personal jealousy. I have argued here that the contest was neither so isolated nor so insulated an event. Each pianist's musical style and social network established a particular position for him within a fractured Parisian world, so that an apparent instance of musical gamesmanship became infiltrated with aesthetic and social competition. Liszt's career predates the full development of mass culture in important respects, and he is often misunderstood as the pianist of the homogeneous bourgeois masses. As the rivalry shows, his reputation derived from his nearness to the intellectual and political elites of Paris, who remained the city's cultural trendsetters. By offering up his poor opinion of Thalberg's compositions in print, Liszt styled himself as a public intellectual and hence claimed his place among those elites. From that point forward, he was not just a pawn in a struggle for social power, but an active contributor to that struggle.

2

Warhorses: Liszt, Weber's *Konzertstück*, and the cult of Napoleon

If other concert halls are salons in which exquisite, sumptuous pleasures are offered, those of Liszt are battlefields, and his successes are victories and triumphs. The feeling conveyed by this image comes over everyone who hears him, and hence he has rightly been called, so often and from so many directions, the Napoleon of the piano.

Franz von Schober, 1843[1]

We use the word "warhorse" to designate a weighty, highly virtuosic composition, typically a violin or piano concerto that is well known and demands strong rhetorical and interpretive skills. It is a "work," a musical object already there, ready and waiting for the interpreter to come along and master it. Yet the metaphor of the warhorse does not in fact originate in the musical work. It is rather the drama of virtuosic *performance*, regardless of musical content, that gives rise to battle imagery. Nowhere is this more evident than in the nineteenth century's favorite image of the virtuoso Liszt, of which Figure 2.1 is an example. The symbolic fusion of the horse with the miniature keyboard – both of them dominated and mastered by Liszt – suggests how his virtuosity could serve as a displaced image of heroic military valor. Liszt authored a bravura conception in which the virtuoso struggles with technical difficulties or with the orchestra, heroically dominates the instrument, and victoriously sweeps away the audience. By amplifying vertical gestures into the keys, introducing stormy embellishments, and mimicking the musical drama with facial expressions and physical movement, he made virtuosity an agonistic spectacle of domination and triumph that invited listeners to imagine the performance as a battle, the virtuoso as a valiant warrior.

---

[1] Franz von Schober, *Briefe über Franz Liszts Aufenthalt in Ungarn* (Berlin, 1843), 4: "Sind andere Concertsäle Salons, in denen ausgesuchte schwelgerische Genüsse dargeboten werden, so sind die seinen Schlachtfelder, und seine Erfolge sind Siege und Triumphe. Das hier bildlich gegebene Gefühl ergreift Jeden, der ihn hört, und darum ist er wohl so oft und von so vielen Seiten der Napoleon des Klaviers genannt worden."

Figure 2.1 Caricature from the *Miroir drolatique*, 1842

The latent homology between military spectacle and virtuosic performance gave rise to one of the most important and least recognized dimensions of Liszt's public identity during his concert career. Contemporary writers repeatedly drew upon battle and military imagery to evoke the atmosphere conveyed by his playing. In press reports we encounter countless comparisons to the great military conquerors of antiquity. In France he was dubbed "le général Liszt," and his reputation as the "Napoleon of the piano" was already widespread early in his concert career. Yet this phenomenon cannot be attributed to the antagonistic drama of his performances alone, as another look at the caricature will make clear. An equally significant element of the image is the *identification* it establishes between the Liszt and the horse. The animal's

79

proportions are so exaggeratedly small that it appears to be an extension of the rider's body (and implicitly of his potency and masculinity).[2] If we see a warhorse, then, it is only by virtue of the rider, equipped as he is with a Hungarian sabre, matching shield, and military cap. Liszt's military aura, indeed, stemmed from several components of his personality and public identity that, like the sabre of honor, were only obliquely related to his pianism.

Recognizing the military dimension of Liszt's public identity will bring us closer to understanding his phenomenal, fascinating popularity. Biographers in the hagiographic tradition present this popularity as a natural consequence of his genius, while those looking into society for an explanation turn reflexively (and often in an implicitly congratulatory tone) to his "sex appeal." In an attempt to develop a more precise "archeology" of Liszt's popularity, I will first discuss conditions that disposed audiences to celebrate him as a battle hero or military general. Military heroes and rituals figured heavily in the public spaces of the 1830s and 1840s, moving audiences to react admiringly and vociferously to spectacles of heroic valor, as they do in the caricature. At the same time, literary romantics were fostering a cult of Napoleon whose influence spread beyond social and political boundaries, and which made the French hero a symbolic fulcrum of the pre-1848 era. Contemporary writers constantly drew Liszt into this orbit of military and Napoleonic representations, reading images of heroism and battle into his performing style, his personality, and his visual appearance.

In the second part of this chapter I show how Liszt actively contributed to his military aura, which was otherwise sustained in critical reception and public discourse. He placed at the forefront of his repertory a composition – the *Konzertstück* in F minor for piano and orchestra by Carl Maria von Weber – through which he could distinctly incarnate the virtuoso as military hero. The *Konzertstück* is a programmatic concerto whose hero is a warfaring knight, and it climaxes in a military march. Liszt greatly enhanced the military impact of the march by introducing in his performances substantial alterations to Weber's score. His changes not only inflected the narrative content of Weber's piece, but wrenched it out of its narrative discursive mode and turned it into an onstage drama in which the pianist took the leading role. Liszt's *Konzertstück* brought together musical and performative semantics in service of a potent military image, and delivered it with sensational success to a public eager for such representations. It became, in every sense of the word, his warhorse.

---

[2] Arguably, the horse provides the muscular physical body that Liszt – with his bony limbs and drooping fingers – seems to lack. Additionally, it is only the horse's body that can adequately balance out Liszt's dramatically rendered head.

Consideration of Liszt's military aura draws attention to one aspect of virtuosic performance that has often been overlooked or suppressed: its violence. The violence of bravura virtuosity – which Liszt brought out to an extreme degree – cannot simply be siphoned off from aesthetic issues, for violence was central to his entire performative aesthetic. In the third part of this chapter, I offer a cultural interpretation of this violence. Historian Peter Gay has argued that acts of "cultivated aggression" – violent rituals carried out within some "civilizing" framework – were a central need of the nineteenth-century bourgeoisie. I argue that Liszt's novel performing style, filtered through military imagery, provided his audiences with an outlet for aggressive impulses, while simultaneously drawing legitimate justification – what Gay calls an "alibi" – from the ideology of music's civilizing or elevating effects. Far from remaining safe within the bounds of the aesthetic, Liszt's military aura engaged with some of the most turbulent and dangerous impulses tugging away at the bodies and minds of his audiences.

1.   Liszt's military aura

Liszt's military aura appeared to emanate from within, but it ultimately originated in the disposition of his audiences. His status as a wandering artist, his appearance before an orchestra, the shape of his head, and his reputation for having a strong will were all mutually disjunct elements of his public identity, but each of them in its own way invited audiences to map military or Napoleonic meanings upon him. Liszt's military aura was thus the cumulative effect of several unrelated semantic strands originating in his cultural environment. In this section we consider first the broadest elements – the celebration of ancient conquerors, and the public presence of military bands – before turning to the cult of Napoleon, which mediated his military aura most directly.

The imperial conqueror

Tales of the great conquerors of antiquity formed an integral part of the popular culture of Liszt's contemporaries. Caesar and Alexander, in particular, were a ubiquitous presence in popular literature and educational curricula.[3] The cult of Napoleon dovetailed with, and to some extent depended upon, this mythologization of the ancient conquerors. Stendhal began his *Mémoires sur Napoléon* (1836) with the bold claim that "we are concerned here with the greatest man who has appeared in the world since Caesar," and in the same breath drew further parallels

---

[3] Rudolph Schenda, *Volk ohne Buch: Studien zur Sozialgeschichte der populären Lesestoffe, 1770–1910* (Frankfurt am Main, 1970), 335–40.

with Alexander.[4] Already during his virtuoso travels, Liszt had acquired a mythic public identity that drew him into the orbit of these conquerors. Newspapers and journals constantly informed the European public about his restless travels, his triumphs in the concert hall, and the elaborate civic processions with which he was greeted and honored (the *Revue et gazette musicale* and *Allgemeine musikalische Zeitung* were especially dutiful chroniclers of his path). Such images of his virtuoso glory brought to mind the familiar stories of antiquity:

> To get an accurate idea of what happened at Lyons, it helps to recall Alexander the Great and his entry into Babylon . . . The joy of the Babylonians stands comparison with the jubilation of the people of Lyons . . . [After the procession] Franz Liszt appeared at a balcony, and as he brandished his grand sabre he announced in Hungarian: "People of Lyons, I am pleased with you!"[5]

Although satirical in intent, this passage registers an imaginative link that contributed to Liszt's military aura. It is in fact a double link, since the last words paraphrase Napoleon's legendary pronouncement: "Soldats, je suis content de vous." French audiences were particularly prone to making this link, partly because of the special importance of Napoleon in French culture, but more importantly because the Parisian press had obsessed over Liszt's notorious sabre of honor. One French journalist was able to remember, fully seven years after the fact, Liszt's enthusiastic reception by the mob in the streets of Pest:

> When you have the honor of seeing your horses detached and your carriage dragged by students, and seeing your person sabred with a grand sabre by a Hungarian magnate, you are entitled to think of yourself as a sort of Napoleon.[6]

Reports of Liszt's triumphs abroad were arguably more important in the formation of public identity than his playing itself. Most people who heard Liszt play, after all, heard him only once or twice, whereas in the press they could encounter him repeatedly. The discursive form of foreign reports, furthermore, was as important as their content in encouraging people to link Liszt's glory with that of famous conquerors, for the reports rendered his glory distant, conceivable only in the imagination. They abstracted Liszt's glory from material or historical contingencies, thus consigning his public identity to the realm of myth. His "greatness," like that of the conquerors to whom he was compared, was in part a function of his absence and inaccessibility.

[4] Marcel Heisler, *Stendhal et Napoléon* (Paris, 1969), 104.
[5] *Ménestrel* 11/33 (14 July 1844).
[6] *Mode*, 5 January 1847, 13–14 ("Louise"). This article is found in the "Second scrapbook" of Marie d'Agoult, at the Bibliothèque municipale de Versailles.

Military bands

Liszt's reputation for having invented the solo recital can obscure the fact that he continued to perform with orchestras in almost every city he visited, especially in the larger houses and at special festivals.[7] This fact needs emphasis here because the very spectacle of him seated in front of an orchestra, regardless of the music, was already charged with military significance. Comparisons of the orchestra to an army were an old trope by the turn of the nineteenth century. In eighteenth-century sources, military metaphors turn up repeatedly in descriptions of large instrumental ensembles, and nearly every example equates the orchestral leader – usually the keyboard player – with the head of an army.[8] As orchestral conductors became more common in the first half of the nineteenth century, journalists continued to favor the metaphor of the general leading his army, a tendency most pronounced in the writings of Berlioz. The metaphor even turned up on one of the rare occasions (during his concert career) when Liszt ventured to conduct an orchestral concert from the podium: "We had often heard and read that our Liszt, so highly celebrated as a piano virtuoso, was pretty poor as a conductor – or, to put it another way, nothing much as a captain of his troops."[9]

Although journalists risked wearing out the metaphor, the comparison of orchestras to armies, and of conductors or soloists to military leaders, was kept alive by the pervasive presence of wind bands in the everyday lives of his audiences. Such bands appeared regularly in parades, at public festivals, or at popular concerts held in parks and restaurants.[10] Berlioz noted that "if you observe people in towns under Austrian domination, you will see them flock to hear a military band and listen avidly to its rich German harmonies."[11] The ears of an English journalist were saturated enough with military marches that when he heard Liszt play his *Marche hongroise*, he felt that Liszt "made the noble instrument he played on ring out like a brass band."[12] Such bands serenaded or greeted Liszt in almost every city he visited, sometimes with arrangements of

---

[7] The institution of the solo recital, in fact, did not take root until long after Liszt had left the concert platform, perhaps as late as the 1870s. Until then, virtuosos rarely performed in public concerts without an accompanying orchestra for at least part of the program.

[8] John Spitzer, "Metaphors of the Orchestra – The Orchestra as Metaphor," *Musical Quarterly* 80/2 (1996), 238–45.

[9] *Allgemeine musikalische Zeitung* (February 1844); quoted without specific date in Michael Saffle, *Liszt in Germany: 1840–1845* (Stuyvesant, NY, 1994), 166.

[10] The most thorough study of military spectacle in the early nineteenth century is chapter 8 in Scott Hughes Myerly, *British Military Spectacle: From the Napoleonic Wars through the Crimea* (Cambridge, MA, 1996).

[11] *The Memoirs of Hector Berlioz*, ed. D. Cairns (London, 1969), 209.

[12] *Wolverhampton Chronicle*, 2 December 1840; quoted in *Liszt Society Journal* 10 (1984), 7.

his own compositions.[13] With colorful uniforms, ordered lines, and an authoritative leader, their appearance mirrored that of a miniature army. Military bands were, in the most literal sense, orchestra and army in one.

With rare exceptions (such as the Beethoven monument festival of 1845), Liszt led his accompanying orchestras, and in contrast to his contemporaries he used hand gestures and eye contact to communicate actively with the ensemble. This leadership role had the potential to cast him as a military figure, and his repertory only reinforced it. Three of the core pieces in his piano/orchestra repertory – the *Hexaméron*, Weber's *Konzertstück*, and the *Marche hongroise* – all feature military musical *topoi*.[14] An anecdote from the Parisian concert season of 1837 illustrates how the visual and topical combined to construct Liszt's military aura. That season Liszt performed Weber's *Konzertstück* twice with orchestra: first at a Berlioz benefit concert that took place at the Conservatoire, then later at his own benefit concert at the Opéra. At the Opéra performance he had to leave the orchestra in the pit rather than bring it onto the stage, probably because his concert filled in the entr'acte of a ballet performance. Liszt was unsettled to find that at the Opéra, audience enthusiasm was markedly lower than at the Conservatoire. His friend Ernest Legouvé attributed it specifically to the loss of the militarized visual spectacle:

You play across who knows how many violins, basses, horns, trombones; in order for your voice to reach us, it must travel above all that orchestral bacchanal! And you are surprised at the result! But why, dear friend, did you produce such a prodigious sensation two months ago, at the Conservatory, with the same piece?

13 In Dublin, where the aristocracy and the military remained in a strong traditional alliance, Liszt's accompanying orchestra was "a very fair band chiefly composed of amateurs and men from the regiments quartered there." Among the "amateurs" were "several lords, colonels and captains . . . besides the military brass instruments" (diary of John Parry, entries from 17 and 18 December 1840; quoted in *Portrait of Liszt: By Himself and his Contemporaries*, ed. A. Williams [Oxford, 1990], 151). Given the military makeup of this "orchestra," it is not surprising that at the rehearsal they made him repeat his performance of the march in Weber's *Konzertstück*, in which the orchestra is temporarily orchestrated as a wind band.

14 Also in his repertory were various other *Marches hongroises* (among which the Rakocsy has a special place), Berlioz's *Marche au supplice*, Moscheles's *Marche d'Alexandre*, Wallweiler's *Marche héroique*, marches lifted from Glinka's *Life of the Tsar* and *Russlan and Ludmilla* and from Rossini's *Maometto* and *Moïse*, and marches worked into the *Puritani* polonaise or the finale of the *Norma* fantasy. To these we could add those included in variation sets by other composers, those that he improvised, or even "Beethoven's Grand March and Chorus," as his performance of the *Choral Fantasy* was once billed. The "Programme général des morceaux exécutés par F. Liszt à ses concerts de 1838 à 1848" (Weimar Liszt-Archiv, Ms. Z15), compiled by one of Liszt's assistants after he moved to Weimar, has an entire category for "Marches." The list includes marches by Lembert, Sultan Abdul-Medjh Khan, and three *Marches héroiques* by Schubert that I have not found among his concert programs.

Because out in front, with the whole orchestra behind you, you had the air of a colonel of the cavalry at the head of his regiment, in full gallop, sabre in hand, and drawing these cavaliers, whose enthusiasm was only the accompaniment to his own enthusiasm. At the Opéra, the colonel had left his position and put himself in the line of his regiment![15]

Legouvé's comments demonstrate not only the potential of Liszt to incarnate the virtuoso as a military hero, but also the power of Liszt's military aura to win the popular favor of his audiences.

The cult of Napoleon

However directly Liszt's military aura was indebted to the familiar spectacle of wind bands and to the legends of ancient and modern conquerors, these two threads were not strong enough or specific enough to consolidate a military aura around him. The frame of signification most directly responsible for militarizing Liszt was, rather, the cult of Napoleon. This cult, which had its origins among the English romantic *literati*, bloomed in France when Napoleon died in 1821. Over the next two decades, writers, historians, biographers, and artists constructed the myth of Napoleon and produced a massive body of Napoleoniana for popular consumption as well as learned contemplation.[16] The Parisian revolution of 1830 gave the cult renewed impetus, inspiring Berlioz to undertake three compositional projects on the subject of Napoleon in the course of the 1830s.[17]

In Paris the cult of Napoleon sank in so deeply that it affected people's everyday behavior. Frances Trollope commented in 1835 that all of the students at the *École polytechnique* were walking and dressing like Napoleon, and a front-page article in the *Gazette musicale* identified "The Napoleon" as a ubiquitous social type:

[15] Ernest Legouvé, "Liszt et Thalberg," *Ménestrel* 56/19 (11 May 1890), 145–47. Quoted in *Liszt en son temps*, ed. P. Huré and C. Knepper (Paris, 1987), 205. This article seems to be a free paraphrase of one Legouvé had written decades earlier. See the quotation on p. 105.

[16] Beatrice Farwell, *French Popular Lithographic Imagery, 1815–1870* (Chicago, 1989), 11 vols., IX: 16. See also Schenda, *Volk ohne Buch*, 341.

[17] D. Kern Holoman, *Berlioz* (Cambridge, MA, 1989), 130, 149–50, 274. Berlioz also composed a poem on Napoleon's death, probably in 1833: "Drapeaux, voilez vos couleurs éclatantes / Soldats, baissez vos armes triomphantes / Ô France, Mère des héros / Pleure / Pleure / Napoléon n'est plus!" (ibid., 150). There is little evidence to determine the extent of Liszt's own participation in the idolization of Napoleon. Given his social and intellectual affiliations (Berlioz and Hugo, for example), it is likely that he was fully involved in it. His projected *Symphonie révolutionnaire*, at least, shows that he was caught up in the public and political fervor that was so closely tied to the cult of Napoleon, and he seemed flattered when Lady Blessington pointed out his resemblance to the young general.

[Napoleons are] that class, made up of many people in the civil sphere, whom we see overcome with the silly pretension of imitating, copying, and aping the great man . . . Today the common ambition is turned toward Napoleon; it is he who serves as the standard measure, him who is chosen as the model and type . . . [There is now] an innumerable, infinite, immense race of Napoleons in all political, literary, musical and industrial categories. Everywhere you go you bump into a Napoleon; the Napoleons travel the streets, in carriage, on foot or by horse, and most often by foot.[18]

These words might be seen as a response to the wave of Napoleon-mania that swept through Paris in 1840, when his ashes were installed at the Invalides. Yet *Gazette* readers could have encountered the idea even before that event: "Napoleon is the man of the age; his glory, his genius, his astonishing good fortunes, his still more astonishing bad fortune, are the constant object of all reflections, of all studies, of all enthusiasms."[19] Liszt was making his reputation in Paris, in short, precisely during those years when Napoleon-centricity was at its height.

Although the cult of Napoleon was most pervasive in France, it also took root in Germany. Some of the German intelligentsia, of course, took a passionate, nationalistic, anti-Napoleon stance. But the cult had siphoned off (however unstably) the historical contingencies that made Napoleon objectionable and converted him into a figure of ahistorical myth, thus rendering him safe for romantics everywhere. Robert Schumann, for example, inscribed two rhapsodies to Napoleon in his diaries.[20] Berlin's leading music critic, Ludwig Rellstab, published quasi-historical fictions about him, thus capitalizing on the thriving European market for Napoleonic biographical anecdotes.[21] And the young Heinrich Heine, circulating among the cutting-edge romantics in Berlin, was an avid, unconditional fan of Napoleon.

In Germany as in France, the cult was not confined to the *literati*, but extended to the less educated population. In small towns one could find all manner of Napoleonic commodities – poems, portraits, songs, and figurines[22] – while in rural areas his portrait adorned nearly every household and children were heard reciting from memory the names of Napoleon's marshals.[23] The cult of Napoleon, then, reached its arms into

[18] Paul Smith, "Les Napoléon," *Revue et gazette musicale* 8/16 (25 February 1841), 121–22.
[19] *Revue et gazette musicale* 6/67 (12 December 1839), 535.
[20] John Daverio, *Robert Schumann* (Oxford, 1997), 293–94. The Napoleon poems appear in his *Tagebücher* (Leipzig, 1971–87), 3 vols., II: 355–56, II: 59, and II: 375–86.
[21] A concise summary of the development of the cult of Napoleon in Germany in the 1830s and 1840s is presented in Otto W. Johnston, *The Myth of a Nation: Literature and Politics in Prussia under Napoleon* (Columbia, SC, 1989), 177–89.
[22] Otto Bähr, *Eine deutsche Stadt vor hundert Jahren: kulturgeschichtliche Skizzen* (Berlin, 1926), 179–80.
[23] O. Elben, *Lebenserinnerungen, 1823–1899* (Stuttgart, 1931), 25; quoted in Schenda, *Volk ohne Buch*, 343. Elben is writing about the region of Swabia.

the international sphere and affected a wide social spectrum. For these reasons it had the capacity to mediate Liszt's reception across social and geographical boundaries.

Physiognomy

It would seem absurd today to claim that Liszt looked liked Napoleon, but his contemporaries came close to doing precisely that, justifying their claims with reference to the "science" of physiognomy. Physiognomists examined the shapes of men's heads and facial features, and proposed that such features revealed the person's moral makeup – characteristics such as benevolence, intelligence, fantasy, or decisiveness. In the early nineteenth century the credibility of physiognomy was hardly questioned, and its basic tenets (propagated in a vast esoteric literature) were familiar to both lay and educated people. From its origins in the eighteenth century, it focused its gaze upon the heads of "great" men, and Napoleon, being one of the "greatest," naturally occupied more attention than others.

It is not clear where the notion of Liszt's resemblance to Napoleon originated, but by 1840 it was already an idea in wide circulation. Robert Schumann wrote of Liszt's physical appearance:

> People have already tried to describe it in various ways, with the artist's head being called Schiller-like or Napoleon-like ... He looks especially like Napoleon as we often see the young general portrayed – pale, gaunt, with a significant profile, the expression of the whole culminating in the head.[24]

Schumann betrays his indebtedness to physiognomy by mentioning two "great men" with similar heads. But in describing Liszt's profile, he extends the resemblance beyond physiognomy proper and hints that Liszt's bearing at the keyboard itself recalled familiar silhouette portraits of the famous general ("as we *often* see the young general portrayed"). A few months after this article was published, a Hamburg critic made a remark on Liszt's performance of the Hummel Septet that seems directly indebted to Schumann: "And did he not sit there like a hero, with a striking resemblance to the youthful Napoleon?"[25] It is likely that this critic's impression was grounded partly in the corporeal stillness Liszt assumed when he performed the Septet.

---

[24] *Neue Zeitschrift für Musik* 12/30 (10 April 1840), 118 (R. Schumann). Schumann probably read the comparison to Schiller in Theodor Mundt, *Spaziergänge und Weltfahrten* (Altona, 1838), 2 vols., I: 317–18. We might conjecture that Mundt, whose impressions of Paris were formed in 1837, had been circulating in salons where Liszt's physiognomy was an object of discussion, in which case the comparison to Napoleon might already have come up.

[25] *Hamburger neue Zeitung*, 4 November 1840 ("Juvenis"). The relevant concert took place on 2 November.

Liszt's resemblance to Napoleon received a ringing confirmation when he visited London in 1840. From there he reported to Marie d'Agoult: "Lady Blessington affirms that I resemble Bonaparte and Lord Byron!!!"[26] Liszt was especially excited to hear this because Lady Blessington was an acknowledged authority on matters Byronic and Napoleonic. She had been a close associate of Byron, whose resemblance to Napoleon – both physical and personal – formed an integral part of his own self-constructed legend. In addition, Byron was the writer with whom Liszt by his own admission felt the closest affinity. Blessington's observations, then, consolidated the Liszt–Napoleon–Byron nexus and crowned it with the legitimacy of scientific physiognomy. Her leading position in London's *beau monde* also ensured that the comparison would be disseminated into various social circles and eventually into the press. This may account for the appearance of a physiognomic description in a Birmingham paper a few months after his London visit:

He is a very good-looking young man, pale, thin, and intellectual; with a fine forehead, good nose, and well cut mouth; not a little resembling the portraits of Bonaparte, when a captain of artillery. He is plainly, in his department, a man of great genius and originality.[27]

Every one of these quotations relates Liszt's appearance specifically to the *young* Napoleon ("young general," "youthful Napoleon," "Bonaparte" [as opposed to "Napoleon"], "Bonaparte, when a captain of the artillery"). This is not only because of Liszt's own age (twenty-nine) and youthful looks, but because the cult itself placed extra weight on Napoleon's identity as a young military hero. The enthusiasms shown by Berlioz in his memoirs, or by Julien Sorel in Stendhal's *Le rouge et le noir*, always come to a climax when they imagine their hero in battle. Such a bias within the cult was unavoidable, for the myth of Napoleon had to hide the hero's dark shadow – the egotistical and despotic emperor who recklessly sacrificed so many men in pursuit of worldly glory. Emphasizing the young, exclusively military Napoleon was a convenient way to deflect attention away from the unsavory

---

[26] *Correspondance de Liszt et de Madame d'Agoult*, ed. Daniel Ollivier (Paris, 1933–35), 2 vols., I: 447; emphasis added.

[27] *Birmingham Journal*, 28 November 1840; quoted in *Portrait of Liszt*, 148. In England, the resemblance became a firmly embedded element of the Lisztian mythology. Sir George Grove, upon meeting Liszt in 1868, was struck by "a great general likeness to Napoleon *when young*. The instant I shook hands with him, the words came to the tip of my tongue, 'the young lieutenant of Engineers' (Carlyle, somewhere about Napoleon)" (C. L. Graves, *The Life and Letters of Sir George Grove* [London, 1903], 164; quoted in *Portrait of Liszt*, 427–28; emphasis added). Grove presents his reaction as though it were completely spontaneous, but in light of Liszt's actual appearance at fifty-seven, it seems more likely that he is transmitting a motif, painfully outdated, from the cluster of oral myths that had consolidated around Liszt.

imperial Napoleon. Liszt's resemblance to Bonaparte thus contributed a specifically *military* dimension to his public identity.

Even by the standards of physiognomy, one can see resemblances between Liszt and Napoleon only with a generous leap of the imagination. Liszt's contemporaries were willing to make this leap because they discerned a strong *character* resemblance between the two men, and wished to see their intuition confirmed by physiognomic science. They admired Napoleon as a paragon of decisiveness, a man who followed his own inner path regardless of the opinions of those around him:

The Napoleon [*le Napoléon*] begins with an idea . . . he believes in his moral force, neither more nor less than he believes in his genius. When he wants or does not want to do something, the universe throws itself at his feet, without shaking him up. When he makes a resolution (and he is making one at every moment) the devil is not going to make him change his mind. If the real Napoleon had listened to the advice of the vulgar, would he have gone to Toulon, would he have conquered in Italy, in Egypt?[28]

Liszt's public persona matched this formula to the letter. Through his many published essays – in which he voiced often critical opinions about contemporary art, politics, and mores – he projected an attitude of confidence, pride, independence, and moral conviction, and these qualities, confirmed by his behavior in the culture of salons, became central to his reputation.

An untitled lithograph that appeared in the *Gazette musicale* in the early 1840s (Figure 2.2) offers a portrait of Liszt intended to convey his decisive, uncompromising nature. The commentary accompanying the portrait makes telling references to Napoleon: "At the center of all the pianistic celebrities, with his arms crossed like general Bonaparte, who would not recognize Liszt with his Napoleonic look [*regard napoléonien*]?"[29] There may be a trace of physiognomy in this comment, but the writer is more likely responding to Liszt's facial expression. His severe, condescending look – conveyed by a tense mouth and a direct, almost accusatory gaze – sets him apart from the modest, if not deliberately effeminized, faces of the other virtuosos. Robert Schumann, using explicitly physiognomic language, singled out the same facial features in arguing for the Napoleonic side of Liszt's personality:

People have already tried to describe [Liszt's appearance] in various ways, with the artist's head being called Schiller-like or Napoleon-like, and since all extraordinary people seem to have in common a trait – namely that of energy

[28] Smith, "Les Napoléon."
[29] Henri Blanchard, "Pianistes célèbres (jeune école)," *Revue et gazette musicale* 10/11 (12 March 1843), 93.

Figure 2.2 Nicolas Maurin, 1842. Left to right: Rosenhain, Wolff,
Döhler, Henselt, Chopin, Liszt, Dreyshock, Thalberg

and strength of will in the eye and mouth – this comparison seems somewhat appropriate.[30]

In several portraits (such as Figures 2.2 and 2.3) the outer corners of Liszt's mouth are distinctly turned up as if to signify his determination and counteract the softer features of his face.[31]

Liszt's crossed arms form a second Napoleonic motif in Figure 2.2. In keeping with the demand that Liszt appear like the *young* hero, the arms recall "general Bonaparte," not the emperor Napoleon. In the 1830s, European readers were accustomed to seeing Liszt in this pose. In Kriehuber's 1838 portrait (Figure 2.5), the arms appear nearly identical to Figure 2.2. Crossed arms also take on an important role in the well-known portrait by Henri Lehmann (Figure 2.3), which apparently takes Ary Scheffer's earlier portrait (Figure 2.4) as its starting point. Given the Napoleon-saturated environment of 1830s Paris, it is possible that the crossed arms are an explicitly Napoleonic motif. More important, however, is the air of nobility and determination the arms convey, which signify those character traits most similar to Napoleon's.

When writers compared Liszt to Napoleon, they intended a gesture of praise, an acknowledgment of his superior charisma, intelligence,

---

[30] *Neue Zeitschrift für Musik* 12/30 (10 April 1840), 118 (R. Schumann).
[31] Other examples of this tendency can be found in Ernst Burger, *Franz Liszt: A Life in Pictures and Documents* (Princeton, 1989), 101, 125.

Figure 2.3 Liszt portrait by Henri Lehmann, 1839

and character. Yet because Napoleon's identity was itself contested and unstable, the comparison always ran the risk of turning back on Liszt. His detractors, who existed in no small number, could also make use of his Napoleonic "strength of will." The Paris-based composer Stephen Heller rarely had kind words for Liszt's compositions or pianism, and he was equally critical of his personality: "[Theodor Döhler] is a fine young man, and although a great pianist, he is quite simple and modest. How different from that roman emperor, or conqueror, or however

Figure 2.4 Liszt portrait by Ary Scheffer, 1837

you like it, whose signature reads Liszt I!!!"[32] Heller makes his point simply by invoking the ill-reputed, megalomaniacal emperor (Napoleon *le premier*).

---

[32] Stephen Heller, *Lettres d'un musicien romantique à Paris,* ed. J.-J. Eigeldinger (Paris, 1981), 119 (letter dated 1 May 1844). Heller used the same epithet in at least one other letter.

Figure 2.5 Liszt portrait by Josef Kriehuber, 1838

A Parisian journalist suggested in 1841 that "If historical parallels were still in fashion, [Liszt] could easily be posited as the Napoleon of the piano; but Napoleon is a name already worn out by pretenders of every kind."[33] The reader is asked to believe that Napoleon is *passé*, or that Napoleon is *cliché*. But the writer makes this gesture to cover up his humiliating inability to avoid Napoleon – the pervasiveness of Napoleon as a symbol in the present. Liszt's audiences were immersed in Napoleonic imagery and had absorbed the basic assumptions of physiognomy. They idolized (and could therefore also de-idolize) the character traits he seemed to share with the French hero – a bold will, an energetic commitment to action, and an uncompromising sense of integrity. This motivated them to read Napoleon into the morphology of his eyes and mouth, into his facial expressions, and into his appearance in profile at the keyboard. Writers deliberately characterized Liszt with reference to the young, pre-imperial Napoleon, and thus constructed him as a military hero. What remains to be seen is how the wild, violent emotions of Liszt's performing style in themselves turned his concerts, as Franz von Schober put it, into battlefields, adding another layer to his militarized public identity.

2.   Liszt and Weber's *Konzertstück*

Liszt's military aura came to a climax in his performances of Carl Maria von Weber's *Konzertstück* in F minor for piano and orchestra. The weight of the *Konzertstück* in Liszt's virtuoso repertory has never been recognized. In the 1830s he programmed it more often than any other composition, using it for nearly every public concert he gave in Paris, Lyons, and Geneva, as well as many private concerts. Already in 1840 a Vienna critic credited him with having made the *Konzertstück* famous,[34] and throughout his concertizing he tended to program it whenever an orchestra was available (he also sometimes played it without orchestra). We know of performances from 1831 to 1847, making it by far the longest-standing composition in his repertory. Its special importance to Liszt is suggested by the fact that he featured it for his single Parisian benefit concert of 1837. The rivalry with Sigismond Thalberg was at its peak, and so far as he knew this would be his only chance to challenge Thalberg in public.

Liszt's performances of the *Konzertstück* also stand out for the impression they made on audiences and critics. Night after night audiences

---

[33] *Artiste*, Ser. 2, VII/16 (1841), p. 269 (A. Specht).

[34] *Allgemeine Theaterzeitung*, 11 February 1840, p. 146 (H. Adami), quoted in D. Legány, *Franz Liszt: unbekannte Presse und Briefe aus Wien, 1882–1866* (Vienna, 1984), 79–80. Adami refers to "the Konzertstück of C. M. von Weber, which has become so famous through him" ("das durch ihn so berühmt gewordene Concertstück von C. M. von Weber").

broke out in applause, sometimes even coming to their feet, at his delivery of the climactic march, and only rarely was he spared the task of encoring the march and finale. No other composition in his repertory generated so much commentary from critics, and superlatives abound to an extent that is rare even by the standards of the usual Liszt concert review. The Parisian critics, who had the opportunity to hear him on several occasions, remembered these performances fondly: "the Conservatoire hall has not forgotten the applause that the public made ring out for this concerto three years ago. On Sunday Liszt, ripened through trials, surpassed himself again."[35] Almost a year after this concert, the ears of another critic were still ringing with the sounds of "the sublime concertino by Litz [*sic*], performed last winter at the Opéra with such passionate intensity."[36]

The centrality of the *Konzertstück* in Liszt's repertory and in the experience of his audiences can be attributed to many factors. At a practical level, its simple, sight-readable orchestral writing perfectly suited the needs of the itinerant virtuoso, which is one reason why Liszt may have used it so often. The length and full orchestral accompaniment in themselves gave it special weight in his concert programs. Critics and musicians took special interest in the *Konzertstück* because they considered it a "classical" composition by an established master. In addition, its internal variety of mood and tempos, together with the narrative pattern created by its form and *topoi*, provided the perfect outlet for the coloristic and dramatic orientation of Liszt's virtuosity.[37] Yet the success of the *Konzertstück* owes most to the impact of the third-movement march. This is the passage writers repeatedly singled out for commentary and praise and, perhaps in response to this success, Liszt sometimes excerpted the march for separate performance or encored it.[38] To understand the power of this virtuosic moment – perhaps the greatest in all of

---

[35] *Revue et gazette musicale* 4/13 (26 March 1837), 104 (E. Legouvé). In the early 1830s Berlioz had heard it often enough that he could write: "Weber's Concertstück, played with the irresistible fire that Liszt *always* brings to it, scored a triumph" (*The Memoirs of Hector Berlioz*, 223; emphasis added).

[36] *France musicale* 1/1 (31 December 1837), 6.

[37] Several writers commented on the encyclopedic quality of Liszt's playing of the *Konzertstück*. Joseph d'Ortigue wrote: "We feel a need to speak once again of Liszt and his magical, passionate, fiery performance, inexhaustible in its forms and prodigious in its variety. All of these qualities he made evident in the concerto for piano and orchestra of Weber" (*Journal de Paris*, 27 March 1837). Henri Blanchard, using equally generic superlatives, noted Liszt's range of expression in the Weber piece: "there is no point of comparison in the playing of any other virtuoso that can help give an idea of this rapidity, this grace, united with such grandeur, force, and powerful sonority" (*Revue et gazette musicale* 11/15 [14 April 1844], 132).

[38] At Harriet Smithson's benefit of 11 November 1833, Liszt performed a "Marche concertante de Weber" (*Revue musicale* 7/44 [30 November 1833], p. 347). One month later, according to *L'artiste* (Ser. 2, VI/22 [1844], p. 263), he performed a "Largo, marche et

Liszt's repertory – we need to take a closer look at Weber's composition and Liszt's way of delivering it.

Story and music

The highly anomalous form of the *Konzertstück* is best understood through a brief review of its genesis. In 1815 Weber began to write a piano concerto, but his thoughts were quickly diverted toward a dramatic idea:

> I have an F minor piano concerto planned. But as concertos in minor [keys] without definite, evocative ideas seldom work with the public, I have instinctively inserted into the whole thing a kind of story whose thread will connect and define its character – moreover, one so detailed and at the same time dramatic that I found myself obliged to give it the following headings: Allegro, Parting. Adagio, Lament. Finale, Profoundest misery, consolation, reunion, jubilation.[39]

At this early stage he was apparently preserving the form of three separate movements, with an amorous theme linking them together. This outline intimates, however, the demise of his planned concerto structure. No ingenious handling of the form of a concerto finale would enable him to represent the four psychological states he lists here. The planned finale, in fact, outlines an operatic scene – a two-phase solo aria, a transition in which the hero enters, and a joyful closing duet. Weber's dramatic idea won out over the concerto. The completed composition, which appeared only six years later, fuses together four elements of his original outline – lament, misery, reunion, and jubilation (the parting and consolation disappear) – to form an uninterrupted musical narrative.

The substance of Weber's narrative has been transmitted by his colleague Jules Benedict, who claimed that Weber named the narrative events as he played the newly completed composition for him. Benedict's account follows both Weber's letter and the progress of the composition convincingly, and there is little reason to doubt its authenticity. The narrative is a simple medieval romance: a noble lady sits in her manor, suffering as she awaits the return of her knight, who is off fighting in the crusades. Just before she collapses in utter despair, the knight and his army return triumphant from the distance. The lovers embrace, and a general celebration breaks out. Table 2.1 outlines the correspondence of Benedict's narrative to the four sections of the composition.

---

finale brillant . . . composé par Weber," meaning the last two movements of Weber's original. In the later years of his career he sometimes excerpted the march from his solo piano arrangement.

[39] Letter to Rochlitz, 14 March 1815; quoted in John Warrack, *Carl Maria von Weber*, 2nd edn. (London, 1976), 245.

Table 2.1 *Program and layout of the* Konzertstück

Music	Benedict's program
1. A slow, mournful introduction in F minor, representing the lady's longing for her beloved (Weber's "Lament")	The lady sits in her tower: she gazes sadly into the distance. Her knight has been for years in the Holy Land: shall she ever see him again? Battles have been fought: but no news of him who is so dear to her. In vain have been all her prayers.
2. An agitated Allegro passionato in F minor representing the lady's hallucination of her lover's death on the battlefield (Weber's "Profoundest misery")	A fearful vision rises to her mind; – her knight is lying on the battle-field, deserted and alone; his heart's blood is ebbing fast away. Could she but be by his side! – could she but die with him! She falls exhausted and senseless.
3. A military march in C major that gradually fades in, representing the return of the hero and his vassals (Weber's "Reunion")	But hark! what is that distant sound? What glimmers in the sunlight from the wood? What are those forms approaching? Knights and squires with the cross of the Crusades, banners waving, acclamations of the people: and there! it is he! She sinks into his arms.
4. A joyful, rondo-like movement in F major and 6/8 time, the key and meter suggestive of the pastoral mode (Weber's "Jubilation")	Love is triumphant. Happiness without end. The very woods and waves sing the song of love; a thousand voices proclaim its victory.

Source: Jules Benedict, *Weber* (London, 1881, 5/1899), 66; quoted in Warrack, *Carl Maria von Weber*, 245.

Weber's narrative was no secret to Liszt's contemporaries. The critic Henri Blanchard pointed out that Weber mentioned the narrative on the title page of some of the early editions, and he was able to rattle off the episodes effortlessly:

... the poem by Weber named *Concert-Stück*, that medieval legend in which the author of *Freischütz* wanted, as he wrote under the title, to narrate a return from the crusade. And one indeed hears and sees in this melodic and harmonious narrative the sorrows of the noble lady in the feudal manor, her streaks of hope, the distant march of the high baron and his chevaliers who arrive, the joyful cries of the vassals, the servants, the embraces of the return, and the explosion of common celebration.[40]

---

[40] *Revue et gazette musicale* 12/14 (6 April 1845), 106 (H. Blanchard). This is a review of Maria Pleyel's concert.

Familiarity with Weber's narrative was bred by the *Konzertstück*'s outstanding reputation and the frequency of its performance. Traveling virtuosos rarely played concertos that were not their own, but several of them, following the lead of Liszt and Marie Pleyel, made an exception for Weber's piece. One Belgian reporter even complained about the *Konzertstück*, "not because I fail to recognize the merit of this fine composition, but because it seems to have been played too often in recent times by great artists."[41] In London, Liszt battled with the administration of the Philharmonic Society over whether he should be permitted to play the *Konzertstück* in the wake of recent performances by Moscheles. As early as 1833, Liszt called it "the famous *Conzertstück* of Weber,"[42] and a decade later it was sufficient to refer to "the famous concerto of Weber."[43]

Although it is likely that many people in Liszt's audiences knew something about the narrative, such knowledge was not a prerequisite for hearing the *Konzertstück* in dramatic or narrative terms. Admittedly, it is entirely possible to hear the first two sections as a concert allegro, without having any idea that it is a programmatic composition. But the transition from the Largo affetuoso to the Allegro passionato, an extended crescendo on the dominant, hints at a narrative design. This hint is ringingly confirmed in the third section – three statements of a military march at progressively louder volume. The march begs the listener for a hermeneutic interpretation, for it dispenses with all generic expectations of the concert allegro or concerto, and its military *topoi* have an almost iconic directness that contrasts with the preceding music (the first statement of the march is scored for military band). The march thus breaks the concert allegro as a possible interpretive framework and installs narrativity in its place.[44] Weber's musical discourse does not, however, clarify the *content* of the narrative, even if the march *topoi* imply a military context. Liszt's performance of the *Konzertstück* closed this hermeneutic gap. His performing style constituted a level of discourse in itself that offered up a displaced image of heroic military valor. Furthermore, he embellished Weber's score in such a way as to encourage his audiences to identify him with the military hero who so triumphantly returns in the march.

---

[41] Report from Brussels in *Revue et gazette musicale* 10/9 (26 February 1843), 71. Other pianists who played it in public at this time include Leopoldine Blahetka, Henri Litolff, and Adolf Henselt.

[42] Letter to Valérie Boissier, 14 November 1833; in Robert Bory, "Lettres diverses inédites de Liszt," *Schweizerisches Jahrbuch für die Musikwissenschaft* 3 (1928), 15.

[43] *France musicale* 5/48 (27 November 1842), 405. In editions from the later nineteenth century, including Liszt's, there are no longer references to the programs.

[44] Each of the three transitions between sections also contributes to the piece's narrativity. In a more general sense, the uninterrupted flow of the piece as a whole is already narrativistic.

Liszt's rendition of the *Konzertstück*

For a piece that served as one of Liszt's warhorses, the piano writing of the *Konzertstück* is surprisingly non-Lisztian. Its predominantly right-handed passagework, outlining scales and arpeggios with single-tone figurations, belongs to the Viennese "brilliant" style of the early nineteenth century. Liszt made the piece his own by introducing a wide range of embellishments. According to his friend Caroline Boissier, he felt a need to update Weber's rather thin cadenzas: "He thinks the entrances in this piece are somewhat meager, and makes an effort to enrich them."[45] Embellishment was of course standard practice for concert virtuosos, but the richness of Liszt's performance stood out against the original score:

> Mr. Liszt changes many things in this concerto; he makes simple passages more difficult, and perhaps also more brilliant, through doublings and the like, and he often introduces a wealth of striking ornaments and decorations.[46]

Liszt's 1883 edition of the *Konzertstück* includes several ossia passages that probably represent his own performance decisions. In many cases he picked up a right-hand figure, doubled it at the octave, and redistributed it among the two hands so that they are playing octaves or chords in rapid alternation (Example 2.1).[47] Such embellishments not only enriched the sonority, but also rewrote the performer's bodily choreography. Whereas the body of Weber's virtuoso sweeps along the horizontal axis of the keyboard, Liszt's arms and wrists are constantly approaching the keyboard vertically. By transforming rapid fingerwork into vertical gestures, Liszt offered a spectacle of domination and violence that, in the special circumstances of the *Konzertstück*, displaced to an image of heroic military valor.

Liszt's embellishments to the *Konzertstück* went far beyond local enrichments of sonority. He made two large-scale changes to Weber's score, both of which magnified the military impact of his performance and forged an identification between him and the battle hero of the narrative. The first change took place at the soloist's first entrance (Example 2.2). Weber introduces the soloist as the orchestra's discursive partner. The pianist does nothing but complete the syntax, with a slight prolongation, of the orchestra's cadence. In the thematic statement at measure 25, the piano duplicates what the orchestra stated at the beginning, right down to the chord voicings. The soloist will soon

---

[45] Caroline Boissier, *Liszt pédagogue: Leçons de piano données par Liszt à Mademoiselle Valérie Boissier à Paris en 1832* (Paris, 1927), 32.

[46] *Allgemeine musikalische Zeitung* 42/14 (1 April 1840), 297.

[47] Liszt's edition was published by J. G. Cotta in Stuttgart. Examples of his embellishments are printed in Dudley Newton, "Liszt and his Glass," *Liszt Society Journal* 13 (1987), 55ff.

Example 2.1 Ossias from Liszt's 1881 edition of Weber's *Konzertstück*

initiate a digressive movement, but in these opening moments he occupies a space already established by the orchestra; he behaves as an obedient servant to the orchestra's discursive logic. If a narrative is underway,
it is being told by the orchestra and piano as a unit.

In place of Weber's languid stretch of dominant harmony, Liszt executed a dramatic, stormy cadenza, as is evident from one of Clara Schumann's diary entries: "On the thirteenth Liszt played *Konzertstück* by
Weber; at his entrance he broke 3 strings on the Graf [piano],"[48] and from
a newspaper report that appeared in Leipzig a few days later: "how he
seizes it forcefully and gigantically *right from the first measures*."[49] Robert
Schumann, who knew Weber's narrative, suggested that Liszt's cadenza
conjured up a bellicose atmosphere for the unfolding of the story: "Liszt
attacked the piece from the beginning with such force and grandeur of

---

[48] Berthold Litzmann, *Clara Schumann: ein Künstlerleben, nach Tagebüchern und Briefen*
(Leipzig, 1910), 3 vols., I: 162–200 (diary entry from 13 April 1838). She may have
singled out the Graf piano because they were known for their endurance.

[49] *Leipziger allgemeine Zeitung*, 26 March 1840 (R. Schumann); emphasis added. The concert
under review took place on 24 March.

Example 2.2 Weber, *Konzertstück*, first piano entrance

expression that a charge on the battlefield seemed to be in question."[50] It is possible that Liszt intended the cadenza as a virtuosic vignette of the hero in battle, the image responsible for the lady's suffering. That he was thinking along these programmatic lines is suggested, at least, by the fact that he borrowed a motive from Weber's finale for his cadenza.[51]

Whether or not Liszt's cadenza was programmatically conceived, it entirely upset the discursive order of Weber's score, for the performing

---

[50] *Neue Zeitschrift für Musik* 12/30 (10 April 1840), 119 (R. Schumann).

[51] Boissier wrote: "he brings to the beginning of the piece a recurrent motive in the finale that sounds like the Oberon motive, and caresses it until, his playing ever increasing toward the conclusion, he plays it on the last pages with passionate wildness" (*Liszt pédagogue*, 32).

Example 2.2 (*cont.*)

forces are no longer working in tandem in the way that Weber's entrance implies. The cadenza asserts the soloist's independence from the orchestra, and its virtuosic intensity focuses the listener's attention on Liszt as a center of dramatic action. The performer is not an individual character, but a locus of subjectivity, or expressive zone, through which characters and events materialize. This effect was reinforced by Liszt's much-discussed (and much-lamented) facial expressions, which mimicked the emotions or characters implied by the music he played. After the cadenza, Liszt was not the narrator or co-narrator of Weber's romance, but a dramatic actor playing the roles of both the lady and the knight. It is telling that Boissier's highest praise for Liszt's *Konzertstück* consists in a comparison to one of the world's leading actors: "Everything had its meaning, its expression, it was a veritable psychological treatise. If Talma had wanted to demonstrate a role by explaining it, he certainly could not have penetrated deeper into Racine and Voltaire than Liszt penetrated Weber."[52]

Liszt's establishment of a dramatic scene in the opening cadenza had important consequences for the march that forms the climax of the *Konzertstück*, for it encouraged his audiences to identify him with the battle hero implicit in the music and explicit in Weber's narrative. Such an

[52] Boissier, *Liszt pédagogue*, 44.

Example 2.3 Weber, *Konzertstück*, march

identification was powerfully reinforced by Liszt's second major alter-
ation. In Weber's score, the first statement of the march is pianissimo
and is orchestrated for winds and timpani, creating the impression
of a marching army and wind band sounding from the distance. The
march is then restated in its entirety with an enriched orchestration, so
that the army seems to be approaching the scene. At the end of this
second statement, the piano breaks in on the dominant, and with an
octave glissando up the keyboard it ushers in a fortissimo statement of
the march by the full orchestra (Example 2.3). The glissando signifies,
bluntly enough, the appearance of the hero. But here the piano drops
right back out: the orchestra alone takes over the portrait of the knight
as he marches toward his beloved. In presenting the hero, that is, Weber

does not differentiate the soloist and orchestra discursively: they are telling the story together.

Liszt dispensed with this musical equivalent of narrative distance, and recast the climax to transform himself into the battle hero who appears so triumphantly. He achieved this with two changes. First, he replaced Weber's glissando with a rapid run up the keyboard in octaves. Rudolph Apponyi described the stunning visual impact of this moment:

He is especially amazing in a passage, written entirely in octaves, which he plays with such rapidity and such force that the hands seem to multiply. It was impossible to follow with my eyes their rapid, inconceivable motions; they flew from one end of the piano to the other.[53]

From this description it is evident that Liszt probably played a chromatic scale, with the hands alternating octaves, controlled entirely from the wrist. The constant repositioning of the hands between white and black keys, combined with the high velocity of the hands, create the dizzying visual effect Apponyi describes (in piano competition videos, the camera people never miss a chance to capture this effect). Liszt's chromatic octave surge expanded the sonic and visual dramatic amplitude of the gesture that marks the appearance of the hero. The listener could no longer see *through* Liszt to the narrative, for he had *become* the hero who appears over the horizon.

Liszt's second change followed inexorably on the heels of these octaves. He joined the orchestra for its climactic, fortissimo statement of the march. Reviewers repeatedly praised his ability to make the piano project out over the full orchestra – probably by means of double octaves and densely voiced chords (the upper system in Example 2.3 represents approximately Liszt's way of executing it). Joseph d'Ortigue devoted little space to Liszt's concerts in his biography, but he did wish to single out this effect:

In the *Conzertstück* of Weber for piano and orchestra we saw him take possession of the entire orchestra with his instrument, and cover the hundred voices of the orchestra with his thunder, and a thousand bravos broke out in the hall at this moment.[54]

Ortigue's words "take possession" spell out the dramatic implications of Liszt's acoustical feat. The virtuoso emerges as the disciplining leader of the orchestra, offering a performative parallel to the image of a battle

---

[53] Rudolph Apponyi, *Vingt-cinq ans à Paris* (Paris, 1913), 3 vols., II: 179 (journal entry from 18 April 1832).

[54] *Revue et gazette musicale* 2/24 (14 June 1835), 202 (J. d'Ortigue). Apponyi's description is confirmed by another reporter, who claimed that the march was played "at the wonderful re-entry toward the end, after having risen up the piano with brilliant octaves in both hands" (*Revue et gazette musicale* 4/13 [26 March 1837], 104. [E. Legouvé]).

hero marching with his vassals. Ernest Legouvé was reminded of "an army general in action, sabre in hand, riding his horse at full speed, at the head of his squadrons, whom he carries along with him; and the entire hall saluted the chivalrous triumph with four salvos of applause."[55] Legouvé emphasizes here military meanings as they are implicit in the dynamism and drama of the performance ("in action," "riding his horse"). The military coding may originate outside of Liszt's playing – in the march *topos* and the visual appearance of the orchestra with a leader – but his virtuosity absorbs and even magnifies them.

At the highpoint of the *Konzertstück*, then, Liszt was transformed into a military hero through a variety of signifying channels: musical coding, performing forces, Weber's narrative, his alterations to the piano score, and the generally dramatic orientation of his performing style. This military aura touched a nerve in Liszt's audiences, steeped as they were in the lore of Napoleonic, Caesarian, or Alexandrian battle valor, and the march became one of the greatest moments in all of his virtuoso performances (to measure from the enthusiasm of audiences and critics). This performative dimension of his militarized aura complemented an already-existing public discourse comparing his appearance and character to that of Napoleon. When Robert Schumann first heard the *Konzertstück*, he made the connection:

> He carried this on with continually increasing power, until the passage where the player seems to stand at the summit of the orchestra, leading it forward in triumph. Here indeed he resembled that great commander to whom he has been compared, and the tempestuous applause that greeted him was not unlike an adoring "Vive l'Empereur."[56]

Here the Napoleonic resonance spreads out beyond Liszt to envelop the entire concert event, since the audience's behavior recalls the great public receptions of the French hero.

3.   Virtuosity and violence

> *... this hero of the air with variations, this Napoleon of the fantasy ...*
> La caricature, 10 July 1842

If Liszt's performances offered up a displaced image of heroic military valor, and thereby joined a broader culture practice of celebrating

---

[55] *Revue et gazette musicale* 4/13 (26 March 1837), 104 (E. Legouvé). One of Schumann's accounts of this passage sounds strikingly similar, but is probably unrelated to Legouvé's: "he then joins in with the march, drawing the orchestra with him, clearly audible over the accumulated forces [*Massen*]; in this way he draws them along with him toward the conclusion like a victorious army general" (*Leipziger allgemeine Zeitung*, 19 March 1840).

[56] *Neue Zeitschrift für Musik* 12/30 (10 April 1840), 119 (R. Schumann).

conquering heroes, we might pose the question why the image of domination or conquering was so highly valued, or why it was so pleasurable for his audiences. Historian Peter Gay offers a compelling answer to this question in *The Cultivation of Hatred*. Gay argues that rituals of "cultivated aggression" formed one of the principal elements of bourgeois experience in the nineteenth century. Through them the bourgeoisie found an outlet for sexual and aggressive impulses that their particular moral codes had placed under taboo. Gay identifies a wide range of such practices – from gruesome student duels to sports events, satires, and nationalist writings. These aggressive behaviors were accepted – indeed promoted and celebrated – as long as they were coupled with a sanitizing "alibi" that figured them as ultimately of positive ethical value.[57] The student duel, for example, was legitimated by its strict code of rules and by its origin in the tradition of chivalry.

Liszt turned the virtuoso concert into a spectacle of cultivated aggression, and his unprecedented popularity can be attributed in part to this fact. The aggressiveness of his playing was protected by the alibi of "art," with its much-trumpeted civilizing mission, and this alibi continues to shield Liszt's virtuosity from full view. I will consider separately three different "axes" along which Liszt's performing style communicated violence. First and most simply, Liszt's extensive vertical attacks into a motionless, passive instrument – the "piano-as-object" – appeared to be merciless. A second kind of violence emerged when, because of Liszt's convulsive bodily motions, the piano seemed to be a resisting enemy to be dominated or tamed. This pattern of struggle and domination could also emerge in Liszt's relationship to his accompanying orchestra, thus forming the third axis along which his playing could figure violence.

The piano as victimized object

It has long been observed that Liszt shifted keyboard technique away from the fingers and toward the wrists and arms. With extended, double-fisted chordal passages, cascades of octaves executed by alternating hands, and radical jumps across the keyboard, he developed an entirely new performing choreography accenting vertical motion into the keys. The violence inherent in this approach to the keyboard was recognized by contemporary journalists, who commonly drew on predator imagery as they described it. As Liszt appeared on stage in Königsberg, a local reporter wrote, he threw his handkerchief to the floor and without delay "fell upon the keys like a vulture."[58] The bird-of-prey image resulted

[57] See the introduction in Peter Gay, *The Cultivation of Hatred* (New York, 1993).
[58] Erwin Kroll, *Musikstadt Königsberg* (Freiburg i. B., 1966), 151. Kroll does not cite his source.

partly from the physiognomy of Liszt's hands: "his fingers we have heard likened to talons on account of their thinness and length, pouncing upon the keys of the pianoforte with the eagerness and velocity of an eagle"[59] – and was enhanced by the positioning of his arms and fingers: "his hands usually hover in the air and the fingers point from above downward, often in a straight line."[60] His restless jumping from one region of the keyboard to another, furthermore, could evoke a rapacious hunt: "Imaginary tone-pictures emerge in full armor from the forehead of this *Jupiter tonans* of the piano; he reaches into the keys with a powerful grip, pouncing upon them with lion leaps."[61] In this passage violence is figured not only at the visual level, but also in the overwhelming sonority ("tonans") of Liszt's virtuosity – sound mutates into a militant Athena.

This level of violence – almost exclusively visual in origin – was easily isolated and exaggerated by his critics. A zealous opponent in Berlin called him "the greatest key-chopper, the most enraged piano-shatterer and string-breaker of our century,"[62] and a Leipzig critic who disliked his performances of classical repertory wrote that "his power is essentially a destructive and wild demon that assumes a Mephistophelean

---

59 *Doncaster Gazette*, 11 December 1840; quoted in *Liszt Society Journal* 11 (1986), 47. This comparison seems to be borrowed from an article in the *Bath Herald* of 5 September 1840: "a prodigious length of forearm and finger complete his *personnel* . . . In the spirit-stirring, energetic, and startling, when he puts forth the full powers of the instrument, his forky fingers appeared winged, and to fly with eagle force and swiftness, and then no storm can match the wild, tumultuous freaks – the tempestuous *con furia's* of this performer" (*Liszt Society Journal* 8 [1982]). During the provincial tours newspapers were borrowing from each other a great deal. It is possible that Lavenu, the impresario of the tour, was passing on a collection of reviews to newspaper editors in the various towns in order to promote their concerts.

60 *Signale für die musikalische Welt* 2 (March 1844), 68. Caroline Boissier, who knew Liszt when he was just twenty, was struck by the sleek beauty of his hands, but this did not prevent her from imagining them as objects of destruction: "His small, slender hand sometimes obliterated [*anéantissait*] the piano with its vigor, at other times floated lightly over the instrument" (*Liszt pédagogue*, 38); "His fingers [are] by turns light, soft, velvety, then terrifyingly energetic" (C. Barbey-Boissier, *La Comtesse Agénor de Gasparin et sa famille: Correspondance et souvenirs 1813–1894* [Paris, 1902], 2 vols., I: 143); "His small hands are at once delicate and tapering, and so flexible that they carry out whatever is demanded of them. With all that, they are powerful enough to break the keys at will" (ibid., 1: 185–86). Boissier also pointed out that Liszt was not in favor of the traditional curved position of the hand (*Liszt pédagogue*, 16). This resolutely vertical positioning of the arms and fingers is one of the principal features singled out for exaggeration by contemporary caricaturists (see for example Burger, *Franz Liszt*, 86, 89, 146, 142).

61 *Allgemeine privilegirte schlesische Zeitung*, 7 February 1842.

62 *Neuigkeits-Bote*, 10 March 1842. The article quotes these words from Maxmillian Langenschwarz, who apparently had a satirical series entitled "Schneider Ritz." The "Schneider Ritz" apparently published a "colossal" satire on Liszt. The original German reads: "den grössten Tasten-Hacker unseres Jahrhunderts, den wüthendsten Klavierzerschmetterer und Saitenzerplatzer."

form."[63] These reactions stand, however, at the margins of Liszt criticism. Most often his violence was praised indirectly, quietly folded into the adulatory rhetoric of the concert reports:

When Liszt throws his hands upon the keyboard, they do not sing, they shout, they thunder, under the impression. He does not touch, he grasps; he does not untwist the hidden chains, he drags them out.[64]

The negative comparisons in this passage ("not sing," "not touch") reveal how radically Liszt was dispensing with the traditional performer–keyboard relationship, in which the performer "touches" the piano and makes it "sing." A pianist who drags out the chains and makes the keys shout under his hands is nothing less than a torturer of his instrument, and the reader is asked to admire such behavior. Liszt's violence is also highlighted in an often-cited passage by Moritz Saphir:

[Liszt is] a kindly monster, who treats his beloved – the piano – now sweetly, now tyrannically, decorates her with kisses, tears her to pieces with sensual bites, embraces her, plays with her, pouts, scolds her, strikes, grabs her by the hair, then hugs her all the more sweetly, more intimately, more passionately.[65]

Saphir consciously attempts to balance violent and tender elements here, and to recuperate the aggression with the concluding rapturous embrace. Yet by including an image of abuse, if not rape, these words only magnify the violence and undo the rhetoric of recuperation.

Liszt's tendency to break piano strings and keys in performance, which motivated him to keep two pianos on stage, contributed substantially to the violent tone of his concerts. When Friedrich Wieck first heard him play, he could describe the concert as little more than a series of destructive acts:

After he annihilated Thalberg's Érard in the first piece, he played the fantasy on a C. Graf, broke two brass strings, fetched himself the second walnut C. Graf from the corner and played his etude, after which he, having once again broken two strings, said aloud to the public that it [the etude] had not succeeded and he would like to play it again. As he entered, he vehemently threw his gloves and handkerchief on the ground in front of the piano . . . It was the strangest concert of our life.[66]

---

[63] *Zeitung der elegante Welt*, 17 December 1841. "Seine Kraft is wesentlich ein zerstörender und verwildener Dämon."

[64] *Birmingham Journal*, 28 November 1840; quoted in *Liszt Society Journal* 10 (1984), 6.

[65] *Humorist*, 21 April 1838 (M. Saphir). A Dresden critic noted that the public was excited by the damaged instruments: "he could have smashed ten pianos: it was heavenly, divine!" (*Neue Zeitschrift für Musik* 20/48 [10 June 1844], p. 188 ["W. J. S. E"]).

[66] Friedrich Wieck, *Briefe aus den Jahren 1830–1838*, ed. Käthe Walch-Schumann (Cologne, 1968), 93–94.

Clara recorded a similar mix of fascination and revulsion, mentioning the damaged instruments on several occasions in her diaries.[67] Because he broke strings so easily, he usually had no choice but to continue playing (in mid-performance he once pushed a technician who was trying to repair the instrument off stage). In this situation the spectator was never allowed to forget Liszt's aggressive relationship to the piano-as-object: whether or not the instrument–victim would survive became an issue to be worked out in the course of the virtuosic drama. Battle imagery offered a suggestive analogy for this violent action:

> After the concert, Liszt remains like a conqueror on the battlefield, like a hero at his chosen post of honor. – The conquered piano lies at his feet. Broken strings appear here and there like shredded standards. The horrified instruments take cover in their cases.[68]

The piano as resisting enemy

In the passages discussed thus far, Liszt appears as an uncompromising aggressor, lunging into a helpless, passive object with predatorial hands and arms, often at the considerable expense of the instrument–object. This image is drawn mainly from the visual dimension of his playing: extensive vertical attacks into the keys. Yet vertical attacks formed only a preliminary step toward a deeper and more dynamic level of violence. In performance Liszt played out an agonistic drama in which the virtuoso struggles against resisting forces and ultimately triumphs over them through an act of violent suppression. His restless bodily motions call his mastery in question, and transform the piano into an animated, recalcitrant opponent, rather than a dead object lying on the stage. Musical sound plays a role in this transformation; the dense, chaotic field of sound emerging from the piano takes on an independent existence that itself threatens to escape the virtuoso's rational and physical control. This drama of domination depends upon the sheer vertical violence for its effect, but it is ultimately far more powerful, for it gives Liszt's domination the appearance of an ongoing, generative spectacle rather than a foregone conclusion. This drama of domination, we will see, was the most important source of the military metaphors that clustered around Liszt.

Liszt's contemporaries most often articulated his performative drama of struggle and domination through two metaphorical fields: battles and storms. Heinrich Heine described a Parisian soirée at which "Franz

---

[67] Litzmann, *Clara Schumann*, I: 198–99. It is possible that these words are partially or completely those of Friedrich Wieck, since he sometimes dictated entries to her diary.
[68] *Humorist*, 21 April 1838 (M. Saphir).

Liszt, having been persuaded to go to the piano, lifted his hair above his soulful face, and waged one of his most brilliant battles. The keys seemed to bleed."[69] Heine's attention to the keyboard suggests that he may be responding principally to the visual dimension of Liszt's playing, but in other documents the military metaphor applies unequivocally to the confused, overloaded blanket of sound-information that his bravura produced: "Listen! Now it is the sigh of a lover / Now the tumult and crash of armies."[70] Having established this agonistic environment in sound, Liszt appeared to be an active, struggling participant in the battle, an effect that can be attributed largely to his convulsive body.

To untangle the complex interaction of performer and sound in producing an image of domination, consider the following description of his performance of the Etude in D minor (later entitled *Mazeppa*):

> an etude from the realm of D minor, a Kaulbachian ghost-battle, in which Liszt goes to the field alone against concentrated, hostile, demonic difficulties, in which he vanquishes the army of the rebelling chords, in which he tramples easily the Lernean tone-ranks, in which he barricades the entire kingdom of sounds, captures the most unruly figures and leads them to unity, in which he throws the main idea into the high tide of tones with ever-increasing tempo, and in which this main idea shoots now above the tide, now below it, like an enormous sea-creature, but always remains master and conqueror.[71]

Liszt's military presence is here figured along two different axes: at one moment he is demonstrating a warrior's valor over the enemy forces ("vanquishes," "conqueror"), while in the next he shows the *disciplining* power of a military general who must engineer his troops ("master").[72] In both cases he is pitted against a swarm of imaginary beings – the multiplicitous, dispersed sounds of his music transformed into animate, independent creatures. Liszt's physical struggle at the keyboard casts these sound-creatures as a force of resistance, and his performance becomes a drama in which he must overcome them. This quotation also points

[69] From *Nuits florentines*; quoted in *Liszt en son temps*, 197. The soirée seems to have taken place in May 1836. In the continuation of this passage, Heine remembers the piece being an improvisation on a passage from Ballanche's *Palingénésie*. Heine's account of Liszt's performance at the Liszt–Thalberg "duel" of 1837, in addition, makes it out as an apocalyptic jousting tournament (*Heinrich Heine und die Musik: publizistische Arbeiten und poetische Reflexionen*, ed. G. Müller [Cologne, 1987], 106).

[70] *Le Glaneur du haut-Rhin*, 20 July 1845; quoted in Roch Serra, "Liszt en Alsace," *Liszt Saeculum* 41/42 (1988), 8.

[71] *Humorist*, 22 November 1839 (M. Saphir).

[72] "He seems to tear the very soul out of the instrument – he calls into requisition every sound, and combination of sounds, of which it is capable" (*Scotsman*, 23 January 1841; quoted in *Liszt Society Journal* 13 [1987], 67).

to a drama of resistance and domination at the sonic level: the main theme ("main idea," associated with Liszt) must fight to avoid becoming engulfed in the proliferating figuration ("the tide"). Yet the threat that Liszt might lose the battle is never real, for at a purely material level his dominion over the piano, over the passive instrument–object, is unquestioned. This explains how he *"always remains* master and conqueror" amidst the twists and turns of the drama.

In the sphere of musical representation, battles and storms have been closely related since the late eighteenth century. The mimetic codes for representing them were almost identical – agitated, rumbling tremolos, dynamic swells, rapid runs, and staccato broken chords. It is therefore not surprising that Liszt's playing could evoke storms as well as battles. In the following account of a storm scene he improvised, nature metaphors pass over to military metaphors without a sense of discontinuity: "the hurricane subsided, the winds were hushed, the waves were stilled, and like a raging battle-host when the excitement of the onslaught is passed, each reclined in gentle confidence upon the bosom of his comrade and his brother."[73] In the case of the storm metaphor, Liszt's musical sound conjures up forces of nature rather than enemy armies or unruly squadrons, but the virtuoso is still characterized by his coercive action over animate, external bodies:

> Byron I would like to name you, you dominator; powerfully
> You travel into the storm, yourself a part of the storm!
> You tear the strings from the soul, and every fiber shudders before you,
> And like the strings, my obeying heart is often swept away.[74]

As with the "Kaulbachian" battle, Liszt is both within the dramatic scene and outside of it, both struggling with nature and controlling it, but nevertheless leaving a *resultant* impression of having entirely mastered it. His physical manipulation of the piano strings leaves conspicuous traces with the poet's flight of fantasy ("you tear the strings"), showing that the raw, aggressive attacks of his playing never cease to influence the discourse. This poem was printed alongside a poem on Thalberg that also uses storm imagery, and the differences point to the uniqueness of Liszt's virtuosic conception:

---

[73] *Musical World* 13/220 (11 June 1840), 361–64. During his tours of the English provinces, Liszt accompanied John Parry's performances of the ballad *The Inchcape Bell*. The improvised storm that he interpolated into the narrative was often singled out as a highlight of the concerts.

[74] *Thalia* 88, 21 November 1840. "Byron möcht-ich dich nennen, Du übergewaltiger, machtvoll / Fährst Du im Sturme dahin, selber vom Sturme ein Stück! / Reissest die Saiten der Seele, dass jegliche Fiber Dir schauert, / Und, wie die Saiten, erreisst oft auch der Horchenden Herz!"

> Thunder rumbles, the ancient glaciers of the alps crack open,
> Lightning flashes, and the stream plunges wildly from the rock,
> But the sun shines upon the giant peaks, the nightingales sing.[75]

Thalberg creates a storm in sound, but nothing speaks of his presence *within* the discourse. His virtuosity, which nearly froze the body and minimized or smoothed out vertical motion into the keys, did not insert him into the scene he evoked, and there is consequently no violent action that would give rise to violent imagery.

When used in connection with Liszt, then, storm imagery was always cast within a narrative of struggle and victory, with the virtuoso himself as the principal character. The mechanisms of this narrative paradigm are unusually clear in a written account of his performance at a Parisian soirée in 1836. At this event, apparently, he initiated a competition with an actual storm taking place outside the house:

No one notices that the [outside] storm has grown more violent; the sounds that he draws from the piano muffle those of the thunder, and, frail though they look, his fingers possess a strength capable of stifling the noise of the tempest. He "plays a storm." On hearing a roll of thunder, he murmurs to Albertine: "I shall hold my own." And indeed he confounds and enraptures us, putting us into a state of ecstasy such as we have never known before. "I win, I am the master," he seems to say . . . The piano was not strong enough; two or three strings were unable to withstand him.[76]

In this narrative, the outdoor weather adds romantic atmosphere but does not change the fundamental terms of Liszt's performative drama. For as we have just seen, the storm he conjures musically can take on an existence independent of him, and in opposition to him ("You travel into the storm, yourself a part of the storm!"), just as the outdoor weather does in this example. Here Liszt is the dramatic protagonist to which the storm plays antagonist. He is vulnerable to being overtaken by it and thus reassures Albertine that he will be the victor. And, importantly, his sheer power over the piano-as-object – signaled here by references to his strong fingers and the broken strings – contributes to the impression of violent confrontation and victory.

The impression of Liszt's triumphant victory did not depend upon storm or battle codes within the music. His bearing at the keyboard, his dramatic struggle with the instrument, and the sound that emerged from the piano were in themselves sufficient to evoke these metaphorical contexts, regardless of what he was playing. One of the richest passages

---

[75] Ibid. "Donner rollen, es kracht urewiges Eis auf den Alpen, / Blitze zucken, und wild stürzet vom Felsen der Bach! / Aber die riesigen Kulmen beleuchtet die Sonne, es flöten Nachtigallen."

[76] Robert Bory, *Une retraite romantique en Suisse* (Lausanne, 1930), 36; quoted in *Portrait of Liszt*, 79. The extract is from the journal of Albertine de la Rive-Necker.

ever written about his military aura was a response to a solo recital that included no military-coded compositions:

He who understands Liszt also understands why and how the Bastille was stormed, he suspects the promise of future redemption. Suspects? Why, he more than suspects. For who is more a mirror image of that time, its virtues as well as its flaws? And – strange to say! – Liszt is also outwardly a portrait of our times; for who might represent it better than Napoleon heading the Italian army? It is his profile, and from that very era, that we saw, and which by the feeble light of our theatre, arose a strangely picturesque, almost magical fashion in dark, sharp contours on the light backdrop . . . that proud, dignified, immobile head, steadily soaring over the wild roar of the battle. He fought the great Hydra of the revolution as it raged and sobbed and clamored to the skies, and into its wide, white-toothed jaws he stretched his hand – he fought and won. To destroy it? Oh, no! To place it, tamed and armed, upon the throne of the world.[77]

This writer sees Napoleon first in Liszt's silhouette, a merely physical, static parallel. But through the sonic and visual dynamism of Liszt's performance, this apparition soon becomes an animate Napoleon "soaring over the wild roar of the battle." At this point in the passage it becomes unclear whether Liszt is being discussed in terms of Napoleon, or Napoleon in terms of Liszt. It would seem to be Napoleon who "fought the great Hydra of revolution," but it is Liszt who reaches into the Hydra's "white-toothed jaws," a monstrous metamorphosis of the piano keys. This merging of the two heroes, which is rooted entirely in Liszt's performative dramatization of violent struggle and triumph, makes Schumann's comments on the *Konzertstück* march seem almost trivial.

The piano–orchestra axis

Liszt's relationship to the accompanying orchestra could add yet another layer of struggle and victory to his performances. Writers often described an agonistic spectacle in which the pianist – the unquestionable underdog in the contest – fights to be heard over the massive orchestra, and finishes victoriously. This may seem to contradict what we have encountered in the *Konzertstück*, where Liszt's acoustic dominion over the orchestra figures him as the orchestra's leader – an image of perfect cooperation. Yet there is in fact no contradiction, for the same conditions that enable him to play the orchestra's leader also enable him to play the orchestra's mortal adversary. In the following passage, the climax of the *Konzertstück* is interpreted in such agonistic terms: "Liszt's fight with the orchestra offered a spectacle still more interesting than when

---

[77] Review of the 17 July 1841 concert in *Foedrelandet*, 19 July 1841; quoted in Bengt Johnsson, "Liszt in Copenhagen," *Liszt Society Journal* 21 (1996), 3–4.

he restated the 'ball' scene of Berlioz."[78] Another writer characterized Liszt's acoustical domination in the march as a violent takeover:

> You can form an idea of his immense power when I say that in the tutti of the March of the Weber piece, where the entire orchestra plays Fortissimo, he simply plays along, but so incredibly strongly that his sound *conquers* the entire orchestra and *pushes* it totally into the background; for this he is awarded a thunderous "Bravo" from the auditorium as well as from the orchestra, which stops playing in order to express its enthusiasm.[79]

With this clever piece of stagecraft (which can only have been planned), the drama of Liszt's victory is taken to its logical conclusion. Not only does the audience rejoice in witnessing the violence, but the orchestra exults in its own annihilation.

Liszt's apparent competition with the orchestra did not originate in a dramatic conflict between alternating solo and tutti forces. Such a soloist-vs.-orchestra plot only became normative in the concert pieces of the later nineteenth century. Liszt, like his virtuoso contemporaries, played compositions in which the orchestra has a decidedly subsidiary role (as in most of Weber's *Konzertstück*), with moments of conflict appearing only rarely. A sense of struggle came from other elements of the performance: the acoustic relationship of solo and tutti, and the visual dynamism of his performing style:

> When one hears Liszt play with orchestra, surging waves of sound coming from the other instruments roar around him, and then he enters with his playing, courageous and inspired, and the whole army of instruments seems to bow humbly and powerlessly to his commanding will alone, so that he appears to us once again so great and wonderful in his art.[80]

Here Liszt's relationship to the orchestra, like his relationship to the keyboard, establishes a drama in which the performer's mastery is first threatened (in this case by the orchestral sound), then vigorously reasserted through a gesture of victorious domination (conveyed by both his heroic bearing at the instrument and his acoustical prominence above the orchestra).

Battle imagery was the most suggestive metaphorical analogy to Liszt's drama of struggle and victory. The above quotation could be an account of the march of the *Konzertstück*, but it is in fact a response to

---

[78] *Monde musical* 10/19 (9 May 1844), 74.

[79] *Didaskalia* 18 (10 August 1840), 313; emphasis added. Berlin critic Ludwig Rellstab effused about "the astonishing force with which he dominates the entire orchestra in the march-like tutti" (*Franz Liszt: Beurtheilungen-Berichte-Lebensskizze* [Berlin, 1842], 24).

[80] *Allgemeine Theaterzeitung*, 7 December 1839, 1197–98 (H. Adami). Quoted in Legány, *Franz Liszt*, 69–71.

Liszt's performance of Beethoven's Concerto in C minor. Since this concerto has no military codes, the battle imagery applies exclusively to the performative level of discourse. A march *topos* such as that found in the *Konzertstück* was thus not a necessary condition for displacing Liszt's virtuosity to battle imagery. In Berlin, to offer a confirming example, one critic identified a piano–orchestra drama in Liszt's performances of his fantasy on *Oberons Zauberhorn*:

The way he once again emerged as the brilliant victor – now harnessing the orchestra, then carrying it away with himself – could have been anticipated, but in the moment of the act it provided an ever-increasing delight.[81]

There is no battle metaphor here, but when the same author later summarized Liszt's concerts at the opera house – which included several other piano/orchestra pieces – he mapped a military image onto the drama he had witnessed: "[these concerts] gave him the opportunity to show his victorious force in battle with an accompanying orchestra and chorus."[82]

Liszt's bravura performances, whether solo or with orchestra, presented his audiences with a drama of violent struggle and domination that repeatedly displaced to an image of heroic battle valor, even when the music lacked military *topoi*. This displacement was rooted in what we might call a "military imagination" – a network of military and Napoleonic symbolism his audiences brought into the concert hall, and through which they could potentially filter the information of Liszt's performance. The battle trope was more than a mere subjective, imaginative elaboration of Liszt's virtuosity, for it performed necessary cultural work. It allowed audiences to enjoy the violence of his playing without casting moral suspicion upon their pleasure. If Liszt's virtuosity resembled battle valor, it was consequently laudable, for the high ethical value of outstanding military prowess was never in question. To imagine Liszt as a military hero was to confront the violence of his playing head-on and channel it in a morally favorable direction. The battle trope thus offered a second "alibi" for his aggressive, dominating bravura style.

Liszt's popularity, such a salient element of his virtuoso identity, has been given plenty of attention by his biographers. We hear much about enthusiastic crowds, elaborate civic receptions, and fainting women. But this popularity is never explained, and we are left to suppose that it

[81] *Neue Zeitschrift für Musik* 16/33 (22 April 1842), p. 130.
[82] Ibid. A chorus is mentioned because Beethoven's *Choral Fantasy* was on the program. At this concert Liszt's heroic domination of the orchestra was magnified by his practice of positioning the piano on a raised platform, which he tended to do in large concert spaces.

needs no explaining – that it was the inevitable outcome of his genius. I have argued here, to the contrary, that his popularity was embedded in cultural conditions specific to his time period, among which the cult of Napoleon is possibly the most significant. His success was not guaranteed by his outstanding musical talents alone, but by his way of addressing musical virtuosity, consciously or not, to the symbolic needs and desires of his audiences. In his performances of the *Konzertstück* – one of his greatest warhorses – he incarnated the virtuoso as military hero and thereby tapped into a network of military and Napoleonic symbolism familiar to his audiences and capable of arousing their enthusiasm. The sonic and visual language of his performing style, furthermore, was so remarkable and unfamiliar as to push writers into hermeneutic elaborations in which military imagery appears again and again.

Liszt's bravura has often been characterized as "Faustian" or "Mephistophelean," on the basis of its "diabolical" orientation. However useful these comparisons are, they contain his virtuosity within the realm of romantic fantasy, in effect removing it from any sphere of human activity beyond the imaginative or aesthetic. If we call Liszt's playing "Napoleonic," however, we draw attention to its worldliness – its refusal to escape entirely into a Faustian realm of fantasy. Napoleon was a romantic hero, but he was also an actual historical figure whose heroism was of the most material sort, leaving trails of blood all over Europe. Liszt's virtuosity, likewise, possessed a raw physicality – violent, dominating gestures into the keys, and a drama playing out the heroic conquering of a resisting force (figured variously as sound, instrument, or orchestra). This spectacle of aggression could not have been recognized as such, for it required the defensive mechanism of an alibi. But traces of violence pervade written evocations of Liszt's playing – praised by his fans, lamented by his opponents – and military prowess was one of its leading metaphorical expressions. Liszt's audiences applauded him in the belief, supported by the alibi of art, that this civilized them, while in fact they were applauding those very aggressive impulses against which civilization poses itself.

3

The cosmopolitan as nationalist

*He is here, the modern Homer, whom Germany, Hungary and France, the
three greatest countries, claim as a child of their land.*

Heinrich Heine on Liszt, 25 April 1844[1]

In the summer of 1844 Liszt was touring the French provinces, as he
worked his way from Paris to the Iberian peninsula. In Marseilles, at a
banquet given in his honor, he opened the piano and discovered that
it was an Érard. He refused to perform on the instrument, chiding his
audience for not providing a piano by the distinguished local piano
manufacturer Auguste Boisselot, and declaring his exclusive devotion
to Boisselot's instruments during his provincial tour. Liszt was showing the public of Marseilles, with a touch of good humor, how to affirm
their regional pride. By favoring the Boisselot instrument over his usual
Érard, he temporarily suspended his long-standing association with the
French capital and aligned himself with the local public. For a fleeting moment the Marseilles audience was pulled out of the shadow of
that formidable cultural metropolis, Paris. "As you can easily imagine,"
wrote a Parisian journalist, "this heartfelt speech was received with frenetic bravos, and without further ado Franz Liszt was naturalized as a
Marseilles citizen."[2]

This anecdote illustrates one of the central strategies by which Liszt
formed a bond with audiences throughout his concert career. He tapped
into their sense of loyalty to a community, paid tribute to that community, elevated their spirit of pride, and thereby made the concert into
an extraordinary, memorable event. He was willing to transform his
image – his dress, gestures, repertory, touring strategies, and even performing style – to reinforce the impression that he belonged, like a
brother, to his audiences. They responded by joining him symbolically to
their communities, whether with honorary citizenships (as in Marseilles
and many other cities) or with precious gifts and prestigious honors.
Liszt's affiliation with specific communities was a two-way process,
benefiting both him and the community's leaders.

---

[1] *Heinrich Heine und die Musik*, ed. Gerhard Müller (Cologne, 1987), 154–55.
[2] Anon., "L'Artiste cosmopolite," *Ménestrel* 11/40 (1 September 1844).

In the next two chapters I examine Liszt's relationship to the larger communities to which his audiences felt they belonged: national communities, on the one hand, and the transnational, cosmopolitan European community on the other. At several periods of his career he won the sympathy of his audiences by inspiring patriotic or national feeling in them. Especially in Hungary and Germany, he willingly participated in rituals of nationalistic significance organized around him. Both of these nations honored him as a compatriot whose support of nationalistic causes lent weight to the spiritual and cultural aspirations of the emerging nation, and these affiliations had a decisive influence on his future career in Germany and in Hungary. In addition, both nations made efforts to "naturalize" him – to make Germanness or Hungarianness an attribute of his person and of his art. Quite apart from these national affiliations, Liszt was also perpetually tied to an elite, transnational community, which felt that he belonged by virtue of his elegant (implicitly Parisian) personality, his itinerant lifestyle, and his cosmopolitan philosophical pronouncements.

The contradictions in Liszt's national identity stemmed from the powerful link between language and nationhood in nineteenth-century thinking. In contrast to Wagner, who struck his contemporaries as through-and-through German, Liszt was difficult to locate geographically and linguistically. His mother country was Hungary, but he could barely speak a word of Hungarian. His mother tongue was German, but already in his teens he spoke French far more fluently, and his German deteriorated. Uprooted both linguistically and nationally, Liszt was easily available for national appropriations, since no one could authoritatively claim that he "naturally" belonged to them. The art of piano virtuosity, furthermore, was non-verbal, making him available for national investments that literary authors and actors could never have accepted due to their dependence on language.[3] Yet for the same reasons, Liszt was an unstable, problematic figure for such appropriations. Too many nations had claims to make upon him, and those claims were sometimes perceived as unconvincing or forced.

All communities define themselves in opposition to other communities, real or imagined, and the story of Liszt's national affiliations reveals this oppositional, negative aspect of community formation in an extreme degree. The enthusiasm of the Marseilles audience, for instance, was a direct result of their imagined relationship to the cultural community of Paris. By making himself available to so many communities, Liszt often

---

[3] There were of course markers of nation in his performing repertory. But no one would have claimed, for example, that he was Hungarian because he played the Rakocsy March, or even because he played it particularly well. Nationally colored compositions were a basic part of every virtuoso's repertory.

put himself on both sides of the boundaries audiences built to mark out their identities. As a consequence, his affiliations to national movements ignited some of the most inflammatory controversies ever fought around him. His reception in Pest in 1840, which was burningly nationalistic in tone, drew criticism all over Europe, partly for its perceived anti-German and anti-Slav implications, and partly because it seemed anti-cosmopolitan or "provincial." And his affiliations with German national(ist) culture, as I show in chapter 4, virtually ruined his Parisian reputation, owing to the francophobic character of German nationalism in the 1840s. Liszt's relationship to various communities thus raised ideological conflicts between nationalism and cosmopolitanism, between individual nations, and even between alternative national conceptions within a single nation. These chapters show Liszt and his audiences working through ideas of what a nation ought to be, and how an artist can be brought in to represent it.

Because Liszt's national affiliations follow a roughly linear "development," with a consistent pattern of reaction and counter-reaction, this chapter takes the form of a chronological narrative. I begin with a discussion of the period before 1840, when Liszt was viewed chiefly as a Parisian and cosmopolitan figure. I then focus on his reception in Hungary in 1840, which culminated in the famous "sabre of honor" concert. Traditional biographies have presented this event in an idealized manner that conceals the considerable social conflicts it provoked, conflicts in which Liszt was perilously embroiled. I show that the Hungarians celebrated him in a manner that recalled an antiquated, quasi-feudal ideology of nation, and that this drew vocal criticism from advocates of a more liberal, state-based nationalism in Bohemia, Germany, and France. In attempting to "Hungarianize" Liszt, the audiences of Pest got him into controversies that nearly ruined the reputation he had so carefully built up in Paris.

Prelude: Hungarian origins

Liszt's Hungarian descent was given some emphasis in his earliest public concerts, chiefly because he was under the patronage of a group of Hungarian noblemen. These nobles had gathered together a six-year stipend, in response to the successful public concert he gave in Pressburg in 1820. The stipend was an entirely traditional gesture of patronage. With it the elites asserted their status as cultural, political, and economic leaders, but with little sense of nationhood.[4] Liszt acknowledged the

---

[4] According to the report in the *Kaiserliche-königliche priviligirte städtische Pressburger Zeitung* (28 November 1820), the audience was a "numerous assembly of the local high nobility and several artistic patrons in the residence of his excellency the Duke Michael

source of his patronage two years later, at his first public concerts in Vienna, by appearing in Hungarian garb. As the Viennese journalist and publisher Pietro Mechetti later recalled:

It was thirteen years ago that a completely inconsiderable boy, whose Hungarian outfit pointed to his homeland – when he was already playing such a trifle as Hummel's B minor concerto from score, and had enjoyed the instruction of Czerny and Salieri – went from Vienna to Paris with his father. He grew up under serious, many-sided studies, and aroused in France, England, and Switzerland astonishment and amazement at his extraordinary achievements.[5]

At this early moment in his career, therefore, he was distinctly marked as Hungarian. Yet Mechetti's mini-narrative is aimed at demonstrating precisely Liszt's transcendence of his nationality. It tells the familiar story of the provincial genius – the "completely inconsiderable boy" from an inconsiderable place, who has become a cosmopolitan figure through "many-sided studies" and through experiences in the major European cities. This transformation was clearly expected: the Hungarians apparently had no desire, at this point, to make him a national symbol. Yet this same Hungary, having sent him off into the world to become worldly, would try to recover him from his cosmopolitanism when he returned in 1840, by dressing him up in the Hungarian national costume.

There is one piece of evidence suggesting that Liszt (or at least his father, who was guiding his career) accepted his role as an "ambassador" for Hungary in these early years. In 1823, having recently capped off his Viennese studies with a pair of public concerts, he and his father returned to Hungary briefly, to give a few concerts before departing for Paris. Supposedly, a poster advertising the concert he gave in Pest on 1 May read:

I am a Hungarian and know no greater pleasure than to present honorably the first fruits of my development and education as an initial offering of the most sincere affection and gratitude before leaving for France and England; steady, hard work and travels may bring what is still lacking in my playing to greater perfection, and perhaps place me in the fortunate position to have become a branch to adorn my beloved country.[6]

There are reasons to doubt the authenticity of this advertisement. We only know about it from a source dated May 1846. Its author claims he has not himself seen the poster, but has rather reproduced it from a

---

Eszterhazy." The concert was thus a highly elite affair, and took place in the political center of Hungary.

[5] *Wiener Zeitschrift für Kunst* (5 May 1838), 429–32 (P. Mechetti). Quoted in D. Legány, *Franz Liszt: unbekannte Presse und Briefe aus Wien, 1822–1866* (Vienna, 1984), 37–41.

[6] *Humorist*, 16 May 1846.

Hungarian paper that had reprinted it when Liszt was in Pest in 1840. The Hungarian journal that published it in 1840 claimed, for its part, that the poster had turned up in the hands of a bookseller who had carefully preserved it since 1823. No copy of the poster has survived, whereas several posters of his other concerts from his time period still exist. In light of the document's evident value in making Liszt into a Hungarian patriot, it seems suspicious that it has "vanished." The document's wording, too, is questionable, mapping out Liszt's fate with uncanny precision, as though the writer already knew the future course of his career. Furthermore, there is no evidence that a trip to London was necessarily in the works in 1823, and it seems very unlikely that anyone would have proposed that a piano prodigy might eventually become a national hero, not even in Hungary.

The poster, I would suggest, is not evidence of Liszt's lifelong mission to serve the Hungarian nation, but precisely the opposite: it was a fabrication of the Hungarian press in 1840, and its purpose was to compensate for Liszt's long absence from, and irrelevance to, Hungary. It sought to legitimate the appropriation of Liszt, when he returned to Pest in 1840, as a national symbol. The Hungarian national movement had gained astonishing momentum in the years between 1823 and 1839. By this time, however, the Hungarians had lost Liszt to cosmopolitan Europe, as epitomized by Paris. One writer at the Pest newspaper *Honmüvész* recognized the loss as Liszt's Parisian reputation grew, and in 1834 he criticized his Hungarian readers for having been "indifferent" to Liszt while his talent was developing.[7] The same writer had even found it necessary, the previous year, to *introduce* Liszt to his Hungarian readers with a brief biography.[8] When he returned in 1839, then, the Hungarians were in need of a way to reclaim him, a strategy for bridging the gap between the Liszt of then and the Liszt of now. Nothing could have suited this purpose better than words of patriotic dedication dating from Liszt's last visit to the country, and these very words suddenly appeared in an anonymous bookseller's drawer. It is not impossible that the poster announcing his 1823 concert is authentic, but it is clearly no evidence of an unbroken bond between Liszt and Hungary. This

---

[7] *Honmüvész* 8/3 (1834), no. 64. The content of this article is summarized in Lajos Koch, *Liszt Ferenc bibliográfiai kísérlet/Franz Liszt: ein bibliographischer Versuch* (Budapest, 1936).

[8] Ibid. Franz von Schober, in his pamphlet on Liszt in Hungary, attempted to portray Liszt's relationship with Hungary as an unbroken one: "with that support [the noble patronage] he remained forever in contact with his fatherland, enough that a manly feeling of gratitude became interwoven with the childhood memory of home, and his heart never lacked motivation to decorate romantic Hungary with the most beautiful colors" (*Briefe über F. Liszts Aufenthalt in Ungarn* [Berlin, 1843], 8).

document, whatever its real status, was used in constructing Liszt as a Hungarian patriot. I will later examine other aspects of this construction, but it is first necessary to examine the development of his cosmopolitan persona in Paris and Vienna.

1. Liszt the cosmopolitan: Paris and Vienna

During the early years in Paris, Liszt's nationality was a non-issue, affecting his reception in no substantial way. There were so many foreigners in Paris, especially in the musical world, that he did not stand out in his environment. Contrary to long biographical tradition, Liszt's foreign nationality was not the reason he was rejected from admission to the Conservatory; the reason was much more prosaic: lack of open places. The difficult pronunciation and orthography of his name (in French) rendered him slightly exotic, yet his patrons ironed out this linguistic wrinkle dubbing him "le petit Listi," thus adopting him in an unmistakably Parisian manner. Liszt's identity in Paris was thus not marked as Hungarian. As Sophie Leo put it in her memoir of Restoration Paris, Liszt was considered German because "In those days . . . Magyars and Czechs were not yet at all in fashion."[9]

By the mid-1830s Liszt was aligned with local culture as a "child of Paris," and this *cultural* aspect of his identity completely eclipsed his ethnic origin. He had come to be viewed as Parisian through his association with the musical, literary, and philosophical romantics of Paris, through his activities as a man of letters, and through his poses as a dandy or as a world-weary, wandering *artiste*. At the same time, he had been circulating without interruption in the salons of the highest aristocrats of Paris, where he developed elegant manners and a witty conversational style that marked him as a member of the Parisian cosmopolitan elite. These two sides to his identity – the romantic and the aristocratic – were to some extent contradictory, but both of them were coded Parisian. Furthermore, there was little difference between being considered "Parisian" and being considered "French," because contemporary notions of a French national character (with the exception of southern France) were based on the behavior and expressions of the Parisian *literati* and aristocrats.

Liszt's new national color – his Frenchness – was most strongly noted in the early years of his concertizing, when people outside of France

---

[9] Sophie Leo, *Erinnerungen aus Paris, 1817–1848* (Berlin, 1851), 190. In the 1830s Cristina Belgiojoso, herself exiled from Italy for her connection to revolutionary politics, had stunning success in Paris with various events she mounted in support of her fellow exiles. This is another sign that nationalism was becoming *à la mode*.

were encountering him for the first time. It was indeed not long after stepping outside the francophone world that Liszt's Frenchness became an issue. In Milan he was disappointed to find that it would be difficult to succeed with a public concert. He published an article criticizing the Milan public for its lack of musical sensitivity, attention, and its ignorance of instrumental music, problems he considered endemic to a musical culture fixated on opera. Whether or not he wrote the article (its authorship is not entirely clear), its authorial voice is that of a Parisian intellectual, with its characteristic authority in matters of refinement and taste, and its condescension toward less "civilized" cities.[10] Liszt was setting himself up as an outsider, marking himself for Frenchness.

Journalists thematized Liszt's Frenchness the moment he reentered the arena of cosmopolitan concerts, with a group of concerts that took place in Vienna in the spring of 1838. It is well known that Liszt initially went to Vienna under the pretext of sympathy for his Hungarian compatriots, who had just suffered severe flooding in Pest and Ofen. Yet Liszt's Hungarian nationality was barely noted during this initial visit to Vienna. Much more attention was given to his French qualities. Heinrich Adami, writing about the first concert of the series, felt that Liszt's virtuosity was drenched in French romanticism:

When one hears Liszt play, one is unwittingly reminded that his musical performance is directed at a public which recognizes Victor Hugo as its greatest poet. In his entire manner of composing and playing is something which I might designate with the name "wild romanticism," which the French in all branches of art have produced in such great excess. As if chased by a whirlwind, almost uncanny and energetic masses of tones raise themselves, light and shade stand always near each other, the most full-voiced phrases follow directly upon sweet, charming, ingratiating motives, and out of this mixing of extremes will develop the most astonishing effects.[11]

Because the Viennese audiences were simply not accustomed to French romanticism, either in the musical or literary worlds, the strong and dramatic juxtapositions of Liszt's playing seemed to point to a foreign origin or evoke a foreign environment – Paris. Audiences found this unfamiliar and slightly exotic spectacle entirely absorbing, and they packed the halls for seven more concerts. It was, however, less easy to win over the intellectual establishment. Pietro Mechetti, the critic for the high-toned *Wiener Zeitschrift*, was disturbed by the unleashed, irrational forces of French romanticism, and saw Liszt as its most dangerous representative:

[10] Franz Liszt, "À Lambert Massart," *Revue et gazette musicale* 5/35 (2 September 1838), 345–52.

[11] *Allgemeine Theaterzeitung*, 21 April 1838, 355–56 (H. Adami). Quoted in Legány, *Franz Liszt*, 24–27.

And so now a kind of "jeune France musicale" has been founded, which calls itself a romantic school . . . To define the inner essence of [Liszt's performance manner] is impossible. It is, to begin with, similar to the tendencies and effects of this *école*, but it sets out, with its verve, on an even more unmeasured course than ever before.[12]

In Vienna Liszt flaunted his connection with the French romantics by playing pieces that had a literary basis. He told Marie d'Agoult that he would play the "Bal et marche" from Berlioz's *Symphonie fantastique* even though the Viennese public would not understand it, as though he were cultivating his exotic appeal. When he returned to Vienna in 1839 he performed a fantasy on Dante's *Divine Comedy*. The fantasy was so redolent of the aesthetics of French romanticism that even one of his most effusive supporters showed signs of dissatisfaction:

A short program would certainly have been desirable for the greater comprehensibility of this imaginative piece, which is capable of so many interpretations. The whole thing seemed to me something like an improvisation to which Liszt had felt inspired after a reading of the "divine comedy," a collection of related ideas chasing each other, often breaking off quickly, exchanging one mood with another, bold in outline, aphoristic in execution, on the whole standing very close in character to the new romantic school as it has formed in France. Of this it is known that the tendencies of this school have found favor nowhere in Germany, and have won the taste of only a smaller part the French public.[13]

The fantasy was not only beyond the public taste of the Viennese, as the author points out, but also grated on the philosophical sensibilities of the *literati*. Another writer found the aesthetic premises of this fantasy essentially French and could not accept them:

This strange and intelligent tone picture seems to fall into the school of the French romantics. I will not deny my prejudice against the tendencies of this school, which are perhaps beyond the boundaries of music. Music to me is a *self-sufficient text* [*selbständiger Text*] and not a running commentary for a program.[14]

The Dante fantasy was not seen or heard again until Liszt's virtuoso career was over, and the *Symphonie fantastique* was soon dropped from his repertory as well. Liszt filtered out such self-conscious announcements of his connection to French romanticism as his travels became more diverse. Yet at this early stage he seems to have been happy to come across as an outsider, and audiences took a keen interest in this exotic import – a living example of French romanticism.

[12] *Wiener Zeitschrift für Kunst, Literatur und Mode*, 5 May 1838, 429–32 (P. Mechetti). Quoted in Legány, *Franz Liszt*, 39–41.

[13] *Allgemeine Theaterzeitung*, 7 December 1839, 1197–98 (H. Adami). Quoted in Legány, *Franz Liszt*, 69–71.

[14] "Rückblick auf Liszts Fragment nach Dante," *Allgemeine Theaterzeitung*, 25 February 1840, 194 (K. Tausenau); emphasis original. Quoted in Legány, *Franz Liszt*, 72–73.

Liszt also seemed French to the Viennese by virtue of his manners, which were emphasized by aristocrats who brought him into their salons. The fact that he spoke French far better than German made it easiest for him to circulate among the French-speaking aristocracy. The Viennese aristocrats, for their part, had every reason to want Liszt in their company: in him they gained a piece of the trend-setting cosmopolitan elite of Paris. Just as the intellectuals saw Frenchness in his literary and aesthetic presence, so the aristocrats looked for Frenchness in his breeding and social manner:

> Great lords fight for the honor of inviting him and receiving him with homage. It is here where his Parisian upbringing becomes quite useful. With friendly uninhibitedness he moves in the world long known to him [i.e. the aristocratic one] – eloquent, cheerful, indeed gallant; if one can at first expect aberrant behavior here or there, the animated nature of the young artist soon reconciles any small misunderstanding, and one begins to find pleasure in his company, all the more because he shows perfect French, which is generally spoken here.[15]

Liszt's Frenchness bonded him to the high elites of Vienna, but this relationship was not without its problems. The "small misunderstanding" and "aberrant behavior" referred to in this passage are traces of a significant intrigue that affected perceptions of his nationality.

Early in his visit to Vienna, Liszt was invited to the salon of Princess Metternich. He was hesitant to approach her for an introduction, preferring that she make the effort to come to him. When she finally did, her first words to him were: "You've been giving concerts in Italy – have you made good business?" Liszt's famous reply was: "Princess, I make music and no business," and he immediately took his leave.[16] This well-known anecdote was only the beginning of a prolonged struggle. The princess took offense and used her power to turn the court circles against Liszt.[17] Toward the end of his concert series, however, Liszt's popularity had become so immense, and Archduchess Sophie had been such a steady supporter of him, that the empress wished to invite him to give a concert at the court.[18] Inviting Liszt to court was easier said than done, since a court concert was a political event as well as a musical one. Liszt's Parisian connections, as well as his behavior toward Princess Metternich, implicated him in liberal or radical political sympathies that the

---

[15] *Allgemeine musikalische Anzeiger*, 21 June 1838, 97–100. Quoted in Legány, *Franz Liszt*, 32–33.

[16] Karoline Bauer, *Nachgelassene Memoiren von Karoline Bauer* (Berlin, 1881), 3 vols., III: 405.

[17] In May he wrote to d'Agoult: "I am being adulated... with the exception of a dozen quite influential individuals, who are even furious at my success. Princess Metternich is more on my side than in the first days. Thalberg is better for those people" (*Correspondance de Liszt et de Madame d'Agoult*, ed. D. Ollivier [Paris, 1933–35], 2 vols., I: 228).

[18] This account is based on two unidentified articles, probably from the later nineteenth century, in the Weimar Liszt-Archiv, Kasten 280.

court obviously could not be seen to endorse. The empress's dilemma was brought to the attention of the minister of public and secret security, Graf Sedlnitzky, by way of Archduke Rudolph: "The empress has just told me that she had the idea of allowing the pianist Liszt to play a concert at her palace. But she has heard so many things about his behavior and his connections in Paris that she can't make up her mind . . . She asked me for advice on what she should do."[19] Sedlnitzky researched Liszt's background and offered an extensive reply in which he exculpated Liszt from any suspicious political activities, even his connection to Lammenais ("participation in the political machinations of the self-styled Abbé and his party was never undertaken by him"). Sedlnitzky did report that Liszt's Parisian experiences, especially his friendship with George Sand, rendered him morally questionable, but he did not consider this threatening: "He is indeed vain and superficial, affecting the fantastic manners of today's young French, but apart from his artistic value he appears much more to be a good-natured, insignificant young man."[20] The final recommendation was to allow the concert to go on, but to exclude him from consideration for an honorable membership to the Hofkapell.[21]

Sedlnitzky's defense of Liszt shows that Paris, or at least *Paris romantique*, was seen by the Viennese authorities as a hotbed of political and moral corruption. As a product of France, therefore, Liszt was potentially dangerous: he could carry the anti-authoritarian contagion inside the imperial walls, reveal the contagion on stage through his romantic performing style, and perhaps infect his audiences with it. At the same time, the court needed Liszt, since alongside his romanticism stood the witty Parisian manners so valued by resident aristocrats. If the court did not join in the general adulation it risked losing its aristocratic alliances and appearing narrowly self-absorbed, or worse yet, tasteless. It needed to acquiesce to the demands of belonging to cosmopolitan Europe, even

---

[19] Ibid.; letter dated 25 April.   [20] Ibid.

[21] When the concert was finally arranged, this process had already been going on two months, and Liszt was relieved: "The first court concert is set for the first days of the week. After all the intrigues, all the cabals which I recounted to you, it's a genuine small triumph for me. I don't have to explain myself to you on this matter. You know me" (*Correspondance de Liszt et de Madame d'Agoult*, I: 229). The matter that didn't need explaining was that giving a concert at court was the final blow to Thalberg. The Princess and her retinue had hung on to Thalberg in their campaign against Liszt, and Liszt was glad to have removed the last barrier. His appearances at court were in fact not sufficient to erase his image as an exotic Parisian with doubtful ideas and morals. As he returned to Vienna in late 1839, he heard rumors that the princess had again turned against him: "[Eskeles] has told me about Princess M and about the hatred she holds toward me (something that I hear everywhere)" (*Correspondance de Liszt et de Madame d'Agoult*, I: 304; letter from November 1839).

if it meant embracing a potentially revolutionary figure. Liszt was simultaneously a support for and a threat to legitimate power.

Moritz Saphir, the editor of the popular, middlebrow journal *Der Humorist*, had an entirely different way of dealing with Liszt's nationality. While many of his colleagues were hammering in the theme of Liszt's Frenchness, he wished to claim Liszt for the German middle classes that made up the readership of his journal. In the review of his first concert of 1839, he criticized Liszt for not addressing the audience in German: "According to the program a second etude was supposed to follow. Why did Liszt announce this change in the French language? Why did the German artist not speak German to the German audience?"[22] As this quote shows, reconstructing Liszt as an Austrian would have to be in large part a process of erasure – eliminating the "French" traits he was putting on display. By this point he was more comfortable speaking French than German. To Saphir it appeared, however, that he spoke French to address the high elites of Vienna, with their comparatively cosmopolitan orientation, rather than the German-speaking middle classes among whom patriotism was more prevalent.

Saphir also wished to separate the taste of the Viennese middle-class public from that of Paris. The Viennese audiences, he claimed, were not enthusiastic about the same Liszt who had become famous in Paris; they saw and reclaimed another, truer Liszt, one the cosmopolitan Parisians had been too flippant to recognize:

Even though the rush to his brilliant concerts here is comparable to other places, in terms of artistic recognition there has never been such an important, true and unfeigned understanding and respect for the genius as here; for here one does not go to concerts out of *bon ton* or fashion, which is for the most part what happens in London and Paris, but because one has true feeling for the beautiful.[23]

In order to show the special bond between Liszt and his Viennese audiences, Saphir emphasized the place of Beethoven and Schubert in Liszt's repertory, music he felt the Viennese could uniquely appreciate. And indeed, Liszt did play much more Beethoven and Schubert in his first two Vienna series than in all his previous concertizing, something that can only be seen as an attempt to address the tastes of the Viennese audiences. Another writer at the *Humorist* portrayed Liszt's performing style as ideally suited to the music of the Viennese masters. He conveniently singled out the "Ave Maria" and "Ständchen" transcriptions – exceptional for their lack of virtuosity – in his commentary:

[22] *Humorist*, 20 November 1839 (M. Saphir).
[23] *Humorist*, 7 December 1839 (M. Saphir).

The character of the playing, which so clearly reflects his own character and his honorable nationality, has been described before . . . [The Schubert transcriptions] were neither variations nor potpourris; they were the simple, wonderful songs of the wonderful departed one . . . An estimable reviewer has compared Mr. Liszt with Victor Hugo . . . Today he was *Victor* in every respect, but I did not find any *Hugo*. Not the slightest trace of that wild, unrestrained romanticism.[24]

The writers at the *Humorist*, then, constructed Liszt as a "German" pianist by downplaying the romantic aspects of his performing style and the non-classical element of his repertory, both of them implicitly or explicitly coded French. And they went further, proposing a fundamental unity between Liszt's nationality, his character, his performing style, and the taste of the Viennese audiences. As Liszt took his leave of Vienna in May 1840, the *Humorist*'s parting message brought these elements together, while failing to suppress traces of his French identity:

Consider the affectionate reception, the real and inner admiration that was shown to your great genius in the friendly city of the Kaiser. It can only enrich your pride to have celebrated triumphs that few previous artists celebrated in the city that counts Mozart, Haydn, and Beethoven among its own! Yes, be proud to be a national son [*Landessohn*] of Austria, even though the charming city on the Seine draws you away![25]

The appropriative force of this passage is particularly stunning in light of the fact that the nationalistic celebrations surrounding Liszt in Pest had occurred just a few months earlier.

After a brief period when the prodigy Liszt appeared in public as a Hungarian, then, his national identification was completely overtaken by his development in France. When he returned to the world stage in Vienna, his persona and performing style seemed steeped in Frenchness. He was simultaneously the quintessential romantic *artiste* and the quintessential cosmopolitan aristocrat, both of them Paris-identified social types. The *Humorist* made a forced attempt to peel away these layers of Frenchness and reveal a German virtuoso for the Viennese middle classes, but this does not seem to have been taken up by other writers. Liszt continued to be seen as a Frenchman at least until 1842, and in some respects never ceased to be seen that way. But already in 1841 he was beginning to shed this national affiliation as he grew closer to Germany and more distanced from France (this development is traced in chapter 4). What is important to recognize for present purposes is the degree to which Liszt's Hungarian origin had been eclipsed by his immersion in the culture of Paris. For the Hungarians would in 1840

---

[24] *Humorist*, 27 April 1838.   [25] *Humorist*, 28 May 1840.

Figure 3.1 Liszt receiving the sabre of honor in Budapest, 1840

try to make him into a national hero, and to many people outside Hungary it appeared to be an entirely artificial appropriation.

2.   The Pest episode: Liszt and the sabre of honor

In the winter of 1839–40, Liszt appeared in Hungary for the first time since his childhood. He had since become Europe's most famous virtuoso and an admired writer. In 1838 he had given a well-publicized charity concert for the victims of a devastating flood in Pest, and soon thereafter he had published an article expressing the profound emotions toward his fatherland that this catastrophe had awakened in him. When he appeared in Hungary Liszt was celebrated as a lost son and a national hero. The patriotic enthusiasm occasioned by his visit culminated in a concert at the Hungarian National Theatre, where a group of six men – three noblemen and three civic officials – appeared on stage and presented him with a valuable "sabre of honor" (Figure 3.1).

Liszt's reception in Pest became one of the most famous episodes of his career, matched in its legendary status only by the "Lisztomania" that swept through Berlin in 1842, and by the Liszt–Thalberg "duel" of 1837. Like the Paris and Berlin episodes, its fame was mixed with notoriety. It provoked controversies in the local and international press, and eventually brought biographers to defensive stances. The enthusiasm of the Hungarians was reported extensively in foreign papers, and Liszt helped publicize his Hungarian identity by wearing the sabre in public. The elegant Frenchman and romantic *artiste* was now presenting himself to Europe, on the first of his major international concert tours, as a sabre-rattling Hungarian patriot. Writers picked up on the irony of this, printing a host of derisive comments, the focus of which was less Liszt than the Hungarian public. Hungarians were criticized for their nationalistic fervor and their excessive demonstrations of honor toward the virtuoso. The word "Lisztomania" had not yet been coined, but the idea was now in place, and the sabre of honor was its summary representation.

The story of the Pest episode has always been told in a defensive tone, and a quick overview of its history will explain why. In 1840 Liszt published an editorial responding to a writer at the Parisian *Revue des deux mondes*, who considered the sabre a bizarre and distasteful demonstration of enthusiasm on the part of the Hungarian audiences. Liszt explained that in Hungary the sabre, as an element of the national costume, was chiefly a symbol of nationhood and not an object of war. He pleaded that the emotions that moved the Hungarians to give him a sabre were patriotic and noble, not militant or aggressive. The apparent success of this defense motivated Liszt to publish it as often as possible, and in as many European capitals as possible. It found its way into all the early biographies (Christern, Duverger, Schilling, and Neumann), as well as a book by Chorley. In 1842 Liszt's friend Franz von Schober published a series of articles explicitly aimed at defending Liszt and the Hungarians, and in 1843 these articles were collected and published as a separate volume, *Briefe über F. Liszts Aufenthalt in Ungarn*.[26]

In all biographies published since the 1840s, this defense has been repeated without question and without any further research. The most recent retelling of the Pest episode, that of Alan Walker, is no exception.[27]

---

[26] Franz von Schober, *Briefe über F. Liszts Aufenthalt in Ungarn* (Berlin, 1843). The articles appeared in the *Blätter für Musik und Literatur*.

[27] There is a still more recent, but sketchy, discussion of the Pest episode by Dezsö Legány ("Liszt in Hungary, 1820–1846," in *Liszt and His World* [Stuyvesant, NY, 1998], 3–16), where the same idea is repeated: "Liszt was ridiculed in Western Europe, because the people who lived there did not know that, according to the Hungarian constitution of that era, only noblemen were allowed to carry swords" (10). In addition to simplifying the objections to the sabre, this passage misleads by emphasizing that Liszt was ridiculed, when in fact the Hungarian audiences were the main object of ridicule. It should also be clarified that in Hungary non-noble military personnel were allowed to wear swords; what was exclusive to noblemen was the *sabre*.

Stepping up the defensive tone of his predecessors, Walker presents the negative reactions to the Pest episode as a grand and offensive misunderstanding of the sabre's intended meaning. He encourages his readers to view the Pest episode within a narrative of Hungary's awakening to nationhood:

For one hundred and fifty years she had been oppressed by Austria. Her language was banned, her culture undervalued, her material resources plundered . . . [The honors bestowed upon Liszt] can only be understood once we see them as part of that general striving for a nation to assert itself through its leading individuals.[28]

This rhetoric is derived from romantic nationalism, and is utterly out of date. It characterizes the nation as an innocent victim (partly by feminizing it), and as a spiritual force that asserts its own will beyond human control. In this tragedy-tinged narrative, the nation is an unquestioned moral good that legitimates and ennobles the public enthusiasm for Liszt.

Such an exaggerated desire to immunize Liszt or his Hungarian audiences from censure has resulted in an inadequate understanding of just how nationalism was relevant to the Pest events. It is usually implied that all or most of the people in Hungary participated in and were served by Magyar nationalism, and that the enthusiasm for Liszt was therefore inevitable. Yet the Pest episode, so glorious on the surface, was from the beginning steeped in controversy, leaving a dark stain that biographers have repeatedly suppressed. The controversy revolved around conflicts *within* Hungary over its national identity. Liszt was forcefully taken up by the dominant, romantic nationalists, who were notorious for breaking into fits of xenophobia. The manner in which they celebrated Liszt – including the presentation of the sabre – drew attention to their xenophobic habits, and thus provoked opposition from the more liberal intellectuals who supported a civic national identity. Furthermore, there existed in Pest a contingent of non-nationalistic, cosmopolitan aristocrats who celebrated Liszt in an entirely different spirit. The Hungarians, then, did not unite under the banner of the nation to honor their virtuoso. On the contrary, nationalism divided them and even generated conflict.

Appropriating Liszt for the cause of Magyar nationalism was doomed from the start to appear forced and artificial. When he arrived in Hungary, his persona was so rich in French and cosmopolitan traces that it was difficult to find any sign of Hungarianness. Just after his visit to Pest a writer at the *Pesther Tageblatt* described his persona and artistic disposition as French through-and-through, even though the press had been emphasizing his Hungarianness in the preceding weeks:

[28] Alan Walker, *Franz Liszt* (Ithaca, 1987–97), 3 vols., I: 320.

His temperament was formed in the intimate company of the intelligent Dude-vant [i.e. George Sand] . . . and the most spiritual men of France; and in the Parisian salons he learned fine and elegant manners, so rare in artists, to such an extent that he impressed people as a man of society just as he did as an artist . . . [His playing] demonstrates immense technique and brilliant spirit, but it tends too much toward the eccentricities of the new French Romanticism . . . he knows how to make effects in his playing with true French coquettishness.[29]

The Liszt presented here is the same figure observed in Vienna: the Parisian *artiste* with aristocratic manners. If he was going to be claimed as a Hungarian and a patriot, these layers of Frenchness would have to be downplayed if not ignored.

The Magyar nationalists, for the most part, took the route of ignoring his Frenchness, and Liszt helped out by dressing up in the expensive Hungarian national costume. But to many outside Hungary, such the-atricality appeared narrow and jingoistic. In Paris, as will be explained in detail later, the main objection to the behavior of the Hungarian nation-alists was that they had suppressed Liszt's obvious cosmopolitan signif-icance. For this reason Franz von Schober, in his retrospective defense of the Hungarian public, felt it necessary to de-emphasize Liszt's French-ness, particularly as it was evident in his performing style. He isolated a single, telling change in performing style that had occurred in the short span of a year:

even the tougher critics recognized that he had become even more extraordi-nary during his absence and that he had fortunately stripped away those fits of forcefulness and randomness that belonged to the French school, and that had in the past often harmed his playing.[30]

A few pages later, Schober spelled out the implications of this change for Liszt's reception in Hungary: "in his art there was no distracting sign of a foreign nationality, and [the Hungarians] could declare his inspiring achievements Hungarian without injury to Magyarism."[31] The irony of this comment is that Liszt's playing, by losing its French traits, would have been considered by his contemporaries more "Viennese" (or "German"), not more Hungarian, since there was a pedigreed Viennese school of pianism.[32]

---

[29] *Pesther Tageblatt*, 2 February 1840.

[30] Schober, *Briefe*, 13. This idea had been promoted by Moritz Saphir, who as shown above was set on constructing Liszt as a German.

[31] Schober, *Briefe*, 24. The "foreign nationality" referred to here is implicitly French.

[32] It should be noted that Schober evidently feels no need to filter out Germanness from Liszt's pianism. This is significant because the Magyar nationalists considered Germans a "foreign nationality." Evidently Schober held a more liberal, inclusive idea of the Hungarian nation than most of the Magyar nationalists.

Liszt's inability to speak Hungarian only added to the strain of making him into a national hero. Development of the Hungarian language was the fundamental goal of the national movement's cultural branch, and the Hungarian National Theatre in which Liszt was granted the sabre was a kind of temple to the Magyar tongue. When time came for him to deliver a speech in acceptance of the sabre, an unanticipated problem arose. The most sensible alternative to delivering the speech in Hungarian would have been to speak German, since most of the audience would have understood it, but German was not allowed on the stage of the National Theatre.[33] After pausing to discuss the problem with the presiding officials, Liszt resolved to give his intensely patriotic speech in French, a language known to few members of the audience. This required a prefatory apology to the audience, one that failed to conceal how awkward the situation was.[34] And because most of the audience did not understand his French, a full outburst of applause had to wait until his speech was translated into Hungarian.[35] Thus, at the very climax of his Hungarianization, Liszt was plunging straight back into his French identity. At the moment the Hungarians were most trying to bring him *inside* their country, his alien qualities revealed themselves most fully. Liszt was apparently somewhat unsettled by this lapse. As he departed from the city he promised "to return to your midst soon, and until then – to learn Hungarian."[36] He was determined to close the obvious gap that still existed between himself and his homeland.

Liszt's French persona may have worked against those who wished to claim him as Hungarian, but it lured those people who harbored a more cosmopolitan outlook: the conservative Hungarian aristocracy. This important dimension of Liszt's Hungarian reception has always been overshadowed by attention to the nationalist fervor he inspired. Enthusiasm for Liszt was shared by the Magyar nationalists and the conservative aristocracy alike, but their symbolic investments in him were recognizably different. Julia Pardoe, a witness of the Pest events, observed that

the entire population was carried away by one common feeling, for while the royalists worshipped the *artiste* who had earned for their country a name among the *virtuosi* of Europe, the reformers saw in the *man* a patriot who loved that country better than his own fame.[37]

Pardoe's comments show that the "one common feeling" – the enthusiasm for Liszt – stemmed from two different sources. "Royalists" valued him because he gave them visibility and recognition on the international, cosmopolitan stage. He allowed them to transcend their nationality.

---

[33] Schober, *Briefe*, 38. [34] *Der Adler*, 17 January 1840. [35] Schober, *Briefe*, 43.
[36] Ibid. [37] Julia Pardoe, *City of the Magyar* (London, 1840), 3 vols., II: 353–54.

"Reformers" on the other hand, observing the noble emotions he demonstrated toward his country of origin, felt reinserted into their nationality
through him. Pardoe made this same distinction in her description of
the serenade that greeted Liszt the night he arrived in Pest:

> They had welcomed him not only as the first native Hungarian who had won a
> European reputation by his art, but also as a Magyar to whom his country was
> a holy and an honoured idol, shrined in his heart of hearts.[38]

In 1840 most "royalists" in Hungary were wealthy, powerful, and conservative aristocrats, who owed their strongest loyalties to the Viennese
court and can be considered a subset of the Viennese aristocracy. A few
of them supported liberal reform, but they were still vastly outnumbered by conservatives.[39] As a class, the conservative aristocrats were
"denationalized," immersing themselves in the cosmopolitan culture of
Vienna in the winter season and angling for the favor of the imperial
court.[40] The spiritual leader of the reform movement, Istvan Széchenyi,
considered it indispensable to "renationalize" this class, since they possessed most of the country's political power. But in 1840, when Liszt
came, a great many of them remained in their "denationalized" condition. The royalists did possess a conception of the Hungarian nation, but
it was defined in feudal, patrician terms: the nation was synonymous
with the Magyar aristocracy, an elite community unified by ancestry and
language. They did not subscribe to the populist vision of the Magyar
nationalists. These so-called "estates nationalists" conceived of "the people" not as a group of free and equal citizens with rights, but as a peasan-
try that would submit to the benevolent authority of their lords.[41]

Hungary's cosmopolitan aristocrats, especially the women who
tended to serve as social leaders, were attracted to Liszt's Parisian bearing, and they received him just as the Vienna aristocracy had. His bonds
with the local aristocracy were already evident in Pressburg, his first
stop in Hungary. In Pressburg, Schober reported, "Liszt drew especially
the aristocracy to himself and won the favor of its women through his

---

[38] Ibid., II: 347.

[39] In the upper house of the Diet, conservative magnates outnumbered liberal ones four-
fold. George Barany, *Stephen Széchenyi and the Awakening of Hungarian Nationalism, 1791–
1841* (Princeton, 1968), 348. Barany is my main source for information about Hungarian
history in this time period. A briefer account of this period is presented by Barany in
A History of Hungary, ed. Peter F. Sugar, Péter Hanák, and Tibor Frank (Bloomington,
1990). Another useful overview is in Andrew C. Janos, *The Politics of Backwardness in
Hungary, 1825–1945* (Princeton, 1982).

[40] I use the word "denationalized" because, in the decades prior to the Congress of 1815,
the Hungarian aristocrats had taken several steps to promote Magyar language and
culture. The heavy censorship imposed within the empire after the Congress, however,
restricted Magyar cultural development. See Barany, *Stephen Széchenyi*, 150–52, 310.

[41] This is the term used by Barany (*Stephen Széchenyi*, 281).

kindness, through a certain elevation in his manner, and through the majestic grace that he commands."[42] Yet because the Diet was in session when Liszt made his visit, there were also in Pressburg aristocrats representing the liberal opposition, and under the guidance of Count Louis Batthány they – however small in number – latched onto him as well. He was thus received equally well, but with different symbolic investments, by different factions within the Hungarian aristocracy.

Liszt was escorted from Pressburg to Pest by a group of magnates, many of them representing Magyar nationalism. Yet in Pest, too, he was taken up by the larger aristocratic society in which conservative and cosmopolitan interests predominated. The first event he attended was a large private dinner given in the Casino by "the entire resident nobility."[43] Here Liszt's Hungarianness was celebrated, but not to such an extent that patriotism and nationalism trumped the entire event. Schober even hinted that, at this event, the Magyarist demonstrations at the dinner had an awkward effect:

while all table conversation was carried out in French and German, toasts with long speeches were directed to him in the Hungarian language, more out of consideration for the national feeling than for him, since he did not understand them at all.[44]

Liszt's attraction to Pest's aristocratic society, Julia Pardoe noted approvingly, had mostly to do with his Paris-formed social persona:

Barons were in his train; and the fairest Countesses, who count among the fairest of all Europe, contended for his smiles . . . I was particularly struck by his manner at a ball given to him by the ladies of the *haute-volée*, where he was little less than deified.[45]

This passage confirms that the cosmopolitan investments in Liszt were not only concentrated in the conservative aristocrats, but in the women among them, while the nationalist investments were more relevant to the politically active male aristocrats. It even seems that, within aristocratic society, gender shaped the axes of investment to a greater degree than political orientation.

There was nothing at all unusual about Liszt's reception by Hungary's cosmopolitan aristocracy, with women at the forefront. It was similar to

---

[42] Schober, *Briefe*, 26. "Dass Liszt durch seine Liebenswürdigkeit, durch eine gewisse Hoheit in seinem Benehmen, durch die majestätische Grazie, die ihm zu Gebote steht, sich vorzugsweise die Aristokratie zu eigen machte und die Huld ihrer Frauen davontrug, steigerte noch die Allgemeinheit seines Triumphes, da die Ungarn gewohnt sind, alles mit äusserem Glanze und mit ihren bevorrechteten Stände in Verbindung zu setzen. Mehrere Magnaten begleiteten ihn nach Pesth . . ."

[43] Ibid., 32.   [44] Ibid., 32.

[45] Pardoe, *City of the Magyar*, II: 348. Pardoe's cosmopolitan orientation is also evident in her condescending attitude toward the nationalistic enthusiasm for Liszt.

his reception in Vienna before the trip to Hungary, and it resembled his reception in Prague soon after the trip to Hungary. The aristocracy's role in Liszt's Hungarian reception needs special emphasis for several reasons. First, it counters the image, transmitted in biographies, of Liszt's Hungarian audiences as a monolithic mass of Magyar nationalists and sympathizers. The conservative aristocrats may not have been especially numerous in relation to the Hungarian audiences as a whole, but they had enormous power in shaping the reputation of visiting artists and were therefore an important contingent in his reception. Second, it shows that Liszt's French, cosmopolitan qualities continued to be evident in Hungary, so that constructing him as a through-and-through Hungarian (as the Magyar nationalists did) was bound to be an awkward and imperfect project. That is, Liszt could only be made Hungarian under considerable pressure exerted by his salient Frenchness. Finally, Liszt's appeal to aristocrats needs emphasis because the sabre was a part of their feudal symbolic apparatus, and it represented their conception of nation much more successfully than it represented the national conception of the liberal reformers. This is a crucial reason the sabre became such a problematic symbol.

Hungarian nationalism in 1840

In order to understand the symbolic valences of the sabre, an overview of Hungarian nationalism is in order. Hungary's nationalism was distinctive, and conflicted, because of the country's ethnic and linguistic diversity. Political leadership was exclusively in the hands of the Magyar nobility, but the majority of the population, about two thirds, was non-Magyar, most of them descended from German and Slav immigrants who had not adopted Magyar language and customs (Liszt's ancestors are an example). In general the non-Magyar populations supported what I will call a "civic Hungarian" national identity: they wished to belong to the Hungarian nation by virtue of civil rights and democratic privileges, and they embraced the ethnic diversity of its people.[46]

Intellectuals in Hungary had been articulating this civic ideal of nationhood since the eighteenth century, but by 1839, when Liszt arrived, romantic nationalism had taken over. Whereas civic nationalists understood the nation as a sort of contract between multiple individuals, the romantic nationalists imagined the nation as a metaphysical or spiritual essence – specifically a Magyar essence inherent in Magyar language and customs. The difference is not just one of ideas, but also

[46] I borrow the term "civic national identity" from Raimond Nicholas Tullius, "The Construction of a Civic National Identity: Magyar and Swabian Nation-Builders in Hungary, 1760–1848" (BA thesis, Harvard University, 1996), 5–6.

of attitude. The romantic nationalists were in principle democratic, but their ideology was laced with cultural imperialism. As nationalism gained speed in the 1830s, many of them became convinced – contrary to Istvan Széchenyi, the founder of the movement – that the nation could only prosper if non-Magyar populations were compelled to adopt Magyar language and customs. Part of this idea stemmed from a fear, planted by the father of modern nationalism, J. G. Herder, that the Magyar race would eventually be absorbed by the Germans and Slavs. Slavs and Germans vocally resisted such an imposition of Magyar culture, and the Magyar nationalists often reacted back with open hostility. Tensions were particularly high in large cities such as Pest because they were dominated by non-Magyars, and the most passionate Magyarists broke out into virulent demonstrations of xenophobia.[47] In his pamphlet on Liszt, Franz von Schober called these extremists "Magyar fanatics" (*Magyar Fanatiker*).

The romantic nationalists, or "Magyar nationalists" as I will call them, were neither primarily nor uniformly racist. Their ideology was fundamentally liberal and democratic. But ethnic chauvinism was nevertheless a strong tendency within their program, influencing students and *literati* and thereby the national culture they were developing.[48] Schober had little patience with them, asserting that

the Magyar fanatics . . . run their course carelessly, despotically, and often opportunistically, and they combine this with a racial pride comparable only to that of the Spanish . . . [For this reason,] in Hungary everything with a Magyar tinge is sought after and exalted, and achievements of any kind that bear the Magyar stamp are received enthusiastically, often overvalued, and favored over those which, though originating in Hungary and therefore equally as national, bear a German stamp.[49]

And Schober was not the only contemporary observer to describe the effect of Magyar-centrism on the reception of performing artists. Another journalist claimed that

Germany has no national costume and no national pride, and any artist from Malabar or Haiti is to them better than a German artist. In Hungary it is different; in their eyes, anyone who is not Magyar is a "blasted Swabian," and though they may be courteous toward that foreign artist, their heart beats twice as fast when they occasionally stumble upon a great artist that is not a "Swabian."[50]

The word "Swabian" in this context means simply a German-speaking inhabitant of Hungary. Both of these passages make it clear that

[47] Barany, *Stephen Széchenyi*, 302–09; Janos, *The Politics of Backwardness*, 43.
[48] George Barany has called this period of Hungarian nationalism the "gentry chauvinism" phase (*Stephen Széchenyi*, 287).
[49] Schober, *Briefe*, 22–23.   [50] *Europa* (1840/1), 477.

Magyar-centrism was widespread in Hungary, and that an excessive enthusiasm for Liszt was almost preordained. But both also adopt a critical, resistant tone, showing that this chauvinism was not universally accepted. Indeed, critics who supported a civic national identity for Hungary were prepared to attack any demonstrations of xenophobia they perceived among the Magyar nationalists.

The conflict between civic Hungarian and Magyar national conceptions motivated many of the earliest critiques of the events in Pest. On two occasions Liszt was held directly responsible for playing into the chauvinistic attitudes of the Magyar nationalists. The first occasion was the "sabre of honor" concert of 4 January. A German journalist interpreted Liszt's choice to deliver his acceptance speech in French as support for the xenophobes, claiming that "he did it in order to win the favor of the Hungarians, by tying himself to the Magyar fanatics and affecting a contempt for Germans and Slavs."[51] This accusation was probably unwarranted. Schober clarified that Liszt spoke French simply because German was not allowed in the Hungarian National Theatre. Yet the unwillingness of the committee to make an exception for German on this occasion, when it was clearly the most sensible course of action, does come across as an instance of Magyar-centrism.

The second occasion on which the problem of Magyar xenophobia emerged was his final concert in Pest, that of 12 January. As Liszt was going through the themes offered by the audience for an improvisation, he pulled out of the vase a popular, often-heard folk tune.[52] According to a Czech journalist it was a Bohemian folk song, and when Liszt played the tune to measure the audience's vote, it was greeted with laughter from the Magyarist contingent of the audience. Liszt immediately consigned the melody to the "no" pile, a gesture that was greeted with a murmur of discontent, presumably on the part of the Slavs in the audience. At this point, Liszt apparently attempted to break the tension by making a joke and burning the slip of paper in the nearest candle flame, but this action, unfortunately, was wildly applauded by the Magyar enthusiasts. The Czech writer considered these gestures not only anti-Slav but also anti-German, apparently drawing on the solidarity the two groups shared as supporters of civic Hungarian nationhood. In his outrage, the journalist had the news disseminated to several German papers, and demanded that Liszt publicly apologize.

Franz von Schober went to some length to defend Liszt against this accusation, but his defense is not very convincing. His most important claim is that the song was not Bohemian, but was "the honorable old German Augustin [tune]."[53] Schober put his own authority heavily into

---

[51] Schober, *Briefe*, 48; emphasis added.   [52] This episode is related in ibid., 48–50.
[53] Ibid., 50.

question on the previous page, however, when he wrote uncertainly of this melody: "It is *possible* that it was of Bohemian origin; to me it *seemed* as if it were the well-known, beloved Augustin."[54] The "Augustin," a student song with a Latin text, seems almost too conveniently to exculpate Liszt from any participation in anti-Slav or anti-German activity. Schober also dubiously transfers the guilt for burning the slip of paper onto an audience member:

a man sitting near the piano fished the slip in question out of the notes, unfolded it and held it to the nearest light. "I take the liberty, given the apparently general mood, to take action and carry out a little trial." To applause and bravos the harmless notes which had caused the anger were transformed into ashes.[55]

But would a man have sat anywhere near the piano? In Pest as in Vienna, Liszt's piano was surrounded by rows of seats occupied by the women of the high aristocracy, and the first rows of seats in the orchestra were typically reserved for women as well.[56] Furthermore, it is hard to imagine, in the worshipful environment that surrounded Liszt, that anyone would have simply taken charge of the stage in this manner.[57] Schober was a very close friend of Liszt who was unquestionably biased in his favor. The dubious aspects of his defense lend further credence to the possibility that Liszt was involved in some Magyar-centric mishap at this concert.

Ideological tensions, these examples show, were clear and present in the Hungarian reception of Liszt, sometimes even in the concert hall. And it is these tensions, not a mere misunderstanding, that made the sabre an object of inflammatory controversy. Objections to the sabre were objections to the idea of nationhood that the sabre, as an ostentatious mark of Magyardom, seemed to represent. But how did the Magyar nationalists come upon the idea of presenting Liszt with a sabre? As it turns out, the sabre was not a natural choice, but a rather unexpected

---

[54] Ibid., 49.

[55] Ibid., 50. The author at first suggests that the identity of the melody was not clear. Later in this report it is crucial to Liszt's defense that it was certainly not the Bohemian tune, but the Augustin, as though he is stretching the evidence here to defend Liszt. This casts further doubt on the veracity of the report, and makes it more likely that this was a defensive article.

[56] Ibid., 39.

[57] Schober makes one last point (ibid., 50). He argues that Liszt and his audiences were not laughing at the song because it was Bohemian, but because it was stylistically out of place next to the Beethoven and Mozart melodies that had already been chosen for the improvisation. This argument is unlikely because Liszt commonly used popular and folk material in his free improvisations. An example would be his Vienna concert of 16 February 1840, in which his improvisation included a Strauss waltz and "the Austrian folk song" (*Sammler*, 22 February 1840 [M. Saphir]).

one – the product of a chain of compromises that ended up compromising the intentions of the givers.

The sabre

The Magyar nationalists were faced with the task of making Liszt "essentially" and "naturally" Hungarian against the odds. It is true that Liszt's liberal political sympathies were known, and that this made him popular among the reformers, but his liberalism had a decidedly French tinge.[58] It is also true that during his visit to Pest he gave charity concerts for Hungarian institutions and even began a fund for the establishment of a conservatory. Yet these gestures of support could not be touted as Hungarian in character. To make Liszt into a national hero, the nationalists could do little but emphasize the one thing that made him unquestionably Hungarian: his birth in Hungary. Thus began an emphasis on race that caused many problems.

The first thought of the nationalists was to furnish him with a Hungarian title of nobility demonstrating his Magyar blood. (Liszt's actual paternal lineage was German, but this was not known at the time.) Count Batthány had already submitted a petition for the title before Liszt arrived in Pest, but only after his arrival was it highly publicized in the papers. Liszt's lineage was traced back to a sixteenth-century noble family, and steps were taken, unsuccessfully, to have the title ratified in Vienna.[59] The reformers probably hoped that Liszt would appear in his concerts with his coat of arms on his costume, for Liszt asked Marie d'Agoult to rush him a prospective design. Had it been conferred, the title would have made Liszt a full-blooded member of the feudal, Magyar brotherhood. But since it failed, the reformers cast about for an alternate symbol, and they happened upon the idea of presenting him with a sabre.[60] As a marker of noble social status in Hungary, the sabre could serve as a substitute for the missing coat of arms.[61]

---

[58] This point was emphasized by Pardoe (*City of the Magyar*, II: 345).

[59] The documents "proving" Liszt's Hungarian lineage were published in the *Pesther Tageblatt*, 21 and 28 December 1839.

[60] That the resistance of Vienna to the title was unexpected is suggested by a letter from Liszt to d'Agoult of 19 December 1839, in which he sounds confident that he will receive the title "within a month" (*Correspondance de Liszt et de Madame d'Agoult*, I: 346–47).

[61] The idea that the sabre was compensation for the title of the nobility appears in an article from the *Hamburger neue Zeitung*, 10 November 1840; the article is a summary of Liszt's defense in the *Revue des deux mondes*. Berlioz also interpreted it this way: in his report for the *Journal des débats* (19 January 1840), he wrote that Liszt's coat of arms had been emblazoned in gold on the sabre. In recent times the sabre had also been granted to *Notabilitäten* who were not necessarily noble, but such exceptions were not common enough however for the sabre to have lost its aura of nobility.

The sabre was thus a compromise, entailed first by Liszt's lack of a connection with Hungarian culture, and secondly by the refusals of the Viennese bureaucracy to grant the noble title. What was crucially lost in this compromise was every trace of the liberal political principles of the reformers. The sabre did not just indicate that Liszt was born *in* Hungary, but that he was *born Hungarian*, part of the Magyar ancestral stock. The coat of arms, with its emphasis on race and the privileges of noble birth, reeked of the conservative "estates nationalism" against which the reformers defined themselves. The sabre, even more dramatically, hearkened back to a feudal social order in which military and political power were held simultaneously and indivisibly by a small group of noble lords. By making Liszt Hungarian only by virtue of his Magyar birth and not by virtue of cultural or linguistic belonging, the sabre represented the conservative, racial element of Magyar cultural nationalism, and downplayed its liberal side.

In the context of nationalist tensions, the sabre could easily be seen as a symbol of Magyar fanaticism, especially to those with some remove from the scene. In Vienna's journal *Der Humorist*, a writer scorned the "pompous and solemn" manner in which Liszt was given a crown of laurels at his 11 January concert in Pest:

Without contesting Liszt's right to distinctions of this kind, such demonstrations always have something comical to them, and especially as *they originate in only a small part of the public*, they lose much of their significance. Even less appropriate was the gift that Liszt received from *his enthusiastic admirers* on the occasion of his concert at the Hungarian National Theater. This consisted of a – sabre.[62]

The critical tone of this article is clearly aimed at the fanatics. By mentioning the sabre in the same breath as the crown of laurels, the author shows that the sabre was not only seen as a military object, but also as a sign of the excessive enthusiasm of the Magyar nationalists. Moritz Saphir, editor of the *Humorist* and a close friend of Liszt, attached a rare footnote to this article in order to make it absolutely clear that *only* the extreme Magyarists, not the entire public, were responsible for the excesses:

It is the real duty of a worthy journalism, when the propagation of such ridiculous excesses makes it necessary, to speak out: such an inflation of art *originates only from a few individuals*, who are indeed worthy and admired but effusive and extreme; and therefore one cannot pass off the paroxysms of *some enthusiasts* as the normal condition of either an entire glorious nation or an entire cultured city.[63]

---

[62] *Humorist*, 18 January 1840 (the article is signed "Fatalis"); emphasis added.
[63] M. Saphir, in ibid.; emphasis added.

Saphir's ire toward the Magyar fanatics here is entirely consistent with his agenda, described earlier, to construct Liszt as a specifically "German" virtuoso.

Apologists for the Pest episode have always argued that objections to the sabre were raised because it was misinterpreted as an object of war, when it was actually a sign of social status. This was to some extent true in Paris, as I will later show. But in the areas closer to Hungary and more in touch with its customs, the specific meaning of the sabre was clear. In these places, knowing that the sabre was part of the national costume was the source of the objections, not an answer to them. For the sabre symbolized a conservative, openly elitist, and pre-modern conception of nation that many found objectionable. It was not only the Germans within Hungary who objected. Members of the intellectual class – writers such as Julia Pardoe, Franz von Schober, and Moritz Saphir – harbored a more cosmopolitan perspective and distanced themselves from the chauvinistic Magyarism that tainted the Pest episode, even as they attempted to defend Liszt and his Hungarian audiences.

Liszt's Hungarian audiences, in sum, were far from a monolithic mass of nationalists ready to celebrate their native son. I have discussed three different attitudes toward nation – a conservative estates nationalism supported mainly by aristocrats, a civic Hungarian national identity supported mostly by non-Magyar ethnic groups, and a dominant, culture-centered Magyar nationalism – each of which wanted Liszt to represent something different. By playing along with the Magyar nationalist contingent, Liszt inadvertently provoked a conflict he may have been powerless to anticipate. There is no need to regret the controversy that ensued, for such conflicts were bound to emerge in a country whose identity, fractured by ethnic diversity and by radically varying degrees of loyalty to the empire, remained so uncertain. Indeed, a parallel conflict seems to have broken out when Liszt visited another ethnically diverse locale in the empire, Zagreb, in 1846.

Interlude: Zagreb, 1846

Understanding this episode requires a brief summary of the national situation in Zagreb. Some months after Liszt left Pest in 1840, the Hungarian radical Lajos Kossuth was released from prison and began the vigorous agitation that brought Hungary to the revolution of 1848. Under the influence of Kossuth's propaganda, the persecution of Hungary's non-Magyars reached acute levels. The Croatians were especially hard hit by this trend because the Magyar nationalists, in an attempt to build up leverage against the imperial regime, were set on achieving cultural supremacy in the main Croatian city, Zagreb. In resistance to the Magyar supremacists – for whom I will borrow the contemporary term

"Magyarons" – the Croatians mounted a cultural national movement of their own centered in Zagreb. This national movement was referred to as "Illyrian" because, although Croat-led, it enlisted the solidarity of Slovenians and Serbs.

According to the account written by music historian Franjo Kuhač, Liszt's visit to Zagreb involved a small-scale struggle between the Magyarons and the Illyrians.[64] It is unclear to what extent Kuhač's narrative is based on factual information. It is evidently an "imaginative" reconstruction to some degree, but this may represent a historiographic priority of his generation (his book was written in 1903) rather than a lack of factual support. Whatever its "truth value," Kuhač's story faithfully reveals the conditions under which Liszt could be used to negotiate the conflicting claims to nationhood that existed in the ethnically non-German regions of the Austrian empire.

Shortly before Liszt arrived in Zagreb in July 1846, the Illyrian movement had been given a significant boost by the success of the first Illyrian national opera, Vatroslav Lisinski's *Ljubav i zloba*, at the National Theatre in Zagreb. The opera's success (Kuhač writes) provoked the Magyarons to mount a major *non*-Illyrian cultural event as a counterweight. Their first thought was to invite an opera troupe from Germany or Italy, but this was quickly dismissed on the basis that such a troupe could have had no effect on the public unless they sang in Illyrian. An irresistible alternative presented itself: Liszt was in the area, and he had just received a Hungarian noble title. Nothing could have more perfectly counterbalanced the recent attention to Illyrian culture. The Magyarons thus invited him to Zagreb, escorted him there from Rogatac, and surrounded him during his entire stay with a team of carriages and lackeys.

That the Magyarons were motivated to invite Liszt specifically by Lisinsky's opera is the least plausible element of Kuhač's narrative.[65] Yet even if untrue, it is entirely plausible that the Magyarons attached themselves to Liszt in an act of cultural warfare with the Illyrians. The one surviving press report indirectly supports this. It appeared in the newspaper *Danica hrvatska, slavonska i dalmatinska*, which represented Illyrian national interests.[66] Liszt was serenaded by the local *Musikverein* at his hotel the night before the concert. The report claims that the *Verein* wanted to perform a piece from Lisinski's opera, but could not because, unfortunately, Lisinsky had left Zagreb and the score was unavailable.

[64] Franjo Kuhač, *Vatroslav Lisinski i njegovo doba* (Zagreb, 1904), 73–75. To my knowledge this account is unknown to the English-speaking world and is the only account in Croatian. I would like to thank Nada Bezić and Mirjana Šimundža for translating this document.

[65] Kuhac tells this story in the context of a book on Lisinski, which may have led him to force a causal connection between the two.

[66] "Franjo Liszt u Zagrebu," *Danica hrvatska, slavonska i dalmatinska* 32 (July 1846).

This detail of the report rings false, even defensive. It is scarcely cred-ible that no one in the *Verein* or elsewhere could have tracked down an excerpt from the leading opera of the day. What the *Danica* article seems to be evading is the admission that the Magyarons, in surround-ing Liszt's hotel, had taken control of his reception, and would not have allowed an "Illyrian" composition to be performed at his balcony.[67] The national newspaper was not a place to concede the victory of the Magyarons.

The *Danica* report also sheds some light on Liszt's concert. The Illyr-ian audience, it explains, received Liszt with enthusiastic applause: "This unusual visit is evidence that our national public has a feeling for fine art." The specific reference to the *national* public may repre-sent simply the Illyrian orientation of the newspaper in general. Kuhač, however, puts a nationalist spin on this comment. He takes the desig-nation "national public" to imply political opposition on the part of the Illyrians. He claims that the Illyrians would normally have restrained themselves from joining in the enthusiasm for Liszt, as a protest against his appropriation by the Magyarons. But they were more concerned, he continues, to preserve the reputation of the Zagreb public as one that could recognize the merit of great artists, and so they applauded with full force.

Kuhač, I would conclude, noted an element of Illyrian defensiveness in the *Danica* report, and chose to elaborate the Zagreb episode around the theme of national tensions. In the process he may have exagger-ated the importance of cultural politics in Liszt's reception there. Yet he also seems to have had information about the role of the Casino members – anti-Illyrian Magyarons and aristocrats – that lends support to his interpretation.[68] Even if we were to conclude that his account is entirely fictional, it reveals two important aspects of Liszt as a poten-tial symbol for national movements. First, the non-verbal character of his art made him easier to appropriate for nationalistic purposes than singers, actors, or writers. Language and literature were the cultural core of most national movements, including that of the Illyrians, and when the Magyarons thought of inviting an opera troupe (surely a fab-rication by Kuhač) the problem of language arose. Liszt however posed

[67] Neither of the parties had an ally in the leader of the *Musikverein*, Juraj Wiesner von Morgenstern, who was Austrian. If Morgenstern was neutral with regard to the Illyrian and Magyar national movements, this would have worked to the advantage of the Magyarons, since their main goal was to draw attention away from Illyrian nationalism by whatever means possible.

[68] The *Danica* reported that tickets for Liszt's concert were triple the normal price. Liszt's concerts were most often double the usual ticket price. The especially high ticket price of the Zagreb concert is further evidence that the event was lorded over by the wealthy members of the Casino.

no such problems, and this is a crucial reason the Hungarians had been able to celebrate him in Pest in 1840, in spite of his evident French cultural identity. Second, audiences with conflicting national factions had to balance out their enthusiasms in the concert hall so as to avoid collusion with their opponents. The Magyars were in the forefront of Liszt's reception in Pest in 1840 as well as in Zagreb. We encountered one example of a segment of the Pest audience withdrawing its applause to protest against the apparent Magyar-centrism that prevailed in the hall. The Illyrian public may have been inclined to make a similar gesture at Liszt's Zagreb concert, as Kuhač suggests.

3.   European reactions to the Pest episode

The relevance of the Pest episode extends well beyond Hungary and its internal divisions. In the European press, too, the sabre of honor became an object of intense debate, and once again the debate revolved around competing ideologies of nationhood. In this international arena the contest was waged not between alternative nationalisms, but rather between cosmopolitanism and nationalism generally. Paris, the proud center of cosmopolitan culture, thus served as center stage for the debate. It is true that Parisian critics and satirists misunderstood the meanings attached to a sabre in Hungary. Liszt's biographers have traditionally taken this as an occasion to correct, and dismiss, the misunderstandings. Yet the misunderstandings are worth attending to, since they tell us much about the values of the international worlds Liszt was moving through.

Parisian discussion of Liszt's reception in Pest damaged Liszt's international reputation to a degree that has never been fully recognized. It was the first of two major blows to his Parisian reputation, and was therefore serious business. Before delving into the content of the debate, then, I would like to situate it in the history of Liszt's relationship to Paris. As discussed in chapter 1, Liszt devoted extensive time and energy in the late 1830s to preparing a dramatic, triumphant return to Paris, which he intended specifically for the year 1840. He entrusted to Marie d'Agoult, who was in Paris for the winter of 1840, most of the responsibility for preparing this return and managing his publicity in the Parisian journals. Through her efforts, news of the events in Pest – namely the noble lineage and the sabre of honor – soon reached Parisian readers. Liszt surely intended these reports to tantalize the Parisian audiences, but they totally misfired, drawing only ridicule toward him and the Hungarian audiences. As Liszt had learned many years earlier, no adverse publicity was more damaging than mockery from the Parisian press. The Pest reports did so much harm, in fact, that d'Agoult suggested aborting his intended comeback during the 1840 concert season.

Liszt did not agree that this was a serious threat, and at first did not accept her suggestion that he decline to give a public concert.[69] But when he arrived in Paris and had a better chance to measure the public temperature, he seems to have retreated. Instead of making the dramatic comeback he had planned, he avoided confronting the general public altogether. He made two private appearances on his Parisian "home ground" – the salon of Cristina Belgiojoso – providing piano accompaniment for classic choral works. The one concert he offered for his own benefit, at the Salle Érard on 20 April, was by invitation only, a ticketing practice he had never used before. The invitation-only policy made sure that whatever opposition had gathered in Paris would not taint his reception.[70] The review of this concert written by d'Agoult (and published in *L'artiste*) makes it clear that Liszt fully intended to give a public benefit concert shortly thereafter: "Before making himself heard by the general public, he wanted to see the result of his efforts confirmed by a small circle made up of his friends."[71] The rest of this review, which probably represents what Liszt wanted to see in print, describes the artistic maturity Liszt had achieved during his three-year absence. Such an emphasis suggests that he wanted the public concert to serve as his long-awaited comeback. The best explanation for why he did not follow through with the public concert is that he sensed public opposition and did not want to risk failure.

We are accustomed to imagining Liszt riding effortlessly from one triumph to the next. But here he was, at the peak of the 1840 concert season, in the city where he had developed as an artist, and where he had a great many friends in various social spheres, and he felt he could not pull off even a single public concert. Apparently the Parisians had reacted so badly to what they had heard about Pest that they utterly spoiled his master plan – his intention of retaking the Parisian publics as a finished, worldly-wise virtuoso and *artiste*. The damage did not end there. Journals such as the *Caricature*, the *France musicale*, and

---

[69] *Correspondance de Liszt et de Madame d'Agoult*, I: 407.

[70] In a letter to d'Agoult from February 1846, Liszt wrote that she had misjudged the negative inclinations of the Parisian audiences in 1840, and that he had fully succeeded, presumably judging from his Salle Érard concert and the positive press it generated (*Correspondance de Liszt et de Madame d'Agoult*, II: 351–52). I am arguing, however, that the concert succeeded *in spite of* the mood of the Parisian audiences, through control of the admission. Liszt's disingenuousness here was motivated by his desire, evident elsewhere in the letter, to convince d'Agoult that he was in no way a charlatan and that the Parisian audiences recognized this. Whereas in 1846 she was almost certainly motivated to claim such a thing out of malice, she had no malicious intent at all in 1840. The article she published in *L'artiste* (series 2, V/18 [1840], 315–16) that season shows that she was doing everything she could to help his reputation.

[71] *Artiste*, series 2, V/18 (1840), 315–16. This article is unsigned but was written by Marie d'Agoult.

especially the *Ménestrel* satirized the sabre relentlessly throughout the 1840s, presenting Liszt as a virtuoso on military parade, and renaming him "General Liszt." This extreme reaction cannot be explained simply as a misunderstanding of the sabre. There were many other issues at stake, namely Liszt's Parisian reputation, a cosmopolitan ideology that prevailed among the French intelligentsia, and a stereotype of Hungary as a conservative or backward nation.

The militant sabre

There is a simple explanation for why the Parisians initially fixated on the militancy of the sabre: poor communications. French journals and newspapers had no regular correspondents in Pest, at least for the coverage of culture and the arts. Liszt therefore had to become his own correspondent. He sent detailed reports to d'Agoult, and she passed them on to Berlioz for a write-up in the *Gazette*. When the *Gazette* refused to print it, Berlioz turned to his other outlet, the *Journal des débats*, and for this paper he had to write a *feuilleton* rather than a dry report. To meet the demands of the *feuilleton* genre, he made all kinds of cuts and conflations of the Pest events.[72] The article, which appeared in the 29 January issue, summarizes Liszt's speech in acceptance of the sabre as follows:

> Mr. Liszt responded in French to Count Festetics that he would preserve the sabre as the object most dear to his heart, and that if necessary he would use it, as every loyal Hungarian must, in defense of his beloved king and his country; and that if divine providence carried out its most ardent vows, he would dedicate his meager talents exclusively to his mother country.[73]

This summary follows only the first and last paragraphs of Liszt's speech as it was transmitted in other sources.[74] Berlioz presented the sabre exclusively as an object Liszt might conceivably use on the battlefield. The middle of the speech, where he says that the sabre "is placed at this moment in weak and pacific hands," and interprets the gift as recognition of Hungary's cultural mission, is left out entirely. The Parisians, then, had little reason to think the sabre had any symbolic resonances other than military ones. They had no alternative reports to fill the gaps in Berlioz's version of the story.

Berlioz's emphasis on the sabre as a militant object, which he transmitted to his Parisian readers, was not just a personal quirk, but stemmed in

---

[72] This article conflates, for example, two episodes: Liszt's attendance of a performance of *Fidelio* on 10 January, and the 4 January concert in which he was granted the sabre. In a letter to Liszt, d'Agoult noted that Berlioz had rearranged the details, but found his *feuilleton* successful nevertheless.

[73] *Journal des débats*, 29 January 1840.

[74] An English translation of the entire speech is found in Walker, *Franz Liszt*, I: 325–26.

part from a well-worn stereotype of Hungarian national character. An 1844 book satirizing various national types described the typical Hungarian as a nobleman whose social status is signified by his "proud eye" and, more emphatically, by his "martial demeanor":

The Hungarian is born a brave soldier, just as Titian was a born painter, Joseph Haydn a born musician, and Michelangelo a sculptor. To see the marvelous dexterity with which he manages a weapon, you'd be tempted to think . . . he was born from his mother armed from head to foot. At three Mozart played the piano; at three a Hungarian draws the sword [*tire le mur*].[75]

This stereotype was drawn not only from contact with Hungarian expatriates in Paris, but also from a more general European perception of Hungary as a conservative, aristocratic, pre-modern nation. Liszt himself romanticized the Hungarian nation as a preserve of noble, feudal virtues. In his French-language acceptance speech for the sabre, he described Hungary as "a nation whose bravery and chivalry are so universally admired," and in a later defense as "that country of antique and chivalrous manners." With these comments he was merely repeating the clichés of his day. Even as far away as Copenhagen we find Liszt described as "a Magyar, a scion of that grand, chivalrous, wild, valiant stock of heroes."[76]

The image of Hungary as a medieval nation, filled with proud, sabre-wielding Magyar nobles, was obviously very far from the truth. It had become widespread because the popular highlights of Hungarian history were battles, some of them in the distant past, that been waged in resistance to Ottoman and Habsburg imperial domination. False or exaggerated as this perception of Hungary was, it could not have failed to shape French reactions to the sabre. To Parisians, the sabre seemed to be the natural way for such a nation to express its recognition of a hero, and Berlioz's surgery on Liszt's acceptance speech had reinforced this perception. French audiences, then, *did* understand the sabre as a symbol of Hungarian nationhood, but by virtue of its militant connotations rather than its place in the national costume. The militancy of the sabre was not in itself objectionable: indeed, the supposed chivalry and bravery of the old Hungarian nation was implicitly valorized. But the romanticization of these virtues was contingent upon their distance, their outdatedness, their otherness from the modern, liberal French order. In attaching a sabre to Liszt – who was a paragon of modern French culture – the Hungarians threatened to close off this distance.

---

[75] *Les étrangers à Paris*, ed. Janin, Beauvoir, Desnoyers, et al. (Paris, 1844), 84. This article was contributed by Stanislas Bellanger. Given that Liszt had been known in Paris as a second Mozart, it is possible that the latter sentence is written with him in mind.

[76] *Foedrelandet*, 19 July 1841, quoted in Bengt Johnsson, "Liszt in Copenhagen," *Liszt Society Journal* 21 (1996), 3–4.

The problem with the sabre was not its militancy per se, but the incongruity of a feudal symbol and a modern, progressive virtuoso.

Because Liszt kept a low profile on his 1840 visit to Paris, there is little journalistic material directly addressing objections to the sabre. The two earliest press comments, however, both interpreted the sabre primarily as a military object, and both criticized it as an inappropriate gift for a representative of the arts. The first came from the editor of the *Gazette musicale*, Schlesinger, who apparently found the sabre of honor ceremony distasteful and declined to publish the report Berlioz had submitted. Instead he published his own brief report (26 January), which chided the Hungarians for a bestowing a gift that was "flattering, but very strange for a man of peace."[77] This point was echoed in the *France musicale*, whose London correspondent compared the sabre with a precious inkwell that had recently been offered to Thalberg:

It is true that the Hungarians just offered to the famous pianist Liszt a sabre of honor; but you might think that, in keeping with the pacific ideas that govern today, an inkwell of honor is a more suitable gift for an artist than a sabre, especially at a time when no country is in danger.[78]

This writer wishes to protect not only the arts, but also the liberal social order – "the pacific ideas that govern today" – against the militancy of the sabre. No charge is leveled against Liszt. The culprit is the Hungarian nation, which has let its militancy intrude upon an artist, and by extension upon the peaceful, civilized environment of liberal society.

The *Revue des deux mondes* debate

The clearest articulation of the problems surrounding the sabre appeared only in the fall of 1840, flaring up in the *Revue des deux mondes*, a prestigious literary and intellectual journal. The comment that incited Liszt's rebuttal appeared in an article lamenting the degeneration of good taste in the arts. At the article's close, the author drew attention to the disproportionate interest contemporary audiences took in virtuoso performers, concluding that "we will leave Petrarch in the street to bring Elssler to the capital; we will let Beethoven and Weber die of hunger to give a sabre of honor to Mr. Liszt."[79] These words are directed at neither Liszt nor the Hungarian public, but at superficial taste and excessive enthusiasm in general, and that of the Parisian public in particular

---

[77] *Revue et gazette musicale* 7/8 (26 January 1840), 67. This was not the only occasion on which Schlesinger refused to support Liszt; see Jacquéline Bellas, "La tumultueuse amitié de Franz Liszt et de Maurice Schlesinger," *Littératures* 12 (1965), 7–20.

[78] *France musicale* 3/7 (16 February 1840), 78.

[79] *Revue des deux mondes*, 15 October 1840. An English translation of this article appears in Walker, *Franz Liszt*, I: 327–28.

("*we* will leave . . . *we* will let . . ."). In his response, Liszt insisted that the emotions of the Hungarian nation, as expressed in the sabre, have nothing to do with the superficial enthusiasm of the Parisian public. The patriotic symbolism of the sabre, he argues, ennobles and justifies the enthusiasm of its givers. Hungarian patriotism, as Liszt presents it, is inherently good.

Liszt's defense is usually presented as the last word on the subject of the sabre, as though he had completely disarmed his Parisian critics and the case was closed. But the writer at the *Deux mondes* came back immediately with a counter-response that has been ignored or dismissed by biographers.[80] This counter-response deserves attention because it clarifies more than any other document the Parisian objections to the sabre, and helps explain why the debates remained unresolved for years thereafter. The writer at the *Deux mondes* adhered to a thoroughgoing cosmopolitan ideology, and felt that this was the only ideology Liszt could reasonably represent:

No, Mr. Liszt, you are neither French nor Hungarian; you belong, like all virtuosos, to all lands where the immortal voice of melody is understood. Today it's the grand duke of Tuscany who honors you, tomorrow it will be the queen of England, another day the empress of Russia . . . You accumulate all trophies, you mingle all crowns, and rightly so, because your art has no nationality for you, it speaks not a language, but *the languages,* as St. Paul puts it . . . Yes, Mr. Liszt, without your philosophical and religious sentiments, the piano has made you a man of humanity; this is why we persist in thinking that the homage at Pest is a much less national thing than you suppose it is, and that these magnates you speak of were music lovers in disguise who should have perhaps made a gift of some magnificent piano instead, and reserved the sabre of Mathias Corvin or Zriny for another occasion.[81]

The Hungarians who gave Liszt the sabre are indicted here for capitalizing on Liszt's international fame to serve their own patriotic agendas, thereby reducing his universality. Liszt belongs to Hungary by birth, but to the transnational community by his artistic achievements, and his art should never be subordinated or reduced to his national origin. In this cosmopolitan outlook, the arts have a higher moral value than the nation. Insofar as Liszt based his defense on the unimpeachable moral value of the nation, his position was incommensurable with that of the writer at the *Deux mondes.*

There is reason to believe that the cosmopolitan ideology advocated in the *Deux mondes* was supported by a majority of educated Parisians,

---

[80] Walker (*Franz Liszt,* I: 328) mentions it only in a footnote, and dismisses it as a sarcastic, personal attack.

[81] *Revue des deux mondes,* 15 November 1840, 612.

for it was consistent with the liberal, pluralistic conception of nation that prevailed in France. A liberally conceived nation could, in theory, be realized anywhere, since it was based on ideas of citizenship and democratic participation, regardless of ethnicity and language. It was in this sense a national conception with a cosmopolitan scope, and it was in fact being transplanted to other parts of Europe.[82] The sabre of honor, as Liszt's defense made clear, symbolized a feudal conception of nation based on patriarchal, aristocratic Magyar lineage. It was a nationalism that seemed inward-turning rather than outward-reaching. Because the idea of nation implied by the sabre was ethnically and geographically concrete – because it was Hungary-specific – it ran contrary to the universalistic, cosmopolitan ideology advocated by Liszt's adversary and by the majority of Parisian intellectuals.

The debate between Liszt and the *Deux mondes*, then, was not a matter that could be cleared up simply by explaining the patriotic significance of the sabre. It was a conflict between different attitudes toward nationhood. This is one reason the sabre continued to draw criticism and ridicule in France long after Liszt had explained its patriotic significance. Yet the *Deux mondes* writer had a second bone of contention, this one aimed directly at Liszt:

There is something singular in these fatuous patriotic demonstrations in men who want not only to come and ask us for applause and decorations, but even pretend to be involved in all our movements and live with France in a *fraternal communion*, as they put it. Is being a pianist sufficient ground to have a nationality that one adorns according to the situation, or takes on at one's leisure? "I am a Frenchman, notice my philosophical and social passions; I am a Hungarian, look at my sabre."[83]

This critique of Liszt had a precedent. In 1838 Heine had published an article in the *Gazette* in which he chided Liszt for the diversity of his political and philosophical affiliations.[84] The *Deux mondes* writer was affirming, with considerably less humor, Heine's implication that Liszt lacked true ethical or intellectual convictions, that he was an ideological chameleon, adopting whatever identity or symbolic purpose made him attractive to his audiences. The sabre of honor was an extreme example

---

[82] The Belgian and Polish uprisings of 1830 took their inspiration from French liberalism. Liszt's reception in Copenhagen in 1841 shows that the liberal movement there looked to France for inspiration. In Hungary, Count Louis Batthány was making reforms heavily tinged with French liberalism (Barany, *Stephen Széchenyi*, 348–49).

[83] *Revue des deux mondes*, 15 November 1840, 612. The phrase "communion fraternel" is an allusion to Liszt's involvement with the Saint-Simonian movement.

[84] "Lettres confidentielles," *Revue et gazette musicale* 5/5 (4 February 1838), 41–44. This article was also published in his book *Über die französische Bühne* (1838). For the German-language version, see *Heinrich Heine und die Musik*, 104–06.

of this flexibility. The Parisians had known a Liszt who espoused republican and sometimes radical-utopian political principles. They now saw him defending what they perceived as his incorporation into Hungary's feudal aristocracy. This leap from the far left of the ideological spectrum to the far right was too abrupt for the Parisians to tolerate. Liszt seemed to be "playing at" nationality; he was betraying his French intellectual roots.

Civilizing enthusiasm

Philosophical objections to the sabre, however strong they may have been, do not fully explain why the Parisian audiences shied away from Liszt when he returned in 1840, forcing him to cancel his intended public concert. The restraint of the Parisian publics can also be attributed to a new attitude toward demonstrative enthusiasm that crystallized in response to the Pest episode. Liszt had just been celebrated lavishly in a country that, as we have seen, was perceived as politically backward, out of step with the liberal, progressive social order of modern Europe. If the Parisians showed enthusiasm toward Liszt comparable to that of the Hungarians, they risked losing their reputation as the cultural and political vanguard of Europe. Parisians were by no means alone in their concern over the behavior of the Hungarians. After the negative publicity generated in the Parisian press, it was becoming imperative to resist "Lisztomania" in order to belong to the order of "civilized" Europe.

Julia Pardoe's comments on the sabre of honor ceremony reveal a sense of distance from the events, and show how predictable the Parisian reaction was. She had lived in Hungary and understood exactly what the sabre meant there, and she found it ridiculous by the standards of "civilized" Europe:

There is probably not another country in the world where it could have occurred without provoking laughter, but the Hungarians are far too earnest in their excitement to induce ridicule. In Paris such a scene would have dwindled from bombast into twaddle; in London it would have commenced with an uproar and ended with dinner; and in both it would have afforded food for pasquinades and party-spirit during the month ensuing; but here all was real, unadulterated, genuine enthusiasm.[85]

Pardoe here encourages her readers to refrain from mockery by characterizing the enthusiasm of the Hungarians as charming, innocent and unsophisticated – in a word, provincial. She places herself outside and above the excitement of Pest as a reaffirmation of her cosmopolitan sophistication.

---

[85] Pardoe, *City of the Magyar*, II: 353–54.

In the months that followed the Pest episode, journalists in several parts of Europe repeated Pardoe's distancing gesture. Her intuition about comic reactions to the sabre became a reality. Surprisingly, the Hungarians were the first to comment. A Pest correspondent for the German-language journal *Europa* pleaded:

No one here remained calm, not even this writer; yet I had from time to time small moments in which, despite my enthusiasm, the activity appeared to be slight madness. Now that they have awakened from the initial rush, the majority of the people here also truly share this opinion, and I haste to make this known so that level-headed Germany, deceived by the clanging of the sabre of honor given to him or the thunder of the canons of honor for him, will not consider all of Pest a great madhouse.[86]

Although this author is trying to counter the prejudices of his German readers, his continuation of the discussion risks reinforcing them. As an explanation for the common euphoria of the Liszt days, he characterizes the Hungarians as a "most excitable, easily enthused populace, in which national pride is the dominant passion."[87] This was exactly the kind of rhetoric Pardoe used to convince her readers that the Hungarians were provincial in their treatment of Liszt. A major theme of her book, in fact, is that the Hungarians have an "excitable character," and she calls upon it to explain their reception of Liszt.[88]

The *Europa* writer ended up demonstrating, above all, the difficulty of separating the Hungarians from their provincial reputation. The article, furthermore, appeared too late to mitigate German reactions. Liszt had already gone on to appear in Vienna, Prague, Dresden, and Leipzig wearing the sabre, accompanied by a few Hungarian hangers-on who sent cries of "Eljen!" up to the stage as he performed. In all of these places the patriotic significance of the sabre was well understood.[89] What disturbed critics was not so much the militancy of the sabre but wild audiences. Saphir, writing just after the Pest episode, felt it necessary to interrupt abruptly one of his typical streams of praise:

But stop! Too much is unhealthy! . . . His memory will survive in every heart illuminated by art, without us making ourselves ridiculous through absurd, slobbering praise or comical honors.[90]

Even in Hamburg, a city Liszt had no intention of visiting, the news of Pest prompted critical reactions, as though the public had to be armed against similar behavior:

---

[86] *Europa* (1840/1), 477. The report is dated "End of January 1840."
[87] Ibid.   [88] Pardoe, *City of the Magyar*, II: 345–46.
[89] See for example *Dresdner Wochenblatt*, 30 March 1840, and Alexander Buchner, *Franz Liszt in Böhmen* (Prague, 1962), 74–75.
[90] *Sammler*, 6 February 1840 (M. Saphir).

Will we Hamburg people also let ourselves get carried away to Pest-like homages? It is said that the Alster would be colorfully lined with flags during the entire period of Liszt's visit; people would unharness his horses and draw him to the "Alten Stadt London" and compel him to give French speeches from a window of this hotel. It is not agreed whether the Sabre of Honor takes the form of a cuirassier's sword or a Damascan blade.[91]

The last sentence is a particularly telling articulation of the sabre's ambiguity. If it is a cuirassier's weapon, it belongs to the occident, to central Europe, to civilized society. But if it is a Damascan weapon, it belongs to the orient, to the untamed, pre-civilized world. This same ambiguity suddenly became important to assessments of Liszt's audiences. Was the audience behavior civilized or fanatical? Was it cosmopolitan or provincial? As Liszt began his international tours and generated unheard-of levels of enthusiasm, the European audiences could not afford to leave these questions unanswered.

Despite these reactions to the Pest events, Liszt was able to put on successful concerts until he reached Paris. The Parisian publics had a greater stake in withholding their enthusiasm, for Paris was by common consent the center of civilized, cosmopolitan Europe. If they wished to preserve their leadership position vis-à-vis European culture, they could not afford to have their enthusiasm take a form similar to that of the Hungarians. Thus Théophile Gautier, reviewing Liszt's second private concert, wrote:

We don't know if the Parisians will grant Liszt sabres of honor, or if the high-placed women will fight for the honor of possessing a piece of the gloves that touched his magic hands, as in Vienna; but these stories, which before seemed to us exaggerated in spite of our esteem for Liszt's talent, now seem entirely authentic and plausible.[92]

Gautier is careful here to imply that the Parisian audiences are above the bizarre demonstrations of the people of Vienna and Pest, so that Paris can be reaffirmed as a site of cultural supremacy. His purpose is to show that the enthusiasm of the Parisians stems from refinement and sophistication, not from patriotic over-excitement (Pest) or fetishistic obsession (Vienna).

As these examples show, after Pest audiences began watching themselves, monitoring their excitement, policing their pleasures. The enthusiasm of the Hungarians had been declared illegitimate, if not laughable, in the international press. There now existed a category "bad enthusiasm," against which European audiences would define and legitimate their own responses. It was easy to construct "bad enthusiasm" around Hungary because of contemporary stereotypes of the national character,

[91] *Telegraph für Deutschland* (April 1840), 252.   [92] *La presse*, 27 April 1840.

which seemed wholly confirmed by the sabre. Press writers represented "bad enthusiasm" using the image of the sabre until Liszt's Berlin visit of 1842, when it acquired the name "Lisztomania" and was represented through images of Liszt's female admirers. In either form, it was a tool by which European audiences affirmed (and in the same gesture made vulnerable) the legitimacy of their enthusiasms.

Earlier we saw that in Hungary Liszt was celebrated according to a chauvinistic form of Magyar nationalism that provoked opposition in the lands bordering Hungary. This examination of the European reactions to the Pest episode reveals another brand of chauvinism, a chauvinism implicit in the cosmopolitan outlook. Europeans, especially the Parisians, were ready to reify stereotypes of Hungary as a backward, provincial nation for the sake of preserving their own "civilized" self-image. It needs to be emphasized that this stereotyping of Hungary often took the form of praise – the Hungarian nation was lauded, not demonized, as a preserve of noble, ancient virtues and customs. The stereotype was only devalued when the stability of the civilized–provincial binary opposition was threatened. This is what occurred when Liszt, the consummate French cosmopolitan, suddenly appeared on the European stage as a full-blooded Magyar patriot and citizen. Neither the Magyar nationalists nor the European critics showed themselves to be unimpeachable. Both groups wanted Liszt to belong to them and to represent their ideological interests. They used Liszt to affirm their principles and their identity, but they also used him to invalidate alternative principles and identities. Liszt typically acquiesced, if sometimes ironically, to their wishes, and he therefore became part of the territory where contemporary ideologies of nationhood were debated.

4

Liszt and the German nation, 1840–43

What fatherland! There is no fatherland; for me it is everywhere.

Franz Liszt[1]

In 1848, Franz Liszt, just thirty-seven years old and recently retired from the concert stage, moved to Weimar to take up full-time his duties as court Kapellmeister. Weimar was at the time the epicenter of classical German culture, as represented by Goethe and Schiller, and in the course of his tenure Liszt would devote himself to honoring and preserving that culture.[2] In Weimar he would also become a figurehead of the so-called New German School of composition. The rapidity of Liszt's transformation into a major institution of German culture has never raised an eyebrow, but the dates are extraordinary. In 1840, Liszt had never set foot in northern or central Germany. His public identity at this point was variously marked as "French," "romantic," "cosmopolitan," and even "Hungarian" (these are all discussed in chapter 3) – everything *but* "German." Yet as early as 1842, the Weimar court offered him their Kapellmeister chair, a position he accepted in a part-time capacity ("in ausserordentlichen Dienst"). Liszt thus metamorphosed into a candidate for German national culture in a remarkably short span of time. In the years 1840–43, indeed, his public identity underwent the most radical change of his performing career, as he became deeply involved with German culture and the institutions (not the politics) of German nationalism.

The story of this extraordinary transformation, which significantly influenced the course of music history, remains untold. Beginning with a concert given on 23 August 1841 to benefit the reconstruction of the Cologne cathedral, Liszt came to be celebrated as a figure in German culture and a supporter of German cultural nationalism. Liszt actively cultivated the affiliation with Germany by associating himself with several institutions and groups with a nationalist bent: men's choirs, charities, members of the royalty, intellectuals, freemasons, and students.

---

[1] Marcel Herwegh, *Au soir des dieux* (Paris, 1933), 177n.

[2] On Liszt's relationship to this cultural legacy, see *Liszt und die Weimarer Klassik,* ed. Detlef Altenburg (Laaber, 1997).

Perhaps without being aware of it, he was rapidly paving the way toward his 1842 appointment in Weimar. German critics contributed to the national affiliation by emphasizing the Germanness of Liszt's artistic makeup, of his personal character, and of his audience's attachment to him.

In this chapter I trace Liszt's richly textured affiliations with the German cultural nationalist movement, hence continuing the national theme of the previous chapter. It should be noted immediately, however, that Liszt's relationship to Germany cannot be discussed in the same manner as his relationship to Hungary. Hungarian nationalism – that is, the dominant cultural Magyar variety – was a far more unified, homogeneous phenomenon at the political and social levels. German nationalism was by comparison diffuse and fragmented. Many historians have, in fact, found the term "nationalism" inappropriate for *Vormärz* Germany, since there was not yet a program for the political unification of the states.[3] Although it is sometimes important to separate and recognize the independence of the cultural and political branches of the German national movement, I am not persuaded that the term "nationalism" ought to apply *only* to political objectives, and will therefore retain the term in this discussion of the *Vormärz* period. Because German nationalism was relatively decentralized, Liszt could not be appropriated for it with a single gesture, as had happened in Pest. He could become a part of German nationalism only by force of accumulation – giving a little bit for the nation in each of the locales he visited. The story of Liszt's involvement with German nationalism is more loosely structured, and thematically less unified, than the Hungarian parallel, and this is probably why it has gone unrecognized.

Leipzig and Dresden

Among all Germans, the person from Vienna probably spares his hands the least, and raises the slitted glove with which he, in idolization, applauds Liszt. In north Germany, as said earlier, it is otherwise.

Robert Schumann[4]

Liszt's visit to Dresden and Leipzig in March 1840 was his first encounter with northern German audiences. In terms of public and critical opposition, it was one of the worst episodes of his career. The source of the opposition was not Liszt's national identity per se. Yet Liszt's playing and personality appeared utterly foreign, incongruous with the customs and values of the Leipzig public, and this outsideness was in some cases

---

[3] Celia Applegate, "How German Is It? Nationalism and the Origins of Serious Music in Early Nineteenth-Century Germany," *19th Century Music* 21 (Spring 1998), 274–96.

[4] *Neue Zeitschrift für Musik* 12/26 (27 March 1840), 102–03 (R. Schumann).

figured in national terms. Liszt stepped into Leipzig with the French, cosmopolitan persona that had served him so well in Vienna and Prague,
and proceeded with his elite-oriented concert arrangements as usual.
He had not at all planned to make the adjustments necessary to succeed
with the Leipzig public, which was far more conservative, classically
minded, and uniformly bourgeois – more stereotypically German – than
his previous audiences.

Liszt approached Leipzig with great confidence. In the past, his public concerts in large cities had usually been prepared by at least some
private salon appearances in aristocratic or artistic society. These private events had offered him the opportunity to show off his brilliant
personality as well as his virtuosity. He thereby created a strong social
bond with the elites, and he could depend on this core of supporters to anchor the success of his public concerts. This was precisely
what he did in Dresden before moving on to Leipzig. But in Leipzig
he played his first concert the same day that he arrived (17 March),
and he had had no chance to measure the inclinations of the public.
Furthermore, there was no substantial aristocratic contingent in the
concert-going public that might have assured him a certain degree of
success.

The Leipzig public had already developed a bias against Liszt before
his first concert. They were turned off by his ticket policies, which they
felt showed no regard for Leipzig customs. First, his ticket prices were
extremely high, going far beyond what they were accustomed to paying
at the Gewandhaus, even for outstanding guest soloists.[5] Second, the
publisher who was handling his ticket sales refused to give complimentary tickets to the guest singers. This probably did not represent Liszt's
wishes, but the public believed he was responsible, and the assisting
artists withdrew from the concert in protest. Third, the first few rows of
the Gewandhaus were designated as *Sperrsitze*, special seats available
for an elevated price.[6] Liszt thus introduced a prestige hierarchy into a
hall whose seating design was intentionally anti-hierarchical.

This disregard for the customs of Leipzig's concert life provoked sharp
criticism in the local press, and the news spread quickly to several other

[5] For the first concert, pre-sale tickets were originally set at 2 Thaler, thus approximately
four times the price of the usual Gewandhaus concert (16 Neugroschen; 1 Thaler =
30 Neugroschen). The price was reduced to 1 Thaler pre-sale when it became clear that
the orchestra would be unable to participate. To offer a standard of comparison, we could
note that Clara Schumann's Gewandhaus concert of December 1841, which included
orchestra and vocal soloists, cost 20 Neugroschen. Liszt gave a concert the same month,
also with orchestra, that was nearly twice the cost: 1 Thaler, 8 Neugroschen.

[6] *Humorist*, 30 March 1840; this is a reprint of an article that had appeared in the *Dresdner
Wochenblatt*.

north German cities.[7] Liszt was accused of making his concerts into greedy speculative ventures. This was a misunderstanding of a considerable scale. Liszt's high ticket prices were not primarily motivated by a desire to accumulate money, but by a wish to give his concerts an elite social profile. The high prices, restrictions on complimentary tickets, and hierarchical seating arrangement gave his concerts an air of exclusivity that would lure the high elites into the relatively open social space of the public concert. Leipzig was the first city Liszt visited whose social structure, lacking a substantial nobility, could not support this strategy. The public was not as stratified socially as in other cities, where social leadership was in the hands of financial and noble elites. Failing to understand Liszt's miscalculation, the Leipzig critics evaluated the ticketing policies according to a bourgeois moral standard in which extensive financial gain was suspect. In his disregard for this moral standard, Liszt appeared to want to place himself outside of, or alienate himself from, the customs and values of the Leipzig public.

The bias Leipzigers had formed against Liszt did not prevent them from attending his first concert. They still had faith that his music making might be worth the price. Yet they did receive him coldly when he first appeared, and their faith was severely shaken by the first piece they heard him play: the Scherzo and Finale of Beethoven's sixth symphony. Applause for this piece was so weak that even Schumann, Liszt's major supporter in the press, could not avoid mentioning it in his report. The *Allgemeine musikalische Zeitung* reviewer was astonished that he had chosen the Beethoven as an opener: "The impression of this piece on the public was also not favorable, and it contributed mostly, in any case, to lessening somewhat their receptivity."[8] Both this writer and Schumann attributed the negative audience response to the impossibility of satisfactorily reproducing an orchestra or a symphony on the piano. They were either missing the point or generously concealing it, for Liszt had fully succeeded with his "Pastoral" transcription in Paris, Vienna, and Prague. The problem was not the medium, but the style. Liszt was importing into the Gewandhaus an idea of Beethoven vastly different from the one to which the Leipzig public was accustomed. It was a Beethoven heavily filtered through Liszt's cosmopolitan virtuoso identity and through his French romanticism. They could not be merely indifferent to this foreign presentation of Beethoven; they had to resist it. A particularly harsh critic attributed to him "a demonic desire

---

[7] A report that appeared in *Das Rheinland* noted that at least ten other newspapers had reported the ticketing scandal. See Lina Ramann, *Franz Liszt als Künstler und Mensch* (Leipzig, 1880–94), 3 vols., II: 65.

[8] *Allgemeine musikalische Zeitung* 42/13 (25 March 1840), cols. 261–66.

to dissolve, to tear to shreds this work of a divine procreativity [i.e., Beethoven], to mix up confusedly its tempos, to hunt dead the spirits living within it. That is Liszt's accomplishment."[9]

The remainder of this début concert consisted of non-classical repertory that audiences found easier to applaud. Yet the damage done by his "Pastoral" was severe. Among the pieces on the program, only the Beethoven had the potential to override the public bias against him. Instead it heavily reinforced the opposition, and the public managed to enact a "boycott" of the concert he had scheduled for the next day. According to one report, the second concert was cancelled because only fifty-four tickets had been sold.[10] This may well have been an exaggeration, but poor ticket sales were almost certainly the cause of the cancellation. Liszt canceled it under pretense of a sudden fever, but Schumann, who was with him daily, considered the fever a strategic fiction, a "politische Krankheit."[11]

While he was in bed, or in retreat, Liszt's company was composed exclusively of a few musicians. To Schumann, who was principal among them, Liszt complained about Leipzig's lack of elegantly dressed countesses and princesses.[12] It was perhaps dawning upon him that the lack of a socially active contingent of aristocratic women was partly responsible for his bad reception. As he prepared to make up his canceled concert, rescheduled for 24 March, he turned on his social skills and endeared himself to what there *was* of high society in Leipzig. Schumann wrote on 25 March: "The past few days there has been nothing but dinners and lunches, music and champagnes, dukes and beautiful

---

[9] *Zeitung für die elegante Welt*, 20 March 1840.

[10] *Dresdner Wochenblatt*, 25 March 1840.

[11] On 20 March, Schumann wrote to Clara Wieck in Berlin: "I quite believe that he is and was exhausted; it was in any case a political illness: I can't explain it all to you" (Berthold Litzmann, *Clara Schumann: ein Künstlerleben* [Leipzig, 1910], 3 vols., I: 414). Walker has challenged the view that Liszt's illness was feigned by citing a letter Liszt wrote to Marie d'Agoult, in which he explains that he had to cancel the concert because he was overcome with a fever at 3:00 that afternoon (Walker, *Franz Liszt*, I: 349). There is no reason to assume, as Walker does, that Liszt could only be telling the truth in this letter. Liszt had personal and professional motivations for reporting "selectively" to d'Agoult: their relationship was shaky and she was still managing his publicity in Paris. One internal detail of the letter casts some suspicion on the reality of his illness. He wrote that "The fever completely left me yesterday" – that is, the day after the canceled concert. Liszt rarely recovered from illnesses so quickly, and most tellingly, he stayed in bed for at least a couple of days longer. We cannot prove that Liszt was covering up the truth, but Schumann, who harbored no malice toward Liszt and strongly supported him during his stay, is a more reliable source for the interpretation of the canceled concert. The cancellation was probably caused by a combination of physical exhaustion and bad publicity, not a debilitating illness.

[12] Litzmann, *Clara Schumann*, I: 416. Letter from Schumann to Clara Wieck, dated 22 March.

women; in short, he has turned our entire life upside down."[13] Instead of adapting himself to the bourgeois mores of Leipzig, Liszt was making Leipzig adapt to him. This social strategy, along with a studied avoidance of Beethoven, and an exculpatory article published in the *Leipziger allgemeine Zeitung* the morning of the concert, helped him counter the opposition and make his second concert a relative success.[14] Yet the utility of his social brilliance was necessarily limited in Leipzig, and the entire public had not been converted. When Clara Wieck heard him six days later, she was struck by how unenthusiastic the audience was: "here in Leipzig people did not know just how great [*hoch*] Liszt is; the public was much too cold for this artist."[15] Her implicit comparison was the Viennese audiences, whose enthusiasm for Liszt she had witnessed in the spring of 1838. The journalistic opposition, furthermore, did not come to an end.[16]

The cosmopolitan and French elements of Liszt's personality were very much in evidence from the beginning of his Leipzig visit, and this contributed to the sense that he was an outsider. Schumann was in a better position than anyone to observe this, since he was constantly in Liszt's company. Already in their first days together in Leipzig, Schumann wrote, they had become "quite rude to each other, and I often have good reason, because Vienna has made him far too capricious and spoiled."[17] Their points of disagreement become clearer in a letter of four days later:

Liszt arrived here aristocratically spoiled and kept complaining about the lack of fancy dresses and countesses and princesses, so that I became cross and said to him that we too have our aristocracy, namely 150 book stores, 50 presses and 30 journals, and that he ought to take note of it. But he laughed, did not bother to respect the customs here, etc. and so he is now faring horribly in all journals etc.; then my concept of aristocracy may have dawned upon him, for he was never so kind as in the past two days, in which he has been torn to pieces.[18]

Schumann and Liszt were trying to reconcile two very different sets of values. Liszt, fully cosmopolitan and aristocratic in orientation, could

---

[13] Ibid., I: 419–20. The letter is dated 25 March.

[14] The article, written by Schumann, appeared in the *Leipziger allgemeine Zeitung*, 24 March 1840, and attributed responsibility for the ticketing mistakes (probably correctly) to the person handling the ticket sales. After the concert, Schumann noted with a touch of self-congratulation that "The slashers and smashers have been quieted down" (Litzmann, *Clara Schumann*, I: 420).

[15] Ibid, I: 420.

[16] An article in *Nordlicht* from 13 April 1840 began: "Liszt has left Leipzig, and it's a good thing . . ." Its author (signed "H.") even found the defense published in the *Leipziger allgemeine Zeitung* inappropriate.

[17] Litzmann, *Clara Schumann*, I: 413; Robert to Clara, 18 March 1840.

[18] Ibid., I: 416; Robert to Clara, 22 March 1840.

only see Leipzig in terms of lack because its social life was so sleepy, and he apparently treated it with some disdain.[19] Schumann tried to win him over to Leipzig by drawing his attention to one of the city's most bourgeois characteristics: the depth of its intellectual, reading culture. Schumann's pride in the *Bildung*-seeking, literary culture of Leipzig was surely shared by most of the residents. Any traces of French cosmopolitanism (which is implied by Schumann's references to Vienna) they might have perceived in Liszt's personality would thus have emphasized his outsider status in Leipzig, and perhaps even turned some people off. Clara Wieck found a "coquettish" side to his personality that she preferred to forget about,[20] and Schumann found "glitter, too much" in his performing style.[21] Both of these elements were, if not necessarily French, at least "other," foreign to the values of the Leipzig public.

In spite of the emphasis on Liszt's Frenchness and his outsideness with relation to Leipzig, Schumann took some steps to construct him as German in character. In a review of the first Dresden concert (16 March), he praised Liszt's musicianship highly, then turned attention to his personality:

In addition, Liszt is a substantial person in every respect! Each of his statements carries the stamp of genius, of cultivation [*Bildung*], of wide reading [*Belesenheit*], of deep thought [*Durchdenkens*]. It is most interesting to hear him discuss literature, music, and art, whether in the French language, which he speaks with the highest elegance, or in the German. This is proven by what he writes (in the *Revue musicale, Revue des deux mondes*).[22]

Liszt's Germanness is not thematized explicitly in this passage, but the high value placed on such traits as "Bildung," "Belesenheit," and especially "Durchdenken" is something quite new. Previous writers, when they described Liszt's personality, tended to focus on behavior: his social manner, his elite bearing, the wit of his conversational style, or the people who surrounded him. Schumann does not ignore Liszt's Parisian elegance, but it is mentioned in passing, relegated to a subsidiary clause. He zooms in on Liszt's language, and evaluates it as content rather than as behavior. Liszt is valued here primarily as an insightful reader, thinker, and writer – a man of letters. Schumann also filters out the social character of his own relationship to Liszt: he is an autonomous, "interested listener." Such disregard for Liszt as a social being, in favor of Liszt as

---

[19] Liszt preserved a certain disdain for Leipzig. His ultimate alienation from the Schumanns was caused by his near-derogatory use of the word "Leipzigerisch," and by his praise of the cosmopolitan Meyerbeer over the more "German" Mendelssohn. See Walker, *Franz Liszt*, II: 341.

[20] Litzmann, *Clara Schumann*, I: 421; diary entry of 31 March.

[21] Ibid., I: 413; Robert to Clara, 18 March 1840.

[22] *Leipziger allgemeine Zeitung* 68 (19 March 1840), 969 (R. Schumann).

an intellectual being, was in effect an effort to "defrancify" and germanize Liszt's personality. Schumann may well have been attempting to make Liszt more appealing to the Leipzig readership by emphasizing personal qualities (*Bildung, Belesenheit, Durchdenken*) they would more readily admire.

Schumann's authorship also helps us confirm the specifically germanizing impulse of the article. It was he who had countered Liszt's complaints about the lack of an aristocracy with the argument that Leipzig's many booksellers were an alternate "aristocracy." That is, Schumann felt the Leipzigers defined their eliteness with reference to their dedication to learning, rather than in terms of social behavior. The same values guided his presentation of Liszt's personality as that of a reader, writer, and thinker, and it was implicitly pushing Liszt toward the German pole of a German–French dichotomy, not to mention to the bourgeois pole of a bourgeois–aristocrat opposition. Schumann makes another germanizing gesture in his *Neue Zeitschrift* article on Liszt's concerts. Directly after a comparison of Liszt to Napoleon, he writes: "Liszt's resemblance to the late Ludwig Schuncke is also striking, and extends deeper into their art, so that as Liszt played I often thought I heard things from the past."[23] The mention of Schuncke comes almost as a recuperation of Liszt's Germanness, in case the Napoleon comparison brought in too many French overtones. And by emphasizing the specifically musical resemblance to Schuncke, Schumann helps compensate for the blunder of Liszt's rendition of the "Pastoral" symphony. If Liszt was not the perfect Beethoven player, at least his playing transmits a German spirit like that of Schuncke.

Liszt's first experience in northern Germany was, in summary, a clash of cultures. He stepped into the conservative, classically minded, bourgeois culture of Leipzig with the accustomed attitudes and habits of his French, cosmopolitan identity. For the first time he was not greeted with open arms by an aristocratic public that sought avidly to make him its own. He found, rather, a public stamped with distinctly bourgeois values. This public found it difficult to accept his cosmopolitan identity, traces of which they found in his playing, his personality and his ticketing policies. At the same time, in Schumann's writings we can see the beginnings of Liszt's construction as a figure exemplifying German culture. In our discussion of Frankfurt and Berlin, we will see more examples of Liszt's personal character being described in terms that are implicitly germanizing and defrancifying. The Berlin reception will furnish, furthermore, another case of Liszt seeming to reincarnate the spirit of a dead German figure.

---

[23] *Neue Zeitschrift für Musik* 12/30 (10 April 1840), 118–20 (R. Schumann).

Schumann's details, however, were in no way able to cancel out Liszt's obvious Frenchness and turn the tide of public opinion. He tried to convince Liszt to go on to Berlin from Leipzig, but Liszt, shaken up by the press scandal, declined and decided to head back to more familiar territory, Paris. Liszt left Leipzig with a troubling sense of defeat. Things were different however, when he next appeared in the city, in December 1841. His success led him to write to Marie d'Agoult: "My little Battle of Leipzig is more than won . . . There is no longer any opposition possible against me."[24] Later in the same letter he wrote a sentence that is very significant in showing his awareness of a growing relationship with the German national movement: "My popularity and, I would dare say, my little importance in Germany is crescendo-ing. At this point I don't even have anything more to fight against."[25] Liszt's significance had indeed developed since his first Leipzig visit, and continued to grow for some years. How had he turned the Leipzig public around? The answer lies not in Liszt alone, but in changes within Germany, particularly the sudden flowering of a national movement in the early 1840s. The historical circumstances behind this flowering are worthy of close attention, for they affected Liszt's career in direct ways.

German nationalism and xenophobia in the early 1840s

Liszt began his concertizing in Germany at a crucial moment in the history of the German national movement. Two events of the year 1840, the Rhine Crisis and the ascension of Friedrich Wilhelm IV to the Prussian throne, gave the movement great impetus. The Rhine Crisis was precipitated by a complicated shift in the balance of European power that occurred when Egypt rebelled against the Ottoman Empire (in 1839–40).[26] This shift worked to the disadvantage of the French. The French Prime Minister, Adolphe Thiers, grasped to recover strength by demanding the return of territories on the west bank of the Rhine that had been accorded to the German confederation in the settlement of 1815. In the weeks that followed there was a tense political standoff, during which an outbreak of war, supported by many people on both sides, was a very real possibility. Although France soon backed down and the event had no substantial political effect, the Rhine Crisis had a decisive impact on the course of cultural nationalism in Germany. It aroused very intense patriotic and anti-French emotions among the

---

[24] *Correspondance de Liszt et de Madame d'Agoult*, ed. Daniel Ollivier (Paris, 1933–35), 2 vols., I: 185.

[25] Ibid, II: 186.

[26] A summary of the Rhine Crisis is found in Cecilia Hopkins Porter, *The Rhine as Musical Metaphor* (Boston, 1996), 4, 38–48.

people of the Rhineland, and these emotions eventually spread to other parts of Germany. Whereas previously nationalism had been cultivated primarily among the educated and prosperous middle classes, it was now spreading to the population as a whole and becoming a mass movement. The Rhine crisis has even been called the origin of modern German nationalism.[27]

A central cultural medium in which these newly awakened patriotic and anti-French sentiments were expressed, and disseminated to other regions of Germany, was the Rhine song. The first and most influential of these songs written specifically in response to the Rhine Crisis was "Der deutsche Rhein," by a Bonn jurist named Niklaus Becker. Each stanza of the poem begins with the phrase "They shall not have it, / The free German Rhine" ("Sie sollen ihn nicht haben / Den freien deutschen Rhein"). The poem was published in several Rhenish newspapers in September and October 1840, and its instant success led to at least a hundred different musical settings in the next few months alone.[28] Mendelssohn noted in November that the craze for Becker's song had reached Leipzig and Berlin.[29] Becker's song became so important as a symbol of pan-German nationalism that it was dubbed the "Colognaise," as a counterweight to France's "Marseillaise."

Becker's song established an entire genre of poetry and music centered on the Rhine as a national symbol, inspiring a particularly voluminous wave of imitations in the year 1840. The Rhine had long been idealized and romanticized in German poetry, but the new poems were more decisively nationalist in tone. More importantly for the sake of Liszt's involvement with German nationalism, the songs were virulently anti-French, demonizing the alien other in the manner too familiar from later nationalisms. One of the most successful examples of the genre, Max von Schneckenburger's "Die Wacht am Rhein," takes directly from Becker a defiant attitude toward the French:

> So long as a droplet of blood still glows,
> And a fist still draws the sword,
> And an arm still cocks the rifle,
> No Frenchman shall set foot on thy shores.
> Dear fatherland, have no fear,
> The watch on the Rhine stands fast and true.[30]

---

[27] Adolf Klein, *Köln im 19. Jahrhundert* (Cologne, 1992), 211: "Die Folgen der Rheinkrise waren jedoch in Deutschland tief daurend. Damals begann hier der moderne Nationalismus."

[28] Horst Johannes Tümmers, *Der Rhein: ein europäischer Fluss und seine Geschichte* (Munich, 1994), 222ff.

[29] See the letter cited in Hopkins Porter, *The Rhine as Musical Metaphor*, 49–50.

[30] Ibid., 54.

165

Ernst Moritz Arndt closed a poem in praise of Becker's song with the following words:

> Now roar joyfully, Rhine:
> Never shall a Frenchman
> Be watchman over my treasure!
> On and on may that resound.[31]

In both of these examples the anti-French phrase appears at the climax of the poem, thus concentrating the poem's import in its most xenophobic moment. Georg Herwegh, in his popular "Rheinweinlied," highlighted the anti-French sentiment by employing a Becker-like recurring phrase: "The Rhine shall remain German" ("Der Rhein soll deutsch verbleiben").

The wave of nationalist feeling that followed the Rhine Crisis was complemented by the ascension of Friedrich Wilhelm IV to the Prussian throne in October 1840. His apparent commitment to reforming the outdated monarchical style of his predecessor, and his promises to address more directly the needs of the German people, inspired euphoria and optimism among German liberals. Shortly after his coronation, the journal *Europa* commented:

The new king of Prussia has much going for him in the public opinion; people are placing their hopes in him; in all parts of Germany they expect from him powerful reforms and help for pressing difficulties; the children of our time, whose bywords are justice and humanity, say of him: he is one among us, he strives forward.[32]

Part of Friedrich Wilhelm IV's popularity stemmed from his devotion to German nationalism. At Berlin University he gave posts to Jacob Grimm, the leading German folklorist, and to E. M. Arndt, the leading patriotic poet of the "Wars of Liberation" generation. In 1846 he arranged for the publication of the complete works of Frederick the Great, around whom a nationally inflected cult had been initiated in Prussia in the 1830s.[33] Most tellingly, he sent a gift of 1,000 Thalers to Niklaus Becker

---

[31] Ibid.

[32] *Europa* (1840/4), 120. Friedrich Wilhelm IV preserved this reputation for some time. Ludwig Jagemann, in a portrait of Berlin, wrote that "Just as Fri. Wil. IV intervenes powerfully in greater matters, so he is in the course of constructing a more up-to-date arrangement in Berlin itself . . . He is a monarch who understands his time. Therein lies his distinction" (*Deutsche Städte und Deutsche Männer* [Leipzig, 1846], 2 vols., II: 16–17).

[33] Michael Hughes, *Nationalism and Society: Germany 1800–1945* (New York, 1988), 81. From 1832 to 1834, J. D. E. Preuss published a nine-volume biography of Frederick the Great that, in Hughes' words, "re-established Frederick as an all-German hero figure." The cult of Friedrich was a German counterpart to the French cult of Napoleon, which had been revived forcefully after the revolution of 1830.

in appreciation of "Der deutsche Rhein," and had the song performed at his court.[34]

The synergistic effect of the Rhine Crisis and the rise of Friedrich Wilhelm IV brought the Rhineland into a newly intimate relationship with Prussia. In the years after 1815, the Rhineland had enjoyed a degree of autonomy from Prussia, even though it officially lay within Prussian jurisdiction. Economically and politically it was the most liberal and developed part of the confederation, largely because it still followed the Napoleonic Code. Its inhabitants had no reason to resent the French, from whom their prosperity had been derived. However, faced with the threat of repossession by France, the Rhineland shifted political alignments, turning against France and fostering solidarity with Prussia.[35] Friedrich Wilhelm IV helped cement this alliance by promoting the reconstruction of the Cologne cathedral, which was a central symbol of the German national movement. At the Cologne *Dombaufest* of September 1842, an elaborate celebration of the reconstruction, he made a speech describing the cathedral as the "door to a new, great and good era for Germany."[36]

The years 1840 to 1842, in sum, dramatically changed the face of the German national movement. The Rhine Crisis brought together regions of the confederation that previously were relatively independent, supporting a vision of a larger, trans-regional Germany that contrasted with earlier, more localized forms of patriotism. It also gave rise to a body of Rhine songs that provided cultural material for the propagation of nationalist sentiment. In Friedich Wilhelm IV, liberal nationalists within Prussia had a ruler who was apparently sympathetic to their cause, and the effectiveness of his reforms seemed to materialize in the completion of the Cologne cathedral. Nationalism of the pan-German variety was on an upswing. Its supporters were optimistic and inspired.

This environment is not so much background as *foreground* to Liszt's German concert activities. Liszt was friendly with the Prussian king, he played concerts for the reconstruction of the Cologne cathedral, and he set two anti-French Rhine-song texts. On two occasions he even ran into the Rhine Crisis head on. As he was travelling through Belgium toward Germany in October 1840, he was unexpectedly stopped at Dinant because the next town, Namur, was closing its gates at night for security purposes.[37] And as he planned his concert in Cologne in August 1841, the archbishop (one of the leaders of the *Dombauverein*)

---

[34] Klein, *Köln im 19. Jahrhundert*, 212; Hopkins Porter, *The Rhine as Musical Metaphor*, 50.

[35] Tümmers, *Der Rhein*, 224. See also Hughes, *Nationalism and Society*, 23, 75, 81–82.

[36] Hughes, *Nationalism and Society*, 81.

[37] "Liszt à Dinant," *Revue et gazette musicale* 7/64 (15 November 1840), 548–49. In this article the Rhine Crisis is referred to as "la question de l'Orient." Liszt took advantage of the delay and gave a performance. The article concludes: "And so the annoying

asked him politely if he would refrain from wearing the sabre of honor: such a nationally charged concert had to be kept free of militant symbols.[38]

Cologne

Liszt had concertized in the Rhineland (Mainz, Ems, Wiesbaden, Frankfurt) in the weeks that followed the Rhine crisis of 1840, but he did not get involved in any way with the French–German tensions. These earlier concerts had little potential to become significant for the German national cause, for several reasons. The summer and fall were the "off season" for musical and social events, and high political tensions probably reduced the attendance at public entertainments. As a result, at least two of the Rhine locales he visited showed poor turnouts for his concerts. In compensation, he lured to his concerts the high, cosmopolitan aristocracy and royalty that had gathered at the baths of Baden-Baden and Ems for the summer, with whom he had recently been consorting. The audience at his Frankfurt concert of 7 August was very elite: "the majority were foreigners, among them several high powers [*Herrschaften*]."[39] In Mainz, similarly, he gave a concert for a small audience of elites drawn from various towns; indeed the concert was delayed because some of the most distinguished guests (probably a prince and his lackeys) had not yet arrived.[40] Liszt's cosmopolitan persona and public were still very strong, making it impossible to bring him into connection with the wave of national sentiment that was sweeping through the Rhineland.

There was no sense that Liszt would become significant for Germany when he was playing there in 1840. The situation was very different, however, when he returned there in the fall of 1841, the moment that properly marks the beginning of his ties to the national movement. The Rhine Crisis was over and the national movement was brimming with energy, especially in the Rhineland. Around 15 August the Cologne *Liederkreis* paid Liszt a surprise visit at his island retreat, Nonnenswerth. After treating him to a musical serenade, doubtlessly including some Rhine songs, they requested that he give a concert for the sake of the

question of the Orient gave an immense, unexpected pleasure to the city of Dinant, as the cataclysm of universal war threatens." This writer was not exaggerating: two days before the article was published, Thiers had given a speech in parliament calling for war to be declared (Hopkins Porter, *The Rhine as Musical Metaphor*, 40).

[38] *Correspondance de Liszt et de Madame d'Agoult*, II: 178. Liszt's reply was: "For my performances as for your offices, the sabre is not at all necessary."
[39] *Frankfurter Konversationsblatt* 250 (9 August 1840), 1001.
[40] Michael Saffle, *Liszt in Germany, 1840–1845* (Stuyvesant, NY, 1994), 102.

reconstruction of the cathedral.[41] Liszt accepted without hesitation and gave the concert on 23 August. This warm-hearted gesture of charity for one of Germany's most important cultural and national symbols was received with immense enthusiasm. Two days before the concert, he was picked up by a group of civic officials together with a singing society (the *Liederkreis*), and until the concert he was feted to an extent unrivalled even by the Pest episode, as they escorted him to Cologne.[42] The *Liederkreis* was singing national songs the entire way, and with hundreds of singers they performed a newly composed cantata based on his melodies.[43] At an afternoon banquet Liszt toasted the *Liederkreis*, and tapped into their national sentiments by remarking "that this institution was entirely national and had no equivalent in England, France, nor even in Italy."[44] As the ship approached Cologne, Liszt was greeted by a fireworks display whose highlight was a set of colored glasses reading "Vive Liszt," and a massive crowd accompanied his carriage to the hotel.[45]

These celebrations were covered more widely than the Cologne concert itself. Almost overnight, Liszt was a hero in the Rhineland. A Rhenish reporter wrote that his celebration in Cologne "proves to Liszt that he understood how to acquire a new country [*patrie*] among us, where the most lively sympathies, the most sincere enthusiasms are aroused in his name."[46] Riding the wave of this success, he continued to concertize in the region through September and October. At the end of October he was brought to Bonn for an elaborate birthday celebration that had been prepared in his honor. The celebration took on a nationalist tone when a new poem, composed for the occasion, was sung to the melody of a well-known *Rheinweinlied*.[47] Liszt was being honored partly for his dedication to the Beethoven monument in Bonn, but the nationalist fervor of the Rhineland was probably an even stronger factor.

The Cologne episode was a landmark in Liszt's reception. Never had he been received with such enthusiasm without the slightest preparation

---

[41] This event was recorded by Marie von Czettritz, who was also living at Nonnenswerth. See *Portrait of Liszt: by Himself and his Contemporaries*, ed. Adrian Williams (Oxford, 1990), 169.

[42] The *Journal des débats* of 1 September 1841 contains a full account of the events from its Cologne correspondent.

[43] The *Allgemeine musikalische Zeitung* 43 (1841), col. 822, reported that 380 singers participated. This number must be exaggerated. It is probably derived from the total membership of the *Kölner Liederkreis*, and the assumption that every member participated in the celebrations.

[44] Ibid.   [45] *Courrier musicale*, 9 September 1841.

[46] *Journal des débats*, 1 September 1841.

[47] Marion Lienig, *Bürgerliche Musikkultur in Bonn* (Bonn, 1995), 107. The melody was taken from "Bekränzt mit Laub," by M. Claudius and J. André. The birthday celebration took place on 31 October.

in the press or in private salons. Newly awakened nationalist sentiments were sufficient to mobilize the entire Cologne public around him. Such unreserved, total veneration was something he had never achieved, and would never achieve, in France. In a letter to Cristina Belgiojoso from October 1841, he wrote that, although he was becoming weary of his concert career, he had found some consolation in "the warm and cordial sympathy that I found on the Rhine this autumn."[48] Liszt's evident satisfaction with what had happened in Cologne motivated him to foster his relationship with the German national movement, especially its Prussian–Rhenish branch, as I will show below. Yet the relationship was already being created independently of his efforts. The first German-language biography of Liszt, by J. W. Christern, appeared shortly after the Cologne episode, and it described Cologne as the climax of his virtuoso successes.[49] The book was evidently written and published in haste. Christern was anxious to make Liszt's charity for the Cologne cathedral better known to German readers. More importantly, he wanted to invest special significance in Liszt's relationship to Germany. He claimed, for example, that Liszt had given concerts in several southern German capitals during his Italian period.[50] This could only have been a conscious fabrication, a piece of propaganda that would make the Cologne episode seem more historical, more inevitable, less isolated or arbitrary.[51] The Leipzig/Dresden episode was obviously not suited to this purpose, and Christern silently passed over it.

The story of Liszt's charity for the cathedral does not end with the Cologne concert. Less than six months later he was in Berlin and he gave another charity concert for the cathedral (9 January 1842). By making this gesture in the Prussian capital, and probably in the presence of Friedrich Wilhelm IV, Liszt consolidated his relationship to the Prussia-led national movement.[52] Berlin's chief music critic, Ludwig Rellstab, launched into an unusually rhapsodic flight in praise of Liszt's dedication, proclaiming that "He has helped build the national masterwork!"[53]

---

[48] *Autour de Madame d'Agoult et de Liszt*, ed. D. Ollivier (Paris, 1941), 183.

[49] J. W. Christern, *Franz Liszt: nach seinem Leben und Wirken* (Leipzig/Hamburg, 1841), 37.

[50] Ibid., 32.

[51] Liszt gave concerts in Munich, Stuttgart, and Augsburg as he and his father traveled from Vienna to Paris in 1823. Christern was evidently transposing these facts to a later part of his career.

[52] The king first heard Liszt at his 5 January concert (*Spenersche Zeitung*, 18 January 1842). It is possible that he remained in the city for some days, and that Liszt intentionally planned the concert to coincide with his presence. As noted earlier, the king was closely associated with the reconstruction of the cathedral, and it is difficult to imagine that he would not have attended this concert.

[53] Ludwig Rellstab, *Franz Liszt: Beurtheilungen-Berichte-Lebensskizze* (Berlin, 1842), 16–17. This book collects all the articles Rellstab published in the *Vossische Zeitung* relevant to Liszt's visit.

The news soon reached other parts of Prussia. A Breslau report praised Liszt for dedicating his art "to the greatest undertaking of our time, the completion of the most exalted monument of German art and divine humility [*Gott-Ergebenheit*], the Cologne Cathedral."[54] Liszt also played a concert at the *Dombaufest* of September 1842, which was a kind of apotheosis of the cathedral as a national symbol. Friedrich Wilhelm IV made himself the symbolic center of the entire festival, leading one historian to describe it as "an orchestrated theatrical demonstration of the Christian–monarchical principle combined with Prussian–German national enthusiasm."[55] The king and queen were at Liszt's concert, and in keeping with the royalist tone of the events he opened with his "God Save the Queen" fantasy. Liszt's cumulative activities for the cathedral made him into a hero of the national movement. As he was touring Prussia in early 1843, a journalist proclaimed that, in the distant future, "The Cologne Cathedral will bear the insignia: 'Liszt helped build Germany's fame and honor.'"[56]

Frankfurt

Liszt's first concert for the Cologne cathedral, we have seen, was the beginning of his relationship to German nationalism, specifically the Prussian–Rhenish wing of the movement. And he fostered this relationship over the next two years by giving further concerts for the cathedral, cultivating his friendship with the Prussian king, and giving many concerts in other Prussian cities. Liszt, however, did much more in the fall of 1841 to develop his relationship to the national movement. Just one month after the Cologne concert, he gave a charity concert (25 September) for the Mozart Foundation in Frankfurt.[57] After the concert, the *Frankfurter Konversationsblatt* published a lengthy essay about the nationalistic goals of the foundation, and claimed that Liszt's concert would contribute immensely to the achievement of those goals. The essay articulates a thoroughgoing pan-German national agenda centered on language and culture:

[The Mozart Foundation] has the advantage, in comparison to all other German foundations, that it is essentially national, that it extends its effect not only over all of Germany, but also over the peoples [*Volksstämme*] torn away from their fatherland by cruel fate, and whose German nationality has already been heinously taken into control by a reprehensible politics. But this is not the only

---

[54] *Allgemeine priviligirte schlesische Zeitung* 38 (7 February 1842), 156.
[55] Hughes, *Nationalism and Society*, 81.
[56] *Frankfurter patriotisches Wochenblatt*, 18 February 1843.
[57] Liszt gave a second concert for the benefit of the Mozart Foundation on 15 November 1842.

national side of the living spirit that lives in the statutes of the Mozart-Stiftung. The fundamental idea [*Grundgedanke*] is also purely national [*rein national*], for its goal is to make it known to the fatherland that it is the chosen home of the most exalted music and the greatest composers, not just in the past, but also in the coming centuries.[58]

This nationalism does not bear the same imprint as the Prussian nationalism of Friedrich Wilhelm IV. It aspires to German unity in the more abstract realm of the *Geist*, whereas the Prussian king imagined the nation in concrete, political terms – a nation obedient to a paternalistic monarch and defined against the French.

The author of this essay felt that Liszt's concert was a major step toward the fulfillment of the Mozart Foundation's national mission. His explanation is worth quoting at length:

the concert . . . signifies a new phase in the history of this organization, which is unique in Germany. The veneration which an artist known and admired throughout Europe has brought to the efforts of the *Liederkranz* will soon have the effect of raising the undertaking to its national significance . . . The more we become convinced of the beauty of the idea the Mozart Foundation is based on, the more we lament the unhealthy provincial spirit, the insane jealousy between the different German states and cities, so that the foundation has not yet received general recognition and support from the German people. Germany has been compared with an eagle whose feathers are the various German states. This is certainly a pretty picture, but its truth disappears when one considers that every undertaking that reaches out over the entire fatherland breaks down into foolish splintering, so that the collective spirit which has awakened in the better part of the people breaks as if over a rock.

This lack of spiritual unity, which can exist quite well without political unity, is the reason the Mozart Foundation is, unbelievably, sometimes seen as a Frankfurt foundation and is for this reason not supported. For this reason the concert given by Liszt is an extraordinary step forward and perhaps the most significant since its founding. Praise and grateful recognition are due to this great master from a distant country, above all from the musical authorities for having passed his name on to members of the foundation.[59]

---

[58] *Frankfurter Konversationsblatt* 277 (7 October 1841), 1106–07.

[59] Ibid. Celia Applegate, building on a recent trend in German historiography, has argued that German nationalism in the early nineteenth century was not as concerned with state-building as some musicological studies have implied. She advocates the view that at this historical juncture, the German nation was conceived as a cultural and linguistic milieu, rather than a political order (see "How German Is It?"). The *Frankfurter Konversationsblatt* article confirms her argument to some degree; its author considers "spiritual unity" a fully legitimate goal of the Mozart Foundation, even "without political unity." At the end of the article, however, he views "spiritual unity" as a precondition for the establishment of a state in the distant future: "We have no capital city and Friedrich Rückert's ideal of one . . . will probably not be realized in this century; but because of this lack, Germany, and preferably all men who believe in a great future, should work

Liszt's international fame and high public visibility, in short, contain within themselves the power to remove the main obstacle to Germany's spiritual unity: regionalism. He is useful to the national cause precisely because he is cosmopolitan, publicizing the institutions of German cultural nationalism to all of Europe. This strategy for relating Liszt to the national cause – in which his autonomy from Germany is respected or even exaggerated ("the great master from a *distant* country") – is exceptional in his German reception. Most German writers preferred, as the Hungarians had, the strategy of tying him to the nation with some kind of spiritual bond. Such writers cited his personal dedication to the nation (in the case of the Cologne cathedral), or constructed his personality and performing style as essentially German in character. This second strategy, with its focus on Liszt's personality and emotions, had a much greater potential to mobilize national enthusiasm in concert audiences. It was the style of romantic nationalism. The Mozart Foundation's strategy was comparatively unromantic, rooted in enlightenment liberal ideals.

Already during this visit to Frankfurt, Liszt's social networks were beginning to change in a way specific to Germany's social conditions. In the major cities he had previously visited – Vienna, Milan, Paris, Prague, Pest, London, Dresden – his concerts emerged out of private salon appearances in the homes of aristocrats and other elites. At his public concerts this was symbolized by the *cercle de distinction*, a small number of seats placed around the piano occupied by elite women. At the intervals Liszt typically conversed with these women, transforming the concert platform into a kind of salon-on-stage. His charity concerts in Cologne and Frankfurt, in contrast, were both engineered by and symbolically led by the local singing societies (the *Liederkreis* and *Liederkranz*, respectively). These societies, more generally known as *Männergesangvereine*, were composed exclusively of men, and their members came mostly from various levels of the bourgeoisie, with the petty bourgeoisie in a slightly higher proportion than the other levels.[60] They harbored a decidedly nationalist orientation. At meetings they sang patriotic songs or (after 1840) Rhine songs written in a quasi-*volkstümlich* style.[61] This was the social milieu in which Liszt was circulating in Cologne, Frankfurt, and at his birthday celebration in Bonn. It was radically different from the elite milieu that he was accustomed to,

---

toward making the spiritual ties that bind us together ever stronger, more varied, and more indivisible, by means of personal influence, word, and book."

[60] Dieter Düding, *Organisierter gesellschaftlicher Nationalismus in Deutschland (1808–1847)* (Munich, 1984), 253–56.

[61] On the *volkstümlich* musical style, see Hopkins Porter, *The Rhine as Musical Metaphor*, 124–68.

but he embraced it and was embraced by it. Liszt was quickly learning a social style that would be crucial to his reception in Germany.

Liszt's visit to Frankfurt brought him most decisively into this male, bourgeois social milieu. Most of the credit can be given to Wilhelm Speyer, a Frankfurt businessman who had been one of the most important members of the city's musical life since the 1830s. He was the head of the Mozart Foundation and was involved with the *Liederkranz*. He also had a reputation as a composer of simple, popular songs and vocal quartets of the type sung by singing societies.[62] Speyer was Liszt's main contact in Frankfurt, and he tried to get Liszt involved in the German bourgeois institutions. He encouraged Liszt to compose vocal quartets, and when Liszt eventually did publish his *Vierstimmige Männergesänge* (1843), he dedicated one of them to Speyer. Speyer also convinced Liszt to give the charity concert for the Mozart Foundation, and probably wrote the *Frankfurter Konversationsblatt* article that explained its national purpose.

The most interesting way in which Speyer influenced Liszt was to convince him to join the freemasonry. On 10 September, Liszt formally requested to join the Frankfurt lodge "Zur Einigkeit" (of which Speyer had long been a member), and Speyer served as one of his sponsors. This was the beginning of a close association with freemason organizations. Five months later, when he was in Berlin, he was admitted to the "Eintracht" lodge and immediately promoted to its third level. In 1843 he joined a lodge in Iserlohn, and in 1844–45 he developed further connections in Zurich and Bordeaux.[63] The freemasons were neither nationalistic nor particularly German, but the social milieu of the freemason meetings had much in common with those of the singing societies: they were all male, they suspended all distinctions of social class, and they carried out rituals for cultivating intimate, brotherly feeling. Speyer, then, was bringing Liszt into contact with a sphere of social activity utterly different from the cosmopolitan, aristocratic circles to which he was accustomed. Liszt's entry into the Frankfurt freemasonry suggests that he was now ready to become a different kind of social being in order to bond himself with Germany.

When Liszt returned to Frankfurt in October 1843, he had effected a spectacular transformation of his social manner. With chameleonic brilliance he shed the elegant manners he had learned in France and among the European aristocracy, presenting himself instead in the guise of German *Herzlichkeit*. This major turnaround was observed, publicized,

---

[62] See Edward Speyer, *Wilhelm Speyer der Liederkomponist, 1790–1878* (Munich, 1925).

[63] Philippe Autexier, "The Masonic Thread in Liszt," *Journal of the American Liszt Society* 22 (1987), 3–18.

and perhaps exaggerated by Carl Gollmick in a lengthy article that appeared in the *Frankfurter Konversationsblatt*.[64] The article reports on a soirée at the home of Speyer, attended only by the host and his family, Gollmick, the singer Pischek, and Liszt. That such a small, private soirée should have been allotted so much space in the press is entirely exceptional. Its public interest lay exclusively in the fact that Liszt was showing himself to be German in character. Gollmick had developed his first impressions of Liszt in 1840, but the Liszt he met at Speyer's house was remarkably different:

My previous impression that Liszt was only a calculating diplomat soon disappeared. In fact I found in his behavior that ever-attractive openness [*Freimüthigkeit*] and a chivalrousness in his being that surprised me . . . I admired his flow of speech [*Redestrom*], in which he intermingles things old and new, things important and trivial. Yet his conversation is clear, for one sees many healthy ideas, like bright stones on the ground. And he has become altogether calmer, for he no longer embodies the Babylonian confusion of tongues as he did before.[65]

The image of the "calculating diplomat" is the surest indication that Gollmick previously considered Liszt's social persona cosmopolitan and artificial. The lively, animated conversational style of the earlier Liszt, incubated in the Parisian salons, was gone. His speech was no longer an extroverted kind of behavior, but a way of communicating clear, "healthy ideas." Gollmick also admired Liszt for the way he fostered intimate relations with the other people at the soirée, implicitly contrasting it with the more formal relationships at elite social events. After performing a Speyer vocal quartet with the other men present, Liszt sprang from his seat, "took the composer and singer by the head and smothered both with kisses."[66] He even expressed the view that the soirée was a better environment for the exercise of his art than the concert hall or the salon: "[He said that] when his inspiration can flow freely in all directions, and is understood by a few capable minds, then he soars in his element." The French–German opposition along which much of Gollmick's portrait is structured becomes explicit later in the article: "The tempo of his life is strepitoso . . . but he still has enough German sensibility remaining to rein in and moderate French exaggeration."[67] Finally, Gollmick identifies this change of sensibility in his performing style:

---

[64] *Frankfurter Konversationsblatt*, 4 and 5 November 1843.   [65] Ibid.   [66] Ibid.

[67] Ibid. In this passage Gollmick is paraphrasing comments that Liszt made over the course of the evening, suggesting that Liszt himself may have thought of his sensibility in national terms.

In the past I believe I remarked that Liszt, when seated at the piano, was affected with his mimicry. In fact it is not so. It is part of his being that his features speak while he is playing, like a person who is thinking vivaciously or reading an interesting book.[68]

Liszt's facial expressions, previously interpreted as French, refined affectation, are reinterpreted here as marks of a contemplative, bookish sensibility that is implicitly coded German. The face has remained the same, but its symbolic value has mutated.

Gollmick's article, particularly the latter point, represents a deliberate construction of Liszt as a person of German sensibility. He presents the Liszt he met at Speyer's house as the true, unadulterated Liszt. He does not allow for the social flexibility that enabled Liszt, for example, to reclaim his ties to the aristocracy when he returned to Paris in 1844, or to Vienna in 1846. At the same time, it is important to avoid a radical nominalist interpretation, according to which Gollmick's article tells us nothing about Liszt, but merely reflects the author's priorities. For in the early 1840s Liszt was actively adapting his persona to suit the different social situations he was encountering in Germany. In Leipzig, as described above, he had found it difficult to adapt his cosmopolitan socializing habits to the city's very different social complexion. Three years later, however, he was able to make himself the leading light of an intimate gathering in the bourgeois home of Speyer. Liszt had not lost his cosmopolitanism or his French qualities; he could reassume them at will. But he had developed an alternative social persona that facilitated his reception in German, bourgeois, male-centered contexts.

Liszt's own participation in his germanization is illustrated by another detail of the Speyer soirée. Inspired by the singing of Speyer's folkish vocal quartet, he jumped to the piano and offered a musical parade of *Volkstümlichkeit* and nationalism:

He entertained us with Polkas, Mazurkas, and Hungarian dances in the most piquant chromatic embellishments, and on top of that cheered out the celebratory passages in their national songs; then he jumped up and imitated with his stamping some Hungarian step-dances with all the high spirits of an opium-induced state of mind.[69]

It is probably not coincidental that Liszt was playing songs from Hungary, Poland, and Bohemia, Europe's most heated nationalistic centers. He did not need to play specifically German folkish music to raise the national sentiments of Speyer, Gollmick, and Pischek. The celebration of folkishness was itself enough to mark a German and nationally minded

---

[68] Ibid. On Liszt's "affected mimickry," see Gollmick's article in the *Frankfurter Konversationsblatt*, 16 and 17 August 1840.

[69] Ibid.

sensibility, as opposed to its cosmopolitan, implicitly French counter-part. A few weeks after the Speyer soirée, Liszt was invited to a soirée at the home of Karl von Leonhard in Heidelberg, where his behavior was similar. According to Leonhard, Liszt was in high spirits, breaking out spontaneously into song and happily playing music to which the guests could dance.[70]

J. W. Christern discussed Liszt's personality and behavior at some length to support the overall germanizing purpose of his 1841 biography. He claimed that "There is nothing obstinate or bizarre in his behavior," evidently a filtering-out of Liszt's well-established reputation for having adopted the eccentricities of the French romantics.[71] His image of Liszt's speech is even more surprising:

Liszt usually speaks quickly, shortly, abruptly; he often gets tangled up in his speech, the words fail him, his mind is too lively, or the picture too fiery, to be able to find a calm expression; in these pauses he looks determined and serious, the forehead contracting as if about to turn dark and angry; but he smiles as soon as someone decides to help him with some words for his thoughts, and says "Yes, yes!" as he quickly nods his head.[72]

Christern probably formed this impression from listening to Liszt con-verse in German, in which he had lost his fluency and eloquence. When he spoke French, by all accounts, he was never short of words. On the contrary, Schumann said that Liszt spoke French "with the highest ele-gance," and there are many anecdotes demonstrating his sense for witty rejoinders.[73] By ignoring the linguistic problem, Christern can claim that Liszt's pauses are in his nature, part of his character. The result is an image of Liszt in anguished contemplation of difficult ideas, a very strong contrast with the clever, debonair conversationalist observed in other contexts. Christern, furthermore, emphasized Liszt's lack of the aloofness typical of famous men:

When he loses his preoccupations, he is completely free and easy and forgets all distinctions with which he has been deified. One need only give a slight indication that one is in the mood to hear him play for the dance, and he goes ahead without further ado.[74]

Christern's portrayal of Liszt as a person of unaffected manners, intel-lectual engagement, and a cheerful, warm-hearted social presence has much in common with Gollmick's portrait. Both writers downplayed

---

[70] K. C. von Leonhard, *Aus unserer Zeit in meinem Leben* (Stuttgart, 1854/56), 2 vols., II: 261. Leonhard insisted that he wanted Liszt as a social guest, not as musical entertainment.
[71] Christern, *Franz Liszt*, 41.   [72] Ibid.
[73] See, for example, *The Autobiography of Charles Hallé*, ed. Michael Kennedy (London, 1972), 106.
[74] Christern, *Franz Liszt*, 42.

aspects of his persona that might be coded French, in an effort to show how appealing Liszt could be to their German readers.

Liszt did one more thing to strengthen the ties he was developing to German nationalism. Having been drenched in the sounds of male singing societies, he wrote two compositions for four-part men's choir, both of them based on nationalistic texts. One of the texts was the most famous patriotic song of the post-1815 period, Ernst Moritz Arndt's "Das deutsche Vaterland." Written in 1813, when German nationalism was largely anti-Napoleonic, it includes a strong dose of anti-French senti-ment. Its popularity was renewed in the wake of the Rhine crisis, and was often performed in a setting by Gustav Reichardt.[75] Liszt organized the music using the standard "Rhine song" technique of a recurring phrase, so that each strophe ends with the refrain: "Das ganze Deutschland soll es seyn." The second text Liszt set was Herwegh's *Rheinweinlied*, a text so popular that it was set by at least fifteen other composers. Its recurring phrase, "The Rhine shall remain German" ("Der Rhein soll deutsch verbleiben"), was typical of the anti-French tone of the Rhine songs.

Liszt began including these patriotic settings in his concerts at Jena, Leipzig, and Dresden in December 1841.[76] It is possible that he was using the songs to win over the Leipzig public that had resisted him on his pre-vious visit. They were certainly the ideal vehicle through which to show that he was more than a French cosmopolite, and that he understood the tastes and sentiments of Leipzig's bourgeois audiences. Yet there is another, more likely strategic purpose for the Rhine songs: preparation for his postponed visit to Berlin. When the Schumanns had tried to get him to visit Berlin in the spring of 1840, he declined because he con-sidered the city "too significant," and felt that he would have to give more concerts there than he was able to within his time constraints.[77] Clearly he had already thought about a strategy for Berlin. His contin-uing preoccupation with Berlin is evident in a letter to d'Agoult from November 1840, after a successful concert series in Hamburg. He con-sidered success in Hamburg no great achievement, and felt that "Berlin

---

[75] Hopkins Porter, *The Rhine as Musical Metaphor*, 29.

[76] Liszt gave a performance of his setting of "Das deutsche Vaterland" on 1 November 1841, the day after his birthday celebration there. It was evidently a piano arrangement. This is another piece of evidence suggesting that he was brought to Bonn to recognize his nationalist gestures, in addition to his support for the Beethoven monument.

[77] Litzmann, *Clara Schumann*, I: 418. During his visit to Halle, which immediately preceded the Berlin episode, Liszt was treated to a performance of his "Rheinweinlied" setting by the university students. In his speech of thanks, Liszt promised them that "he would bring back two new song settings when he returned from Berlin, which would sound more beautiful than this one" (*Europa* [1842], 219–20). This is strong evidence that he was aiming his patriotic songs at his activities in Berlin.

has an importance of a completely different kind."[78] Liszt's sense of Berlin as a city of special significance may sound prescient, given his actual reception there in 1842, but his real concern was Berlin's tough-minded music critic Ludwig Rellstab, who was a harsh critic of virtuoso pianists and had a bias against Liszt even before hearing him.[79] Rellstab was especially frightening because he had an effective monopoly on music criticism in the city, and his writings were popular. The affiliations with German nationalism that he had developed in the fall of 1841 provided the leverage from which Liszt could reasonably launch a successful concert series in Berlin, the center of the Prussian nationalist renaissance of the early 1840s. Armed with his newly composed Rhine songs, and about to venture Berlin, Liszt had every reason to write the words already quoted above: "My popularity and, I would dare say, my little importance in Germany is crescendo-ing. At this point I don't even have anything more to fight against."[80]

Berlin

Liszt started playing the music of Bach, Handel, and Scarlatti in public for the first time during his visit to Berlin, and he hardly ever touched such repertory thereafter. Previous to his Berlin visit, the oldest music in his concert repertory was by Beethoven.[81] At his first concert (27 December) he boldly programmed Bach's lengthy *Chromatic Fantasy and Fugue*, and each of his next four benefits included a different "baroque" piece: a Handel fugue and variations, two Bach fugues, and Scarlatti's "Cat's fugue" (most of them in minor keys). This uncommonly systematic programming practice, together with the novelty of the repertory, suggests that Liszt was trying to make a deliberate statement with his baroque pieces. He probably hoped that by showing a commitment to serious, learned music, especially Bach's, he might deflect criticism from Rellstab and the connoisseurs. This interpretation is supported by the fact that he dropped the baroque pieces later in the concert series (and indeed, for the rest of his career), when Rellstab had clearly been won over. Yet Liszt could have pleased the serious-minded critics with Beethoven

---

[78] *Correspondance de Liszt et de Madame d'Agoult*, II: 43.

[79] For Rellstab's views on virtuoso concerts, see "L'état actuel de la musique à Berlin," *Revue et gazette musicale*, 6 May 1838, and his review of Thalberg's etudes in *Iris im Gebiete der Tonkunst*, 20 December 1839. Rellstab admitted that he had harbored a bias against Liszt before he came to Berlin, simply because he was a virtuoso (Rellstab, *Franz Liszt*, 2).

[80] *Correspondance de Liszt et de Madame d'Agoult*, II: 186.

[81] There is one exception. On 23 March 1840, in Leipzig, he played Bach's concerto in D minor for three harpsichords, with Felix Mendelssohn and Ferdinand Hiller performing the other solo parts. This was obviously a tribute to Bach's association with Leipzig.

and Weber, as he always had. To explain why he turned specifically to baroque music in Berlin, we need to consider his special affiliation with the Prussian monarchy.

Because the musical canon has achieved a certain stability and homogeneity today, Liszt's baroque pieces are usually put under the umbrella of his classical repertory. In programming Handel, Bach, and Scarlatti, however, Liszt was trying to present his Berlin audiences with a distinctly *antiquated* sound that contrasted with the more recent serious music of Beethoven, Weber, and Mendelssohn. Every one of the six concerts for which he programmed "baroque" music included a fugue, together with a Bach prelude, a Bach fantasy, a Scarlatti sonata, or variations by Handel. The fugue was the indispensable element because it was the clearest marker of the music's antiquity. To the ears of his audiences, this severe music sounded learned and traditional, while the music of Beethoven and Weber sounded modern and new (even on the rare occasions when it was fugal).

In Berlin, this antiquated sound was linked to the mythology of the Prussian monarchy. If France's national hero was a modern, forward-looking figure who belonged to the nineteenth century, the national cult in Prussia was formed around Frederick the Great, an absolute monarch who was decidedly pre-modern, belonging firmly to the earlier eighteenth century. As noted above, Friedrich Wilhelm IV was actively promoting the cult of Frederick the Great as he advanced the cause of Prussian nationalism. In a typical mix of liberalism with conservative monarchism, he was defining the glory of modern Prussia with reference to a pre-modern, pre-French Revolution era. Liszt programmed Bach, Scarlatti, and Handel, then, as a tribute to ancient Prussian glory under Frederick the Great. This strategy was particularly felicitous because Frederick the Great's skills as a flutist and composer were legendary. Berlin audiences might well have felt that the antiquated sounds they were hearing were just like those that came from Frederick's flute or his pen. Indeed, Bach's well-known personal association with the Prussian monarch would have made this seem incontrovertible.

In Berlin, Liszt wasted no time in affiliating himself with the Prussian royalty and with Prussian nationalist sentiment. The first concert attended by the royal family was Liszt's third, on 5 January. In the presence of the king, Liszt brought out for the first time his "Rheinweinlied" and thus imparted to the concert a nationalistic tone. Critic Ludwig Rellstab seized upon the national tone of the Rhine song and began a forceful construction of Liszt's character as German:

What pleases us, much more than its inherent value, is the German spirit, or rather the German cast of mind [*Gemüth*] that it demonstrated – a noble enthusiasm combined with warm affection. The song, as well as the very attractive general disposition of the artist, showed us that his true, most inner center belongs to us like a brother, and that the slight effects from the foreign country are only sprouts in relation to this stem, only incidental . . . Liszt has a German-formed sensibility [*deutsch ausgebildeten Sinn*].[82]

Rellstab clearly perceived Liszt's French qualities – the "slight effects from the foreign country" – but in response to the "Rheinweinlied" he was anxious to push into the background Liszt's Frenchness, so he could claim him as a German "brother."

Liszt tied himself even more closely to the Prussian national mythology at the concert he gave four days later (9 January). This was his charity concert for the Cologne cathedral, the nationalist icon with which Friedrich Wilhelm IV had been associating himself. It was thus already steeped in nationalist and royalist Prussian ritual, but Liszt found a way to raise the stakes. He began the concert with a quartet for piano and strings composed by Prince Louis Ferdinand of Prussia. Louis Ferdinand was a nephew of Frederick the Great who died at the Battle of Saalfeld in 1806, and whose musical and military skills were highly reminiscent of his uncle. In this performance Liszt showed an uncommon degree of physical restraint, as he sometimes did in his performances of Beethoven.[83] By suppressing his own performative presence, he made more room for the presence of the lost battle hero to assert itself. Rellstab took this as another occasion to germanize Liszt:

Related spirits recognize each other over the gap of centuries, over the cleft of the grave; the former, a knightly prince who was an early victim of the iron age, and the amazing artist with whom we are now so occupied, have such a close affinity [*Verwandtschaft*] that we can hardly be surprised how intimately and deeply the musical creation of the long departed was mirrored in the soul of the living.[84]

Liszt's performance of the quartet, as Rellstab perceived it, forged a spiritual bond between Liszt and the heroes of the Prussian national mythology. As a response to this gesture, the royal family gave Liszt manuscripts of compositions by Frederick the Great and by Louis Ferdinand. Later in the year, he reciprocated by composing an *Élégie sur des motifs du Prince Louis Ferdinand de Prusse*, and dedicating it to Princess Augusta.

Rellstab did not continue promoting Liszt's innate Germanness very long. He eventually settled on the view that Liszt's disposition was a hybrid of German and French elements.[85] This shift in his view corresponds directly to Rellstab's growing disapproval of Liszt's

---

[82] *Vossische Zeitung*, 5 January 1842 (Rellstab, *Franz Liszt*, 10).
[83] Rellstab noted Liszt's physical restraint (Rellstab, *Franz Liszt*, 16).
[84] Ibid., 16.   [85] Ibid., 48.

performances of Beethoven, Bach, and Weber. In the early reviews, Rellstab had insisted that although Liszt played Beethoven with unaccustomed liberties, these liberties were permissible because his individual approach was convincing on its own terms. The more he heard Liszt, however, the less he could accept the liberties. In response to a performance of part of the "Hammerklavier" sonata at his tenth concert (6 February), Rellstab wrote:

> More and more we see that there is a palpable gap between his life- and art-viewpoint, developed in completely different zones, and ours; over this gap a bridge of understanding (if I may be allowed the metaphor) may here or there be built, but it entirely prevents a closer fusion [*Verschmelzung*].[86]

Liszt's Frenchness, alluded to here as a "completely different zone," is no longer a mere leaf on the German stem. It is now seen as a fundamental hindrance to his understanding of Beethoven, and moreover to an understanding between the virtuoso and his Berlin public. In a retrospective essay on Liszt's visit, Rellstab preserved this viewpoint. He discussed at length Liszt's absorption of the Parisian environment in which he developed, "with its explosions in art and life smashing all moderation." Yet he also wanted to preserve part of Liszt for Germany. Aesthetically, he wrote, Liszt "keeps himself free from the excess of hyper-romanticism, which in Paris blew its nervous, overstimulating wind his way,"[87] and his personality possesses a French "liveliness, yet without losing a German modesty and warm-heartedness."[88] Rellstab's revision of his earlier, more positive and germanizing opinion of Liszt was motivated in part by a desire to separate himself from the Berlin public, whose enthusiasm for Liszt was attracting mockery from other parts of Europe.

The *fons caritatis* concert

After Liszt's concerts of 5 and 9 January, the nationalist flames were kept burning around Liszt by Wilhelm Wieprecht, co-director of the *Männergesangsverein* and director of the royal military band. He was in all likelihood involved with the performance of Liszt's "Rheinweinlied" at the 9 January concert. Liszt soon gave him the score of his setting of "Das deutsche Vaterland," and within a few days Wieprecht had made a free arrangement for wind band.[89] On 10 February, Wieprecht

---

[86] Ibid., 23.   [87] Ibid., 41–42.   [88] Ibid., 49.

[89] *Briefe hervorragender Zeitgenossen an Franz Liszt*, ed. La Mara (Leipzig, 1895), 3 vols., I: 38. Wieprecht's letter to Liszt about the "Vaterlands-Lied" is dated 20 January. Such arrangements were usually made in order to serenade Liszt. When Liszt passed through Berlin in 1844, he was serenaded by a military corps with a potpourri that combined his *Ungarischer Sturmmarsch* and the *Grand galop chromatique* (*Europa* [1844/2], p. 45).

got Liszt involved in a concert whose nationalist pageantry was even more saturated than the "sabre of honor" concert in Pest. It was billed as a charity concert for the Berlin *fons caritatis*, but its charitable purpose was clearly not in the foreground. One reporter mistook the theatre for the beneficiary, and found the real interest of the concert to lie elsewhere: "[the concert,] beyond the charitable goal, had a national significance and an artistic emphasis quite as attractive."[90] The event was, indeed, a double concert in which Wieprecht shaped the "national significance" and Liszt shaped the "artistic emphasis." The artistic and the national came together at the concert's culmination, when Liszt conducted the *Männergesangsverein* in a performance of his "Das deutsche Vaterland." This event was the climax of Liszt's growing affiliation with Prussian nationalism, and is worth describing in detail.

The Wieprecht–Liszt concert was not connected to either of the two concert series Liszt gave for his own benefit, which were at the *Singakademie* and the Royal Opera. It was set, rather, in the royal theatre, and it belonged to what was becoming an annual Berlin tradition. A concert for the *fons caritatis* had been given the previous year in the same theatre, and its tone was likewise highly nationalistic: "at that concert all Rhine-song compositions were performed, and the Becker-Rhine-song enthusiasm ultimately contributed a good part to the filling of the hall."[91] The annual *fons caritatis* concert was thus a public ritual of Friedrich Wilhelm IV's monarchical brand of nationalism: it combined the spirit of social reform – conveyed by the charity function – with nationalist sentiment, and set them in the royal context of the theatre. In 1842, Liszt was brought into this web of signification.

The Wieprecht–Liszt concert was a grandiose event that included the royal military band, the *Männergesangsverein*, and Liszt in roughly equal proportions. Since Berlin's military bands were an important component of the representational apparatus of Prussian state power, they set a monarchical tone for the event. They were famous all over Europe for their precision, and they greatly helped Prussia preserve its longstanding reputation as a state of formidable military excellence. On the afternoon of the concert Liszt and Meyerbeer were invited to a display of the band's prowess at the palace of Prince Wilhelm, probably in connection with a rehearsal. Wieprecht led a band of 360 performers in an arrangement of the *William Tell* overture, Mendelssohn's *Meerestille und glückliche Fahrt*, and an array of marches, after which Liszt handed a silver baton over to Wieprecht.[92] With this gesture Liszt made the

---

[90] *Spenersche Zeitung*, 12 February 1842 (J. P. Schmidt).
[91] *Berliner Figaro* 36 (12 February 1842), 143–44 (C. O. Hoffmann).
[92] *Korrespondent von und für Deutschland*, 16 February 1842.

military concert more than a mere ostentatious display of Prussian power; he turned it into a reaffirmation of his own bond to the state.

An even stronger military emphasis prevailed at the evening concert. The winds of the Second Defensive Cavalry Brigade performed a Wieprecht composition called *Military Reminiscence* [*Die militär Erinnerungen* (sic?)], and accompanied a declamation entitled *The Horn-Signal of the Infantry*, which was popular with the Berlin public.[93] In keeping with the state-centered, monarchial import of these military pieces, Liszt performed his fantasy (or improvisation) on "Heil Dir im Seigerkranz," or "God Save the Queen." These pieces were not nationalist in the pan-German sense. They were concerned, rather, with affirming loyalty to the Prussian state, as represented by its military unit. The *Männergesangsverein*, however, was an organization more directly representative of liberal, pan-German nationalism. It performed an arrangement of a well-known Hussar song and a setting of Kücken's "Held Friedrich," a tribute to the valor of Frederick the Great.[94] Both songs included militantly anti-French sentiments, and thus promoted an imagined, national solidarity of all Germans. As we shall see later, these songs created major problems with the Parisian critics the following summer.

Liszt's other pianistic contributions to the program were standard fare: the *Norma* fantasy (encored), the *Erlkönig* transcription, and the *Grand galop chromatique*. It was only at the end of the program that his relationship to Prussian nationalism was sealed. Liszt stood before the *Männergesangsverein* and conducted performances of his "Rheinweinlied" and "Das deutsche Vaterland," both of them having patriotic texts that include anti-French moments. His setting of Arndt's famous hymn to the German nation drew special attention because the text was so well known, and because it had not yet been heard in Berlin. He did not employ the strophic structure and *volkstümlich* style of the Rhine songs for his setting, as his contemporaries had. On the contrary, he through-composed the verses and employed a sophisticated harmonic language, treating it more as an epic of the German nation than as a *Volkslied*.[95] One critic found this style perfectly suitable to the nationalist tone:

The composer, Mr. Liszt, has set the Arndt story in a grand style and in cantata form, and expressed it with profound feeling in tones full of German love for the fatherland, burning for right and duty, zealous for everything great and beautiful.[96]

---

[93] *Berliner Figaro* 36 (12 February 1842), 143–44 (C. O. Hoffmann).

[94] *Spenersche Zeitung*, 12 February 1842 (J. P. Schmidt).

[95] In an unidentified review of the published "Das deutsche Vaterland" (found in the Weimar Liszt-Archiv, Kasten 261), Arndt's poem is referred to as a "Volkslied."

[96] Ibid.

Singled out as especially effective were the recurring phrase "His father-land must be greater" ("Sein Vaterland muß größer seyn"), and the concluding idea that the fatherland of the Germans "must be *all* of Germany" ("das ganze Deutschland soll es seyn").[97] Liszt set both phrases in a declamatory, grandiose style that was closer to the sound of the singing societies than his setting of the verses.[98] The public showed its enthusiasm for Liszt's piece with a shower of flowers and poems, and before the applause came to an end the chorus broke into a "Vivat Liszt," set to music by Wieprecht. No other moment in Liszt's concert career, not even the sabre of honor event in Pest, was so saturated with nationalistic meaning.

The life of "Das deutsche Vaterland" and Liszt's relationship to the German national movement were far from over after this concert. He spent the summer of 1842 away from Germany, but when he returned in September he resumed his national affiliations systematically. The *Dombaufest* concert in Cologne took place on 13 September. On 26 October he conducted a setting of Becker's "Der deutsche Rhein" in Jena, a sign that the Rhine-song culture was alive and well. A few days later, he was made *Kapellmeister in ausserordentlichen Dienst* to the Weimar court, the capacity in which he would most lastingly tie himself to the history of German culture. And shortly thereafter, on 15 November, he gave his second concert for the Mozart Foundation in Frankfurt.

Liszt was still focusing his energies on Prussia, however, and to this end he returned to Berlin in late December. There the *Männergesang Akademie* had named him honorable director on 7 December, and he reciprocated shortly after his arrival in Berlin by conducting them in a private concert (5 January). On 16 February he participated in a benefit concert for the same institution, and its program was thoroughly centered on German music. He conducted the orchestra in overtures by Beethoven and Weber, played Mendelssohn's D minor concerto and his own *Don Giovanni* fantasy, and he led the *Akademie* in three of his choruses. Once again the concert culminated in a performance of "Das deutsche Vaterland," this time arranged with orchestral accompaniment. During this visit Liszt also maintained his relationship with the king, and the royal family attended many of his January concerts. On one occasion he went unusually far out of his way to preserve his link

---

[97] This concluding phrase answers the question asked at the beginning of the poem: "What is the fatherland of the German?" ("Was ist des Deutschen Vaterland?"). The strophes consider individual regions of Germany as possible answers to the question, but in each case it is concluded that "His fatherland must be greater." The conclusion proposes that the German fatherland is something beyond regions, beyond geography – "it must be *all* of Germany."

[98] The unidentified review of "Das deutsche Vaterland" in Weimar Liszt-Archiv Kasten 261 described the setting of the latter phrase as "uncommonly powerful and folkish."

to the king. Before embarking for eastern Prussia in late January, he had accepted an invitation to perform at the Potsdam court. From Breslau he requested a postponement of the court concert in order to allow him to extend the length of his tour. The king refused to postpone, but gave Liszt permission not to appear. Surprisingly, Liszt chose to return to Berlin and fulfill his obligation, and then resumed his tour of eastern Prussia.[99] He clearly did not feel that a court concert was something he could afford to miss.

Six months later, the score of "Das deutsche Vaterland" was published in Berlin, with a dedication to Friedrich Wilhelm IV. The music was now well known in Germany, and the publication helped disseminate it further. Yet not everyone in Germany was convinced that it was a perfect vehicle for the expression of German national aspirations. In a carefully written review of the score, a critic at the *Allgemeine musikalische Zeitung* found fault with Liszt's sophisticated musical language, which he considered inappropriate for the direct, *volkstümlich* character of the poem.[100] Liszt's contemporaries were accustomed to hearing "Das deutsche Vaterland" in Gustav Reichardt's *volkstümlich* setting, or in imitations thereof. Liszt's setting seemed to avoid this modest, indigenous men's-choir style in favor of the advanced compositional language of cosmopolitan Europe. The setting is an emblem of his ambivalent relationship to German nationalism. On the one hand, he was trying to belong to the Germans by picking up a text and a genre that were nationalist in a specifically German sense. Yet he was coming to the German national movement as a figure in cosmopolitan European culture, and his efforts to support nationalism were bound to reflect that fact.

Starting in the late months of 1843, Liszt's relationship with Prussian nationalism began to cool off. Over the next two years his German concerts were concentrated in areas he had left unvisited, especially the southern regions of Swabia and Bavaria. The *Männerchöre* were no longer appearing on his programs. Liszt's connection to German nationalism shifted away from Prussia and toward Weimar, whose classical cultural

[99] Liszt asked Meyerbeer to make the request in a letter of 6 February (*Briefe hervorragender Zeitgenossen an Franz Liszt*, I: 56). Meyerbeer and the court theatre director Graf Redern both advised Liszt to return for the concert, probably sensing that the king would be seriously displeased if Liszt did not follow through with his obligation. Liszt may have harbored a slight resentment against the king for his inflexibility in this matter. In a letter of 17 July 1845 to Therese Bacharacht, he wrote that the Prussian king "has not let himself be excessively gracious and benevolent toward me" (*Franz Liszts Briefe*, ed. La Mara [Leipzig 1893–1902], 8 vols., VIII: 43).

[100] *Allgemeine musikalische Zeitung* 45/40 (4 October 1843), cols. 711–14. Perhaps in response to this criticism, Liszt made a second version of "Das deutsche Vaterland" that is considerably simpler and more typical of the *Männergesang* style. This version is printed in James Thompson Fudge, "The Male Choral Music of Franz Liszt" (Ph.D. diss., University of Iowa, 1972), 351ff.

heritage he was joining. In December 1843, as he was preparing his first season of activities as *Kapellmeister in ausserordentlichen Dienst* in Weimar, he wrote to Marie d'Agoult: "My position here is perfect . . . I am pushing hard for this Germanic appearance. It's an excellent grain of silliness and it kills two birds with one stone."[101] Whatever Liszt might have specifically meant by this, it is at least clear that he is playing at Germanness, and that he sees it primarily as a strategic maneuver. He beams with satisfaction in his new role, and will take the necessary steps to secure it for the future.

German artists and princes were equally as active in drawing Liszt into the cultural institutions of Weimar. Franz von Dingelstedt, a prominent poet and director of the Stuttgart theatre, wrote enthusiastically to Liszt in October 1845 and asked him to join in the establishment of a new journal. The journal had been suggested by the Duke of Baden-Württemberg, who wanted a cultural magazine for aristocrats that would promote communication among the individual German states. Dingelstedt felt it could succeed with the combined efforts of the duke, of Weimar, and of Liszt:

La Revue Allemande . . . The Princess and Prince of Prussia, perhaps the king himself, would become interested because of you; nothing more is needed . . . We would be the heart [*beau centre*] of the German political, literary, and social movement, located between Paris and Vienna. It would be famous.[102]

Dingelstedt's letter shows, once again, that Liszt's utility for the German national movement consisted in the multiplicity of his affiliations – his ties to both Weimar and Prussia. It also reveals the extent to which German nationalism was in the hands of the monarchs, which kept nationalism from becoming anti-authoritarian. Liszt has earned a reputation as an anti-authoritarian, revolutionary virtuoso because of his support for nationalisms in Hungary and Poland, but his involvement in German nationalism lacked this character entirely. He made himself part of the German national movement not by opposing its rulers, but by attaching himself to them. The negative dimension of German nationalism was anti-French and anti-imperialist, but not particularly anti-authoritarian.

Liszt's association with the German national movement, to summarize, was incubated in a brief span of time – from his first Cologne cathedral concert of 23 August 1841 to his departure from Berlin on 3 March 1842. Within this period, in which German nationalist sentiment was exceptionally high, he became involved with several of the

---

[101] *Correspondance de Liszt et de Madame d'Agoult*, II: 310. "Je pousse beaucoup pour cette apparence germanique. C'est une excellente graine de niais und cela fait de deux coups une pierre."

[102] *Briefe hervorragender Zeitgenossen an Franz Liszt*, I: 80; letter dated 27 October.

key nationalist institutions: the *Dombauverein* of Cologne, the Mozart
Foundation of Frankfurt, the king of Prussia, and perhaps most importantly, the various *Männergesangsvereine* – and he actively sustained his
relationship to all of these institutions until the end of 1843. Liszt also
began shifting his social milieu away from elite, cosmopolitan, female-
dominated francophone communities, and toward the more bourgeois
and male organizations of Germany such as the singing societies and the
freemasonry. German journalists began constructing Liszt as a person
with a German disposition, which they saw revealed in his performing
style and his social behavior. There was an element of appropriation in
this attempt to germanize him, for there were still many elements of his
persona that betrayed his cultural Frenchness. But Liszt's relationship
to the German national movement was a combination of appropriation and willing participation. He was aware of his "apparence germanique" and of his "petite importance en allemand," and on several
occasions he went out of his way to develop his ties to the aspiring
nation.

This discussion of Liszt's German nationalist affiliations puts the virtuoso's notable "turn to Germany" in a new light. Biographers have
traditionally presented 1848 as a "clean break" in Liszt's career. The
virtuoso stands on one side, the composer on the other; the international wanderer on one side, the guru of Weimar and leader of the New
German School on the other. Backdating his turn to Germany to the
early 1840s does not just refine the chronology. It shows that Liszt first
became folded into nationalist culture by virtue of his identity as a virtuoso, not as a composer. In the early 1840s his reputation as a composer
was minor, heavily eclipsed by his virtuoso brilliance. He tied himself
to Germany through the advantages that a virtuoso alone can possess:
the capacity to excite mass enthusiasm, the ability to raise funds, the
authority to endorse causes with a high public profile, and, of course,
the ability to exploit personal charisma. The road that led to Liszt's status as a leading composer in the German tradition was thus paved by
the prestige he had gathered through his pianism.

In 1855, William Neumann published a lengthy biography that both
recognized and consolidated Liszt's high position in the German musical establishment. It served Neumann's purposes to present Liszt's current position as the fulfillment of a long-term destiny to serve German
culture. Surveying the virtuoso years, he found his seminal moment in
Liszt's concerts for the Cologne cathedral. In contrast to the audiences
of Paris, Pest, and Vienna, Neumann writes, Germans understood the
true Liszt: "the reception Franz Liszt was accorded in Germany was
much more appropriate to the significance of the artist and the high
inner worth of the man. In the Rhine region . . . the cheerful and clever

populace [*fröhliche und kluge Volk*] greeted him warmly."[103] Neumann was forging a "natural," characterological bond between Liszt and the Germans. His use of the word "Volk" resonates with nationalist overtones, and his modifiers "fröhliche und kluge" betray a wish to separate the Germans from the high-toned, mannered elites who had led Liszt's reception in Paris, Vienna, and Pest.[104] Some decades later, another biographer would point to the Berlin episode (1842) as a stage in the unfolding of Liszt's latent German-ness: "These famous Berlin days brought Liszt into close contact with the German essence [*deutschem Wesen*] and the leading geniuses of the German spirit, and were of great significance for his development."[105] Writings such as these made Liszt's association with Germany sound organic and inevitable – the ideal of romantic nationalism. But as we have seen, it was only through strategic shifts in his social habits, personal affiliations, compositional activity, concert programming, and even personal behavior that Liszt forged his bond to Germany.

French reactions

Both Liszt and the German national movement had everything to gain from their mutual association. There was one party, however, that stood to lose: France. German nationalism, still recovering from the era of Napoleonic domination, was notoriously anti-French in character. In an essay published in 1836, Heinrich Heine argued that German patriotism was cold-hearted, rooted in the hatred of foreigners, whereas French patriotism was open-hearted and welcoming to foreigners.[106] The Rhine Crisis of 1840 only made things worse: "Old horror stories about three centuries of French atrocities against the German nation were revived, along with calls for the return of the lost lands, Alsace and Lorraine."[107] French critics were therefore watchful of how Liszt was becoming involved in German nationalism, and when they heard about the anti-French songs that had been performed at the *fons caritatis* concert in Berlin, they waged a campaign against him. As usual, Liszt

---

[103] William Neumann, *Franz Liszt: eine Biographie* (Kassel, 1855), 77. "Der Empfang, den Franz Liszt in Deutschland fand, war ein der Bedeutung des Künstlers wie dem hohen innern Werthe des Mannes durchaus entsprechender. Am Rhein . . . kam ihm das fröhliche und kluge Volk mit Herzlichkeit entgegen."

[104] It is also telling that, in his biography, Neumann omits the opposition Liszt encountered during his very first concerts in northern Germany – those of Leipzig and Dresden – thereby smoothing out an important wrinkle in his German reception.

[105] Julius Kapp, *Franz Liszt: eine Biographie* (Berlin, 1911).

[106] Hughes, *Nationalism and Society*, 80. The essay, "Why did the Germans Take to the Romantic School?" appeared in his book *The Romantic School* (1836).

[107] Ibid, 78.

attempted to extricate himself from the affair by publishing a defense, and a major press debate was soon underway.

Almost nothing has been written about the debate over Liszt's anti-French sympathies, with the result that its effect on his French reputation in general has been underemphasized. It was the second and most serious nation-related issue to alienate him from Paris. Admittedly, he never lost a certain core of support there, particularly among the aristocracy and among some of the artistic–literary community. But after this episode, the critical opposition became set in its ways and continued to dog Liszt for years. Already in 1841, when he revisited Paris, his reputation was fragile, not only because of the lingering sabre of honor debacle, but also because of a new controversy involving high ticket prices.[108] One journalist, noting the accumulating controversy, wrote that

> Liszt is more French than anyone in terms of education, intelligence, even in his lightness and audacity. And what do you know, he is more contested in France than elsewhere; perhaps that is a way of naturalizing him completely.[109]

Liszt's questionable affiliations with German nationalism were, in a sense, the straw that broke the camel's back. In 1842 Parisian critics began accusing him of "playing at" Germanness, and recognizing a parallel to the Hungarian episode, they revived the sabre as an object of mockery. Yet the urgency was now greater, since for French audiences, Liszt's ties to the German national movement were more immediately troubling than his ties to Hungary.

Word of Liszt's anti-French choral works first reached Parisian readers by way of the journal *La patrie*, shortly after they had been performed at the *fons caritatis* concert in Berlin (10 February). The applause he received in recognition of his philanthropy, the *Patrie* reported, was well earned,

> But that he, according to the *Oberdeutsche Zeitung*, forgets the hospitality and the success that came to him in France to such a point that he wins this applause from compositions on a *Rheinweinlied*, in which the claims of the French to reconquer the Rhine are attacked – that makes us regret the ovations in his honor from the Prussian students, who wanted to unharness the horses from his carriage and carry him around in triumph. Talent should never forget recognition.[110]

---

[108] See Bellas, "Tumultueuse amitié."

[109] *Revue et gazette musicale* 8/26 (1 April 1841), 204–05. Heine, too, reviewing the 1841 concert season, noted that "In spite of his geniality, Liszt faces an opposition in Paris, which consists mostly of serious musicians and awards the laurels to the Kaiser's Thalberg" (*Heinrich Heine und die Musik*, ed. Gerhard Müller [Cologne, 1987], 120).

[110] This passage was reproduced in *Blätter der Vergangenheit und Gegenwart*, 22 February 1842. This is translated from the German translation in the *Blätter*.

This news apparently remained in oral circulation, for two months later the *Guêpes* urged him to defend himself:

Mr. Liszt is a talented man; – but . . . he must refute, in the journals where he has so many things printed, the rumors being circulated, according to which he sings songs at banquets in Germany in which the French are treated slightly worse than dogs.[111]

The controversy did not reach full force, however, until Liszt returned to Paris in June. Léon Escudier, his opponent at the *France musicale*, announced his arrival, and without further ado promised that "In an upcoming issue we will give the translation of a song against the French, recently set to music by the Hungarian pianist, and sung at one of his concerts by the students of young Germany."[112]

In Paris Liszt made no attempt to cover up his association with Germany. On the contrary, he displayed it openly by agreeing to perform for a traveling German opera company that had failed miserably in Paris. The leading aristocrats of Paris organized a soirée to relieve the company's financial burden, and when Liszt assented to participate he became the central attraction. This was the first and most important of the two appearances he made in Paris during his visit. When the concert was announced, Escudier tried to make sure that attention to Liszt's charity did not overshadow his anti-French songs:

It is said that Mr. Liszt proposes to give a concert for the benefit of the German choristers, who are singing at this moment in the Rue Vivienne concerts. This will be an act of charity that does much more honor to Mr. Liszt than his settings of songs against the French, which were sung at his concerts on the other side of the Rhine by the German youth.[113]

This may have provoked, rather than intimidated, Liszt, for at the concert he decided to include a choral performance of his "Rheinweinlied." Liszt's defenders vaunted this as a deliberate challenge to his critics: "As a complete response, Liszt wanted to have the song sung openly in France, and I swear to you that no one was scandalized by it."[114] This writer was being somewhat disingenuous, however, for the concert was not set "en pleine France." It took place at the salon of Colonel Thorn, one of the most lavish party-givers in Paris, and it had been organized by seven leading aristocratic women of various nationalities.[115] Tickets

---

[111] *Guêpes* 3 (April 1842), 280 (A. Karr).   [112] *France musicale* 5/25 (19 June 1842), 225.

[113] *France musicale* 5/26 (26 June 1842), 233.

[114] *Revue et gazette musicale* 9/27 (3 July 1842), 277–78 (P. Smith).

[115] The committee of women was almost self-consciously international. It consisted of the Baroness Rothschild (France), Baroness Stockhausen (Germany), Countess Salvandy (Spain), Countess Plaisance (France), Lady Henriette d'Orsay (England), Baroness Pierres (France), and Countess Rasomoffsky (Russia). See *Monde musical*, 7 July 1842.

were set at an exorbitant twenty francs. It was a highly exclusive event whose tone was set by the cosmopolitan nobility, and demonstrations of national sympathy would have been utterly out of place. Had Liszt programmed the "Rheinweinlied" in a more public setting, the response would surely have been different.

In Germany, Liszt's concert for the opera troupe was used to vigorously reassert his Germanness and his dedication to the national movement. Heinrich Börnstein, apparently a member of the troupe, published a detailed account in the Viennese *Allgemeine Theaterzeitung*, and its rich germanizing rhetoric is worth presenting at some length:

> Some narrow-hearted French journals, which dwell on the quickly ended arguments of the year 1840, on Becker's and Musset's Rhine-songs, and other such things, reproached Liszt's German-national orientation [*Richtung*] and especially the manifestations of it in his German songs. Liszt, an energetic, masculine artistic disposition [*eine energisch-männliche Künstler-Natur*], unaccustomed to retreat in decisive moments ... announced [the "Rheinweinlied"] on the program of the concert as a response. The "Rheinweinlied," a thundering, authentically German tune, is written with national inspiration and ardor, and cannot fail to have an effect. – Not only were there no opponents, but there was general, unaffected applause, despite the gauntlet that had been thrown. – One could see here the good, practical sensibility of the French, who without bothering with passionate journalistic gossip, recognize the right of a German person to feel German and to feel for Germany, and can no more hold it against him than against their love for their own country.[116]

Börnstein not only found Liszt's music purely German in spirit, but also made efforts to germanize his character disposition. In his account of the choral rehearsal for the concert, he implicitly defined Liszt's behavior against the affected, more impersonal manners of the Parisian elites: "Liszt ... received us simply and cordially [*schlicht und herzlich*], not like a patron or benefactor, but like a compatriot receives his compatriots; – the plain [*biedere*] German handshake retained its old, native right." The same German–French dichotomy is just beneath the surface of his untranslatable comment that "Liszt ist eine eben so herzlich-gemüthliche, als geistig-geniale Künstler-Natur" ("Liszt's artistic disposition is just as warm-hearted and good-natured as it is intellectual

The high social status of the audience was confirmed in a German report (*Blätter für Musik und Literatur* 3 [September 1842], pp. 133–36).

[116] This article was reproduced in the *Blätter für Musik und Literatur* 3 (September 1842), 133–36. Joseph d'Ortigue, in his review of the concert, also felt Liszt had captured the German style authentically: "the drinking song, with a text by Herwegh, composed for voices without accompaniment, delighted us with an ever-vigorous tune, a flowing stream of melody, full of candor, a hearty phrasing, an entirely German liveliness. One could perhaps reproach the latter piece for having a style too concerted, too *instrumented* for parts entrusted to the voice. But that is a fault common to musicians of the other side of the Rhine ..." (*Monde musical*, 28 July 1842).

and brilliant"). At the culmination of the article, Börnstein claims nothing less than that "Liszt would be the man to solve the problem of a German opera here; his name would attract Germany's top artists to Paris." His intuition that Liszt could be the leader of a major German cultural institution was confirmed just a few months later by Liszt's appointment at Weimar.

Because the concert for the German troupe had a low public profile, it barely affected the debate over Liszt's anti-French songs. With an opponent as determined as Escudier, Liszt was forced to join the debate in the press. His first step was to attempt getting a defense published in the *France musicale* through the intervention of a friend, a certain M. Masset. Escudier was infuriated and published another attack:

Mr. Liszt has lately complained in quite inappropriate terms about the observations we have made on the subject of his songs against the French . . . If Mr. Liszt had come to us directly, we would have answered him that we need neither inspiration nor advice from anyone to express our antipathy toward an artist who has people applaud verses in which the hero Frederick *slaps the French in the face* [*tape sur la gueule aux français*].[117]

An important change in Escudier's line of attack is the absence of the "Rheinweinlied." Instead he cites the "Held Friedrich" song, which had been performed alongside the "Rheinweinlied" at the *fons caritatis* concert in Berlin. He may have been forced to shift his tactic, for the "Rheinweinlied" had not created a scandal at its Paris performance. From this moment on, Escudier's only strategy could be to *implicate* Liszt in the generally anti-French patriotic tone of the *fons caritatis* concert. He therefore published the texts of the two shamelessly anti-French songs that had been performed at this concert: "Frédéric le Héros" and "L'Hussard de l'an XIII."[118]

In the meantime, Jules Janin had published a lengthy defense of Liszt in the *Journal des débats*. Janin took the strategy of writing a general eulogy to Liszt, emphasizing his charity and accusing the opponents of jealousy: "There is only one way, my dear gentlemen, not to be yellow with envy: and that is to have the talent, the popularity, the brilliance, the indefatigable verve of Franz Liszt; and above all, it is to be generous and charitable like him."[119] Escudier tore up Janin's article in the next issue of his journal. Addressing Janin directly, he wrote: "[Liszt] will take his sabre of honor, the music of his songs against the French . . . Together you will rehearse together this battle cry: *No, you shall not have*

---

[117] *France musicale* 5/27 (3 July 1842), 241 (L. Escudier).
[118] *France musicale* 5/28 (10 July 1842), 245–47 (L. Escudier). Escudier had received the texts from a German correspondent.
[119] This article is quoted in its near entirety in ibid.

the German Rhine."[120] Here Escudier revives the sabre of honor, grafting it onto Liszt's more recent display of German nationalist militancy. Later in the same article he comes up with the epithet "le général Liszt." With these comments, Escudier had invented what became the most pervasive satirical trope in the French press for the rest of his concert career: Liszt as a pianistic Hotspur. It was a fusion of two separate issues that had alienated him from France: his Hungarian national sympathies, and his German national sympathies.

The controversy over Liszt's songs also made the French aware, for the first time, that they had always considered him one of their own. Previously, his relationship to France was more or less "organic" – preserved through his constant contacts with the press, with musicians, and with publishing houses. There had been no need to state what was obvious: that he belonged to France. The anti-French songs, however, raised the possibility that Liszt was rejecting his French identity and shirking responsibility toward the land in which he bloomed as an artist. His defenders thus began referring to him as an "adoptive child of France" who would never stoop so low as to insult France,[121] while opponents such as Escudier saw him as a flagrantly ungrateful child:

Barely two years ago, Liszt had someone request the cross of honor from the French minister; we know this and confirm it. Today France, who made him what he is, who established his reputation, who gave him a name for Europe, who put his first crown on his head, hears the cries of war and contempt rising at its doors.[122]

Previous debates over Liszt in the Parisian press had negotiated his relationship to different factions within the city, thus eclipsing his more general belonging to French culture. The Rhine-song issue shifted this perspective and made people examine his place in the international sphere. For the first time in his Parisian reception, his relationship to France as a whole was a fact of greater importance than his relationship to the different elite groups, to the musical establishment, or to rival virtuosos. Ironically, it was a sign that his attachment to France was weakening.[123]

---

[120] Ibid. The latter sentence is, of course, a paraphrase of the refrain of Becker's famous Rhine song.

[121] *Revue et gazette musicale* 9/27 (3 July 1842), 277–78 (P. Smith).

[122] *France musicale* 5/28 (10 July 1842), 245–47 (L. Escudier). Alphonse Karr was astonished to hear the accusations against Liszt, who "became a Frenchman in France – who received such great hospitality in Paris, who describes himself proudly as the brother of all our *grands hommes*, no matter what they do" (*Guêpes* 3 [April 1842], 280).

[123] Starting in late 1841, the *Gazette* reports on Liszt's travels were shifted out of the "local" subdivision of the miscellaneous "Nouvelles" column, and placed under the "Étranger" heading. This change registers the growing perception that he was no longer a local, Parisian figure.

Ten days after Liszt's concert for the German opera troupe, the debate had reached a level of intensity easily comparable with that of the Liszt–Thalberg affair of 1837:

Litz [*sic*] – this name fills at this moment all of Paris, it excites more passions than all the current political candidates. Only in vain can one speak of order, of unity; thanks to him civil war is brimming, disorder is at a peak, the parties watch each other with a ferocious eye. The first party says that he is the humanitarian pianist, the great prophet of progress, the friend of men . . . But the other party calls him the foreign pianist, the defector of national music, the spy of Pitt and Coburg; they condemn his Hungarian sabre, the Berlin serenades, and above all the more or less Rhenish songs that he set to music.[124]

The debate dragged on for weeks. The *Charivari* republished the texts of the Hussar song and of "Held Friedrich," provoking Liszt to print a defense in the *Monde musical*, on whose editorial board he sat.[125] Answering Escudier's charges to the letter, he claimed that he had "neither composed, nor *patronized*, nor *propagated*, nor *had sung*" the anti-French songs in question.[126] Within two days he had published another letter in which he made a further correction: the Berlin *fons caritatis* concert was not given *by* him, but was given *for* him. The *Ménestrel* granted this, but refused to accept that Liszt was thereby free of complicity in the xenophobic sentiments of the concert:

The concert in which the anti-French couplets were performed seems not to have been given by Mr. Liszt himself, but all the more, in his honor, by a singing society of German patriots. In any case, it is clear that Mr. Liszt, *in accepting to play at this concert*, cannot expect generous honors from France.[127]

The *Charivari* also refused to accept Liszt's defense, and challenged him to acknowledge his guilt:

Mr. Liszt now realizes that his behavior outside France was of such a kind that can only reduce his popularity in France. What he publicly said to the contrary is more an excuse than a refutation; all the more, we hope he will respond, and we wish him success, because there is always time to repent his errors.[128]

Both of Liszt's opponents were probably right to claim that even passive involvement in Prussian nationalism was enough to make

[124] "Les Listophobes et les Listophiles," *Le caricature*, 10 July 1842.
[125] Liszt had never before turned to the *Monde musical* to wage his battles with the Parisian press. He usually did this in the pages of the *Gazette musicale*, or in the editorial columns of the journals that attacked him. Liszt's relationship with the editor of the *Gazette*, however, had recently turned sour (see Bellas, "Tumultueuse amitié"). Schlesinger had already allowed two statements of defense into his journal, and perhaps felt that this was a reasonable limit.
[126] *Monde musical* 3/28 (14 July 1842) (F. Liszt).
[127] *Ménestrel* 9/33 (17 July 1842); emphasis added.
[128] This article was reprinted in the *Gesellschafter*, 26 August 1842.

him responsible for his actions. Their argument would have been much stronger had they mentioned the "Rheinweinlied" as well, which evinced his deliberate, active participation in nationalist discourse. Yet Liszt was a figure of such symbolic potency that every institution or audience with which he came into contact craved his attention, even if this attention was passive or lacking in personal commitment. The initial step of Liszt's involvement with nationalisms was, in fact, always a passive one. He did not go out seeking to become a symbol for the German or Magyar national movements. These movements came to him asking for an endorsement, and they were delighted if that was the only thing they received from him. Only after this initial step had been taken did he start developing the relationship by buying costumes, tailoring his repertory, or changing his social behavior. Liszt's presence at the *fons caritatis* concert represented, at the very least, a passive endorsement of the patriotic, anti-French sentiments that the *Männergesangsverein* was promulgating. Liszt did not feel anti-French, but he knew that the concert had an anti-French tone and he knew he was increasing the event's symbolic weight by being there. And his performance of the "Rheinweinlied" represented an active endorsement of the tone of the concert.

We do not need to conclude from the foregoing discussion that Liszt was morally culpable in his national affiliations with Germany. My point is that he left France without fully answering the objections that had been raised concerning the events in Berlin, and the Parisian critics were not willing to let the issue fade. He was in a corner not because he meant harm to France, but because he wished to be a positive force, and to be recognized as such, wherever he went. Unfortunately, being a positive force in German nationalism, especially in the aftermath of the Rhine Crisis, almost automatically meant reinforcing animosity toward the French. It was beyond his power to erase the anti-French strain from German nationalism. At the same time, Liszt was not a helpless victim of the contradictions of this time. He had a future career to think about, and in the summer of 1842 Germany offered him more promising prospects than France. A frank apology for the xenophobic songs might have jeopardized his position in Germany. He had less to lose from another controversy in the Parisian press, and it was this consequence that he chose to accept.

Fallout

I have presented the matter of Liszt's anti-French songs in depth because it has been barely recognized in writings on Liszt, and its consequences for his future were decisive. It virtually forced him to exclude Paris from consideration as a possible place to settle down, and in this sense moved him more decisively toward the choice of Weimar. The debate in Paris involved a large number of periodicals: for the defense the *Gazette musicale, Monde musical,* and *Journal des débats,* and for the plaintiffs the *France musicale, Charivari, Ménestrel,* and *Caricature.* These journals encompass a wide range of styles and readerships, from the professional and intellectual (*Revue et gazette musicale*) to the satirical and popular (*Caricature*). The public profile of the debate was bound to be larger than that of all previous controversies, including the rivalry with Thalberg, because the issues were easier to understand and were relevant to the non-concertgoing parts of the public. For this reason, it can fairly be characterized as the single most damaging debate of his concert career.

After the summer of 1842, Liszt was the perpetual object of satire in the Parisian press. His brilliant return in 1844 did nothing to hold back the tide of mockery. Satires revolved around two themes: his militancy and his chameleonic adaptability. The theme of militancy was the cumulative result of his Napoleonic aura, the sabre of honor, and the anti-French songs, and the sabre became the favorite medium for representing Liszt as a *virtuose militant.* But as mentioned earlier, satirists first pulled the sabre out of their arsenals *after* the issue of the anti-French songs was well developed. That is, the latent content of the sabre was not Liszt's Hungarian sympathies but his pronounced German sympathies. This explains why one of the most elaborate and most often imitated caricatures, portraying Liszt riding a battle horse in full arms (see chapter 2, Figure 2.1), appeared at the peak of the debate in July 1842, rather than in the aftermath of his Hungarian visit of 1840.

The militancy theme was most insistently propagated by the *Ménestrel.* Its first report on Liszt after the summer of 1842 predicted that his upcoming tour would be a great military success: "What a future of laurels, of sabres of honor and artillery salvos!"[129] It repeatedly referred to him as "general Liszt" or as "the Hungarian general," and these epithets wore off on other satirists. Heine picked up the trope and called him "the furious Roland with his sabre of honor."[130] Liszt's companions and friends were transformed, in this satirical trope, into "aides-de-camp." His manager Gaetano Belloni was the *Ménestrel*'s favorite candidate for this position, but another satirical journal used it to remind readers of Liszt's pro-Prussian sympathies:

Franz Liszt has brought back from Berlin two dozen students who are his aides-de-camp. Joined with his thirty Parisian aides-de-camp, they form a kind of Roman legion that will not let grass grow on the path of enthusiasm.[131]

[129] *Ménestrel* 9/46 (16 October 1842).
[130] *Heinrich Heine und die Musik,* 155. The article is dated 25 April 1844.
[131] *Tintamarre,* 30 June 1844.

Liszt's itinerant concert career was now being caricatured as a series of imperialistic military triumphs. Even at the *Gazette musicale*, where we might least expect a satire of Liszt, one writer found the above quotation worth imitating:

We are waiting for him to travel around Greece like Nero, where he will only need, from moment to moment, some soldiers to extract applause for him, such as those of this emperor-artist usually do.[132]

The *Ménestrel* followed up this line of satire directly, but as usual, with less of an emphasis on the imperial, Napoleonic strain: "In several locales Liszt is taken for the conquerer of Mogador, or for the hero of the battle of Isly."[133]

Liszt as militant virtuoso quickly became a mechanized cliché and lost its biting critical potential. Satires of his adaptability, however, were more serious because they called into question his ethics. As early as 1838, Heine had humorously commented on the variety of Liszt's philosophical "hobby-horses," and when he returned with the sabre in 1840, he was treated unkindly for "adorning a nationality according to the situation."[134] Predictably enough, Liszt's German affiliations were criticized as another example of this tendency. But the consequences for France were now much greater, and the criticism was correspondingly harsher. Shortly after the debate over the anti-German songs, the Berlin *Gesellschafter* reported that

Dr. Franz Liszt has very strongly rebelled against the French journals who say that he wants to be a Frenchman in Paris, a German in Germany, a Hungarian in Hungary, and another person in other countries. Mr. Liszt answered emotionally, bitterly, indeed incourteously, but ultimately with justification.[135]

French critics did not agree that Liszt was justified, and the *Charivari* issued an immediate rebuttal.[136] After he left Paris, criticism of his adaptability took the form of satire, and again the *Ménestrel* was in

---

[132] *Revue et gazette musicale* 11/39 (29 September 1844), 328.
[133] *Ménestrel* 11/48 (27 October 1844).   [134] See chapter 3, fn. 84.
[135] *Gesellschafter*, 26 August 1842.
[136] The *Charivari* responded to Liszt's complaint as follows: "Mr. Liszt can complain less than many others about the press; where is there an artist who has been so favored and worshipped by them? If the press has deserved a reproach in this matter, it is because it has placed an admittedly notable talent too high, by ascribing it to a man who only manages uncommon affectation and significant dexterity in the tips of his fingers, while the press often lets men to whom we are indebted for the most serious progress of art sink unacknowledged into oblivion" (reprinted in ibid.). The last line is a clear paraphrase of the charge made against Liszt by the *Revue des deux mondes* in 1840. Indeed, the *Charivari* was taking its entire polemical position from the *Revue des deux mondes*, which had been the first to criticize Liszt's adaptability to nationalisms.

the forefront. A particularly trenchant assault was prompted by the Marseilles episode described at the beginning of chapter 3.

We have already predicted that, some centuries from now, human intelligence will discover the true titles and qualities of Franz Liszt only with difficulty. Posterity will not know whether Liszt was a great general, or a profound jurisconsult, or an elegiac poet, or a nomadic musician, or a famous preacher. Posterity will be equally baffled at the location of Franz Liszt's real country. Everywhere the great pianist appears he receives homage as a compatriot, as a local glory . . . The humanitarian virtuoso has, for his part, contributed in no small part to complete this illusion. He goes to Russia? Franz Liszt is a Muscovite of pure blood; he has slaves and has knout distributed to them. He goes to Berlin? He becomes a merciless Prussian, he intones arch-teutonic and anti-gaulish couplets. Is he at Marseilles? There's Provençal in his soul and he fraternizes with the *bouill-abaisse*. Transport him into Hungary: he pulls his national sabre out again and turns back into a Hussar. He molds himself to every zone and takes the mold of all patriotisms. It is only in the case of such proud and independent spirits that one finds such suppleness.[137]

This article was with pointed irony entitled "The Cosmopolitan Artist," and it puts a finger on one of the central contradictions of his virtuoso identity: the contradiction between his national affiliations and his cosmopolitanism. For Liszt to preserve his cosmopolitanism intact, he would have had to serve chiefly as an *endorser* of the liberal spirit of national causes, while at the same time asserting his independence from the various locales he was in. This is precisely what his opponent at the *Ménestrel* demanded of him: that he remain a "proud and independent spirit" in his national affiliations. Liszt would not have wanted to be held to any other standard. When, for example, his Polish sympathies put him out of favor with Tsar Nicholas I of Russia, he claimed that "it was a matter of honor with me not to deny [them]."[138]

Liszt and his audiences in Germany and Hungary, however, took a different approach – the approach of romantic nationalism. For romantic nationalism, the nation was something *inside* the individual, something felt instinctively, emotionally, and irrepressibly, something that could not fail to shine through a person. Liszt and his audiences set out to naturalize him, to close off the gap between his uprooted, cosmopolitan identity and the national or regional spirit of the local community. We have seen that the construction of a national identity for Liszt was carried out in several spheres of activity – social behavior, performing style, dress, performing repertory, social affiliations, composing activities – as though he had to be saturated with the nation in order to be relevant to

---

[137] Anon., "L'artiste cosmopolite," *Ménestrel* 11/40 (1 September 1844).
[138] *Portrait of Liszt*, 198. Liszt did, however, feel that the degree and nature of his Polish sympathies had been misrepresented to the Tsar.

the nation. This way of nationalizing Liszt had a popular appeal that the more abstract, cosmopolitan, Enlightenment-based idea of nation could never have gained, and was therefore capable of generating enthusiasm among large publics, or even masses, during his concert tours. The *Ménestrel* rightly pointed out that Liszt "contributed in no small part" to his nationalization. Only in a few particular cases can we clearly identify the nationalization of Liszt as a gesture of sheer appropriation. It was a mutually beneficial process to which both Liszt and his fans willingly contributed.

The conflict between national and cosmopolitan ideologies, however, is not the only issue Liszt's affiliations raised. In these last two chapters we have seen critics fighting over civic, romantic, and feudal conceptions of nationhood, over "provincial" versus "sophisticated" behavior, over the relationship between the spheres of fine arts and politics. As he traveled across dozens of geographic borders, Liszt also cut across the conceptual borders with which his audiences marked out and maintained their identities. These borders remained as unstable as the French–German boundary of the Rhine, as unstable as Hungary's political ties to the Austrian empire. In the concert hall, Liszt's charisma and virtuosity cast a spell over his audiences, reminding them of how exalting it felt to belong to a community, and to affirm that community. But as we look back over his national affiliations, we also find unsettling evidence of that which, in the past and present alike, draws communities and nations apart.

5

Anatomy of "Lisztomania": the Berlin episode

Liszt's visit to Berlin in the winter of 1841–42 was once narrated as the triumphant climax of his concert career. Lina Ramann, his first major biographer, devoted many pages to the episode, establishing a precedent for countless derivative biographies appearing around 1900. Marie Lipsius, the great Liszt devotee, could thus write:

The year 1842 is called the "great," culminating year in Liszt's virtuoso life. Berlin swims in a frenzy of excitement such as it never experienced before or after. The magical playing of things unprecedented takes the city of intelligence beyond moderation and consciousness.[1]

In the same spirit, an early biographer called 1842 "the great year" and claimed that "Liszt's stay in Berlin forms the climax of his virtuosity."[2] More recent accounts of the episode, however, have entirely dispensed with such enthusiasm and triumphant rhetoric. Michael Saffle writes, in a decidedly measured tone, that "The performances Liszt presented during his first visit to Berlin became the most celebrated of his German tours, perhaps the most celebrated of his entire 'transcendental' career."[3] The quotations marks around "transcendental" suggest an unease with the grandiose claims previously made about Berlin. Alan Walker, likewise, resists all rhetoric about the "greatness" of the episode, and devotes considerably less space to it than previous biographers.[4]

Why has triumphalism disappeared from accounts of Liszt in Berlin? The main reason, I would suggest, is that the wars of the twentieth century have shifted attitudes toward mass public enthusiasm. Early biographers were able to interpret the behavior of the Berliners as a reliable index of Liszt's overwhelming genius. But this now strikes us as naïve. We feel compelled to look upon mass public enthusiasm suspiciously when it is directed toward highly charismatic figures, perhaps

[1] Marie Lipsius, *Liszt und die Frauen* (Leipzig, 1911), 96.
[2] Julius Kapp, *Franz Liszt: eine Biographie* (Berlin/Leipzig, 1911), 83–85.
[3] Michael Saffle, *Liszt in Germany, 1840–1845* (Stuyvesant, NY, 1994), 129.
[4] Alan Walker, *Franz Liszt* (Ithaca, 1987–1997), 3 vols., I: 371–74.

especially in the case of Berlin, the center of Hitler's regime. Liszt's audiences are no longer reliable witnesses to his artistic strength. And their credibility has been further injured by diligent biographers, who uncovered numerous caricatures and satires portraying the ridiculous extremes of Berlin's enthusiasm. Audiences now have the potential to compromise Liszt – to embarrass or trivialize him – and thus to subvert the basic laudatory premise of hagiographic biography. Confronted by this situation, Alan Walker has made an anxious effort to defend Liszt against his audiences: "He had suddenly become the victim of his own success and hardly knew how to cope . . . The fuss was entirely the fault of the Berliners."[5] The status of the Berlin episode remains in a kind of evaluative limbo, still recovering from its post-war wounds.

But there was a deep, divisive ambivalence about the Berlin audiences from the very beginning. Contemporary accounts of Liszt's 1842 visit present two opposing images, one positive and one negative. The negative image, which predominated outside Berlin, presented the enthusiasm for Liszt as excessive and irrational – evidence of a grave social illness. The positive image, articulated exclusively by writers within the city, presented the excitement as healthy sympathy for a virtuoso who managed to spread humanitarian benevolence through his art and activities. Although these views oppose one another, they share a focus on the social and moral life of Berlin, leaving aesthetic or musical issues largely to the side. This disregard of the aesthetic leads us to two key questions. Why did the Berlin episode inspire such different contemporary interpretations? And why did the discussions center on social issues? To answer these questions we need to take Liszt, as "man and artist," out of the spotlight, and reexamine the episode within the history of Berlin.

In the *Vormärz* period, Berlin was a city with an uncertain, "double" identity. In some ways it seemed steeped in the past, in other ways it seemed to be an embryo of the future. To Europeans in the more liberal capitals it was a residual outpost of the feudal–monarchical order. Starting in 1840, however, with the ascension of Friedrich Wilhelm IV, many within the German lands looked to Berlin as the kernel of a future German nation built on liberal principles. In this chapter I consider how this doubleness left its imprint upon Liszt's reception in the press. In the first part I argue that the negative vision of the episode emerged from a "progressive consensus," according to which the people of Berlin suffered under a repressive and censorious state apparatus. The enthusiasm for Liszt was, in this view, compensatory, an illusory substitute for the lack of agency and public participation among Berliners. Writers turned repeatedly to the image of illness to articulate their criticism, and the

---

[5] Ibid., I: 373.

word "Lisztomania" was born from this medical conceit. The emphasis on women's role in Lisztomania, deeply embedded in the Liszt mythology, was less a matter of factual representation than an extension of the pervasive theme of illness. The opposing positive of Liszt's reception was organized around perceptions of his benevolence or charity. Friedrich Wilhelm IV's optimistic and popular political rhetoric, with its promise of liberal social reforms, predisposed the Berlin public to appreciate Liszt's various gestures in support of charitable, humanitarian causes, as they saw themselves and their monarch echoed in Liszt's benevolence. But significantly, they found evidence of it not solely in his donations. His personal openness, his behavior toward audiences, and his performing style all became emblems of "charity" as well. Charity was thus, like the cult of Napoleon or the symbols of nationhood, an aspect of Liszt's historical context that he integrated into his performing persona.

1.   Anatomy of Lisztomania

The word "Lisztomania" is used today as a colorful expression to describe the mass public enthusiasm inspired by Liszt. It resonates with echoes of the more familiar word "Beatlemania," and because we are closer to the 1960s than to the 1840s, we might naturally tend to filter our imagination of Liszt's audiences through our images of Beatles fans. Yet when the word "Lisztomania" was coined, the medical valences of the term "mania" were still strong, whereas in modern parlance it designates any popular fashion or craze, and scarcely bears a trace of medical discourse. Understanding the medical connotation of the term is more than an exercise in semantics. It is the first step toward defamiliarizing the enthusiasms of Liszt's audiences and returning our sense of Lisztomania to its historical context.

Heinrich Heine coined the word ("Lisztomanie" in both German and French) as he overviewed the 1844 Parisian concert season, to which Liszt had spectacularly contributed. More than any other writer, Heine devoted himself to understanding the social and psychological roots of Liszt's popularity, and in his protracted attempt to do this, he constantly returned to the discourse of medicine. After witnessing Liszt's marvelous reception in Paris, he wrote: "And what celebration! A true madness, unheard of in the annals of furor! But what is the basis of this phenomenon? Perhaps the solution to this question belongs more in pathology than in aesthetics."[6] As we shall see, Heine asked a doctor about the Liszt phenomenon, and was answered with a feast of pathological esoterica. In the end Heine was skeptical about these elaborate

---

[6] *Heinrich Heine und die Musik*, ed. Gerhard Müller (Cologne, 1987), 156.

diagnoses. But about the symptoms he was certain: the emotional intensity that prevailed in Liszt's concert hall was symptomatic of a "spiritualistic sickness of our time [*Zeitkrankheit*] which vibrates in nearly all of us."[7] For Heine, Lisztomania was a contemporary social condition, an unhealthy state of mind and spirit.

Heine's invocation of the language of medicine in his evaluation of the public response to Liszt was more than a literary conceit. For some time, liberal and radical social reformers had seized upon medical metaphors and integrated them into their rhetoric of social criticism.[8] They divided social phenomena into symptoms and causes – the visible and the invisible – so that they could aim their reforms at the roots of society. Their two-tier apparatus allowed them to combat the traditionalists, who drew attention to symptoms alone. Medical language came to pervade discourse about society so completely that even today we refer to social problems, with hardly a trace of metaphorical awareness, as "social ills," and to their solutions as "panaceas." The discourse of illness flared up violently in writings about Liszt during and after his 1842 visit to Berlin. The public's extravagant behavior seemed so out of proportion with its presumed cause – piano virtuosity – that it could be explained only according to an alternative "pathology." In the manner of Heine but well before him, various critics had diagnosed the enthusiasm as a disease, and within a few months this opinion was being repeated all over Europe.

Why did the theme of illness show up so often and so dramatically in Berlin and not elsewhere? The obvious answer – that the Berliners were uncommonly enamored of Liszt – is convincing if we judge from the extraordinary number of public concerts he was able to give. But this does not explain why this exaggerated enthusiasm was judged to be not only extreme, but "sick" in nature. It is true that a few bizarre incidents – such as two women fighting over a glass he had just emptied – were widely publicized and contributed to external perceptions about the extremity of the Berlin audiences. I will argue here, however, that these incidents were probably fabricated *after* the episode to project the

---

[7] Ibid., 161. Although Heine's thoughts about Liszt's audiences had been pervaded with the framework of medicine, his reception in Paris in 1844 convinced him to discard the medical explanation for something more "prosaic": "It sometimes occurs to me that the whole magic can be explained by the fact that no one in the world knows as well as our Franz Liszt how to organize his successes, or the staging of them." Heine goes on to describe the exorbitant bills Liszt and Rubini had run up buying laurels, flowers, and a *claque* for their recent tour (ibid., 156–57).

[8] The *Oxford English Dictionary* gives an 1855 citation for "mania" from Macaulay's *History of England* that registers the use of mania to designate unhealthy social conditions: "A mania of which the symptoms were essentially the same with those of the mania of 1720 ... seized the public mind."

guilt of Berlin onto women. Illness became a theme in the Berlin episode not because the public's behavior seemed utterly abnormal, but on the contrary, because it seemed perfectly normal for Berlin. Well before Liszt arrived, that is, Berlin society had a reputation among progressive intellectuals for being stifled, straitjacketed, and rigidly hierarchical – in a word, unhealthy. What happened in the winter of 1842 ringingly confirmed this prejudice, and because it involved Liszt, it attained international visibility. Negative responses to the Berlin episode were a form of social criticism, generated by already existing opinions about Berlin and Prussian power.

The progressive consensus on social conditions in Berlin is nowhere better illustrated than in the passage in which Heine coined the word "Lisztomania":

As I some time ago heard about the giddiness that broke out in Germany, and especially in Berlin, when Liszt appeared there, I shrugged my shoulder sympathetically and thought: peaceful, restful Germany can not miss the opportunity to make a bit of permissible uproar, it has to shake its soporific limbs a little, and my kin [*Abderiten*] on the Spree like to tickle themselves with whatever enthusiasm is available . . . It is they, I thought, who make a spectacle of themselves at a spectacle, no matter what the cause is – Georg Herwegh, Franz Liszt or Fanny Elssler; with Herwegh exiled, they turn to Liszt, the unthreatening and uncompromising. That's what I thought; that's how I understood the Lisztomania, and I took it as an indication of the politically unfree situation on that side of the Rhine.[9]

According to this diagnosis, Lisztomania has nothing to do with Franz Liszt in particular. Liszt is merely the temporary occupant of a symbolic space, the "popular public figure" desperately needed by the Berlin public. It is appropriate, however, that Liszt's name appears between those of Elssler and Herwegh, for Liszt was able to combine the virtues of both of these artists. Like Elssler, he was a major performer appearing in public theatres – one of the few places a Berlin citizen could express himself or herself without punitive risk. And like Herwegh, he espoused liberal principles that (as Herwegh's exile proved) were closely watched and little tolerated in the Prussian capital. Better still, his fundamental means of expression was music, whose non-verbal, indeterminate meanings bypassed the difficulties of the censor and the state.

On stage, Liszt did the work of a Herwegh and an Elssler combined: he satisfied needs specific to the restraints on free and public expression under the Prussian monarchy. "Lisztomania" was not, therefore, meant to designate simply the mania for Liszt. It described a symptom of stunted spiritual and intellectual growth in monarchical Germany, as epitomized by Berlin. Heine's opinion was the most explicit

[9] *Heinrich Heine und die Musik*, 157–58.

articulation of an international consensus about Berlin that grounded negative responses to Liszt's reception there. To understand the roots of this consensus, we need to develop a fuller picture of public life in Berlin, and a sense of how it was different from other cities Liszt visited. But before looking more deeply into the conditions of the city, we will consider what in Liszt's virtuoso style might have made the metaphor of illness so tempting as a characterization of his effect on contemporary audiences.

The nerve of Liszt

One of the earliest satirists of Liszt's reception in the Prussian capital called it "the aesthetic St. Vitus-dance of all Berliners."[10] Victims of this dance, named after the religious ecstasies of St. Vitus, were said to jump around wildly and uncontrollably. This image registers the powerful effect Liszt's playing had on the bodies of his listeners. His high-intensity, often frantic bravura manner provoked involuntary physical reactions – shaking, shuddering, weeping. Applause for Liszt, indeed, appears less a gesture of appreciation, wonder, or joy, than a sheer corporal reflex – an outlet for great physical excitement. The effect of his playing passed over into the physical by virtue of its excess: an excess of vibrating sound, of musical information, of visual data – too many stimuli to be processed by the mental or affective faculties alone. Yet Liszt's playing reached into the body of his listener by a still more direct route: their identification with his performing self. For at the keyboard he appeared possessed by the same St. Vitus spirit. One listener described his experience of Liszt's favorite closer, the rousing *Grand galop chromatique*, as follows:

Along with an unbelievable richness of harmony, the tempo of the dance was so fast that one could hardly follow it with the ear, and even less with the eye, for whoever looked at the fingers of the concert-giver got lost in their rapidity, which in their flitting escaped the eye. If dancers were to look into this Lisztian whirl, they would compare it to the Turkish dervishes, who in their whirl-dance soon fall to the ground unconscious.[11]

This passage splits off the spectator from the performer; it orientalizes Liszt for the sake of projecting outward the spectator's bodily stimulation. The separation utterly breaks down, however, when we consider that the genre *galop* – as a variant of the *quadrille* – was internationally one of the most popular and most physical social dances of the 1830s and

---

[10] *Gesellschafter*, 19 February 1842. The *Gesellschafter* quotes this passage from a non-Berlin source.
[11] *Königliche preussische Staats- Kriegs- und Friedenszeitung*, 12 March 1842 (F. Raabe).

1840s. Liszt's virtuosity, then, got into the bodies of listeners not only through an excess of stimuli, but also by reviving sources of pleasure that lay within the experiential sphere of his audiences.

Contemporary commentators most often explained Liszt's effect on the body with reference to nerves. References to nerves show up almost exclusively in response to the bravura mode of his playing. Passages of tender or lyrical expression, less frequently occurring, were said to work their effects upon the heart or soul of his listeners, but rarely the nerves. In a performance of his *Niobe* fantasy, wrote a Vienna critic, "Liszt appeared to us as a tragic god, and through his harmonies made the finest nerves of the breast tremble."[12] The word "harmony" probably designates here only the resonant sonority of Liszt's rich textures, rather than particular chord progressions or modulations.[13] Such an emphasis on sonority derives from the fact that, physiologically, nerves seem to respond to the vibrations of musical sound, without cognitive intervention. The massive sonority Liszt summoned up at the first climax of the *Guillaume Tell* transcription (Example 5.1), a piece with which he opened dozens of concerts, was singled out for its effect on the nerves: "as the distinguished master played the Fortissimo in E minor, there stirred in the listeners feelings that they never felt, or even imagined, coming from this instrument. All fibers were set into motion."[14] This quotation stands out for its isolation of sheer sound as a force of its own; as soon as the sonority exceeds the listener's expectations of the piano's possibility, it ceases to act on him cognitively and passes over into a physical response.

Liszt's virtuosity worked so remarkably upon the body that some writers were driven to deeper physiological investigations of the phenomenon. Henri Blanchard, struck by the enthusiasm of the public at Liszt's Parisian concerts of 1844, proposed a study of "the connection that exists between metaphysics and physiology" with regard to "the art

---

[12] *Wiener Telegraph*, 4 May 1838.

[13] Most music critics in this time period, especially those writing for newspapers such as the *Wiener Telegraph*, used the word "harmony" in only the most generalized sense. Few knew even the most elementary aspects of music theory. Those who did – people such as Fétis, Schumann, and Berlioz – wrote very little about it in their journalism. Discussions of a composer's approach to harmony, or of isolated harmonic gestures, are extremely rare. There is evidence in Liszt's reception that many reporters were in fact quite deaf to harmony. A few who heard his *Grand galop chromatique*, clearly misled by the title, found it harmonically learned or esoteric. The *Grand galop* is extremely simple harmonically, its chromaticism applying to the melody alone. Heinrich Heine's well-known use of the word "harmony" as a characterizing concept for the genre French Grand Opera is typical of its time: its meaning is restricted to the sheer predominance of group singing over solo singing.

[14] *Breslauer Zeitung*, 24 January 1843.

Example 5.1 Liszt's transcription of the *Guillaume Tell* overture, first climax

of piano playing." In a contorted digression on this subject, he could not decide whether the virtuoso's expressive "sensibility" comes from the mind, the heart, or the hysteria (*aponevrose*), but he was unambiguous in his understanding that the audience underwent "frenetic enthusiasm stemming from disturbances pressed on the nervous systems by an artist."[15] It was the very same Parisian concerts that had provoked Heinrich Heine, convinced that the enthusiasm owed more to pathology than to aesthetics, to seek out a professional opinion. He chose to question a doctor who specialized in these female diseases, who

---

[15] *Revue et gazette musicale* 11/17 (28 April 1844), 131–33 (H. Blanchard).

talked variously about magnetism, galvanism, electricity, about the contagion in a hot hall filled with several hundred perfumed and sweating people and innumerable wax candles, about histrionic epilepsis, about the phenomenon of ticklishness, about musical cantharides and other awful things.[16]

This list is conspicuous for its emphasis on the nervous system and on invisible natural forces (magnetism, galvanism, electricity) that act only on the body's nervous fibers. Heine's assisted speculation also introduces two motifs closely related to the theme of nerves: first, the analogy of nervous excitation and electricity; and second, the association of women with nervous dispositions, as if women (but not men) were vessels, whose agitations could not effectively be controlled by mental or moral restraints.

Electricity is a pervasive presence in descriptions of Liszt's playing, registering the highly stimulated state of nerves he aroused in his listeners. Carl Gollmick described a linear electrical current flowing from Liszt out over his audience: "Liszt seemed to me like the highly charged conductor of an electric machine. When he is moved, electrical waves radiate outward. We felt electrified along with him."[17] The bright, piercing sounds he created by exploiting the upper registers of the keyboard lent themselves particularly well to electrical imagery:

the thunder, after muttering at a distance, gathered in strength till it crashed in dreadful peals around our ears commingled with coruscations of the electric fluid, struck out from the highest notes of the instrument, then gradually dying away.[18]

This passage describes one of the weather storms Liszt often improvised on his English tours to illustrate a dramatic recitation. The "electric fluid" of pianistic sound obviously originates in the dramatic image of lightning flashes. It is worth recalling, in this connection, the E minor fortissimo passage from *Guillaume Tell*, which was singled out for its nerve-rending effect. In the mimetic rhetoric of Rossini's overture, this moment represents a violent burst of lightning in the midst of a storm. The right hand crashes down on a high-pitched, tremolo-sustained E minor chord, slowly fades away with a chromatic descent, and returns again moments later. There was thus an element to the sound of Liszt's virtuosity that made electricity a compelling metaphor. Nevertheless, most often electricity was introduced to account for the invisible, dynamic process by which Liszt transmitted his intense nervous state to his audiences. Another writer thus mentioned electrical fluid passing not from the piano into the audience, but from Liszt's body into the keyboard:

[16] *Heinrich Heine und die Musik*, 156.
[17] *Frankfurter Konversationsblatt*, 4 November 1843 (C. Gollmick).
[18] *Wakefield Journal*, 11 December 1840; quoted in *Liszt Society Journal* 11 (1985), 48.

He is the sovereign master of his piano; he knows all its resources; he makes it speak, moan, cry, and roar under fingers of steel, which distill nervous fluid like Volta's battery distills electrical fluid.[19]

This passage demonstrates, furthermore, the close conceptual link between nerves and electricity. In describing Liszt's effect on audiences with the language of electricity, it implies that this effect was like a law of nature; Liszt's playing works upon the body directly and without mediation, through physiological processes that have nothing to do with cognition or consciousness.

In most of the citations above, Liszt's corporeal impact on listeners is valued favorably. Yet for contemporaries, recognizing the physicality implicit in listening to Liszt was doomed to produce cultural anxiety. For there was a risk that the experience of Liszt could become *exclusively* physical, all sensual pleasure, devoid of moral or intellectual engagement. Applause for Liszt thus teetered on the edge of the illegitimate abyss of pure sensuality. Both Heine and Blanchard betray this anxiety in their speculations on Liszt and the human body. Immediately after mapping out a field for the study of "metaphysics and physiology," Blanchard writes that

It would be intriguing to do this study on the art of playing the piano, which we have quite justly from the beginning called *pianism*, which surrounds us, invades us, carries us away and threatens to dominate all classes of society. One of these days I may work on an amusing piece on this new musical cult, on this instrumental Saint-Simonism of which Liszt is at least the high priest if not the Mohammed.[20]

This passage cannot be dismissed because of its humorous tone. Its gentle mockery is defensive, an attempt to temper or control the disturbing force Liszt had worked on the bodies of the Parisian public. Blanchard's rhetoric insistently pushes the body outside of the "us," consigns it to the margins ("new musical cult") or to the orient ("Mohammed"). Heine, too, mapped such physical excitement onto an Other when he attributed Lisztomania to German political conditions. What he saw in Paris in 1844, however, made him change his mind: "But I was wrong . . . this was truly no German-Berlin-sentimental, fake-feeling public before which Liszt played all alone."[21] It was precisely at this moment that Heine turned to his doctor for help: even the applause of the sophisticated Parisians had to have something to do with the body.[22]

[19] Paul Scudo, *Critique et littérature musicales* (Paris, 1850), 2 vols., I: 15.
[20] *Revue et gazette musicale* 11/17 (28 April 1844), 151 (H. Blanchard); emphasis original.
[21] *Heinrich Heine und die Musik*, 156. "Das war kein berlinisch-sentimentalisch, anemfindelndes Publikum."
[22] Heine abridged the contents of the doctor's physical speculations for the publication of the article: "The electrical effect of a demonic nature on a tightly packed mass, the

This mechanism of displacement is centrally important in considering Liszt's female listeners. Writers thematized Liszt's influence on women to delegitimate pleasures that, although shared by audience members of both genders, could not be affirmed or even acknowledged in men because they existed in the body alone. Women were most vulnerable to this displacement because Liszt's playing troubled the nerves, and in the physiological construction of gender difference, nerves held a privileged position. Women's fine, sensitive nerves were thought to make them highly excitable, susceptible to the strong stimuli of Liszt's fiery virtuosity. Men too demonstrated states of high excitation, but such states were attributed to high cognitive faculties such as intelligence or aesthetic understanding, or to extraordinary external pressures – never to a sheer physiological predisposition. The French writer Léon Beaufort brought up this gender dichotomy as he defended the authenticity of Liszt's emotions in performance:

O women! faithful mirrors, sympathetic echoes of all sensibility and passion, I would not demonstrate with an example that which you already well know by the power of response that it [Liszt's nature] holds over your soul – how true, how spontaneous the electricity of his soul of fire is ... But alas! I do not have the softness to write for you alone; and for our denigrating and skeptical sex, our positive and charlatan sex, I can not speak of sincere enthusiasm, of inspiration born in the heart, without raising cries of doubt.[23]

Liszt's virtuosity thus affects women through an inevitable sympathy with his electrified soul, a sympathy predetermined by gender. Men, however, lacking such an uncensored and automatic response, require corroborating evidence from Beaufort, which he promptly offers in the continuation.

The Berlin episode gave rise to dozens of caricatures, anecdotes, and criticisms attributing the excessive enthusiasm to women. There is no need to deny that women were involved in the public enthusiasm, or that they behaved differently from men in relation to Liszt. The media's focus on women, however, should not be taken at face value, as it has been even in recent writings about Liszt.[24] It was first and foremost a

infectious force of ecstasy, and perhaps the magnetism of music itself, of this spiritualistic disease that vibrates in nearly all of us – I never encountered these phenomena so clearly and so frightfully as in the Liszt concert" (ibid., 161).

[23] *Le dilettante*, 2 August 1838 (L. Beaufort).

[24] The notion that women were particularly taken with Liszt – one of the most entrenched elements of the Lisztian mythology – rests largely on the literal interpretation of documents pertaining to the Berlin episode. Robert Walser interprets the caricatures of Liszt in Berlin as historical fact: "Wolf Marshall ... compares today's metal guitarists to Liszt and Paganini in their virtuosity, bravura manner, mystique, attractiveness to women, and experimentation with flashy, crowd-pleasing tricks. These parallels seem very apt when we recall that women swooned and threw flowers to Liszt during his

rhetorical ploy, a mechanism for displacing irrationality to the Other (women), hence delegitimating the sheer physical excitement that all listeners experienced at his concerts. This rhetorical purpose is most easily observed in extreme cases such as the following correspondent's report:

> Praise God! Mr. Liszt has left, the paroxysms of his adorers has reached the limit of madness. At the moment it is raining caricatures to mock the fanaticism of some sectors. A lady was recently arrested in the street, calling Mr. Liszt by the most intimate names at the top of her voice. She was visited by doctors and led like a madwoman to the Charité hospital to be treated there.[25]

This fanciful anecdote is probably extrapolated from a satire of a madhouse for women that appeared shortly after Liszt's visit to the city (Figure 5.1). Such fictions are structured around the perception that Lisztian enthusiasm was generated in and on the body's nerves. Yet they simultaneously deny the ungendered body by coding the response as a female "special case": the overstimulation of frail nervous systems developing into madness or hysteria. By the nineteenth century this was an old game in the European world, but this game was not played in the world of public concerts until a virtuoso with Liszt's nervous, unsettling temperament came along.

Figure 5.2 shows an image, created in the wake of the Berlin episode, that has often been reproduced and has played a formative role in the myth of Liszt's power over female listeners. The image seems aimed at highlighting the susceptibility of the female gender. The most important figure in the audience is the woman holding a cup, which is presumably filled with wine. This drink itself codes her response as sensual, and the way her shawl has come off her shoulder makes sensuality spill over into sexuality. The woman is positioned exactly where the sound comes out of the piano; the angle of the glass suggests that the music passes into it as though it was passing through the bottom of the cup, so that music and drink are co-implicated in the woman's sensual, if not sexual, indulgence. In addition, the position of Liszt's raised hand is such that he seems to be pushing or throwing the music toward her. Because of this, her response cannot be attributed to the power of sound or music in some general, platonic sense, but must have its source in Liszt himself.

Three other women in the picture are drawn with particular care: one fainting (center of the public), another throwing flowers (above right), and the third blowing a kiss to Liszt (lower left). The first two of these are

---

performances . . . The contemporary description [of Liszt] with which I began this chapter could just as well apply to Ritchie Blackmore or Eddie Van Halen" (*Running with the Devil: Power, Gender, and Madness in Heavy Metal Music* [Middletown, CT, 1993], 28).

[25] *France musicale* 5/12 (20 March 1842), 119 (Berlin report).

Figure 5.1 Berlin caricature by Grühnspahn, 1842

Figure 5.2 Berlin caricature by A. Eyssenhardt, 1842

both accompanied by distraught male companions, further reinforcing the gender specificity of the picture's "message." But there is one
other figure who completes a geometrical diamond with the others:
the man in the lower right-hand corner. Just as the women try to
"reach" Liszt with flowers or kisses, this man (perhaps a fop) is trying to "reach" him visually – with his binoculars – and his fascination
with the virtuoso is of no lesser order, and of no different kind, than
that of the women. As if to confirm this, he carries a laurel crown in his
top hat, ready to render his fondness to Liszt in the same way as the
woman in the upper right. Furthermore, while the poor fainting girl has
attracted the attention of the women around her, this man, under whose
nose the crisis is taking place, will not be distracted. With this character,
then, the picture contradicts what it seems to assert: that women alone
are susceptible to such enthusiasm. The emphasis of contemporary journalists on women's susceptibility to Liszt in Berlin was at least partially
a projection of the extreme enthusiasm of the public *as a whole* out onto
its female constituency, for whom such enthusiasms were considered
"natural."

The image of Liszt shaking up the nerves of human masses with potent
waves of electrical energy, an image that transcended the Berlin episode,
gave the rhetoric of social disease a resonant analogy in the very texture

of his concerts. Audiences took great pleasure at entering into an abnormal physical state bordering on the pathological, and they incessantly sought to repeat and prolong the experience. This disturbing fact must have lurked in the minds of many observers as they worried about the link between the peculiar social climate of the Prussian capital and the outstanding reception its residents accorded to Liszt. The metaphors of disease which cropped up so often in contemporary evaluations of the Berlin episode, however, are more directly related to stereotypes of social life in Berlin, and less to scientific speculation about fibers, invisible forces, or charged fluids. Only with a full presentation of the conditions of civic life in Berlin can we fully understand the idea of "Lisztomania."

Public life in Berlin: the liberal consensus

Philosopher Jürgen Habermas has traced the historical development of what he calls the "bourgeois public sphere." This sphere consists of the various forums in which private persons engage in critical debate over questions of political authority. It is opposed to a "representative public sphere," in which the authority of the feudal lord or of the monarch is *represented before* the people it affects, like a piece of theatre, unavailable for interruption or contestation. The eventual displacement of the "representative" by the "bourgeois" public sphere is an obvious fact of history, but the public sphere emerged at different times and in different forms. Historically, Habermas argues, such a forum first reveals itself in the flourishing coffee-house culture of late seventeenth-century London, while in Paris a public sphere becomes recognizable in salons of the mid-eighteenth century.[26] In the German lands, the bourgeois public sphere emerged considerably later, showing its first traces only at the end of the eighteenth century. The development of a politically significant bourgeois public sphere in Germany, in fact, lagged behind that of France and England throughout the nineteenth century.[27] There were, to be sure, pockets of radical thought in the German states. Berlin's own Cafe Steheli was well known for its left-leaning intelligentsia clientele. But without a free press to propagate their views, the sphere of critical

---

[26] Jürgen Habermas, *The Structural Transformation of the Public Sphere*, trans. Thomas Burger and Frederick Lawrence (Cambridge, MA, 1991), 32–35, 70–71.

[27] Peter Gay writes: "the *Bürgertum* in the German states appeared relatively undemanding in the political sphere or, when demanding, unsuccessful . . . Germany managed to delay the accession of the *Bürgertum* until well into the twentieth century" (*The Cultivation of Hatred* [New York, 1993], 218). Norbert Elias has described the German intelligentsia – which became a numerous class in the eighteenth century – as a non-political class, almost driven to pursue academic knowledge by their exclusion from any real influence in the state affairs of their noble employers (Jürgen Rehm, *Zur Musikrezeption im vormärzlichen Berlin* [Hildesheim, 1983], 44).

debate remained largely confined to elite intellectual circles, and could not embrace a larger bourgeois sphere.

The idea that the people of the German states remained monarchical and politically docile, at a time when other European states were facing off with a confrontational bourgeois public sphere, does not belong to historians and sociologists alone. Commentators of Liszt's time also noticed it, and those with a liberal outlook considered it vitally important to criticize what they saw as a backward, or at least sleepy, political order. As the capital of the Prussian kingdom, Berlin was an obvious target for such criticism. Yet Berlin was not just another example: it was the home of the Prussian monarchy, lorded over by an aloof aristocracy, and it epitomized the feudal spirit that progressives most disliked. In a displaced form of political critique, they portrayed Berlin as a dreary, cold, jaded environment. A closer look at this image of Berlin will bring us closer to explaining why the trope of illness became so pervasive.

To many outsiders writing in the 1840s, Berlin society appeared to be rigid and joyless. The mixing of social levels so characteristic of urban society, and so crucial to its liveliness, seemed absent from Berlin. Carnival was intended to suspend the class divisions of everyday life in a spirit of play and collective joy, yet according to a correspondent writing in 1843, the Berliners seemed constitutionally unsuited to such a celebration:

Berlin and a Carnival are inherently opposites of one another . . . Social life moves only in uniform, same-status circles; and woe to him who wants to jump from one to another, he will receive a tough reprimand . . . even socializing evinces a strict, police-like order and regularity.[28]

At the great Carnival balls held in the opera house and playhouse, the correspondent continued, many people took off their masks to avoid mixing with those outside their social circles.[29] This author was most interested, however, in subsuming his observations about Carnival within a more general image of Berlin's "strict, police-like order and regularity." Other commentators found such militaristic regularity in the very layout of city streets, or in the lines of armed guards that stood in front of the gates and palaces of Unter den Linden, the city's promenade.[30]

Berlin was also known as a city with strict laws and strong censorship, rendering any attempt at political organization or opposition futile. Friedrich Wieck encountered this as he organized concerts for Clara in 1839. All notices and changes had to be written five times and go through four authorities before appearing in journals and newspapers, leading

---

[28] *Europa* (1843/1), p. 490.   [29] Ibid.
[30] Ernst Dronke, *Berlin* (Frankfurt a. M., 1846), 13.

him to write to his wife: "The difficulties with police, censors, etc. are endless here."[31] The state's paranoia of political revolution led to the establishment, in the 1830s, of a law restricting the number of people allowed to gather together in the streets. Even more notorious than this law was the prohibition on smoking in public places, also an attempt to curb violent uprisings.[32] Public theatres were one of the few environments in which crowds could gather and make their opinions felt without obvious punitive risk, but the state was known to intervene here as well: in January 1844, Friedrich Wilhelm IV cancelled a planned benefit concert when he heard that the "Marseillaise" and the "Riëgo" hymn were on the program, fearing that the audience would sing along.[33]

In a public environment so restrictive, it was difficult for the middle classes, who had no political power, to feel even a tinge of political engagement, a situation that led to widespread political apathy and conservatism. Ernst Dronke wrote that "the mind of the Berliners is in general very monarchical ... despite their little jokes and anecdotes they remain very loyal to the 'ancestral dynasty.'"[34] Heinrich Heine extended the same observation to apply to all Germans, as he mocked the patriotic propaganda over the anti-Napoleon wars of 1813: "we Germans received orders from on high to free ourselves from the foreign yoke and we flamed up in manly wrath ... we do everything commanded by our princes."[35] Even if Heine was correct that obedience toward monarchs was a trait of the German people as a whole, this tendency was undoubtedly exaggerated in Berlin, where the numerous state officials, most of them noble, presided over public events.[36]

Liberal critics were concerned about the political indifference of the Berlin bourgeoisie and the lack of a flourishing bourgeois public sphere. In 1843 a fledgling Berlin journal urged, in its prospectus, that Berliners develop a political consciousness according to the models of Paris and London:

Berlin adopts all characters and all directions, but has no character or direction. Berlin has no public sphere [*Öffentlichkeit*] like London and Paris, where politics raises its voice and can express its deepest secrets. And because Berlin has no voices, it also has no mood. Berlin has no political consciousness, because it has no historical consciousness.[37]

---

[31] Friedrich Wieck, *Briefe aus den Jahren 1830–38* ed. Käthe Walch-Schumann (Cologne, 1968), 60.

[32] *Europa* (1843/1), 490: "even cigar smoke is suppressed by police control."

[33] Karl August Varnhagen von Ense, *Tagebücher* (Leipzig, 1861), 14 vols., II: 253.

[34] Dronke, *Berlin*, 13.

[35] From *Die romantische Schule* (1835), in *Sämmtliche Schriften*, ed. Klaus Briegleb et al. (1968–76), 6 vols., III: 379. Quoted in Gay, *The Cultivation of Hatred*, 101.

[36] Rehm, *Zur Musikrezeption*, 19.

[37] *Berliner Wespen* (January 1843), 1 (F. Wehl). Habermas's German word for "public sphere" is "Öffentlichkeit."

As negative as these words sound, their author hoped for a regeneration of Berlin appropriate to its status as Prussia's capital. Indeed, the reforming voice here is not entirely inconsistent with the rhetoric of Friedrich Wilhelm IV. Frankly critical voices about Berlin's lack of a politically active public could only come from writers located outside Berlin, such as Heine.

The bourgeoisie compensated for its exclusion from public affairs by engaging in activities and behaviors that simulated agency or influence. One product of this sublimatory process was the legendary *Berliner Witz*. The Berlin wit was an ironic, merciless deflation of anything that pretended to be important. Its privileged discursive media, as Liszt found out soon enough, were jokes, satirical verses, and caricatures. The *Berliner Witz* manifested itself not only in humor, but also in a more general "critical spirit." Ernst Dronke was transmitting common wisdom when he wrote: "Criticism, the negation of every authority, is, if nothing else, a characteristic of Berlin. In its eyes nothing is 'holy,' everything is first examined, criticized and then 'undone' with a droll comment [*Witzwort*]."[38] Unable to vent their political discontents without severe penalty, the bourgeoisie attacked non-political targets and displaced their aggression to the less threatening mode of satire.[39] Dronke felt that the political potential of the *Berliner Witz* would inevitably bloom in the near future.[40]

Wolfgang Rehm has argued that the bourgeoisie of *Biedermeier* Berlin also compensated for their political exclusion with imitations of the aristocracy. They fantasized the possession of social power by holding their own salons, or asserting themselves at the theatre and the opera, venues which were formerly the privilege of the aristocracy.[41] A lack of political agency, in Rehm's view, was responsible for "the theatre-obsession of the Berliners, the almost unbelievable public interest in great artistic personalities," and helps explain the "excessive enthusiasm

---

38 Dronke, *Berlin*, 22. Liszt was himself intimidated by Berlin's critical reputation, which seemed incarnated in the leading music critic Ludwig Rellstab. He had a chance of going to Berlin in the fall of 1840 and in the spring of 1841, but both times he decided to wait until a more opportune moment. He did not want to concertize there until he felt certain of success.

39 Peter Gay has written at length on humor as a form of aggression. A classic example of how the bourgeoisie used humor for aggressive ends was the Parisian revolution of 1830, a "bourgeois" revolution that inspired many caricatures, notably those of Daumier. See chapter 5 in *The Cultivation of Hatred*.

40 Dronke: "The wit should become political, as the entire direction of Berlin is a political one" (*Berlin*, 19).

41 Dronke argued that the royal opera house and other new institutions "give the middle and lower bourgeoisie, with their bad taste, a reflection [*Abglanz*] of the pleasures and the taste of the richer idlers in the aristocratic quarters" (*Berlin*, 339).

of the Berliners for a singer like Henriette Sonntag."[42] This is, once again, a view shared by social observers of Liszt's time. An 1843 article in *Europa* offered the following words about the typical *Bürger* of Berlin:

> his own concerns and affairs go before everything, and the concerns of the state and the world, which cannot raise his income, interest him little. This political indifference makes it such that we cannot yet speak at all of a public opinion, of the kind that the people make manifest; even among the higher classes we find an indifference that seems, to those who come from constitutional countries, truly amazing. It is alone on the boards that portray the world that a public opinion shows itself. *Here the public that freely pays its taxes can make its applause or disapproval manifest*, and the theatre box office is compelled to follow its voice.[43]

A politically disempowered bourgeoisie, then, caught up in its own affairs and alienated from any public interest, finds at the theatre ("the boards that portray the world") a simulacrum of engagement in public matters. This was precisely what Heinrich Heine meant when he claimed that the Berliners "like to make a spectacle of themselves at a spectacle," be it Liszt, Elssler, or Herwegh.[44]

The radical critic Ernst Dronke diagnosed the enthusiasm of the Berliners for public spectacles somewhat differently. Dronke was most struck by the anonymity and looseness of human relationships in Berlin. Like other critics, he saw an unhealthy disconnection among the various social segments of the city, but the focus of his criticism was family life, particularly among the bourgeoisie (what he called the *Mittelstand*). Bourgeois families were being disintegrated by widespread extramarital relationships, which were commonly tolerated, and by students who preferred keeping *grisettes* to marrying and establishing a family. The bonds of the family were so weak, Dronke argued, that people struggled to make superficial, fleeting social connections in public spaces: "one no longer finds the expression of life in the domestic hearth, but outside the house, in the wild, confused bustle of public space [*Öffentlichkeit*], and externalness is once again here the leading characteristic."[45] Nowhere was this tendency better observed than in theatres, concert halls, and comparably public locales:

---

[42] Rehm, *Zur Musikrezeption*, 45.

[43] *Europa* (1843/4), 588–89 ("L . . . q"); emphasis added.

[44] When Friedrich Wieck took Clara to Berlin in 1839, he had already seen many audiences in different parts of Europe, but the enthusiasm of the Berliners took him by surprise. "An enthusiastic Berlin public," he wrote to his wife, "is a frightening one" (Wieck, *Briefe aus den Jahren 1830–38*, 64).

[45] Dronke, *Berlin*, 17–18.

Acquaintances with women are even more easily established. In the theatre, in public places, in gardens and concerts, they arise from superficial contact when someone takes a place next to them at the same table or in the same box; the desire to continue the relationship . . . is expressed and accepted through glances and apparently accidental indications.[46]

The bourgeoisie's pursuit of entertainment and public appearances was so extreme, Dronke continued, that they could not even attend to their basic necessities: "One can never be sure whether the families that rush around at concerts, public entertainments, etc. in velvet and silk might not be giving up their mid-day meal or offering up their most essential needs, beds and furniture."[47]

There were thus differing assessments of why the Berliners pursued their public activities so zealously. For some critics the cause was political exclusion, while for Dronke the cause was moral decay. There was general agreement, however, that the Berliners threw themselves into their public entertainments in compensation for something they fundamentally lacked in their daily lives, be it political agency or close family ties. Their enthusiasm at theatres, concerts, and other public events signified neither artistic sensibility nor warm gratitude toward performers, but rather grave social problems, indeed social malaise. This was the progressive consensus on Berlin, and it provided the foundation for criticism of Berlin's "Lisztomania."

A veritable summary of the progressive consensus on Berlin appeared in the *Neue Zeitschrift für Musik* six months after Liszt's visit. The article is a *Stadtbild* – a city portrait – in which the author, Hermann Hirschbach, attempts to explain why Berlin has not produced any composers of note. Hirschbach does not hesitate to fault an outdated state order:

so little is done for the support of younger talents . . . that truly outstanding talents are intimidated with repression and little by little completely robbed of free expression. All along, only externally brilliant fame has found the useless protection of the state powers, whereas needy but promising talents are neglected.[48]

Hirschbach's manifest purpose here is to criticize royal patronage, which favors foreign artists over native talent, but his larger rhetorical move is more interesting. He forges a link between the state, on the one hand, and the "repression" and lack of "free expression" on the other. This link can only be made rhetorically, for a lack of state patronage is not itself repressive or censorious. He introduces the motifs of repression and censorship more from predetermined disapproval of Berlin's conservative,

[46] Ibid., 28.   [47] Ibid., 13.
[48] H. Hirschbach, "Städtebilder. Berlin," in *Neue Zeitschrift für Musik* 17/44 (29 November 1842), 179–80.

monarchial order than from a desire to explain musical circumstances. His portrait of Berlin also incorporates the other favorite motifs of progressive critics: cold, anonymous social relations; a negative, critical attitude; and the plain physical layout of the city. Most tellingly, however, he links these elements with the mania for virtuosos:

Neither the very prosaic natural environment of Berlin nor the mocking, joking disposition of its people are suited to provide music with fruitful nourishment and inspiration, and this lack of life warmth and personal warmth cuts divisively into all relationships. The often very overwhelming enthusiasm for virtuosos and singers is frequently held against us; this enthusiasm is always only a matter of people, not of the often so ambiguous music.[49]

Although "virtuosos" and "singers" appear here in the plural, there was one virtuoso and one singer who, far more than any others, had given Berlin a bad name. The virtuoso was Liszt. The singer was Henriette Sonntag. A look at the reception of Sonntag will help us see how Liszt's reception exemplified a larger pattern of behavior among the Berlin publics, and why critics were inclined to view it as a "matter of people," not of music.

Sonntag Fever

Opera singer Henriette Sonntag took Berlin by storm in 1826. A compelling account of the Sonntag reads like Liztomania *avant la lettre*. Berlin's public was utterly obsessed with seeing, hearing, and chatting about the opera heroine. Night after night she brought down the house at the Volksbühne with her performance of Desdemona in Rossini's *Otello*. On these nights the royal opera and the royal theatre were as good as empty, and the guards would abandon their posts to go hear her. People wrestled each other to obtain tickets, and those who had never managed to hear her felt like social outcasts.[50] Like Lisztomania, the obsession with Sonntag disgusted some observers. Composer and pedagogue Ludwig Berger was so tired of hearing Sonntag chatter that he fled the city and returned only after she was gone. The social breadth of Sonntag's popularity forms a further parallel to Liszt. She was admired "from the top to the bottom, from the state ministers and ambassadors down to the chambermaids,"[51] just as Liszt was "talked about with delight in the palaces of the great as well as in the cottages of poverty."[52] At the height of Sonntag's visit people were talking about

---

[49] Ibid.   [50] *Nachgelassene Memoiren von Karoline Bauer* (Berlin, 1881), 3 vols., II: 171ff.
[51] Ludwig Rellstab, *Henriette, oder die schöne Sängerin* (Leipzig, 1826), 48.
[52] *Blätter für Musik und Literatur* 3 (March 1842), 51–52 (G. Nicolai). The poor probably attended the performances of Liszt and Sonntag in very small numbers. They were more likely to be able to afford tickets to Sonntag's performances, which took place at

her in every restaurant, every salon, even at the fish and vegetable markets. She had become, to borrow an epithet Rellstab later applied to Liszt, "a phenomenon of public life."[53]

Sonntag's departure from Berlin was a major event in which thousands participated. Liszt's departure, described in nearly every biography, had more ceremonial pomp because it was spearheaded by officials and professors from the university, but in all other respects Sonntag's *Abschied* was equally as immense. After her final performance, she left the theatre and found a curious, restless crowd filling up the entire large expanse of Alexanderplatz. There her trademark red carriage picked her up and began the route back to her apartment, the way paved with flowers and packed with spectators. Everyone pushed to get a last view of her as cheers and salutes poured in from all directions. Outside her hotel window she was serenaded by military bands, while the crowd continued to send up salutes well into the night. The next morning she was accompanied by the highest military escort to Potsdam, where she gave a concert for the king and queen.[54] The manner in which Liszt was honored at the end of his stay corresponds in almost every detail to this description.

The resemblance between the reception of Liszt and that of Sonntag was not lost on contemporary journalists. Those who made the comparison, however, tended to be Liszt's critics. Rellstab, a Liszt supporter, rejected the comparison to Sonntag out of hand: "The mixing-up of these two figures, and the resulting bitter hostility toward the current one (in certain bad journals), reveals only the obtuse narrowness of these opponents."[55] Rellstab's main contention was that Sonntag's artistic achievement was of a lesser order because she had merely repeated the same performance over and over, whereas Liszt had shown astonishing breadth and flexibility in his repertory. But in his vehement denial of any similarity between the reception of Liszt and of Sonntag, Rellstab risked exposing a further parallel. For in the book he had published on Sonntag in 1826, he attributed the bulk of the enthusiasm to the scores of male fans that were hopelessly enamored of her.[56] Liszt's opponents

the Volksbühne and therefore probably had a wide variety of price categories. Liszt's ticket prices rarely reached below the medium price range. In the case of both artists, however, the involvement of the poor was chiefly at the level of public conversation and observation. The poor also appreciated the generous response both Liszt and Sonntag gave to people who visited them and requested money for the aid of destitute families (see ibid. and Rellstab, *Henriette*, 166–67).

[53] "Liszt, ein Ereignis des öffentlichen Lebens" was the title of an essay Rellstab wrote after Liszt's departure, summarizing his visit for foreign readers (Ludwig Rellstab, *Franz Liszt: Beurtheilungen-Berichte-Lebensskizze* [Berlin, 1842], 46ff.).

[54] Bauer, *Nachgelassene Memoiren*, II: 203.

[55] Rellstab, *Franz Liszt*, 45.   [56] Rellstab, *Henriette*, 49ff.

used the same rhetoric, delegitimating the public enthusiasm by pointing to the antics of his female admirers.

It would be hasty to conclude from this that the Berliners were particularly responsive to the "sex appeal" of their public performers. The critics of both Liszt and Sonntag were first and foremost attempting to delegitimate public behavior that seemed extreme and unhealthy. "Sex appeal" was a convenient vehicle for such delegitimation because it was so obviously external to the performer's putative artistic product. Rellstab, at least, clearly subsumed his comments on the male fanatics within this broader delegitimating purpose. He fell short of characterizing Sonntag's reception in terms of illness, but he did call it a "general drunkenness" to which an "uncritical, unknowledgeable public" had succumbed.[57] He was appalled that such a large portion of the public had adopted the wild accolades Sonntag's courtiers were propagating. Sonntag's effect on her public was, however, eventually interpreted in the language of medical discourse. Reflecting on the episode from considerable temporal distance, one witness dubbed the enthusiasm "The Sonntag Fever" and concluded that "that wild Sonntag-enthusiasm was extreme and is a symptom of the sickness [*Krankheitszeichen*] of that time."[58]

I do not want to conceal the important differences between Liszt's and Sonntag's reception in Berlin, but the parallels need emphasis here. They help explain why many contemporary writers who observed the public enthusiasm for Liszt interpreted it as evidence of a more general problem in Berlin, rather than as proof of the artist's overwhelming genius. The public reaction to Liszt was familiar behavior, a replay of events in Berlin's recent past. And they would be replayed once again in 1843, when dancer Fanny Elssler arrived. Observers took advantage of the Liszt episode to register their disapproval of the deeper social conditions it seemed to reveal, and the most consistent strategy for doing this was to employ images of illness.

Criticism from the inside

The diversity of journals and newspapers reporting on cultural events was considerably smaller in Berlin than in other capitals Liszt visited. Most Berliners read either the *Spenersche Zeitung* or the *Vossische Zeitung*, and the music critics at both papers were generally positive in their reports on Liszt.[59] Voices resisting the public enthusiasm were heard

---

[57] Ibid., 48. [58] Bauer, *Nachgelassene Memoiren*, II: 176.

[59] Ludwig Rellstab's attractive style gave the *Vossische Zeitung* greater popularity and authority among Berlin readers. The critic at the *Spenersche Zeitung*, J. P. Schmidt, reviewed most of Liszt's concerts, but his comments are very superficial and contribute little to our understanding of the Berlin episode.

only in the *Gesellschafter* and the *Neuigkeits-Bote,* and both were ready to invoke metaphors of illness. The *Gesellschafter* used a light touch. Its entertaining writer J. Bellegno, exiting from one of Liszt's concerts, overheard a spectator lamenting that Berlin had lost

all measure to judge something's worth. Ignoring or worshipping, underestimating or blind enthusiasm – these are rampant among us like a malaria [*Wechselfieber*], and whoever gets caught up in the whirl and bustle of our paroxysms gets through only one half of the illness.[60]

Bellegno may have contrived this comment to voice his own opinion, but the idea could easily have been blowing through the air of Berlin. The specific symptoms of Bellegno's illness – radical shifts from one extreme to the other – suggest that he is making a social commentary, for according to the diagnosis of Berlin as a socially sick city, there is no moderation in its behavior. The public either remains apathetic because it has no sense of participating in public affairs, or gets overexcited in compensation for its impotence in public affairs; a healthy midpoint between these extremes is not to be observed. Bellegno presents the problem as a matter of aesthetic judgment, a lapse into bad taste. But we can now see this within the larger intellectual context, in which the aesthetic deficiencies or extremities of the Berlin public were attributed to stiff and exclusionary social conditions.

The most socially conscious of all the Berlin journals to report on Liszt was the *Neuigkeits-Bote,* and it too drew upon the language of illness to voice its discontents. The *Neuigkeits-Bote* rarely reported on music, and it became interested in Liszt only when the public seemed to have entirely lost its senses. After four or five weeks of closely packed concerts, it was clear that the enthusiasm of the Berliners was not subsiding: the time had come to intervene and bring the Berlin public to its senses. With missionary fervor, a writer who signed his name "Beta" published a series of attacks on Liszt and the public excitement over him.[61] These articles, which have never been cited by Liszt researchers, are worth dwelling upon, for they lay out the case for the sickness of the Berlin publics more fully than any other writings. Together, in fact, they constitute the most merciless diatribe ever mounted against Liszt.

To Beta it was nearly self-evident that Liszt's playing was of no positive value, and he spent little time explaining why he held this opinion. All virtuosity was in his eyes "the triumph of form over the ideal, divine content." He addressed himself not to aesthetics, but to the malaise from which Berlin now suffered:

---

[60] *Gesellschafter* 36 (28 February 1842), 169 (J. Bellegno).

[61] The editor of the *Gesellschafter,* in which Bellegno's vignette appeared, let moderately critical commentary about Liszt appear in other columns of his journal. For this he was warmly praised by the editor of the *Neuigkeits-Bote.*

the effect of his bizarre, substance-less, idea-less, sensually exciting, contrast-ridden, fragmented playing, and the diseased [*krankhafte*] enthusiasm over it, is a depressing sign of the stupidity, the insensitivity, and the aesthetic emptiness of the public.[62]

Beta preserved his hyperbolic, humorless tone through every sentence of his articles. Fully in line with the liberal consensus, he argued that the Berliners' response to Liszt proved their disengagement from matters of social reform. At the end of his first article, for example, he pleaded with his readers:

In conclusion I ask Berlin once again: Where is your enthusiasm and your heart-felt devotion for events, phenomena, and persons that sacrifice themselves for the good of the people, for national interests, for lively ideals and ideas? No one is considering the question where this sacrifice will come from. Oh Kyritz, my fatherland![63]

Beta wrung his hands over Liszt's influence over the university students and the women of Berlin. Completely reversing the opinion of most critics, he felt that Liszt distracted the students from their pursuit of *Bildung*: "A healthy youth enthusiastic for German spirit and German learning does not prostrate itself to such a virtuoso."[64] The women, he continued, so occupied themselves with Liszt that they lost sight of their domestic duties. After Liszt left, Beta wrote with relief that the women "are once again taking care of children, kitchen, and husband," but their behavior during his presence should "instantly fill with anger the heart of every honorable man of good health."[65] Beta's survey of the social ills contributing to Lisztomania culminated in a dire prediction that the Liszt episode would eventually be seen as a lowpoint in the history of Berlin:

Someday, when the Berlin newspapers and reviews come before the eyes of a later century and they survey the entire Liszt-period in Berlin, this period, in its blackness, will be seen as the darkest blemish of all. It will be said: Only an insane enthusiasm, intensified to an extreme, for a virtuoso whose orientation unceasingly turns art into idolatry; otherwise everywhere coldness,

---

[62] *Neuigkeits-Bote*, 1 March 1842. "Die Wirkung seines bizarren, halt- und ideelosen, sinnlich aufstachelnden, kontrastvollne, zerrissenen Spiels, der krankhafte Enthusiasmus darüber ist ein betrübendes Zeichen der Gehaltlosigkeit und Gefühlsermattung, der ästhetischen Leere im Publikum."

[63] *Neuigkeits-Bote*, 10 February 1842. The same idea appears in an essay from the 8 March issue: "The night watchman blows the fire alarm, but this fire leaves you cold. Your children cry – let them cry, you have to go hear Liszt. Thousands of poor people writhe in hunger and suffering, but the only thing that makes you writhe is having the two-Thaler coins which, saved up or acquired from a loan house, are the keys to the heavenly gates of Liszt's concerts."

[64] *Neuigkeits-Bote*, 8 March 1842.   [65] Ibid.

indifference, discord, diseased forced-feeling [*krankhafte Gefühlsmäche*] and empty splendor.[66]

These words distinctly echo Bellegno's *Wechselfieber*: a diseased condition in which the public is either entirely passive and indifferent, or absurdly excited and enthused. Fortunately, Beta found a few sturdy minds that managed to resist the infection: "the *healthy* part of the populace manages to avenge itself through numerous caricatures, most of them passing from mouth to mouth."[67]

A view from above

Although the liberals were dominant in the criticism of Liszt's popularity, the conservatives also had reason to worry. The monarchy, too, had the potential to lose from the public's absorption in the virtuoso, for as long as he remained in the city the public's eye might be averted from the king. While liberals worried about an excess of monarchical loyalty, then, conservatives worried about a lapse thereof. When after six weeks of concerts it seemed as though the Berlin public would never let Liszt leave, the official newspaper of the Prussian monarchy, the *Königliche preussische Staats-Zeitung*, raised its solemn voice:

Never has a winter been so empty of public entertainments [*Vergnügungen*] as the present one, in which no celebration at court in the higher circles, nor a ball is held. The only respite of the Berliners are Liszt's concerts, which replace everything. Liszt is admired here as no artist ever was, and unfortunately even this immeasurable enthusiasm, although Liszt certainly deserves recognition, evinces an all too great slackness toward higher interests, which are far overshadowed by pleasures, the desire for entertainment, etc.[68]

This writer offers a completely different explanation for Liszt's popularity from that of the liberal critics, and it is a perfectly plausible one. When Liszt arrived in Berlin, the court was in high mourning over the recent death of the queen's mother, resulting in a near shutdown of major public festivities – especially the balls – at which the court displayed itself to the public. Lacking their usual outlets for social conviviality, the Berliners concentrated their activities on entertainments less integral to aristocratic society. The correspondent for the *Telegraph für Deutschland* reported that "The Christmas period has destroyed nearly all social life; at most, people let themselves attend concerts, soirées, theatres, or

---

[66] *Neuigkeits-Bote*, 1 March 1842. "Wenn einst ein späteres Jahrhundert die Zeitungen Berlin's und die Kritiken über Liszt zu Gesicht kommt und die ganze Liszt-Periode Berlin's überschaut, so wird es diesen Zeitpunkt als den dunkelsten Fleck aus allen andern durch seine Schwärze herausfinden."

[67] *Neuigkeits-Bote*, 8 March 1842; emphasis added.

[68] *Königliche preussische Staats- Kriegs- und Friedenszeitung*, 10 February 1842.

exhibitions."[69] Among these compensatory entertainments Liszt's concerts had a central position, eclipsing at least all other musical events in the city.[70] They deflected the public's attention away from "higher interests," by which the *Staats-Zeitung* probably meant the "official" mourning of the court, but perhaps also state affairs in a more general sense.

The consternation of the *Staats-Zeitung* toward Liszt's popularity has much in common with that of the liberal critics. Liszt has become an idol: a figure toward whom the public directs energies that should be directed elsewhere. He is a substitute, and an inadequate one, for something the public needs but lacks. The *Staats-Zeitung*, however, presents this as a temporary situation resulting from exceptional circumstances – the dearth of public entertainments in a period of mourning – whereas the liberals present Lisztomania as an *exposé* of permanent problems lurking deep within Berlin's repressive, monarchical social order. Conservative critics would never have used the language of illness to characterize Liszt's reception, because they did not analyze society into the two levels of symptoms and causes. They only called out for a restoration of the already monarchical orientation of the Berliners, which was in their eyes synonymous with social health. The *Staats-Zeitung's* refusal to probe the social implications of the Liszt phenomenon beyond the surface is painfully evident in a follow-up critique it printed a few days later. Its author compares Liszt's reception with that of Paganini and Sonntag, and thereby opens up the possibility of a liberal critique, but his conclusion devolves into a pointless circular observation: "[the enthusiasm for Liszt] shows us very clearly our situation, and how a piano virtuoso can make himself the center of all publicity [*Öffentlichkeit*] and daily affairs among us."[71]

The irony of the *Staats-Zeitung's* complaint is that the king, queen, and the crown prince and princess were themselves involved in the fuss over Liszt. As discussed in chapter 4, Liszt was actively bonding with the royal family, especially in January, in order to develop his relationship to the German national movement. The royal family received his attentions appreciatively and reciprocated them. Parisians heard from their Berlin correspondent that *"Despite their mourning,* the king and queen wished to hear him several times."[72] Another correspondent reported

---

[69] *Telegraph für Deutschland,* 8 January 1842.

[70] The *Neue Zeitschrift für Musik* confirmed that Liszt had no competition, at least on the musical front, during his first weeks in Berlin: "For the month of January Liszt and Liszt alone has literally absorbed the musical attention of Berlin" (4 February 1842). Liszt's opponent "Beta" was enraged that the classically oriented concerts of Karl Möser were badly attended because of Liszt's popularity (*Neuigkeits-Bote,* 8 March 1842).

[71] *Königliche preussische Staats- Kriegs- und Friedenszeitung,* 17 February 1842.

[72] *Revue et gazette musicale* 9/8 (20 February 1842), 68–69; emphasis added.

that in spite of the lull in aristocratic social life, the prince was orga-
nizing parties with Liszt as the honored guest.[73] The royal family, then,
might well have been considered among those people who let their
fondness for Liszt overshadow "higher interests." But the reports cited
here pertain specifically to the *early* part of Liszt's visit, when his ties to
the court were particularly strong. At this point he was still appearing
before the public as the "court favorite." By mid-February, however, the
wider public had effected a "takeover" of Liszt, compelling him to give
more concerts than he had planned, forcing him to move his concerts
from the *Singakademie* to the more spacious opera house, and even dic-
tating to him the repertory he was to play. It was ultimately the public's
"stealing" of Liszt from the court that provoked the *Staats-Zeitung* to
begin worrying about people's engagement in "higher interests."

Criticism from the outside

Neither of the two Berlin journals that criticized Liszt's reception during
his visit – the *Neuigkeits-Bote* and the *Gesellschafter* – was a particularly
influential paper. But the opinions they expressed, reinforced by numerous caricatures and satires, were picked up in the international press and
became a standard external opinion of the Berlin episode. The two key
elements of this opinion were the focus on the social roots of the phenomenon, and the pervasive use of metaphors of illness. Lisztomania
was identified as a "contagion," and critics started taking measures to
"immunize" their publics against it. Such a political perspective is lacking in local accounts, which, trapped in the discourse of illness, did not
seek global explanations for the symptoms they described. For instance,
a writer in the small Prussian town of Hirschberg waged a battle against
what he called the "Liszt-Fever" when a prospective visit by Liszt was
announced. The town was in a state of excitement, and like Beta of the
Neuigkeits-Bote, he worried that the public was forgetting its duty to
promote civic and social progress:

However all ears are buzzing, all tongues talking, all heads spinning on account
of Liszt. I ask you Lisztian Hirschberg, if for example tomorrow and the next day
and the day after that a petition went around to be signed for contributions to
the formation of a fund to establish a public library, as our humane government
wishes it, how much would you be likely to give?[74]

---

[73] *Korrespondent von und für Deutschland*, 20 January 1842: "His Majesty the Duke of
Nassau, in particular, is amusing himself by hosting brilliant gatherings. Only there
has Liszt been heard in private society. The general public is pursuing its usual habits,
and has been in a consistently lively mood since the new year."

[74] *Priviligirte schlesische Zeitung*, 11 February 1843. Hirschberg was a small town with a
population of 7,000.

This direct address to the Hirschberg public was nothing less than political activism. Liszt had apparently stipulated that a subscription list be drawn up to guarantee sufficient receipts, and the residents were racing to gather subscribers, many of whom were more than happy to pay his elevated prices. The critic therefore focused on the issue of money, reproaching the Hirschbergers for wasting it on art while the city swam in debt and lacked important public institutions. Such an inversion of priorities, he felt, was rooted not in aesthetic appreciation but in an unhealthy public morality: "the Lisztian artistic sensibility is nothing more, at least among the majority, than a fashionable illness [*Modekrankheit*] [that produces] paroxysms of art-fever."[75] The author might well have congratulated himself on his efforts, for the subscription list was ultimately too small to lure Liszt to Hirschberg.

The rhetoric of the Hirschberg correspondent – with its social criticism and medical metaphors – derives directly from the bad publicity that surrounded the Berlin episode. Yet it bears only a dim trace of the politicized, international perspective that made the Berlin episode so notorious to begin with. All reactions to the Berlin episode that were printed in Prussia, in fact, lack the critical edge characteristic of outsiders like Heine, Dronke, *Europa*, and the *Neue Zeitschrift für Musik*. Even Beta of the *Neuigkeits-Bote*, for all of his passionate railing against Lisztomania, suggested that the ideal recovery from it consisted in women returning to their domestic duties and students returning to their books – hardly a threat to the monarchy. Within Prussia it was not easy to point fingers at the police-heavy, monarchical political order of Berlin and hope to get such opinions past the censors. If a writer shared in the critical consensus, he could not have said so very explicitly or with a politicized tone.

Journalists in Prussia, furthermore, were motivated to cut down Berlin out of competition for civic prestige. Seven days after leaving Berlin, for example, Liszt gave his first concert in Königsberg. As Prussia's previous capital and a university town, it carried on a cultural rivalry with Berlin comparable to the old rivalry between Vienna and Prague.[76] To strengthen its edge on Berlin, one Königsberg journalist subtly urged his readers not to indulge in the excesses just demonstrated in the capital:

---

[75] Ibid.

[76] One writer felt that Königsberg was intellectually and culturally far in advance of Berlin, and that in many ways it remained Prussia's capital (*Berliner Wespen* [January 1843], 1–2 [F. Weyl]).

Paris and Berlin have honored him. I do not doubt that Königsberg will join in, without however making more outgoing acclamations, which can be of little satisfaction to an artist like Liszt when they do not flow directly from the most inner feelings.[77]

When Liszt returned to Prussia in 1843, the people of Breslau (likewise a university city) tried to show Berlin that they too knew how to honor a great virtuoso. Their principal music reporter, however, did not want the outstanding reception to be mistaken for the hysterics of the Berliners: "As great as the admiration and general acclaim of the Breslauers for Liszt might have been, they were always only of a purely artistic nature."[78] Both of the above writers imply that the Berlin enthusiasm stemmed from something other than aesthetic sensibility, but they go no further. Their goal of raising Breslau or Königsberg above Berlin (in relation to the reception of Liszt) has been served, and there is no hint of a more global, liberal political agenda.

Outside Prussia, however, informed opinion on Berlin tended to follow the progressive consensus. When Ernst Dronke summarized the prevalent stereotypes of Berlin, only his fictive "Rhinelander" had anything positive to say about the city. The "Pietist," the "Freespirit," the "South German," and others all saw Berlin as degenerate, repressive, or jaded.[79] Among these the "South German" deserves special emphasis, for the press in Bavaria, Swabia, and neighboring regions took pride in the liberal ideology that seemed to be prevailing in the south, and they defined themselves against Berlin: "It is evident that Berlin, which in recent times has made so many temporary starts for freedom, is not at all receptive to the freedom that is blossoming so richly in the south."[80] Prague's German-language journal *Ost und West*, belonging roughly to this south German milieu, was one of the first to lament the Berlin episode in a serious tone, as opposed to a mocking or hyperbolic one:

The measureless admiration with which Liszt was applauded here was not that honorable recognition due to the true artist; it was a veritable adoration, a sad

---

[77] *Königliche preussische Staats- Kriegs- und Friedenszeitung*, 12 March 1842 (F. Raabe); review of Liszt's first Königsberg concert (10 March). The Königsberg university tried to outdo its Berlin counterpart by granting Liszt an honorary doctorate. The same competitive impulse led a Königsberg critic to put up heavy resistance to Liszt's playing of Bach's music, which had been well received in Berlin. The debate over Liszt's Bach playing was carried out in the *Königliche preussische Staats- Kriegs- und Friedenszeitung*, 16 and 22 March 1842.

[78] *Priviligirte schlesische Zeitung*, 9 February 1843 (A. K.).　　[79] Dronke, *Berlin*, 14–15.

[80] *Europa* (1843/1), 490. *Europa* was published in both Stuttgart and Leipzig. The "temporary starts for freedom" of "recent times" are an allusion to the liberal reforms promised by the new Prussian king in 1840, which were propagated intensively and received well by people all over Germany.

sign of our time, and it furnishes proof that there are moral [*geistige*] sicknesses quite as contagious as those of the body.[81]

When Liszt first concertized in Bavaria and Swabia in October and November 1843, the south German critics made a conscious effort to define *their* public's reception of Liszt against that of Berlin. A report on his Munich debut began:

Liszt fever, a contagion that breaks out in every city our artist visits, and which neither age nor wisdom can protect, seems to appear here only sporadically, and asphyxiating cases such as appeared so often in northern capitals need not be feared by our residents, with their strong constitutions.[82]

This author does not specify what makes the Munich audiences immune to the Liszt contagion. In the context of the north/south dichotomy, however, he implies that Munich residents are more resistant because of the more free and liberal social and political environment. Indeed, the paper in which this report appeared, the *Augsburger allgemeine Zeitung (AAZ)*, made social health its leitmotive as it followed Liszt through Stüttgart, Augsburg, and other south German cities. It touted the independent-mindedness and moderation of the southern audiences, always with an implicit comparison to Berlin:

His success in Swabia should perhaps be esteemed all the more because our public, which always wants to see with its own eyes and hear with its own ears rather than go on faith, almost obstinately refuses all vociferous applause.[83]

The liberal orientation of the *AAZ* is also evident in its extra effort to acknowledge Liszt's commitment to liberal social reform. After Liszt had agreed to play a charity concert (25 October) for the home for the blind in Munich, it listed his other liberal achievements and concluded: "We believe this must be emphasized, since such services for an organ of public political life – so rare in our time and matched in this degree by no artist of the present – must never and nowhere be forgotten."[84] The *AAZ* was the most widely read paper in southern Germany, and a powerful opinion-shaper. The Leipzig *Allgemeine musikalische Zeitung*, for one, helped propagate the newspaper's opinions to the European musical community:

Liszt has given concerts in Munich and Augsburg. The southern Germans admired him without letting themselves break out into that diseased [*krankhaften*] enthusiasm that Liszt instilled into certain north Germans.[85]

---

[81] *Ost und West*, 10 May 1842 (Berlin report by Wilhelm Müller).
[82] *Augsburger allgemeine Zeitung*, 20 October 1843 (Munich report).
[83] *Augsburger allgemeine Zeitung*, 25 November 1843 (Stüttgart report).
[84] *Augsburger allgemeine Zeitung*, 22 October 1843 (Augsburg report).
[85] *Allgemeine musikalische Zeitung* 45/44 (1 November 1843), col. 804.

This discussion of the *AAZ* returns us full circle to Heinrich Heine, for the *AAZ* was the paper that published most of his Parisian reports, including the one that included his neologism "Lisztomanie." In the safety of Paris, Heine could afford to be more explicitly anti-monarchical than the liberal *AAZ*, but the *AAZ* shared the view that Berlin suffered from social illness – a suffering never more obvious than in its reaction to Liszt. This progressive consensus, we have seen, was also heard in other parts of Germany, notably Frankfurt and Leipzig. Berlin was criticized within Prussia as well, but in a considerably watered-down form that only implied the liberal ideology so explicit elsewhere. More than a mere political construction, Lisztomania spoke to circumstances peculiar to contemporary life in Berlin: highly punitive laws of censorship, restrictions on free expression in public spaces, the weakness of the bourgeois public sphere, and the self-enclosure of the aristocratic and bureaucratic circles. These circumstances resulted in a pattern of behavior toward major public figures – Sonntag, Elssler, and Herwegh – that resurfaced when Liszt came. Liszt's outstanding reception in Berlin, then, can be attributed as much to the character of Berlin as to Liszt's virtuosity.

2. Charity: the glow of goodness

Social illness was just one of two major explanations for Liszt's astonishing reception in Berlin. The second explanation, and the more surprising one, was that Berlin was responding to the depth of Liszt's charity activities. Parisians, for example, heard from their Berlin correspondent that "*All* of these ridiculous demonstrations have had their *principal* source in numerous donations Mr. Liszt has distributed to charitable institutions."[86] A German correspondent even more explicitly downplayed the role of Liszt's pianism: "Not his virtuosity itself, but the noble utilization thereof . . . has earned him these expressions of sympathy."[87] The extent of Liszt's charity in Berlin was likewise highlighted in large retrospective essays by Gustav Nicolai and Ludwig Rellstab, which will be examined later. Liszt had been playing charity concerts throughout his career, but never did they strike a nerve quite as sensitive as that of the Berlin public.

I will discuss here some of the reasons the Berliners were disposed to respond so positively to gestures of benevolence. But this dimension of the Berlin episode needs first to be evaluated with a wider lens, for charity grounded his popular appeal throughout his career. Biographers have always acknowledged the abundance of Liszt's charitable

---

[86] *France musicale* 5/12 (20 March 1842), 117; emphasis added.
[87] *Augsburger allgemeine Zeitung*, 7 March 1842.

activities, but rarely with any other purpose than proving his superior moral character. I am interested in showing how Liszt used charity *strategically* to shape his public image and win the support of his audiences, especially during his climactic days in Berlin. This requires a closer look at the organizations he was supporting and the moral valences that framed charitable giving, for these were the elements that he was able to manipulate strategically. I also discuss how Liszt's charitable activities were seen as a symbolic reflection of his virtuoso persona. His advocacy of specific humanitarian social and political causes, along with a Christ-like internal glow, became fused with a performance style featuring states of divine or transcendental exaltation, so that he appeared to be enveloped in a halo of goodness. This aura was a major source of his appeal to contemporary audiences.

Liszt exceeded all contemporary musicians in the quantity of charitable causes he supported with his playing. This fact was recognized in his day and has been emphasized by biographers, but it is simplistic to imply that Liszt was therefore a person of especially high generosity. Musicians did not necessarily give charity concerts out of sheer goodness of the heart or social commitment. Any virtuoso who made a significant amount of money in any one place was expected to contribute to charity concerts; it was the unofficial obligation of every instrumentalist or singer of high repute. Paganini, for example, nearly shattered his reputation in Paris when, having made huge sums of money playing concerts there, he refused to participate in a charity concert. Liszt's famous obituary of Paganini, in which he censured the violinist for greed and vanity, brought this strain of public criticism to its culmination.[88] One simple reason Liszt participated in more charity concerts than others is that he played more concerts in general. His fame, furthermore, was a valuable asset for any charitable organization, so that he received an unusually high number of requests to play for charity. Liszt did not want to refuse such requests and risk being criticized as a Paganini. On most occasions he probably agreed to play out of obligation, mixed with anxiety about the consequences of refusal.

The moral engine driving charity concerts was Christian humanitarianism, whose beneficiaries tended to be the poor, victims of natural catastrophes, orphans, fallen families, or penurious artists. Demonstrative, emotive sympathy for the beneficiaries, however, was not the highest priority of Christian humanitarianism. The commitment to help unfortunate people was supposed to come from a sense of religious duty, not from emotional commiseration alone. Charity in the early nineteenth century, that is, was rooted in an Enlightenment-based idea – the benefit of mankind – in which emotions had only a subsidiary

[88] *Revue et gazette musicale* 7/50 (23 August 1840), 435.

role. When people attended charity concerts, they were more likely to be thinking about their ethical selves than about the people who would receive the benefits.

Liszt contributed to dozens of concerts undertaken in the Christian humanitarian spirit, but he developed his reputation for benevolence by cutting off the Enlightenment roots of humanitarianism and replanting them in the soil of romanticism. He made the charity concert into a new kind of event, in which the emotional stakes were raised to a new level and folded into his performing persona. The concert he gave for the poor of Lyons in 1837 serves as an example. This concert endeared Liszt to the political left in Paris, especially his friends in the world of letters, who vilified the French government's violent suppression of the Lyons workers' rebellion of 1831. Liszt's audiences, furthermore, knew of his sympathy for the Saint-Simonian brand of socialism, so that the benevolence of the concert seemed to emanate irrepressibly from within him. The whole charitable purpose of the Lyons concert, then, was bundled up within Liszt's romantic virtuoso persona and layered over with the immediacy of contemporary politics.[89] In performance he seemed to embody the benevolent impulse itself, representing charity to his listeners in an emotionally charged guise that swept them into a vortex of moral edification. Liszt published an essay on the Lyons concert in the *Lettres d'un bachelier* series, where he contrasted his own immense sympathy for the suffering of the poor with the cool, self-satisfied attitude of most donors.[90] It was an argument for bringing the emotion back into charity.

The Pest charity concert

Just eight months after the Lyons concert, Liszt made the most ostentatious charity gesture of his career: he rushed to Vienna from Italy to give a concert for the victims of the disastrous Pest flood. This gesture, I would argue, demonstrates most clearly Liszt's *strategic* use of charity. Such an argument, however, requires a detailed review of the events, since Liszt's motivations for going to Vienna have been a matter

[89] Liszt had even composed a new piece for the occasion, "Lyon," whose revolutionary tone has been discussed by Alexander Main in "Liszt's 'Lyon': Music and the Social Conscience," *19th Century Music* 4 (1981), 3–21.

[90] Liszt discussed Lyons in his letter to Adolphe Pictet, printed in *Revue et gazette musicale* 5/6 (11 February 1838), 57–62. The segment on Lyons is found in English in *An Artist's Journey: Lettres d'un bachelier ès musique*, ed. C. Suttoni (Chicago, 1989), 48–51. The original French version is reprinted in *Franz Liszt: artiste et société*, ed. R. Strecker (Paris, 1995), 89–91. The following excerpt conveys the flavor of Liszt's rhetoric: "Oh, merciless law of social fatality! When will your brazen tablets be shattered by the Angel of Wrath? Oh, you tears, sighs, and groans of the people! When will you bridge the abyss that still separates us from the reign of justice?"

of contention and misrepresentation. In one of the *Lettres d'un bachelier*, Liszt described how, hearing about the disastrous floods in Pest, he was suddenly overcome with a feeling of love for the homeland he had forgotten. His emotions awoke him from the soporific years of pilgrimage and contemplation, driving him to Vienna to raise money for the flood victims.[91] Marie d'Agoult presented the story differently, implying that Liszt was attempting to escape a deteriorating relationship with her, and abandoning her as she expected a child. Alan Walker makes special effort to discredit d'Agoult's story and to reestablish Liszt's version as authoritative:

> Liszt's Vienna concerts are traditionally interpreted as "marking his official return to the stage." But they have a deeper meaning: Liszt's swift response to the catastrophe in Hungary is an indication of his latent patriotism.[92]

Walker's overall priority of defending Liszt's moral rectitude against the criticisms of d'Agoult leads him to exaggerate drastically Liszt's charity. He writes that "between April 18 and May 25 Liszt gave eight concerts which raised the colossal sum of 24,000 gulden, the largest single donation the Hungarians received from a private source."[93] However, it is clear from the contemporary press that only the *first* of his eight public concerts aided the victims of the flood.[94] In addition, Walker apparently arrives at the figure of 24,000 gulden by adding up the *gross* intake of all eight concerts. In fact Liszt netted 1,700 gulden in his first concert, a number only slightly higher than the average net of the remaining concerts, and that was probably the extent of his contribution.[95]

Liszt's concert series, I would argue, was more than a huge fund-raiser and outpouring of patriotic feeling, which is how Walker presents it. To begin with, there is evidence suggesting that that his return to Vienna was not a spontaneous reaction to the floods in Pest. Several weeks before the floods occurred, the Vienna journal *Der Adler* reported that "German papers announce that the famous piano virtuoso Liszt will soon visit Vienna in order to perform in public. A French paper confirms, on the contrary, that he will settle in Italy for a period of some

---

[91] This segment of the article appeared in *Artiste*, 11 June 1839. It is reprinted in English in *An Artist's Journey*, 138–42; the French version is in *Franz Liszt: artiste et société*, 134–36.
[92] Walker, *Franz Liszt*, I: 254.   [93] Ibid.
[94] See, for example, Pietro Mechetti's article in the *Wiener Zeitschrift für Kunst*, 5 June 1838.
[95] The expense sheets for Liszt's Vienna concerts of 1838 as well as those of 1839–40, which were kept by Tobias Haslinger, survive in Weimar, Liszt-Archiv Kasten 133–34. The tendency to exaggerate Liszt's charity in support of his moral character extends back to the early biographies of Liszt. J. W. Christern wrote in his 1841 biography: "He gave concerts, first in Vienna, then in Pest, not for himself, but only to noble, humane ends, for the poor, for the people who lost everything to floods . . . for young artists" (*Franz Liszt: nach seinem Leben und Wirken* [Hamburg/Leipzig, 1841], 33).

years without leaving. How do we make sense of this?"[96] The rumor of Liszt's impending visit was thus in circulation well before the floods in Pest occurred. The source of this accidental "leak" was probably Liszt's Viennese publisher Tobias Haslinger, with whom he was consistently corresponding at the time, and who took care of Liszt's business arrangements whenever he gave concerts in Vienna. As publisher of the *Allgemeine musikalischer Anzeiger*, Haslinger had many contacts with the Viennese press as well as a business interest in generating excitement for Liszt's visits.

Why might Liszt have considered leaving his Italian retreat to give concerts in Vienna? The most obvious answer has been explained in chapter 1: the rivalry with the Viennese virtuoso Thalberg was far from over. To make up for whatever damage his reputation had suffered in Paris the previous season, he would challenge Thalberg on his home ground. Yet this motivation would have been too exposed had he simply arrived in Vienna to give a series of concerts. If he was still worried about Thalberg, it was the last thing he wanted his audiences to know. The rumor was quickly hushed up, and nothing more was heard about a potential visit to Vienna until the banks of Pest and Ofen overflowed. Appearing in Vienna under the cover of a charitable and patriotic cause, Liszt could draw attention away from the fact that he wanted to challenge Thalberg. This is not to doubt that he also felt sympathy for Pest; it is only to show that he had other, less flattering motives as well.

Liszt's decision to place his charity concert *first* in the concert series was anomalous and strategically motivated. Contemporary virtuosos normally gave charity concerts after giving a series of concerts for their own benefit. By beginning with a charity concert, Liszt made it seem as if the entire series flowed from a charitable, patriotic impulse, even though it was in all other respects a normal and financially profitable series for him. The first concert also marked a return of sorts to the European concert stage. By returning to the concert platform in the guise of benevolence, he marked himself as the humanitarian virtuoso, free from the material considerations that other virtuosos often had to struggle with. In this way he set himself apart from the "typical virtuoso." The essay that appeared in the *Lettres d'un bachelier* series, furthermore, highlighted the intense emotions he felt for his homeland and its suffering. It shaped for posterity the perception that his concerts in Vienna were born of a profound humanitarian mission.

Liszt, in sum, was not impelled to Vienna in 1838 solely by a wave of nostalgia and sympathy for his homeland, as he and his biographers have consistently claimed. There were other motivations – a deteriorating relationship with Marie d'Agoult, perhaps a need for money, but

[96] *Der Adler*, 2 January 1838.

most importantly an unsettled rivalry with Thalberg. Liszt's charity gestures were caught up in a rich web of motivations, not all of them exalted,
and only one of which was his sympathy for unfortunate people. He
was using them strategically to shape his special significance for contemporary audiences and to separate himself from his colleagues. An
1841 letter he wrote to Cristina Belgiojoso shows that he was still, at the
height of his career, fishing for new ways to mobilize gestures of charity. Belgiojoso had recently attracted interest in Milan through charity
events. Liszt expressed fascination that "everybody in Paris and here
is talking about your trip to Milan," and asked her whether the beneficiaries were orphan girls, orphan boys, old people, or young people.[97]
His curiosity clearly did not stem from a special interest in these social
groups, but from the attention it drew to Belgiojoso. Liszt was capitalizing on charity the same way he capitalized on the cult of Napoleon or on
opera melodies from *Don Giovanni* and *Robert le diable*. He identified a
disposition embedded in the minds and emotions of the contemporary
publics, and generated public support by addressing his virtuosity to
that disposition.

Starting with his visit to Pest in 1840, Liszt began devoting himself
more and more to raising funds for national and cultural institutions:
the Hungarian National Theatre, the future conservatory of Pest, the
Beethoven monument in Bonn, the Cologne cathedral, and the Mozart
Foundation of Frankfurt. None of these institutions was exclusively
Christian in significance, but Liszt's generosity toward them appeared
to flow from the same selfless source. His benevolent aura was thus
expanding out into the fields of culture and politics, without ever losing its Christian connotations. The theme of benevolence was thus not
unique to Berlin, but it came to a climax when he made his first visit
there. Through a combination of strategy, luck, and Berlin's strong disposition toward charity, the Berlin episode became the apotheosis of
Liszt's glow of goodness. But before returning to Berlin, I will consider
how Liszt's persona and performing style were constructed to project
benevolence, and thereby complement his charity activities.

The glow of goodness

Liszt's personality and performing style were said to exude an aura of
"benevolence," an aura that made his charitable activities seem as if
they radiated irrepressibly from his heart. This was the most significant
sense in which he differed from Paganini. In performance he had all

---

[97] *Autour de Liszt et de Madame d'Agoult*, ed. D. Ollivier (Paris, 1941), 178. The fact that
the beneficiary was *not* being talked about in Paris is a sign of how little the actual
recipients mattered to the members of the *monde*.

of Paganini's dark, Mephistophelean intensity, but he complemented this with another affective mode, a positive outer radiance, that was wholly foreign to the violinist. This radiance struck many contemporaries as "romantic": a yearning or striving for an ideal. Yet it was also laden with implications of Christian benevolence, providing a performative anchor for his legendary generosity. After a brief discussion of how benevolence was perceived in Liszt's disposition and personality, I will discuss two different ways the glow of goodness emerged from his virtuoso performing style.

In previous chapters, we have seen that elements of Liszt's personality appealed to particular social groups. His graceful French manners and verbal wit endeared him to the cosmopolitan aristocracy, while his lively and volatile philosophical musings were admired by the *literati*. Liszt's personal warmth and kindness, however, were cited by almost everyone who met him. He was hardly unique in this respect. People praised his rival Thalberg for the same qualities. What made Liszt's kindness different was that it did not seem to be dictated by rules of decorum or tact. It appeared, rather, to flow over from a deep well of internal good will, regardless of external considerations. Caroline Boissier, who saw him often in 1831, piled up words in an attempt to portray this surplus of goodness: "a young man with the highest faculties, bursting with soul, a noble character, pure and deep, the most sincere, open, most loving soul and the most grand that I have ever met."[98] Richard Wagner was particularly impressed at how Liszt's benevolence could even prevail when he was being confronted:

The whole bearing of the man, and the way in which he tried to ward off the pitiless scorn of [Wilhelmine Schröder-Devrient's] attacks, was something new to me, and gave me a deep insight into his character, so firm in its amiability and boundless good-nature.[99]

The key phrases here are "boundless good-nature" and "bursting with soul," both of them characterizing Liszt's kindness as excess. Like his inspiration, which constantly regenerated and pushed him toward new musical climaxes, his reserves of goodness seemed inexhaustible.

Boissier and Wagner both knew Liszt intimately, but his warm, giving personality had been part of his public profile from an early stage, and many writers in the 1830s emphasized its Christian overtones. It has rarely been noted that Joseph d'Ortigue's lengthy biography of the young Liszt has a polemical purpose. D'Ortigue was deeply interested

[98] Diary of C. Boissier, 17 March entry; quoted in *Liszt en son temps*, ed. Pierre-Antoine Hure and Claude Knepper (Paris, 1987), 140.
[99] Richard Wagner, *My Past and Thoughts*, trans. C. Garnett (London, 1911), 2 vols., I: 144; quoted in *Portrait of Liszt: by Himself and his Contemporaries*, ed. Adrian Williams (Oxford, 1990), 194. The events Wagner relates here took place in late 1842.

in the relationship between religion and the arts, and the latter portion of his biography portrays Liszt as the spirit of Christianity become manifest in music. Liszt's connection to the Saint-Simonians was clearly the source of this idea, but more useful for d'Ortigue's polemical purpose was Liszt's generally benevolent personal disposition, which transcended specific groups or philosophies: "This soul has associated itself, identified itself with a prodigious power of sympathy for everything grand and everything generous in today's society."[100] A few years later, Heinrich Heine poked fun at Liszt's utopian "hobby-horses" – Saint-Simonianism, Ballanche, Lammenais – but admired the moral spirit in which he rode them: "But this untiring longing for light and divinity is always praiseworthy; it stems from his sense for the holy, for the religious."[101] Both writers present this orientation toward humanitarianism and religion as a natural disposition: Liszt is drawn like a magnet toward the highest good.

As Liszt undertook his international tours in the 1840s, he shed much of the explicit Christian utopian baggage discussed by Heine and d'Ortigue. Its vogue was already in decline. But the halo of benevolence continued to radiate out from his performing style, thus preserving his "untiring longing for light and divinity." The musical mechanics by which he produced this glow in performance begin with the "demonic" overtones of his intense bravura moments. Contemporary writers drew on the idea of the "demonic" pervasively to characterize Liszt's bravura playing, and to this day it remains the favorite metaphorical analogy. Several writers, including both Heine and Rellstab, suggested that the demonic mode predominated in the impression he left on listeners. The psychological, literary, and musical roots of demonic imagery deserve an independent study. Here I only wish to describe the mechanisms by which Liszt played off images of the holy and the good against the backdrop of his demonic mode, with its implications of evil and transgression. One way he posed the holy against the demonic was to make abrupt shifts between intense, passionate bravura and tender, melting lyricism.[102] After discussing this process in detail, I will explain how Liszt used musical codes to establish a demonic–holy dialectic *within* his bravura mode. In both cases, the effect of holy transfiguration devolved upon his performing self, transforming his virtuosity into a discourse of demonic possession and exorcism, and culminating in a glow of goodness.

---

[100] *Revue et gazette musicale* 2/24 (14 June 1835), 197–204.

[101] *Revue et gazette musicale* 5/5 (4 February 1838), 41–44 (H. Heine).

[102] Lawrence Kramer has discussed this oscillation and related it to the Bakhtinian carnivalesque. See "Franz Liszt and the Virtuoso Public Sphere: Sight and Sound in the Rise of Mass Entertainment," in *Musical Meaning: Toward a Critical History* (Berkeley, 2002), 85ff.

Celestial blue

From the earliest to the latest years of Liszt's concert career, writers describe his virtuosity as an energetic bravura flight interspersed with quiet, lyrical pauses. It is one of the most commonly recurring patterns in all of the writings about Liszt. In such descriptions, the alternation of lyrical and bravura moments is not smooth and gradual, but sudden, stealing upon the listener unexpectedly. The following example conveys the pattern clearly:

> Now and then the busy hands intermit their astonishing activity; and then come dropping, in pure, clear and simple tones, the unadorned notes of the theme on which the *recital*, as it is called, is constructed; and while you are drinking in the soft and low music, off darts the performer, like a steam engine broke loose, and with a crash as if a whole orchestra were at once bursting into symphony.[103]

The suddenness with which Liszt passes from one mode to the other provokes the writer to rationalize the discontinuity with a metaphorical image, or some other hermeneutic structure that can subsume both modes. Heinrich Adami imported a tiny storm narrative to integrate the bravura and lyrical moments:

> Just as strongly as his playing arouses through its fire, through its boldness and energy . . . he also proves no less through his cantabile that he can console and enrapture. This characteristic of his playing can only make the artist more worthy still, for it allows the listener moments of peace amid the excited race of tones, and additionally shows that a place will not be denied to the most simple and beautiful next to the grandiose. Such intermediate sections are like sunshine after a lightning storm.[104]

Until the last sentence, the two affective modes Adami describes (boldness/energy and cantabile) are disconnected, merely adjacent. The storm image draws attention to the transition itself as an agent of meaning. The sudden interruption installs narrative structure into the virtuosic discourse by inviting the writer to map out concrete narratives as he describes Liszt's playing.

Narrative was one basic instrument through which writers unified Liszt's virtuosic discontinuities. But there was another hermeneutic structure – the dialectic – that could be employed to the same end. Liszt's playing installs a dialectic in his listener's mind by means of the extremely oppositional affective qualities of the bravura and lyrical passages. The shift from one to other is so radical that, so it seems, they *must* belong to some larger, subsuming unity. Unlike narrative, dialectic

---

[103] *Birmingham Journal*, 28 November 1840, quoted in *Liszt Society Journal* 10 (1984), 7.

[104] *Allgemeine Theaterzeitung*, 21 April 1838, 355–56 (H. Adami). Quoted in D. Legány, *Franz Liszt: unbekannte Presse und Briefe aus Wien, 1882–1866* (Vienna, 1984), 23–27.

suppresses the temporal sequence of events. Rather than separate and successive states, the two modes are always implicit in one another, synthesized through an idea that stands above and apart from them. The following example represents how this dialectic process can pass over into religious imagery:

> He coaxes from the dead keys wonderful noises, so bold and terrifying [*erschütternd*], and then so weak and moving, that they make the heart rise in fear, only to then fill it *in the same moment* with joy . . . This diabolic principle, *most closely tied with* a holy artistic inspiration [*heiligen Kunstbegeisterung*] makes his playing . . . indescribable.[105]

The signal difference from a narrative interpretation is the simultaneity of the listener's fear and joy, their coexistence "in the same moment." Liszt's shuttling between bravura and lyricism thus generated meanings in two different ways: through narrative mappings onto the sequence of events, and through semantic mappings onto the oppositional, binary structure of the modes. In the examples given above, these two hermeneutic structures are distinct, but as we shall see, they could operate simultaneously upon the listener in conveying Liszt's glow of goodness.

As these examples suggest, writers favored storm imagery and divine imagery when they were called upon to describe Liszt's playing and its effect on listeners. Different though the images are, they share a common orientation around an opposition of light and darkness. In the following narrative they blend into one another:

> Sometimes, at the height of the torment, a ray of sunshine appears, one of those "celestial blue" cracks you sometimes see among the dark clouds. It is a divine singing voice [*chant divin*], just a few tender, sweet, sensitive tones, thrown there, with their delicious chromaticism, their suave chords which seem to caress the heart.[106]

The link between the metaphors of nature and divinity here is an image of light: the ray of sun that shines through the clouds becomes a radiant signal from heaven. But this light is more than a visual signal. It is also an aural communication, a disembodied utterance, a "divine singing voice." This quality of utterance, of animate vocal presence, is crucial to the effect of Liszt's lyrical moments. His bravura mode lacks all traces of vocal utterance, be it human or divine: singable melody and declamatory rhetoric are completely absent. In this quotation the bravura mode, positioned over and against the lyrical mode, is rendered voiceless and inanimate, qualities well served by images of nature and storms. Hence

---

[105] *Allgemeine Wiener Musik-Zeitung* 6/29 (7 March 1846), 114 ("A. S."); emphasis added.
[106] Diary of C. Boissier, 7 February entry. Quoted in *Liszt en son temps*, 135.

the listener, presented with this animate/inanimate binary opposition in sound, was driven to align Liszt with the animate pole. The divine voice and celestial, redemptive light were perceptually mapped onto his performing presence:

> He can raise up a storm about him, which he finds in the hurly burly of the instrument, so frightful, that he is obscured and lost; but as it dies away, he reappears through a mist, decked in the most radiant colours.[107]

The language of this passage is revealing. Liszt *creates* a storm, but he is not identified with it; indeed, he is soon swallowed up by the sound world he creates. Liszt's bodily and sentient presence returns as the storm "dies away" by virtue of the vocal, animate presence of the sound world that takes over, with which he can easily be identified. He returns in a *chant divin* – transfigured, glowing, a rainbow of goodness.

The series of oppositions described here – in which Liszt is aligned with light, animate presence, voice, and divinity – is the result of a *narrative* hermeneutic operation. Both of the cited passages, that is, give meaning to Liszt's playing by describing a temporal effect ("at the height of the torment, a ray of sunshine appears . . ."; "as it dies away, he reappears . . ."). The storm and the crevice of blue sky, for instance, do not form a conceptual binary pair. They represent, rather, two successive states of a natural scene that reflect the psychological effect of the music. Liszt's lyrical moments, in this operation, are holy not so much by their polar opposition to the bravura, but by their own internal signification of tenderness and benevolence.

The consistent semantic coding of Liszt's tender lyricism as divine, independently of a binary logic, can be shown with a pair of examples. At an early Parisian concert he played Beethoven's Sonata in C sharp minor, with a piano–orchestra arrangement of the first movement that, one imagines, consisted of sustained chords in the strings, creating a "halo" of moonlight around his delivery of the plaintive melody. After this performance, Henry Reeve, a friend of Liszt, wrote: "I took his hand and thanked him for the divine energy he had shed forth."[108] Liszt also radiated divine energy in his performances of Schubert's *Ave Maria*, one of the core pieces of his touring repertory, and the only one that explicitly couples tender lyricism with religious imagery.[109] Franz von Schober,

---

[107] *Leicester Chronicle*, 12 September 1840; quoted in *Liszt Society Journal* 9 (1983), 7.

[108] *Memoirs of the Life and Correspondence of Henry Reeve*, ed. J. K. Laughton (London, 1898), 2 vols., I: 48–49; quoted in *Portrait of Liszt*, 66.

[109] "From the *Ave Maria* the public expected church-like, outward-stretching expanses of sound. But only an organ can produce them. Nevertheless the bell-tones and the chorale-like prayers, lightly accompanied, lightly exhaled and sigh-like, were magical [*bezaubernd*]" (*Frankfurter patriotisches Wochenblatt*, 25 January 1843 [C. W. Spieker]).

describing this lyrical dimension of Liszt's playing, synthesized it with his general aura of radiant benevolence:

Liszt's magical moments liberate and exalt the soul, they are radiations of his beautiful, brilliant, loving being, which without diminishing him, transmit to others, just as light reproduces itself, one flame igniting thousands without losing its own brightness or its own warmth. In this same way the inspiration of his performance passes over to his person, transforms his listeners into his friends and showers his path with a wealth of gifts [*Liebesbezeugungen*] and distinctions.[110]

We will later see that this intimate, transcendent performer–audience bond – in which Liszt becomes a Christ-like medium of divine transmission – was central to the positive view of the Berlin episode.

The *dialectical* hermeneutic constructs Liszt's glow of goodness by a different mechanism. The basis of the dialectical hermeneutic is a stable coding of his bravura mode as demonic or diabolical. In contrast to its narrative counterpart, the dialectical hermeneutic ascribes an animate, supernatural presence to the bravura mode. As Liszt interrupts the bravura with lyricism, a psychological chiasmus takes place, in which the supernatural presence is recoded as holy or good. One Berlin journalist objected to the emphasis on Liszt's diabolical qualities, partly because it did not account for this dialectical effect:

But this force is not quite diabolic, as people have tended to call it, for it suppresses in us all other feelings and ideas and sets itself up as the centerpoint or idol thereof; it dominates us, but it can also transfigure us through its own astonishing dimensions and through its intermittent flashes of sweetness [*Lieblichkeit*].[111]

This writer offers two types of transfiguration, both of them dialectical: one achieved through the sudden appearance of flashes of sweetness, the other achieved within the bravura mode itself ("through its own astonishing dimensions") and therefore independent of the alternation

---

[110] Franz von Schober, *Briefe über F. Liszts Aufenthalt in Ungarn* (Berlin, 1843), 5. "Liszt's Zauber aber befreien und erhöhen die Seele, sie sind Ausströmungen seines schönen, genialen, liebevollen Wesens, die sich, ihm unbeschadet, Andern mittheilen, wie sich das Licht vervielfältigt, an der einen Flamme sich tausende entzunde, ohne dass sie an eigenem Glanze, an eigener Wärme verlöre. Darum geht auch die Begeisterung von seiner Leistung auf seine Person über, verwandelt seine Hörer in seine Freunde und überschüttet seinen Weg mit einer Menge von Liebesbezeugungen und Auszeichnungen."

[111] *Gesellschafter* 11 "Beilage" (19 January 1842), 53: "Aber diese Gewalt ist deswegen noch keine diabolische, wie man sie hat bezeichnen wollen, wenn sie auch alle anderen Empfindungen und Beziehungen in uns niederkampft und sich allein als den Centralpunkt, als das Idol derselben aufstellt; sie beherrscht uns, aber sie weiss uns durch ihre eigene, staunenswerthe Grösse, durch ihre dazwischen aufblitzende Lieblichkeit zu verklären."

of modes. This latter, dialectical process is yet another source of Liszt's glow of goodness. Before examining this paradigm further, however, let us consider some specific music that gave rise to the impression of Liszt's sudden alternations.

One looks in vain through Liszt's concert repertory for passages that exemplify the sudden shift from bravura to lyrical and then back to bravura. His fantasies often show such alternation over longer expanses of time, but the shifts from one mode to the other are usually smooth: gradual build-ups and wind-downs. The suddenness of effect evident in all of the quotations analyzed above is almost completely absent from the scores. Writers were not describing what we see in Liszt's published scores, but contrasts introduced in improvisational contexts, or as extemporaneous elaborations to other compositions. Only one of the above quotations ("He can raise up a storm about him . . . he reappears through a mist") explicitly identifies the piece being played, and it happens to be one of the improvised storms he featured on his English tours.[112] The low level of compositional constraints in improvisational contexts left room for, indeed necessitated, such marked disjunctions as Liszt introduced with his celestial blues. Particularly in the case of an improvised storm, where there is no melody or thematic material to embellish or vary, the improvisation must communicate through strong gestures that beg for a hermeneutic interpretation by the listener. The absence of melody, furthermore, encourages the listener to make the *performer* the site of hermeneutic entry. An improvisation on an opera melody, in contrast, might encourage the listener to enter hermeneutically through the operatic scene, as was often the case with his performances of the *Don Giovanni* fantasy. In his improvisations, then, Liszt becomes for the listener the source of utterance, the appearance of the performer "through a mist" in the lyrical section.[113]

The exordium of the *Hexaméron* (Example 5.2) is the only clear printed example of the bravura–lyric alternation. Following the generic conventions of the virtuoso variation set, the opening has a loose, improvisational character, foreshadowing the melody on which the variations will

---

[112] The first quotation ("the busy hands intermit their astonishing activity; and then come dropping in pure, clear and simple tones") also comes from his English tours, and may be derived from an impression of the storm, although the writer presents it as a general feature of Liszt's playing.

[113] A passage from Heine suggests that Liszt could, through body language, change the relationship of his performing self to the storm imagery: "Before, when he played for example a storm on the piano, we saw the play of light on his own face, his limbs burned as though disturbed by the tempest . . . But now, when he performs the same frightful storm, he himself rises above it, like the traveller who stands at the peak of an alp as it thunders in the valley" (*Heinrich Heine und die Musik*, 119–20; the article is dated 20 April 1841).

Example 5.2 Liszt et al., *Hexaméron: morceau de concert*, opening

be based. Out of the opening bravura chaos there emerges a fragment of Bellini's Puritan march, delivered in full grandiosity (letter A). This is abruptly followed by a very quiet, slow episode, spare in texture, in which the march tune fragment is reintroduced in minor and diverted into relatively free-moving harmonic elaborations (letter B). The episode does not last long: it builds quickly back to the bravura mode and toward an emphatic dominant seventh that announces the arrival of the march theme proper (letter C). The affective rhetoric of the *Hexaméron* opening, although corresponding to the bravura–lyrical–bravura

Example 5.2 (*cont.*)

pattern, does not obviously transfigure Liszt in the central section, principally because it has a minor-mode coloration. He may well have intended the minor-mode digression to represent allegorically the suffering of the oppressed pilgrims, over which they triumph when the full march arrives.

This opening of the *Hexaméron* is the most exact written trace of a practice Liszt probably followed in other improvisational contexts. One of the few moment-by-moment accounts ever written about his playing describes this opening, and it invokes the characteristic bravura–lyrical oscillation:

It begins with a rolling thunderstorm, followed by individual claps; then it clears out into a more peaceful Adagio, interrupted by occasional thunder, but otherwise having a melting sweetness, blowing away in almost fading tones. Suddenly the storm erupts anew, and then begins the battle-duet from "I Puritani," played with unsurpassed beauty.[114]

---

[114] *Gesellschafter* 11 "Beilage" (19 January 1842), 53.

In the ear of this listener, the minor-mode coloring of the lyrical section is not especially important. Its melancholy tone is overridden by the contrast with the preceding bravura, so that it bears a "melting sweetness." It is possible, then, that the lyrical section was heard as a "celestial blue" moment in spite of the minor mode. This description reveals another habit of Liszt's: just as he sprinkled lyrical moments into long bravura sections, so he sprinkled bravura moments into extended lyrical sections. This is evident in the reference to "occasional thunder" amidst the lyrical episode, probably the left hand grace-note figures. Liszt even introduced such gestures into performances of Beethoven's Sonata in C sharp minor, perhaps partially in recognition of its fantasia-like character. It nevertheless irritated Ludwig Rellstab, who expected only literal renditions of Beethoven: "The overheated temperament of our performing artist is not content with this overall romantic coloration. He inserts dark cloud-shadows, pale lightning tremors, distant rolls of the thunder, sudden storm claps."[115]

Liszt's celestial blues, in summary, are a dimension of his virtuosic style that can only be reconstructed from contemporary descriptions of his playing and from one or two examples in his virtuoso repertory. They were probably a stock element of his free improvisations, especially in looser sections not constructed around a melodic thread, and he apparently also introduced them spontaneously as he performed through-composed pieces. They manifest an impulse to destabilize the discourse as soon as a single affect predominates or threatens to cancel out its opposing affect. This insistent way of positioning positive against negative, light against dark, aspires to the simultaneous representation of contrary affective states. The resultant affect is the uncanny *tension* between these contrary poles, a feeling separate from and dissimilar to either pole taken individually. Writers called in the image of the natural storm, that cliché of the romantic sublime, with remarkable consistency in describing this dimension of Liszt's playing. The romantic sublime – in painting the lonely observer gazing out over a vast, dark-hued landscape – is characterized by a feeling of awe or astonishment at the gulf separating human and nature. Liszt's celestial blues (and his terrestrial grays) produced a comparable psychological state in his listeners through sound.[116] His incarnation of the romantic sublime was unique, however, by virtue of his performing presence. He was inserted into the

---

[115] Rellstab, *Franz Liszt*, 7. Ironically, Rellstab was the critic who originated the epithet "Moonlight," a romantic elaboration that probably inspired Liszt's embellishments.

[116] In the classic "romantic sublime" paintings by Kaspar David Friedrich, the human is a tiny presence and nature an overwhelming presence. These proportions are preserved in Liszt's alternating moments: the lyrical moments are brief interruptions of the predominant bravura mode.

discourse in such a way that the celestial blue seemed to radiate out from him.

Demonic dialectics

Liszt's glow of goodness emerged from his performances by another mechanism: a dialectical shift from the diabolical to the holy, a kind of played-out baptism into grace. This shift did not depend upon the aural effect of *chiaroscuro* described above. It took place toward the end of his performances, when the level of high-intensity bravura is sustained over a long period of time. In the following description of Liszt performing one of his own compositions, we encounter two contrary affective states being communicated simultaneously, both *within* the bravura mode:

As the closing strains began, I saw Liszt's countenance assume that agony of expression, mingled with radiant smiles of joy, which I never saw in any other human face, except in the paintings of our Saviour by some of the early masters; his hands rushed over the keys, the floor on which I sat shook like a wire, and the whole audience were wrapped in sound, when the hand and the frame of the artist gave way.[117]

Liszt's bravura has the capacity to be coded holy as well as diabolical: his performing body shudders from the force of religious ecstasy as well as from demonic possession. In this passage his agony is positioned, to a limited extent, prior to his ecstasy (by the phrase "mingled with"), but it catches Liszt in a transitional moment of his performance. Liszt collapsed on stage before concluding his piece, but he was moving toward an eventual triumph of the holy radiance over the diabolical.

The complete trajectory from diabolical possession to holy transcendence is most clearly conveyed in Hans Christian Andersen's account:

he seemed to me a demon who was nailed fast to the instrument whence the tones streamed forth – they came from his blood, from his thoughts; he was a demon who would liberate his soul from thraldom; he was on the rack, the blood flowed, and the nerves trembled; but as he continued to play, the demon disappeared. I saw that pale face assume a nobler and brighter expression: the divine soul shone from his eyes and from every feature; he became as beauteous as spirit and enthusiasm can make their worshippers.[118]

Andersen's narrative, in which Liszt's performance becomes a ritual of exorcism, is exclusively visual, yet the presence of sound can be felt

---

[117] Quoted in *Portrait of Liszt*, 66; this account, from the year 1835, is by Henry Reeve. Another interesting passage on Liszt's Christ-like appearance comes from the notes of Caroline Boissier: "Yesterday he was so pale, his tapered face expressed such suffering, that he had the air of a martyr. Poor young man!" (*Liszt pédagogue*, ed. A. Boissier [Paris, 1976], 43–44).

[118] From *A Poet's Bazaar*; quoted from an 1846 edition in *Portrait of Liszt*, 146.

through the visual details. The first sentence collapses the flow of blood and the flow of musical sound, both of them rushing forth from Liszt's diabolical bravura. As he is transfigured, the source of the outward flow of sound becomes his eyes, recast as a divine radiance. Although the performer is present all along, this progression from the non-sentient body (blood and nerves) to the face recovers Liszt as a self – delivers him from occupation by a foreign, threatening presence. This is a crucial asymmetry within Liszt's demonic dialectic: in the diabolical mode Liszt nearly disappears as a self, but in the holy mode his self is entirely present, hence constructing Liszt's glow of goodness.

Invocations of the diabolical–holy trajectory are obstinately resistant to the musical codes of particular compositions. Heinrich Heine forgot which composition he had heard Liszt play at the famous "duel" with Thalberg. Although Liszt had played his fantasy on Pacini's "I palpiti frequenti," Heine sardonically evoked Liszt's performance as a scene from the apocalypse, poised between heaven and hell:

First Satan galloped into the lists, bedecked in black, on a milk-white horse. Slowly behind him, Death rode on his pale horse. Finally Christ appeared, in golden armor, on a black horse. With his sacred spear he first thrust Satan to earth, and then Death, and the spectators cheered.[119]

Although Heine presents this narrative as a purely psychological, fantastic elaboration of the musical drama, an identification of Liszt with the figure of Christ is heavily implied. Satan and Death are both figurations of his diabolical bravura, but they are not identifiable with Liszt himself: they stand apart from him, or invade him, and the closure of the performance event depends on his eventual triumph. This complex process of signification operates entirely apart from, and can even eclipse, the specific identity of the composition Liszt is playing. Heine was far more compelled by the drama of Liszt's performing style than by the drama of Pacini's opera.

If Liszt's demonic dialectic functions independently of the dramatic or generic codes in the music, there must nevertheless be a musical gesture, a mechanism of opposition, that triggers the shift from diabolic to holy. As an example of such a musical gesture, I take the end of the *Norma* fantasy, one of the more prominent pieces in his virtuoso repertory. The *Norma* fantasy has a level of "allegorical" signification that I deliberately ignore here in order to shed light on the musical logic of the diabolical–holy opposition.[120] Approximately ten minutes into the lengthy fantasy, the melody "Padre, tu piangi?" is heard for the first time in a highly

---

[119] *Heinrich Heine und die Musik*, 106.

[120] Suttoni's study of the early nineteenth-century opera fantasy, in which he shows how Liszt and other composers created a microcosmic image of the relevant opera's dramatic action, has set the tone for many subsequent studies of the genre. Charles Suttoni,

Example 5.3 Liszt, *Réminiscences de Norma*

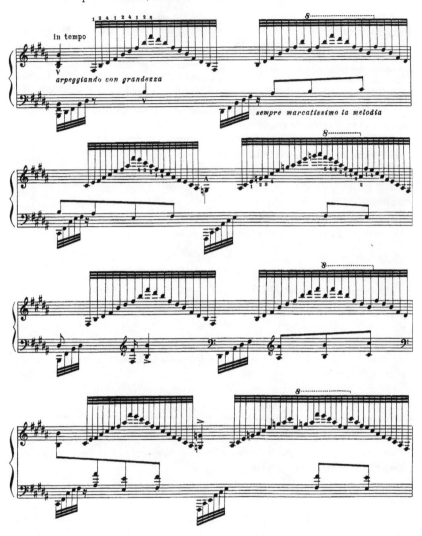

impassioned setting (Example 5.3). This thematic statement is in many respects continuous with the music that precedes it. It preserves the fortissimo dynamic level, the stable B major tonality, and the rich three-tier texture with a melody placed in the center. An important element of this thematic statement for my analysis is the rhythm. The arpeggio figures articulate a half-note span, within which time the pianist's right

"Piano and Opera: A Study of the Piano Fantasies Written on Opera Themes in the Romantic Era" (Ph.D. diss., New York University, 1973).

Example 5.4 Liszt, *Réminiscences de Norma*

hand cuts a strongly curved arc of arpeggiation. The effect is highly suggestive of deep, impassioned human breaths.

After the entire theme has been stated in its entirety, a repetition begins, this time with an anxious undercurrent (*Molto più animato*, Example 5.4). The anxiety soon reveals its source, as the B major bliss is rudely interrupted by a rough, dissonant hammering, which gradually

251

Example 5.4 (*cont.*)

works its way up the keyboard and wrenches the music into a threatening, implacable E flat minor march (*Doppio movimento. Presto con furia*).
These two pages of E flat minor are a classic example of the type of
bravura writers describe as "diabolical." The music is loud and percussive, with arpeggio flourishes, bold double-fisted chords, and constant
shifts of register. The hands and arms must cross each other as they leap
around the keyboard (*marcatissimo con bravura*) or rapidly alternate from
the wrists (*martellato con bravura*). This section culminates in a chord
(VII dim. 7/V) whose dissonance level is increased by its percussive
articulation and its wide-spaced voicing. The A natural in the bass pulls
up the preceding bass tone A flat and implies a movement toward the
dominant B flat, but it prolongs the dissonant chord a full eight measures, thus heavily dramatizing the arrival on B flat (*Meno allegro*).

This arrival on B flat is the crucial turning point. The melody "Padre, tu piangi?" returns, once again in the middle of a three-tiered texture, but it is transformed from its first appearance in three ways. First, it contrasts radically with the preceding music: the move from a volatile minor back to the major mode gives the listener a feeling of profound release. Second, the melody is heard over a dominant pedal that supports a I $^6_4$ chord, which uplifts the listener by intimating that the conclusion is near and the major mode will remain triumphant.[121] Third, the right-hand figure transforms the rhythmic backdrop against which the melody appears. It traces out huge, expansive arcs that span the length of two whole notes, four times the length of the arpeggios that accompanied the original melodic statement. The sense of human breath implicit in the earlier accompaniment disappears, and we hear instead breaths only possible among gods. The new accompaniment thus transfigures the melody, abstracting it from the human realm and inserting it into the divine. The right-hand figuration, furthermore, creates a sonorous aura of the divine: the pedal blurs the scale tones together in a diffuse halo of sound that hovers around the melody.

This segment from the *Norma* fantasy exemplifies some of the musical features – modal contrast, harmonic tension/release, and sonority – by which Liszt could precipitate a shift from a diabolically coded virtuosity to an ecstatic, holy virtuosity, and rendered his performances a spectacle of demonic exorcism. There are undoubtedly many other devices and strategies that could achieve the same result. His diabolical bravura, for example, often included chromatic ascents and descents and harmonic instabilities absent from this *Doppio movimente*, but which are effective when posed against music of strong harmonic stability. The demonic dialectic always begins with the diabolical mode as the prior term, and it gives over to its opposite by the agency of sudden shifts in the musical affect. It is worth repeating that Liszt's performing self was inserted into this discourse of sound asymmetrically. The *Doppio movimente* contains no sounds of the human singing voice, but the human voice returns in the *Meno allegro*, recontextualized within an aura of divinity. As a solo performer, Liszt is aligned by default with the human side of this dichotomy, and like the melody he returns in an aureole of radiance, a glow of goodness. It was this emergence into benevolence that provided the conduit between Liszt's performing style and the social world in which he was situated. But there was another element within his

---

[121] It is also arguable that the B flat pedal resolves the B minor and B major tonalities – enharmonically the flat-six of E flat – that dominate the middle of the fantasy. The difficulty with this interpretation is that the first several minutes of the piece are in G minor and G major, not E flat, putting strain on the tonal conditions that would be necessary to hear the B tonalities as flat-six degrees of E flat.

concert hall – a bond to the audience – that further enhanced his aura of benevolence.

Charity/charisma

During his visit to Berlin Liszt became friendly with his audiences to an unprecedented degree. In his previous concertizing he had always made occasional concessions to the requests of audiences, but in Berlin he was honoring them systematically, and toward the end of his visit the *Berliner Modenspiegel* claimed that this responsiveness was one of the causes of his popularity.[122] Already at his third public concert (5 January) the audience provoked him, after an already long program, to play his *Robert le diable* fantasy. At his January 12 concert he made extra efforts to satisfy the wishes of his audience: he received a request, apparently during the intermission, to play an extra piece before the concluding *Grand galop*, and he turned this request into a masterpiece of stagecraft. He offered the *Erlkönig* and Weber's *Aufförderung zum Tanz*, for which the audience voted with equal measures of applause. After a brief deliberation, he broke the tension by announcing that he would simply play both pieces. The Berlin publics could not get enough of these two compositions, and they demanded them in Liszt's later performances. At the 23 January concert he improvised on the *Aufförderung* at the public's request, and on 30 January he was prevailed upon to do the same with motives from the *Erlkönig*.[123]

Liszt's receptivity to requests was thus already a hallmark of the Berlin episode after the first few weeks, but from there it expanded still further. He had originally planned to stay in Berlin only until early February. As his planned departure approached, however, the university students requested through Ludwig Rellstab that he play a concert at the university with reduced prices, since they could not afford the high prices of his regular concerts. This was a bold and unprecedented request to which Liszt quickly assented (25 January). The professors at university, however, took advantage and swallowed up a large number of the tickets intended for the students. Hearing of the students' anger toward the professors, Liszt announced at the end of his performance that he would give a second concert (1 February), to which the students responded with redoubled enthusiasm. At the second concert, furthermore, he left it up to the students to decide the second half of the program. These displays of generosity and congeniality generated a new wave of enthusiasm for Liszt. The public kept demanding more concerts, and almost half

---

[122] *Berliner Modenspiegel*, 5 March 1842; report on the 28 February *"fons caritatis"* concert.
[123] *Spenersche Zeitung*, 25 January and 1 February 1842. According to the reviewer, the applause was not so strong, in the latter case, as to make an encore inevitable.

of them were for the benefit of charities and institutions.[124] Altogether they managed to keep him in Berlin a full five weeks longer than he had planned.

Liszt's reputation for selflessness, and his easy acquiescence to the wishes of the Berlin public, sometimes got out of hand. Already in January, one journalist warned that if the public kept demanding so many encores they might wear Liszt out.[125] When he agreed to conduct the orchestra for a theatre benefit on 28 February, the *Spenersche Zeitung* printed a request that he perform at least one solo piano piece on the concert, and the audience came to the concert expecting him to fulfill the wish. With about twenty public concerts behind him, Liszt might well have felt this was unnecessary. He avoided the problem by "falling ill" before the last piece, which he was supposed to conduct, and after which he would surely have been brought back for an encore.[126] Liszt's reputation for financial generosity also became unmanageable. He was receiving dozens of visits and letters each day from people begging for money, not all of them from the lower classes of the population.[127]

The Berlin episode was thus permeated with the theme of charity at several levels. Liszt demonstrated his benevolence in direct contributions to unfortunate people, in numerous concerts for charitable causes, and in his congenial deference to the wishes of the public. We might not expect, however, that such gestures could generate public enthusiasm to such a degree that they would be cited as a *principal* cause of the Berliners' enthusiasm. Understanding the disposition toward charity among Liszt's audiences requires an imaginative leap into history. As F. K. Prochaska has written of the nineteenth century: "The degree to which charity saturated people's lives, both as givers and recipients, is difficult to imagine for anyone who has grown up in the shadow of the welfare state."[128] Problems dealt with today by the welfare-state framework were covered in Liszt's time by the moral framework of Christian

---

[124] Kapp counted nine charity concerts among Liszt's twenty-one public appearances (Julius Kapp, *Franz Liszt: eine Biographie* [Berlin/Leipzig, 1911], 85).

[125] *Blätter für Musik und Literatur* 3 (11 January 1842), 9–11 (G. Nicolai).

[126] *Spenersche Zeitung*, 2 March 1842.

[127] This situation was much lamented by the reporter Gustav Nicolai: "It is also the talk of the town that during the presence of the brilliant man in this capital an innumerable pile of written requests came to him, unfortunately not coming from the lower people's classes, in which he was begged for assistance ... What a man, but still more, what a sad reproach to the condition of our civic happiness, which presses many family fathers, some of them very estimable, to claim the assistance of a foreigner passing through in order not to starve in the civilized capital of the so honorable fatherland!" (*Blätter für Musik und Literatur* 3 [February 1842], 21–22). Rellstab made a passing reference to this situation (Rellstab, *Franz Liszt*, 43).

[128] F. K. Prochaska, "Philanthropy," chapter 7 in *The Cambridge Social History of Britain 1750–1950* (Cambridge, 1990), 3 vols., III: 373.

benevolence: "The philanthropic disposition was inseparable from religion in the Christian mind, the word charity itself synonymous with the
conduct of Christ."[129]

Liszt's essay on his visit to Lyons shows how fully humanitarian
benevolence was layered with Christian significance. Through charity,
he writes, "The most elegant ladies employ their charms, turning flirta-
tion into Christian virtue." But Liszt's main theme in the article is the *lack*
of true Christian virtue shown by the Parisians at their charity events:

I have always considered it a duty to associate myself with charitable societies
at every opportunity – except on the day following those concerts in which I had
taken part, I have seen the patrons of the gala praising and congratulating themselves on the amount raised, while I continued on my way, my head lowered,
pondering the fact that when the alms are distributed each family might receive
one loaf of bread to eat and one stick of wood for the fire . . . Eighteen centuries
have passed since Christ preached the Brotherhood of Man, and His Word is
still not really understood! . . . The Providence of God must be announced anew
to the people.[130]

Liszt asserts his own special endowment of Christian virtue by criticizing the tendency of Parisians to attend charity events out of concern for
social distinction rather than from religious motives. Germans tended
to use the same rhetorical gesture. The Berlin writer Theodor Mundt,
who visited Paris in 1837, attended a charity concert in which Liszt
participated, and was struck at how completely considerations of fashion and social visibility overshadowed the presumed purpose of the
event. All the money that went into dress, makeup, and carriages, he
remarked ironically, might have amounted to a hefty charity contribution.[131] Mundt was evidently holding Paris up to the standard he was
accustomed to in Berlin, where a higher sense of moral purpose prevailed at charity events. A Berlin journalist confirmed this in a report on
Liszt's first *fons caritatis* concert, noting that the Berliners were "willing
and generous when it comes to supporting a charitable institution."[132]

Liszt came to Berlin at a time when, perhaps because of the recent
death in the royal house, religious sentiment was unusually high. While
his concerts were underway the *Telegraph für Deutschland* reported that
"in philosophical and free-spirited Berlin there dominates now such an
impenetrably pious atmosphere that a worldly person can hardly fend

[129] Ibid., III: 378.
[130] *An Artist's Journey*, 49–50. For a detailed study of Liszt's philosophical views on religion
and charity, and their intellectual sources, see Arthur McCalla, "Liszt *Bricoleur*: Poetics
and Providentialism in Early July Monarchy France," *History of European Ideas* 24/2
(1998), 71–93.
[131] Theodor Mundt, *Spaziergänge und Weltfahrten* (Altona, 1838), 2 vols., I: 313–18.
[132] *Berliner Figaro* 36 (12 February 1842), 143 (C. O. Hoffmann).

off the infection."[133] The intensity of religious feeling, characteristic of the Pietists who had a strong presence in Berlin, went hand in hand with an increased fervor on the part of the charity organizations in Berlin, who saw their mission as a religious one. Not far from the concert reviews of Liszt in the *Gesellschafter*, for example, there is an editorial column protesting the increasingly Pietistic righteousness of Berlin's charities. The leaders of such charities are faulted for their passionate claims that they alone are the direct workers of God's will, chosen transmitters of divine benevolence, as though God did not also will the misfortunes of the people in need of help. The article also makes it clear that Berlin was sprouting a large number of charities at this time, singling out the often-ridiculed *Organisation against Animal Abuse*, which had recently been formed.[134]

The disposition to Christian humanitarian philanthropy, in sum, was stronger in German cities than in the more cosmopolitan, elite European capitals, where charity was caught up in the struggle for social distinction, and in Berlin the disposition seems to have been especially marked. Liszt's multiple demonstrations of humanitarian benevolence therefore had greater potential to mobilize public enthusiasm in the Prussian capital. Berlin critics gave more attention to Liszt's charity than it had ever received previously. Gustav Nicolai, after listing the sheer volume of performances Liszt gave in Berlin, wrote:

Whoever tries to read between these lines that Liszt covets money is quite mistaken indeed. For when has an artist given so much evidence as he has of Christian sympathy for the misfortune of others, of the purest feeling of benevolence?[135]

Liszt's Berlin activities had clearly convinced Nicolai that he was a paragon of Christian virtue. Yet as we saw in the cases of the Lyons concert and the Pest flood concert, Liszt made charity work for him and his audiences by funneling extra, para-Christian layers of moral purpose into it.

In Berlin, he was able to combine charity specifically with the ideology of liberal reform and Prussian nationalism (discussed in chapter 4) to magnify his appeal. It may sound strange to suggest that Liszt was so clever as to merge his charity with national feeling in Germany, but the possibility did occur to his contemporaries. In 1847, a thoroughly

---

[133] *Telegraph für Deutschland* (February 1842), 101. Although the report is undated, it probably pertains to the time period around December and January. Correspondence reports in papers like the *Telegraph* tended to appear in print about a month after the events they describe. This makes it even more likely that the author is referring to the mood of Berlin after the death of the queen's mother.

[134] *Gesellschafter*, 22 January 1842.

[135] *Blätter für Musik und Literatur* 3 (February 1842), 21.

skeptical observer identified his ostentatious generosity as a strategy for winning enthusiasm specifically in Germany:

I am familiar, through the journals of London and Paris, with the eccentricities of Liszt; I know that in France he played at philosophy, the republic, and socialism, and in Germany at nobility, enthusiasm, generosity, and all this in the best faith of the world.[136]

If this writer had been asked to cite a specific case of Liszt "playing at generosity," he would surely have referred to Berlin. Closer to the Berlin episode, another writer compared Liszt's reception with that of Fanny Elssler, and found that Liszt's benevolence had given him a distinct advantage:

Elssler enjoys the praises mostly of men, and even this in a lesser degree than Liszt, since he, in addition to his artistic fame, knew how to surround himself with an aureole [*Glorienschein*] of benevolence, originality, and generosity.[137]

The singling out of men is an important detail here, revealing that Liszt's benevolent aura was strongly anchored in gestures toward institutions – the university, the *Männergesangsverein*, the freemasons, and the monarchy – that were not explicitly aimed at Christian humanitarian causes.

Humanitarian charity and Prussian nationalism were bonded to each other by their common basis in Christian principles: just as charitable giving was undertaken as a religious duty, so dedication to the Prussian nation was figured through obedience to the divinely ordained monarch, Friedrich Wilhelm IV. The Cologne cathedral, for which Liszt gave a concert on 9 January, is a perfect example of this nexus: it was simultaneously a religious and a national symbol, which is why Friedrich Wilhelm IV so theatrically associated himself with its reconstruction. The ill-fated *fons caritatis* concert of 10 February – discussed in detail in chapter 4 – was simultaneously a pageant of Christian humanitarianism (*fons caritatis* means "charitable fund") and of Prussian nationalism, the latter celebrated in the performance of numerous patriotic songs.[138]

The concert Liszt gave at the Royal Opera House on 19 February for the benefit of the *fons caritatis* was particularly rich in charitable significance. Its uncommonly grandiose program began with Beethoven's "Emperor" concerto and closed with Beethoven's Choral Fantasy. At the end of the Choral Fantasy, according to one report,

---

[136] *La mode*, 5 January 1847 ("Louise"). This article is among the clippings in the "Second scrapbook" of Marie d'Agoult, at the Bibliothèque municipale de Versailles.
[137] *Europa* (1843/1), 34. "Sie [Elssler] geniesst daher grösstentheils nur die Huldigungen der Männer, und auch diese nicht in solchen Grade wie sie Liszt zu Theil wurden, da dieser neben seinem künstlerischen Ruhm mit einem Glorienschein von Wohlthätigkeit, Originalität und Freigebigkeit sich zu umgeben wusste."
[138] For a discussion of the nationalistic tone of this event, see chapter 4, "The *fons caritatis* concert."

the patriotic and artistic enthusiasm developed into the audible desire for and calls for the national song "Heil Dir im Siegerkranz," which was accepted and received with a cheer, whereupon more poems and silhouettes with the byline "Gaudeamus igitur" were thrown down, although all too few of them and a bit too late.[139]

No particular piece on the program was responsible for the "patriotic enthusiasm" of the audience. Patriotism was simply implicit in the charitable tone of the concert, and they wished to hear it made explicit in Liszt's improvisation. The competing request for "Gaudeamus igitur" represents the climax of yet another strain of Liszt's benevolence: his sympathy with the students. The two inexpensive concerts he gave at the university – the second of which included an improvisation on "Gaudeamus igitur" – had so endeared him to the academic community that he was being considered for an honorary doctorate, an unprecedented honor for a virtuoso.[140] The end of this *fons caritatis* concert shows just how completely Liszt's humanitarianism and receptivity to requests had become intertwined with patriotic and intellectual currents prevalent among the Berlin audiences.

The positive view of the Berlin episode was articulated most thoroughly in detailed essays by Ludwig Rellstab and Gustav Nicolai, whose ideas overlap considerably.[141] Both writers saw Liszt's visit as a highpoint in the city's history. In stark contrast to adherents of the progressive consensus, they presented the enthusiasm of the Berliners as worthy and honest – a credit to themselves and to Liszt. Both writers also drew attention to charity in the more expansive sense that Liszt had imparted to it through his support for nationalism and academic learning, and through his readiness to offer money or music at the slightest provocation. Rellstab composed the title of his retrospective essay – "Liszt: An Event of Public Life" – after the idea that Liszt's significance poured out

---

[139] *Spenersche Zeitung*, 21 February 1842.

[140] The university was at the foreground of Liszt's reception toward the end of his visit, most notably in the *Abschiedsgeleit*. It is likely that university professors initiated the motion to elect him to the Prussian *Academie der Künste*, which was celebrated in an immense banquet just three days before this concert (16 February). The honor may, in fact, have been a substitute for the doctoral degree that was notoriously denied to him in Berlin. At the very least, the *Academie* membership functioned to install him in the field of science and learning in the same manner that an honorary doctorate would have. The reasons he was denied the doctorate are not clear, but probably had something to do with the lack of precedent for presenting a virtuoso with such an honor.

[141] Rellstab's retrospective essays are "Liszt in Berlin," which appeared in the *Vossische Zeitung*, 6 March 1842 (Rellstab, *Franz Liszt*, 41–46), and "Liszt: ein Ereignis des öffentlichen Lebens," which he sent to various other German papers (Rellstab, *Franz Liszt*, 46–55). Nicolai was commissioned to write three reports for the *Blätter für Musik und Literatur*, one for each of the January, February, and March editions.

beyond the boundaries of "art criticism" and "art history," and Liszt's all-embracing charity lay at the heart of this idea.[142] After listing his donations in "small as well as large circles," Rellstab writes:

But perhaps – no certainly – this same worthy generosity with his talent . . . has increased the number of his listeners, for it was no longer a mere isolated artistic offering that people wondered at, but they entered into lively, warm contact with the personality of the artist, which exerted an equally powerful force of attraction.[143]

Here Rellstab suggests that Liszt's generosity and personality, which he had already demonstrated in the civic sphere, were part of the concert experience itself, woven into the performer–listener bond. Liszt's intimate, non-hierarchical bond to the audience, epitomized by his receptivity to requests, is thus figured as one mode of his thoroughly amiable and generous attitude toward all people.

Nicolai likewise emphasized the broad social implications of Liszt's visit at the opening of his retrospective essay:

Liszt's appearance in Berlin signifies a segment not just in the history of art, but in the overall chronicle of our city. Previously art embraced only the artist and the initiated with a spiritual bond; it was reserved for Liszt alone to transmit through art the moral and political element of social relations, and so he is everywhere a true member of the public, he is everywhere a native, he is everywhere . . . recognized by all, he gives himself to all people with the same love.[144]

Like Rellstab, Nicolai collapses the boundary between music and money – between the concert hall and the civic sphere of Berlin more generally. Liszt occupies and transcends both spaces as a fount of charismatic benevolence. The ethical model for this unconditional, universal selflessness is none other than Christ. The theme of Liszt's twofold significance – his achievements at both the musical and moral levels – was picked up in the Prussian city of Königsberg, which he visited immediately after Berlin: "Liszt has left us, having received here, as everywhere, the most general admiration, not only for his unsurpassed achievements, but also for his rare qualities of mind and heart."[145]

The positive view of the Berlin episode was thus organized around the theme of charity, intensified by the climate of liberal social reform introduced by the new king in 1840. The public's euphoria over Liszt embodied a healthy civic spirit, guided by Christian virtue, characterized by honor to the monarch and optimism about social amelioration.

---

[142] Rellstab, *Franz Liszt*, 46.   [143] Ibid., 26.
[144] *Blätter für Musik und Literatur* 3 (March 1842), p. 50.
[145] This Königsberg report, dated 20 March 1842, is probably from the *Königliche preussische Staats- Kriegs- und Friedenszeitung*. It is cited in Ernst Burger, *Franz Liszt: A Life in Pictures and Documents* (Princeton, 1989), 145.

This view contradicts that of the progressives in the starkest imaginable way. The one side sees in Liszt's presence an alert, socially engaged public spirit, in harmonious accord with the monarchial order, while the other side sees only a diseased public, driven by their exclusion from political participation to engage in excessive histrionics devoid of moral content. There was evidence to support both views, but in the aftermath of Liszt's departure, only the negative view spread to the international press. As the satires and caricatures rained down, Rellstab felt compelled to pick up his pen and defend the Berliners:

> The enthusiasm for him is therefore worthy, in its inner nature completely different from that weak enthusiasm, rightly mocked, that flares up for merely external events and talents of the day . . . We will not deny that the noble spirit of many, especially women, has been somewhat excessive and has yielded some very bizarre symptoms. Yet all phenomena of this sort should be evaluated not in their details, but in their general outlines. And in this general sense the enthusiasm for Liszt does honor to our capital city; it shows the city felt deeply and truly the extraordinariness of this phenomenon.[146]

It is clear from this passage that Rellstab understands the logic of the progressive consensus, and even agrees that there exists a general problem in the Berlin publics, at least among the women. Their reception of Liszt, however, is in his eyes an exceptional case that stands apart from Berlin's stained history.

Contemporary opinions about Liszt's visit to Berlin were radically polarized. Some saw it as one of the darkest moments in the city's history, others saw it as one of the brightest peaks. These remarkably opposed views stemmed from the doubleness of Berlin's own identity. Around 1800 the city struck visitors as little more than a garrison town, but by 1871 it was the center of the unified German nation, proudly dubbed "das neue Berlin" or just "Neuberlin." The Berlin of the 1840s stood at the cusp of the old and the new. It was both forward-looking in its promise of liberal reform, and backward-looking in its continuation of feudal, monarchical traditions. Cultural observers of Liszt's time tended to see one of these sides at the exclusion of the other, and they made their judgments about Liszt's immense popularity in Berlin accordingly.

But why would Liszt's virtuosity, of all things, bring about such controversies over Berlin's civic identity? The answer lies in the difficulty of "reading" public enthusiasm. Applause, bouquets, and bravos look and sound the same no matter who is producing them. But the *causes* of such demonstrations are invisible; they can only be read back from their outward signs. The cause might be merely sensual and hence illegitimate, or aesthetic and intellectual and hence legitimate. When the

---

[146] Rellstab, *Franz Liszt*, 45.

public gets as excited over someone as it did over Liszt, the question of legitimacy naturally comes to the fore. And music does not help to judge Liszt's legitimacy, for music too is invisible, working upon people in ways difficult to isolate and analyze. As vibrating sound, it has the potential to work invisibly upon the nerves, to shake up the body, and give immediate pleasure. In many ways, Liszt's virtuosity brought this potential of music to its fullest development. Yet music also has a moral or intellectual content, an ability to uplift, inspire, and awaken noble sentiments, and this power is equally as invisible. Liszt's aura of radiant benevolence brought this side of music to a certain climax as well. The two views of the Berlin episode, in conclusion, stem not only from an ambivalence about the city of Berlin, but also from a basic ambivalence about the power of music itself.

Afterword

The nineteenth-century piano soaked up its contemporary musical culture like a sponge. In addition to developing poetic worlds of its own, it became a medium for reproducing operas, symphonies, songs, and chamber music, and faithfully echoed the sounds of orchestras, voices, military bands, harps, and organs. By taking on these genres and instruments, the piano also became a repository of their attendant social meanings. In capable hands, it could now be played to render symphonic grandeur, amorous intimacy, operatic passion, pious religiosity, national pride, the dizzying euphoria of the ballroom. Its pretensions to universality – not just musical but social universality – were greater than any other instrument. It seemed to place an entire universe of human experience at the performer's fingertips.

Franz Liszt made it his mission to exploit the piano's "universal" potential in order to define the virtuoso as a figure of urgency and social relevance. His pursuit of a broader identity for the virtuoso led him to impressive technical innovations. He developed colors, textures, articulations, and sound effects that had never before been heard from the piano. Historians and biographers have given extensive attention to these innovations, but Liszt's audiences paid little attention to such progress. They were interested in the here-and-now of his virtuosity, and Liszt was expanding the range of the instrument to address them in contemporary terms. With his outstanding capacity to absorb every scrap of music he encountered and domesticate it for the piano, he served up salon dances, national airs and anthems, symphony excerpts, art songs, grand opera scenes, *bel canto* arias, military marches, chamber septets, improvised storms, classical sonatas, art songs, fugues, and concertos. This was not the music of the future, but the entire musical spectrum of the present, brought under the expressive control of a single artist.

In pursuit of his aspirations to universal significance, Liszt went far beyond music. He turned his talent for absorption and incorporation toward the social world, and forged charismatic personas out of its raw materials. In this book I have focused on how he built humanitarian, militaristic, national, romantic, and aristocratic elements into his persona and performing style, but this is hardly a complete list. At

263

one point or another he was compared with Faust, Byron, Napoleon, Caesar, Alexander the Great, Kaiser Franz I, Prince Louis Ferdinand of Prussia, Ludwig Schuncke, Thalberg, Mazeppa, Antaeus, Prometheus, Orpheus, Archimedes, Victor Hugo, Hercules, Homer, Christ, Schiller, Roland, Mephistopheles, Leviathan. This jumble of historical, mythological, and literary figures, refracting through his performances, suggest that Liszt embellished and modulated his identity with a prowess and improvisational verve comparable to his treatment of opera melodies.

It is important to acknowledge that Liszt reached for the universal, but like any self-respecting romantic, his reach exceeded his grasp. As he strove to realize the principle of all-inclusiveness, he was bound to inflame the conflicts and divisions – moral, political, social, and aesthetic – that structured his contemporary world. In Paris he delighted romantics such as Berlioz and George Sand, but his style did not win over the dilettantes, who craved a rich vocal sonority. In Germany, he ingratiated himself with audiences by supporting their national sentiments, but the French critics who discovered this attacked him aggressively, and never forgave him. Liszt's elegant, aristocratic manners made him the darling of Paris, Milan, and Vienna, but they met with stiff resistance in bourgeois Leipzig, provoking him to curtail his visit. His virtuoso renditions of Beethoven won him immense admiration among the general public, but professional musicians in London, Paris, Berlin, and Leipzig voiced objections. In all of these ways he anticipated today's star athletes, who are so aggressively pursued by companies that they eventually endorse competing products.

Liszt's public identities multiplied and splintered, then, as a direct consequence of his ambition to transcend them all. He tried to mean everything, only to end up meaning a multitude of things. It is this dialectic – between the ideal domain of Liszt's universal aspiration and the historical realm of his concrete significations – that I have attempted to activate throughout this book. Traditional biography stands exclusively on the side of the "universal" Liszt. By foregrounding a narrative of "inner artistic mission," it consigns public reception, social mediation, and indeed the experiences of thousands of people who heard Liszt, to the margins. This is a particularly fatal flaw in the case of a figure whose manifest goal was to reintegrate the virtuoso with social and ethical life. In striving to make a monument to their hero, biographies have fixed him in stone, immobilizing him in a flattering pose. Liszt was, in many ways, the advocate of dynamism and motion, and he begged to be understood in terms of his contradictions. When Heinrich Heine poked fun at him for jumping from one philosophical school to another, he did not anxiously step forth and iron out his philosophical commitments. Instead he admitted that he had been inconsistent, and pleaded that he too was a creature of history, a victim of the *mal-de-siècle*:

Am I then the only one, in this time in which we live, who is "unsettled" ["mal assis"]. Don't we all sit "unsettled" together, despite our gothic armchairs and our pillows à la Voltaire, between a past that we no longer want to know and a future that we do not yet know?[1]

In recent years, alternative interpretations of the virtuoso Liszt have emerged that proceed from the premises of deconstruction or new historicism. These postmodern studies embrace the transience and diversity of his identities, which can reveal the structures and processes embedded in culture (Kramer), language (Bernstein), or ideology (Leppert). My own interpretation takes its impetus from this critical orientation. I am particularly sympathetic to the postmodern image of culture as a web of complex, indeterminate relationships among nearly all elements in the field of discourse, rather than a group of artifacts that stand out apart from their "context." For the Liszt I have presented here is deeply embedded in his world, constantly negotiating that embeddedness, at times profiting from its advantages and at other times desperately attempting to free himself from it. My effort to discuss Liszt's performing style as a "language" with its own peculiar signifying logic might likewise be considered postmodern, in that it reassigns musical performance to a primary level of meaning production, as against its traditionally reproductive or secondary status.

This study, however, stresses empirical history in resistance to some tendencies of postmodern readings. First, such readings heavily subordinate Liszt's active self-construction to the overwhelming force of cultural processes that determine his historical meaning. This might succeed for most performing artists, but Liszt cared too much about his public image to let his reception run its autonomous course. He could not fully control public perceptions, but he perpetually intervened in the press, and deftly adapted himself to local circumstances, to define and constrain the terms in which he was discussed or debated. Neither were audiences and critics ready to accept all constructions as equally legitimate. They battled out their "bounded" interpretations of Liszt in public and private spaces alike, and it is important not to neutralize such tensions and contradictions in a programmatic search for polysemy or indeterminacy. For all his mutability, Liszt was rarely available to his audiences as a symbol of instability.

Second, deconstructive methods are imprinted with a liberationist politics that has skewed interpretations of Liszt heavily in the direction of the radical or subversive. "Liszt" does appear to have been a site where the antithetical element embedded within the aspirations of dominant culture often came to the fore, and this is certainly a source of his fascination. But it seems naïve to celebrate this antithetical element and

---

[1] Quoted in *Heinrich Heine und die Musik*, ed. G. Müller (Cologne, 1897), 219.

suppress the historical realities that blocked its full emergence. Many of Liszt's virtuoso practices, for example, strike us as inherently critical of the work concept. But he also played his part to instill the work concept by vaunting his dedication to spreading "classical" works, and by dramatizing on a few occasions his faithfulness to the letter of Beethoven's scores. Early in his career, to take another example, he vocally aligned himself with radical utopian political movements in Paris, but when he made his first appearance in the capital of the Habsburg empire and came under the close scrutiny of Metternich's anxious police, they wrote him off as harmless. In this book I have linked Liszt to other domains of contemporary culture, such as Christian morality, militarism, and conservative nationalism, that can be described as "dominant" and make it difficult to advance him convincingly as a liberatory (or liberated) figure.

Carl Dahlhaus has written that "the more comprehensive the knowledge of history that one possesses, and the more obstinately one pursues the search for the premises on which the past rested when it was still the present, the harder to understand, and the more foreign it becomes."[2] Researching Liszt's concerts and reception was for me a process of discovering this apparent paradox. The harder I tried to imagine his virtuoso career "as it was," through an accumulation of detail that would bring it "nearer," the more distant it looked. I began by pursuing the question of how he historically anticipated the modern popular star, only to find that his popularity rested on unfamiliar premises quite specific to the 1830s and 1840s. There is no reason to elevate these premises above other factors not discussed in this book. I have hardly broached, for example, the psychic dynamics of the performer–spectator relationship, which Liszt transformed in ways that are as profound as they are elusive. But I do hope to have shown that historical change has filtered out entire layers of meaning from Liszt's virtuoso legacy, thus provoking historians to define the significance of his performing career according to idealist paradigms such as "instrumental progress" or "compositional development." The greatest performing career in history becomes a great leap forward in the history of the piano, leaving new resources to composers of greater talent, or worse yet, a mere stepping stone to the realization of Liszt's "true" compositional ambitions.

The gravest consequence of working Liszt into idealist paradigms is that his audiences, the very social fabric of his virtuoso career, become wooden and irrelevant. Liszt's audiences: those naïve, unenlightened bourgeois masses who, in their repression, could not contain their rapturous applause in the concert hall, or who, in their earnestness, deceived

---

[2] Carl Dahlhaus, *Ludwig van Beethoven: Approaches to his Music*, trans. Mary Whittall (Oxford, 1991), p. 7.

themselves that shallow piano music was giving them profound experience. The image resounds with a contempt for the middle classes of the nineteenth century that, as Peter Gay has shown, we are all too willing to affirm. But to snicker at Liszt's audiences for their excessive enthusiasm, however sensible from our current perspective, is covertly to admit that we envy them. It is difficult to read about Liszt's career and not feel that our musical culture has in some significant way lost its responsiveness to major virtuosos, and thereby closed its doors to a whole range of musical experience. The prospect of changing this seems extremely low. Yet European audiences were experiencing a similar anomie in the 1820s, as post-classical instrumental styles started to wear thin, and prodigies seemed to be springing up by the dozens. No one then suspected that a figure would come along who would sweep piano virtuosity into the vortex of public life, and give concert audiences something new to care about.

BIBLIOGRAPHY

I. Archival sources

Liszt-Nachlass, Goethe- und Schiller-Archiv, Weimar:

Kasten 261: Miscellaneous press
Kasten 280: Miscellaneous press
Kasten 165: List of attendees of banquet in honor of Liszt
Kasten 133–34: Vienna concert receipts
Kasten 135: Berlin concert receipts
Ms. Z15: "Programme général des morceaux éxécutés par F. Liszt à ses concerts de 1838 à 1848"

Bibliothèque municipale de Versailles: "Second scrapbook" of Marie d'Agoult (Miscellaneous press)
Bibliothèque de l'Opéra, Paris: "Dossier d'artiste: Franz Liszt"

II. Newspapers and periodicals

Abeille musicale	Paris
Adler	Vienna
Allgemeine musikalische Anzeiger	Vienna
Allgemeine musikalische Zeitung	Leipzig
Allgemeine priviligirte schlesische Zeitung	Breslau
Allgemeine Theaterzeitung	Vienna
Allgemeine Wiener Musik-Zeitung	Vienna
Artiste	Paris
Augsburger allgemeine Zeitung	Augsburg
Belgique musicale	Brussels
Berliner Figaro	Berlin
Berliner Modenspiegel	Berlin
Berliner Wespen	Berlin
Birmingham Journal	Birmingham
Blätter der Vergangenheit und Gegenwart	Hanau
Blätter für Musik und Literatur	Hamburg
Breslauer Zeitung	Breslau
Caricature	Paris
Constitutionnel	Paris
Courrier des théâtres	Paris
Courrier musicale	Paris

268

Danica hrvatska, slavonska i dalmatinska	Zagreb
Didaskalia	Frankfurt
Dilettante	Paris
Doncaster Gazette	Doncaster
Dresdner Wochenblatt	Dresden
Europa	Leipzig/Stuttgart
Foedrelandet	Copenhagen
France musicale	Paris
Frankfurter Konversationsblatt	Frankfurt
Frankfurter patriotisches Wochenblatt	Frankfurt an der Oder
Gazette des salons	Paris
Gazette musicale de Paris	Paris
Gesellschafter	Berlin
Glaneur du Haut-Rhin	Mulhausen
Guêpes	Paris
Hamburger neue Zeitung	Hamburg
Honmüvész	Pest
Humorist	Vienna
Iris im Gebiete der Tonkunst	Leipzig
Journal de Paris	Paris
Journal des débats	Paris
Journal des rieurs	Paris
Kaiserliche-königliche priviligirte städtische Pressburger Zeitung	Pressburg
Königliche Preussische Staats- Kriegs- und Friedenszeitung	Königsberg
Korrespondent von und für Deutschland	Nürnberg
Leicester Chronicle	Leicester
Leipziger allgemeine Zeitung	Leipzig
Ménestrel	Paris
Mode	Paris
Monde	Paris
Monde musical	Paris
Musical World	London
Neue Zeitschrift für Musik	Leipzig
Neuigkeits-Bote	Berlin
Nordlicht	Leipzig
Norwich Mercury	Norwich
Ost und West	Prague
Pester Tageblatt	Pest
Presse	Paris
Revue des deux mondes	Paris
Revue et gazette musicale de Paris	Paris
Revue musicale	Paris
Sammler	Vienna
Scotsman	Edinburgh
Signale für die musikalische Welt	Leipzig

Spenersche Zeitung	Berlin
Telegraph	Frankfurt an der Oder
Telegraph für Deutschland	Hamburg
Thalia	Hamburg
Tintamarre	Paris
Vert-vert	Paris
Vossische Zeitung	Berlin
Wakefield Journal	Wakefield
Wiener Telegraph	Vienna
Wiener Zeitschrift	Vienna
Wolverhampton Chronicle	Wolverhampton
Zeitung für die elegante Welt	Leipzig

III.   Primary printed sources: books and correspondence

Agoult, Marie d'. *Mémoires 1833–1854*. Daniel Ollivier, ed. Paris: Calmann-Lévy, 1927.

Ançelot, Virginie. *Les salons de Paris*. Paris: J. Tardieu, 1858.

Apponyi, Rudolph. *Journal. Vingt-cinq ans à Paris (1826–50)*. 3 vols. Paris: Plon, 1914.

The Autobiography of Charles Hallé. Michael Kennedy, ed. London: Paul Elek Books, 1972.

Autour de Madame d'Agoult et de Liszt. Daniel Ollivier, ed. Paris: B. Grasset, 1941.

Bähr, Otto. *Eine deutsche Stadt vor hundert Jahren: kulturgeschichtliche Skizzen*. Berlin: Fraenkel, 1926.

Barbey-Boissier, Caroline. *La Comtesse Agénor de Gasparin et sa famille. Correspondance et souvenirs 1813–1894*. 2 vols. Paris: Plon-Nourrit, 1902.

Bauer, Karoline. *Nachgelassene Memoiren von Karoline Bauer*. 3 vols. Berlin: Louis Gerschel, 1881.

Benedict, Jules. *Weber*. 5th edition. London: S. Low, Marston and Co., 1899.

Berlioz, Hector. *The Memoirs of Hector Berlioz*. David Cairns, trans. London: Victor Gollancz, 1969.

Boissier, Caroline. *Liszt pédagogue: leçons de piano données par Liszt à Mademoiselle Valérie Boissier à Paris en 1832*. Paris: Champion, 1976 [1927].

Börne, Ludwig. *Briefe aus Paris, 1830–1831*. 2 vols. Hamburg: Hoffman und Campe, 1832–34.

Briefe hervorragender Zeitgenossen an Franz Liszt. La Mara [pseud.], ed. 3 vols. Leipzig: Breitkopf & Härtel, 1895–1904.

Chorley, Henry. *Music and Manners in France and Germany*. 3 vols. London: Longman, Brown, Green, and Longmans, 1844.

Christern, J. W. *Franz Liszt: nach seinem Leben und Wirken*. Hamburg/Leipzig: Schuberth, 1841.

Correspondance de Liszt et de Madame d'Agoult. Daniel Ollivier, ed. 2 vols. Paris: Bernard Grasset, 1933–35.

Devrient, Therese. *Jugenderinnerungen*. Stuttgart: C. Krabbe, 1905.

Dronke, Ernst. *Berlin*. Frankfurt am Main: Luchterhand, 1846.

Bibliography

Duverger, Joseph. *Notice biographique sur Franz Liszt*. Paris: Amyot, 1843.
Elben, Otto. *Lebenserinnerungen, 1823–1899*. Stuttgart: W. Kohlhammer, 1931.
Les étrangers à Paris. Janin, Beauvoir, Desnoyers et al., eds. Paris: Charles Warée, 1844.
Franz Liszt: l'artiste, le clerc. Jacques Vier, ed. Paris: Editions du Cèdre, 1950.
Franz Liszts Briefe. La Mara [pseud.], ed. 8 vols. Leipzig: Breitkopf & Härtel, 1893–1902.
Gasparin, La Comtesse Agénor de. *Correspondance et souvenirs 1813–1894*. 2 vols. Paris: Plon, 1902.
Girardin, Delphine. *Oeuvres complètes*. 6 vols. Paris: Plon, 1860.
Graves, C. L. *The Life and Letters of Sir George Grove*. New York: Macmillan, 1903.
Heller, Stephen. *Lettres d'un musicien romantique à Paris*. J.-J. Eigeldinger, ed. Paris: Flammarion, 1981.
Jagemann, Ludwig von. *Deutsche Städte und deutsche Männer*. Leipzig, 1846.
Leo, Sophie. *Erinnerungen aus Paris. 1817–1848*. Berlin, 1851.
Leonhard, K. C. von. *Aus unserer Zeit in meinem Leben*. 2 vols. Stuttgart, 1854–56.
"Lettres diverses inédites de Liszt." Robert Bory, ed. *Schweizerisches Jahrbuch für die Musikwissenschaft* 3 (1928): 5–25.
Memoirs of the Life and Correspondence of Henry Reeve. J. K. Laughton, ed. 2 vols. London: Longmans, Green & Co., 1898.
Mundt, Theodor. *Spaziergänge und Weltfahrten*. 3 vols. Altona: J. F. Hammerich, 1838–39.
Neumann, William. *Franz Liszt: eine Biographie*. Kassel: Ernst Balde, 1855.
Pardoe, Julia. *City of the Magyar*. 3 vols. London: George Virtue, 1840.
Pontmartin, Count Armand de. *Souvenirs d'un vieux critique*. 10 vols. Paris: C. Lévy, 1881.
Rellstab, Ludwig. *Franz Liszt: Beurtheilungen-Berichte-Lebensskizze*. Berlin: Trautwein, 1842.
Henriette, oder die schöne Sängerin. Leipzig: F. L. Herbig, 1826.
Sass, Friedrich. *Berlin in seiner neuesten Zeit und Entwicklung*. Leipzig: Koffka, 1846.
Schloezer, Curd von. *Römische Briefe, 1864–1869*. Stuttgart and Berlin, 1926.
Schober, Franz von. *Briefe über F. Liszts Aufenthalt in Ungarn*. Berlin: Schlesinger, 1843.
Schumann, Robert. *Tagebücher*. 3 vols. Leipzig: Deutcher Verlag für Musik, 1971–87.
Scudo, Paul. *Critique et littérature musicales*. 2 vols. Paris: Amyot, 1850.
Spohr, Ludwig. *Lebenserinnerungen*. 2 vols. Tutzing: Hans Schneider, 1968.
Trollope, Frances. *Paris et les Parisiens en 1835*. 3 vols. Paris: Fournier, 1836.
Varnhagen von Ense, Karl August. *Tagebücher*. 14 vols. Leipzig: Brockhaus, 1861.
Wieck, Friedrich. *Briefe aus den Jahren 1830–1838*. Käthe Walch-Schumann, ed. and intr. Cologne: A. Volk-Verlag, 1968.

IV.   Chronicles and documentary collections

Arnold, Ben, and Saffle, Michael. "Liszt in Ireland (and Belgium): Reports from a Concert Tour." *Journal of the American Liszt Society* 26 (1989): 3–11.

Bellas, Jacqueline. "Un virtuose en tournée: Franz Liszt dans le Sud-Ouest en 1844." *Littératures* 9 (1960): 5–50.

Bory, Robert. *La vie de Franz Liszt par l'image*. Geneva, 1936.

Buchner, Alexander. *Franz Liszt in Bohemia*. London: Peter Nenill, 1962.

Hure, Pierre-Antoine, and Knepper, Claude, eds. *Liszt en son temps: documents choisis, présentés et annotés, précédés de Dionysos, ou Le crucifié*. Paris: Hachette, 1987.

Johnsson, Bengt. "Liszt in Copenhagen." *Liszt Society Journal* 21 (1996): 2–10.

Keeling, Geraldine. "Liszt's Appearances in Parisian Concerts, 1824–1844." *Liszt Society Journal* 11 (1986): 22–34; and *Liszt Society Journal* 12 (1987): 8–22.

Legány, Dezsö, ed. *Franz Liszt: unbekannte Presse und Briefe aus Wien, 1822–1866*. Vienna: H. Böhlhaus, 1984.

Müller, Gerhard, ed. *Heinrich Heine und die Musik: publizistische Arbeiten und poetische Reflexionen*. Cologne: Röderberg, 1987.

[n.a.] "Liszt's British Tours: Reviews and Letters." *Liszt Society Journal* 8 (1983): 2–8.

[n.a.] "Liszt's Playing in London in 1840 & 1841: Some Contemporary Opinions." *Liszt Society Journal* 6 (1981): 16–18.

Newton, Dudley, ed. "From 'The Musical World.'" *Liszt Society Journal* 9 (1984): 31–33.

Newton, Dudley. "Liszt and his Glass." *Liszt Society Journal* 13 (1988): 40–60.

Strecker, Rémy, ed. *Franz Liszt: Artiste et société*. Paris: Flammarion, 1995.

Suttoni, Charles, ed. and trans. *An Artist's Journey: Lettres d'un bachelier ès musique*. Chicago: University of Chicago Press, 1989.

Williams, Adrian. *Portrait of Liszt: by Himself and his Contemporaries*. Oxford: Clarendon Press, 1990.

Wolff, Konrad, ed. *Robert Schumann on Music and Musicians*. Paul Rosenfeld, trans. New York: Pantheon Books, 1946.

V. Secondary sources

Altenburg, Detlef, ed. *Liszt und die Weimarer Klassik*. Laaber: Laaber-Verlag, 1997.

Applegate, Celia. "How German Is It? Nationalism and the Origins of Serious Music in Early Nineteenth-Century Germany." *19th Century Music* 21 (1998): 274–96.

Autexier, Philippe. "The Masonic Thread in Liszt." *Journal of the American Liszt Society* 22 (1987): 3–18.

Barany, George. *Stephen Széchenyi and the Awakening of Hungarian Nationalism, 1791–1841*. Princeton: Princeton University Press, 1968.

Bellas, Jacquéline. "La tumultueuse amitié de Franz Liszt et de Maurice Schlesinger." *Littératures* 12 (1965): 7–20.

Bernstein, Susan. *Virtuosity of the Nineteenth Century: Performing Music and Language in Heine, Liszt, and Baudelaire*. Stanford: Stanford University Press, 1998.

Bélance-Zank, Isabelle. "The Three-hand Texture: Origins and Use." *Journal of the American Liszt Society* 38 (1995): 99–121.

Bibliography

Bory, Robert. *Une retraite romantique en Suisse: Liszt et la comtesse d'Agoult.* Lausanne: Editions SPES, 1930.
Botstein, Leon. "Listening through Reading: Musical Literacy and the Concert Audience." *19th Century Music* 16 (1992): 129–45.
Boulenger, Jacques. *Sous Louis-Philippe: les dandys.* Paris: Calmann-Lévy, 1932.
Burger, Ernst. *Franz Liszt: A Life in Pictures and Documents.* Princeton: Princeton University Press, 1989.
Courcy, Geraldine de. *Paganini the Genoese.* 2 vols. Norman, OK: University of Oklahoma Press, 1957.
Dahlhaus, Carl. *Nineteenth-Century Music.* J. Bradford Robinson, trans. Berkeley and Los Angeles: University of California Press, 1989.
Daverio, John. *Robert Schumann.* Oxford: Oxford University Press, 1997.
DeNora, Tia. *Beethoven and the Construction of Genius.* Berkeley and Los Angeles: University of California Press, 1995.
Düding, Dieter. *Organisierter gesellschaftlicher Nationalismus in Deutschland (1808–1847).* Munich: R. Oldenbourg, 1984.
The Early Romantic Era. Alexander Ringer, ed. Englewood Cliffs, NJ: Prentice Hall, 1990.
Ellis, Katharine. *Music Criticism in Nineteenth-Century France.* Cambridge: Cambridge University Press, 1995.
"Female Pianists and their Male Critics in Nineteenth-Century Paris." *Journal of the American Musicological Society* 50 (1997), 353–85.
The Faces of Physiognomy: Interdisciplinary Approaches to Johann Caspar Lavater. Ellis Schookman, ed. Columbia, SC: Camden House, 1993.
Farwell, Beatrice. *French Popular Lithographic Imagery, 1815–1870.* 11 vols. Chicago: University of Chicago Press, 1989.
Franz Liszt's musikalische Werke. 35 vols. Franz Liszt-Stiftung, ed. Leipzig: Breitkopf & Hartel, 1908–36.
Franz Liszt: Neue Ausgabe sämtlicher Werke. Imre Sulyok and Imre Mezö, eds. Budapest: Editio Musica, 1970– .
Fudge, James Thompson. "The Male Choral Music of Franz Liszt." Ph.D. dissertation, University of Iowa, 1972.
Gavoty, Bernard. *Liszt: le virtuose.* Paris: Juillard, 1980.
Gay, Peter. *The Cultivation of Hatred.* New York: Oxford University Press, 1993.
Guichard, Léon. "Liszt et la littérature française." *Revue de musicologie* 1 (1970): 5–34.
Gut, Serge. *Franz Liszt.* Paris: L'Âge d'Homme, 1989.
Habermas, Jürgen. *The Structural Transformation of the Public Sphere.* Thomas Burger and Frederick Lawrence, trans. Cambridge, MA: Harvard University Press, 1991.
Hall, Jennifer Lee. "The Refashioning of Fashionable Society: Opera-going and Sociability in Britain, 1821–1861." Ph.D. dissertation, Yale University, 1996.
Heisler, Marcel. *Stendhal et Napoléon.* Paris: A.-G. Nizet, 1969.
Herwegh, Marcel. *Au soir des dieux.* Paris: J. Peyronnet, 1933.
A History of Hungary. Peter F. Sugar, Péter Hanák, and Tibor Frank, eds. Bloomington: University of Indiana Press, 1990.

Holoman, D. Kern. *Berlioz*. Cambridge, MA: Harvard University Press, 1989.

Hopkins Porter, Cecilia. *The Rhine as Musical Metaphor*. Boston: Northeastern University Press, 1996.

Hughes, Michael. *Nationalism and Society: Germany 1800–1945*. New York: E. Arnold, 1988.

Janos, Andrew C. *The Politics of Backwardness in Hungary, 1825–1945*. Princeton: Princeton University Press, 1982.

Johnson, James H. *Listening in Paris: A Cultural History*. Berkeley and Los Angeles: University of California Press, 1995.

Johnston, Otto W. *The Myth of a Nation: Literature and Politics in Prussia under Napoleon*. Columbia, SC: Camden House, 1989.

Kapp, Julius. *Franz Liszt: eine Biographie*. Berlin and Leipzig: Schuster & Loeffler, 1911.

Klein, Adolf. *Köln im 19. Jahrhundert*. Cologne: Wienand, 1992.

Koch, Lajos. *Franz Liszt: ein bibliographischer Versuch*. Budapest: Székesfőváros Házinyomdája, 1936.

Kramer, Lawrence. "Franz Liszt and the Virtuoso Public Sphere: Sight and Sound in the Rise of Mass Entertainment." *Musical Meaning: Toward a Critical History*. Berkeley and Los Angeles: University of California Press, 2002.

Kroll, Erwin. *Musikstadt Königsberg*. Freiburg im Breisgau: Atlantis, 1966.

Kuhač, Franjo. *Vatroslav Lisinski i njegovo dob*. Zagreb: Matica Hrvatska, 1904.

La Mara [pseud.]. *Liszt und die Frauen*. Leipzig: Breitkopf & Härtel, 1911.

Legány, Dezsö. "Liszt in Hungary, 1820–1846." *Liszt and his World*. Stuyvesant, NY: Pendragon Press, 1998.

Leppert, Richard, and Zank, Stephen. "The Concert and the Virtuoso." *Piano Roles: Three Hundred Years of Life with the Piano*. James Parakilas, ed. New Haven: Yale University Press, 1999.

Lienig, Marion. *Bürgerliche Musikkultur in Bonn*. Bonn: Bouvier, 1995.

Litzmann, Berthold. *Clara Schumann: ein Künstlerleben, nach Tagebüchern und Briefen*. 3 vols. Leipzig: Breitkopf & Härtel, 1910.

Loesser, Arthur. *Men, Women, and Pianos: A Social History*. New York: Simon and Schuster, 1990 [1958].

Main, Alexander. "Liszt's 'Lyon': Music and the Social Conscience." *19th Century Music* 4 (1981): 3–21.

Marix-Spire, Thérèse. *Les romantiques et la musique: le cas George Sand*. Paris: Nouvelles Éditions Latines, 1954.

Martin-Fugier, Anne. *La vie élégante, ou la formation du Tout-Paris, 1815–1848*. Paris: Fayard, 1990.

McCalla, Arthur. "Liszt *Bricoleur*: Poetics and Providentialism in Early July Monarchy France." *History of European Ideas* 24/2 (1998): 71–93.

Mongrédien, Jean. *La musique en France des Lumières au Romantisme, 1789–1830*. Paris: Flammarion, 1986.

Müller, Gottfried. *Daniel Steibelt: sein Leben und seine Klavierwerke*. Strasbourg: Heitz, 1933.

Myerly, Scott Hughes. *British Military Spectacle: From the Napoleonic Wars through the Crimea*. Cambridge, MA: Harvard University Press, 1996.

Pincherle, Marc. *Le monde des virtuoses*. Paris: Flammarion, 1961.

Pistone, Danièle. *Le piano dans la littérature française des origines jusqu'en 1900*. Paris: Champion, 1975.

Prendergast, Christopher. *Napoleon and History Painting*. Oxford: Oxford University Press, 1997.

Prochaska, F. K. "Philanthropy." *The Cambridge Social History of Britain, 1750–1950*. 3 vols. Cambridge: Cambridge University Press, 1990.

Ramann, Lina. *Franz Liszt als Künstler und Mensch*. 3 vols. Leipzig: Breitkopf und Härtel, 1880–94.

Rehm, Wolfgang. *Zur Musikrezeption im vormärzlichen Berlin. Die Präsentation bürgerlichen Selbstverständnisses und biedermeierlicher Kunstanschauung in den Musikkritiken Ludwig Rellstabs*. Hildesheim: Georg Olms, 1983.

Reich, Nancy B. "Liszt's Variations on the March from Rossini's *Siège de Corinthe*." *Fontes Artis Musicae* 23/3 (1976): 102–06.

Saffle, Michael. *Liszt in Germany, 1840–1845*. Stuyvesant, NY: Pendragon Press, 1994.

Schenda, Rudolph. *Volk ohne Buch: Studien zur Sozialgeschichte der populären Lesestoffe, 1770–1910*. Frankfurt am Main: V. Klostermann, 1970.

Schmölders, Claudia. *Das Vorurteil im Leibe: eine Einführung in die Physiognomik*. Berlin: Akademie Verlag, 1995.

Speyer, Edward. *Wilhelm Speyer der Liederkomponist, 1790–1878*. Munich: Drei Masken, 1925.

Spitzer, John. "Metaphors of the Orchestra – the Orchestra as Metaphor." *Musical Quarterly* 80/2 (1996): 238–45.

Suttoni, Charles. "Piano and Opera: A Study of the Piano Fantasies Written on Opera Themes in the Romantic Era." Ph.D. dissertation, New York University, 1973.

Thematisches Verzeichnis im Druck erschienener Compositionen von Ignaz Moscheles. Leipzig: Kistner, 1862. Reprint London: H. Baron, 1966.

Torkewitz, Dieter. "Die Erstfassung der 'Harmonies Poétiques et Réligieuses' von Liszt." *Liszt-Studien 2*. Munich: E. Katzbichler, 1981: 220–36.

Tullius, Raimond Nicholas. "The Construction of a Civic National Identity: Magyar and Swabian Nation-Builders in Hungary, 1760–1838." BA thesis, Harvard University, 1996.

Tümmers, Horst Johannes. *Der Rhein: ein europäischer Fluss und seine Geschichte*. Munich: C. H. Beck, 1994.

Tytler, Graeme. *Physiognomy in the European Novel: Faces and Fortunes*. Princeton: Princeton University Press, 1982.

Walker, Alan. *Franz Liszt*. 3 vols. Ithaca: Cornell University Press, 1987–97.

Walser, Robert. *Running with the Devil: Power, Gender, and Madness in Heavy Metal Music*. Middletown, CT: Wesleyan University Press, 1993.

Wangermée, Robert. "Tradition et innovation dans la virtuosité romantique." *Acta Musicologica* 42 (1970): 5–32.

Warrack, John. *Carl Maria von Weber*. 2nd edition. New York: Cambridge University Press, 1976.

Weber, William. *Music and the Middle Class*. New York: Holmes and Meier Publishers, 1975.

Wechsler, Judith. *A Human Comedy: Physiognomy and Caricature in Paris.* Chicago: University of Chicago Press, 1982.

Weissmann, Adolph. *Berlin als Musikstadt: Geschichte der Oper und des Konzerts von 1740 bis 1911.* Berlin and Leipzig: Schuster und Loeffler, 1911.

Winklhofer, Sharon. *Liszt's Sonata in B minor: A Study of Autograph Sources and Documents.* Ann Arbor: UMI Research Press, 1980.

INDEX

Index

Index

Index

9834820R0

Made in the USA
Lexington, KY
01 June 2011